Social Origins of
the Irish Land War

Social Origins of the Irish Land War

SAMUEL CLARK

Princeton University Press
Princeton, New Jersey

Published by Princeton University Press, Princeton, New Jersey
In the United Kingdom: Princeton University Press, Guildford, Surrey

Library of Congress Cataloging in Publication Data will be found on the last
printed page of this book

Publication of this book has been aided by a grant from
The Andrew W. Mellon Foundation

This book has been composed in VIP Melior

Clothbound editions of Princeton University Press books are printed on acid-free
paper, and binding materials are chosen for strength and durability.

Printed in the United States of America by Princeton University Press,
Princeton, New Jersey

TO MY MOTHER AND FATHER

Contents

Acknowledgments

Over the many years during which this book has been in preparation I have incurred debts to several institutions and to a great number of people. For their invariably helpful and courteous assistance, I would like to express my appreciation to members of the staffs of the Land Valuation Office, the National Library of Ireland, and the State Paper Office, and especially to Breandán Mac Giolla Choille, who helped to make available several sources that I have used extensively. Most of the maps and figures are the work of Éamonn Dunne, who kindly took a personal interest in this volume. For their sympathetic and considerate assistance, I am most grateful to Joanna Hitchcock and Judith May of Princeton University Press. Financially and in other ways, this project was aided by the University of Western Ontario and by McGill University. The major source of financial support was the Humanities and Social Sciences Division of the Canada Council, which is now known as the Social Sciences and Humanities Research Council. The publication of the book was assisted by a subsidy from The Andrew W. Mellon Foundation.

I am indebted to the publishers of *Irish Historical Studies*, *The Canadian Review of Sociology and Anthropology*, and *The British Journal of Sociology* for permission to reprint portions of articles of mine that appeared in those journals. For permission to quote at length from manuscripts in their possession, I wish to thank the following: the Most Reverend Dr. Thomas Morris, archbishop of Cashel and Emly; the Department of Irish Folklore, University College Dublin; the National Library of Ireland; the Manuscript Department, McGill University Library; and the State Paper Office of Ireland.

A study of this kind, which utilizes many secondary as well as primary sources to answer a specific question, inevitably owes a special debt to the work of other scholars. Doubtless I no longer appreciate how great that debt is, having taken as mine so much of what really belongs to others. Yet I am extremely conscious of how much I have learned from Irish historians, not just about Ireland, but also about the historian's craft. In addition, I feel very keenly the obligation I am under to a number of scholars who read parts or the whole of the manuscript and gave me the benefit of their reactions. I have profited greatly from criticisms, generally both wise and copious, from D. H. Akenson, Desmond Bowen, Kurt Bowen, J. W. Boyle, L. P. Curtis, Jr., Richard Henshel, K. T. Hoppen, P. G. Lane, Emmet Larkin, Joseph Lee, Kevin McQuillan, R. W. Mansbach, M. P. Maxwell, Cormac Ó Gráda, Hereward Senior, Charles Tilly, and Donald Von Eschen.

A longstanding debt remains to the professors at Harvard University who performed the time-consuming task of directing the doctoral dissertation which constituted the initial stage of this project: George Homans, John V. Kelleher, and Barrington Moore, Jr. All three had a profound influence not just on this study, but on my whole intellectual development and on my conceptions of good academic research. I am also heavily indebted to T. W. Moody of the University of Dublin, who provided both encouragement and aid from the very beginning. And it is beyond my capacity to pay full tribute to W. J. Lowe and C. J. Woods, whose contributions to this project went far beyond the obligations of friendship.

I am least able to express my feelings towards James Donnelly and William Feingold. The influence they have had on my thinking, the encouragement and assistance they have given to this undertaking, and the inspiration that they have been to me personally have no equivalent in my experiences.

My wife Claudia, who was never sure why anyone would care what Irish peasants were doing a hundred years ago and could think of a thousand things more interesting to study, nevertheless bore the heaviest burden of all with a patience and devotion that can and should only be repaid in kind.

My largest debt is acknowledged in the dedication.

Samuel Clark

Department of Sociology
University of Western Ontario
January 1979

Abbreviations

H.C.	House of Commons
H.L.	House of Lords
N.L.I.	National Library of Ireland
P.R.O.I.	Public Record Office of Ireland
S.P.O.	State Paper Office of Ireland
T.C.D.	Trinity College Dublin
V.O.	Land Valuation Office of Ireland

IRELAND

Eamonn Dunne · Nov.'78

The Province of
connaught

Sligo

Manor-
Hamilton

leitrim

Killala
Dromore West
Ballina

sligo

Tubbercurry

Carrick-on-Shannon

mayo

Swinford
Castlebar

Boyle

Mohill

Newport

Westport

Castlerea

roscommon

Louisburgh

Claremorris

Roscommon

Clifden

Ballinrobe
Clonbur

Glenamaddy

Tuam

Mount Bellew
Athleague

Athlone

galway

Ballinasloe

Aughrim

Carraroe

Galway

Loughrea

Woodford
Portumna

Social Origins of
the Irish Land War

One · **Introduction**

When the Irish talk about the "Land War," they have in mind either three phases of anti-landlord agitation in the late nineteenth century, or, more narrowly, the first of these phases, which lasted from 1879 until 1882. In this book, the term refers to this first phase. The movement emerged during a severe agricultural depression caused by crop failures and a sluggish market for farm produce. Economic conditions for farmers took a serious downturn in 1877, recovered partially in 1878, but deteriorated again in 1879. Unrest began on a small scale in late 1878, grew slowly during the early months of 1879, and then accelerated in the spring of 1879 when a series of public meetings were held in the western province of Connaught. With the help of nationalist politicians, a "Land League" was formed in County Mayo in August 1879 and the "Irish National Land League" was founded in October.

The agitation remained strongest in western regions, but at times it raged in almost all parts of the country, with the notable exception of the northeast. Tenant farmers resisted evictions, refused to pay their normal rents, and demanded that parliament make extensive alterations to the laws governing ownership and occupation of agricultural land in Ireland. Literally hundreds of public meetings were held during the years 1879-81, and more than five hundred branches of the Land League were formed. There was also more rural violence than at any other time in the second half of the nineteenth century, the chief victims being landlords, land agents, bailiffs, process servers, and tenants who took land from which the previous occupant had been evicted. Most celebrated of all was the organized and systematic ostracism of enemies of the movement, which became known as "boycotting" because it first gained notoriety in autumn of 1880 when the English and Irish press gave extensive coverage to the ostracism of Captain Charles Boycott of Lough Mask, County Mayo. In an effort to combat the agitation, the government enacted a major land-reform measure in 1881, outlawed boycotts, restricted the possession of arms, interned close to a thousand agitators, and eventually, in October 1881, banned the Land League altogether.

In what follows, an attempt will be made to explain this movement. The inquiry will be guided by certain theoretical and methodological assumptions, which are best stated explicitly at the outset, since they have led me to ask questions and explore subjects that most sociologists would not consider when trying to explain a social movement. There are several assumptions, in particular, that are essential for the reader to recognize in order to follow the argument of the book.

First, I believe that rebellions such as the Land War are variants of a broader and more common category of social behavior known as "collective action." By collective action is meant the pursuit of a goal or set of goals by a number of persons. It can refer to a wide range of activities. A band of thieves robbing a bank, a team of neighbors trying to find a lost child, a crew of workers building a bridge, a group of citizens organizing a petition—all are examples of collective action. As the term will be used here, participation may be voluntary or involuntary, so long as people engage in activities that are directed toward the same goal or set of goals. Even a gang of slaves harvesting a crop, or a troop of prisoners repairing a wall, is collective action.

It is ubiquitous. Every day, people join in collective action of some sort as they behave in ways that serve the goals of collectivities to which they belong, from small family units to large formal organizations or even nation-states. Since it is impossible to conceive of a society in which no collective action occurs, a student of social behavior is never called upon to explain the existence, as opposed to the absence, of collective action. What invariably does require explanation, however, are the characteristics of the collective action occurring in a society at a given point in time. Why do certain combinations of individuals rather than other combinations join together? Why do they pursue certain goals rather than other goals? And why do they pursue these goals in certain ways rather than other ways?

Placing rebellious behavior in a category by itself has encouraged most researchers to bend their energies primarily toward explaining this rebelliousness, and to neglect many other, equally fundamental, characteristics of the collective action they are studying. As a result, they frequently fail to appreciate the immense variety that can be found in rebellious behavior. Often social scientists will plot rates of social unrest covering different countries or different periods of time, always assuming that they are measuring the same thing. It is easy, for example, to find studies tracing the effect of modernization on rates of social protest, which most often show (at least by the measures used) that it increases in the early stages of industrialization and declines thereafter. The approach I have taken has been greatly influenced by a school of writers who argue that the effect of modernization on the *magnitude* of protest has been much less important than the effect of modernization on its *character*. These writers claim that modernization has changed the character of rebellion because it has changed the character of collective action, of which rebellion is simply one kind.[1]

The advantage of treating social unrest as a variety of collective action is that one is led to compare the specific unrest one is studying with other cases of collective action. In the present study, the question "Why did the Land War occur?" becomes "Why did collective action take the form of the Land War?" For purposes of comparison, one could analyze collective action in several other agricultural societies and seek to account for the differences between these other examples and the Land War. The alternative, which is adopted here, is to compare rural collective action within the same society at different points in time. Such a comparison will necessitate an investigation of the nature and social basis of collective action in Ireland both in the late nineteenth century and during some earlier period. The earlier period I have selected is the first half of the century, before the Great Famine of 1845-51. By studying rural collective action in this period as well as during the Land War, it will be possible to demonstrate how the character of collective action changed over the course of the nineteenth century.

The premise that rebellion is a variant of collective action leads directly to the second major theoretical assumption of this study: that in order to explain and understand protest or rebellion it is necessary to study social relationships. Rebellion is not an individual enterprise; one rebels with some people and against others. By definition, the basic condition for the occurrence of collective action is that a number of people are persuaded to engage in the pursuit of a goal or set of goals. Usually, though by no means always, they must be persuaded that the goal is desirable, but other

[1] See, in particular, Edward Shorter and Charles Tilly, *Strikes in France, 1830 to 1968* (New York, 1974); Charles Tilly, Louise Tilly, and Richard Tilly, *The Rebellious Century 1830-1930* (Cambridge, Massachusetts, 1975).

kinds of inducements are generally necessary in order to get them
to assume their share of the cost of a collective effort.[2] These inducements may be coercive, as when people are threatened with
punishment if they do not go along. They may involve material
rewards, as is usually the case when the collective action is aimed
at an economic goal. They may consist largely of social approval
from others who consider the activity to be important. Or the inducements may consist merely of the personal self-satisfaction
that people get from doing what they perceive as their duty.

The strength of inducements varies greatly from one individual
to another. It is extremely difficult to make generalizations about
the reasons for which people join in a specific instance of collective action. The assumption on which this study is based, however, is that most often these inducements are channeled through
existing social relationships, that is, through the regular interactions in which people are already engaged. Consequently, the
character of collective action is generally determined by the
prevailing social relationships in a society. Ideas, values and
other states of mind are important, but are mediated by social relationships. People acquire beliefs through existing social relationships, and, as a rule, they act upon them through such relationships. This may seem almost obvious in the case of day-to-day
collective action, such as the activities in which one joins as
the member of a family or of a formal organization. Only recently
have we begun to realize that the same is true of social movements. It helps to stop and ask the simple question: Exactly how
do most people become involved in a social movement? The answer one invariably obtains, if one pursues this question, is that
most people join through the influence of a friend or acquaintance.[3] Like any form of collective action, social movements—and
even crowds[4]—are most often built on pre-existing social rela-

[2] Mancur Olson, The Logic of Collective Action (Cambridge, Massachusetts, 1965).

[3] Luther P. Gerlach and Virginia H. Hine, People, Power, Change: Movements of Social Transformation (Indianapolis, 1970), especially pp. 79-80; Maurice Pinard, The Rise of a Third Party: A Study in Crisis Politics (Englewood Cliffs, N.J., 1971), especially p. 199; and John Wilson, Introduction to Social Movements (New York, 1973), pp. 131-3.

[4] Clark McPhail and David Miller, "The assembling process: a theoretical and empirical examination" in American Sociological Review, 38, no. 6 (Dec. 1973); and Adrian F. Aveni, "The not-so-lonely crowd: friendship groups in collective behavior" in Sociometry, 40, no. 1 (March 1977).

tionships, and so are inevitably shaped by these connections. It follows that if we want to understand a social movement, we should carefully study the patterns of social relationships prevailing in the environment in which the movement occurs. Sociologists refer to these patterns as "social structure." When they talk about kinship structure, religious structure, class structure and so on, they are discussing some of the more salient patterns of social relationships in a society.

I can now briefly outline the kinds of questions that I shall be asking and that should always be asked, in my view, in any attempt to explain a social movement. I shall also indicate some of the basic concepts to be used in this study. One begins by identifying the major social structures in the society and investigating how these structures determined which particular combinations of individuals were likely to engage in collective action. There are really two types of questions here, both of which need answering: First, how did social structures combine people and make it likely that they would engage in collective action? Second, how did social structures divide people, and make it unlikely that they would engage in collective action and perhaps even bring some of them into opposition? In answering the first question, we identify what can be called *integrating* factors—conditions that pulled people together into social groups, whether or not collective action actually resulted. In answering the second question, we identify *segmenting* or *cleavage* factors—those tending to separate people and restrict interaction among them, or if not separated, to set them at odds. We should also examine how these factors intersected with one another. Did different lines of integration and cleavage reinforce one another or did they cross-cut? Did class, for instance, divide the society in the same way as religion or language? Or did it cut in a different direction creating a more complex pattern of social divisions? It is the final topography carved out by the major forces of integration and cleavage in a society that we must be able to describe in order to understand the social basis of collective action.[5]

[5] A tradition of writings in sociology and political science has emphasized these questions. Some of the major works are Karl Deutsch, *Nationalism and Social Communication* (Cambridge, Massachusetts, 1953); L. A. Coser, *The Functions of Social Conflict* (Glencoe, Illinois, 1956); Ralph Dahrendorf, *Class and Class Conflict in Industrial Society* (Stanford, 1959); and S. M. Lipset, *Political Man: The Social Basis of Politics* (New York, 1963). More recent writings include S. M. Lip-

When we are identifying integrating factors we can make a distinction between those based on *communal* structures and those based on *associational* structures. As I use the term, the defining characteristic of a communal structure is that it results from frequent social interaction. Almost invariably communal structures are strongest when they are small, local, and relatively homogeneous (for example, kinship, neighborhood, or tribal groups), though it is possible for communal structures to develop over a wide geographical area on the basis of indirect social interaction. Associational structures, on the other hand, result from common interests. They often consist of groups formed for specifically stated purposes—occupational, religious, political, civic, or economic organizations, including special interest associations. In any case, the relationships are utilitarian. Like communal structures, associational structures may be local or supra-local. Unlike communal structures, however, they can be just as strong when they are supra-local. The distinguishing and most significant feature of an associational structure is that it can bring together people with common interests who are spread over a wide geographical area.[6]

These distinctions are, of course, theoretical. Most social relationships in the real world contain both communal and associational elements. Indeed, it is quite common for bonds of one type to emerge on the basis of relationships that were, to begin with, primarily of the other type. Nonetheless, there are differences in

set and S. Rokkan, "Introduction" to *Party Systems and Voter Alignments* (New York, 1967); W. J. Foltz, "Ethnicity, Status and Conflict" in W. Bell and W. F. Freeman (eds.), *Ethnicity and Nation-Building: Comparative, International, and Historical Perspectives* (Beverly Hills, 1974); and D. J. Grove, "A cross-national examination of cross-cutting and reinforcing cultural cleavages" in *International Journal of Comparative Sociology*, 18, nos. 3-4 (Sept.-Dec. 1977).

[6] For examples of the use of this distinction by students of social unrest see Anthony Oberschall, *Social Conflict and Social Movements* (Englewood Cliffs, N.J., 1973), pp. 119-20; and more especially see Charles Tilly, "Collective violence in European perspective" in H. D. Graham and T. R. Gurr (eds.), *The History of Violence in America* (New York, 1969), and Charles Tilly, "Revolutions and collective violence" in Fred I. Greenstein and Nelson Polsby (eds.), *Handbook of Political Science* (Reading, Massachusetts, 1975), especially p. 505. I depart slightly from their use of these terms by placing greater emphasis on frequency of social interaction as the defining characteristic of communal structures, but the general idea behind the typology is the same. It can be traced to Durkheim's distinction between mechanical and organic solidarity, as well as that of Tönnies between *gemeinschaft* and *gesellschaft*.

the degree to which structures are communal or associational, and these differences are important. By extension, one can make a parallel distinction among cleavage factors between those based on *isolation* and those based on *opposition*. The former result from the absence or infrequency of social interaction; the latter result from conflicts of interest. Again, in the real world, one often finds the two combined. But not always. People may interact frequently and yet have conflicting interests.

Once we have identified the major integrating and cleavage factors in a society, we can then ask how these factors shaped the character of collective action. What social groups were formed by the direction and the intersection of the lines of integration and cleavage we have identified? What active collectivities emerged from these social groups? Who belonged to these active collectivities? What were their goals? And by what methods did they try to achieve those goals? In the final analysis, the measure of the theoretical model is how well one succeeds in answering these questions.

This theoretical model can be placed in the context of the current sociological literature on social movements by briefly reviewing some of the major approaches to this subject developed over the past several decades. For this purpose, three distinct approaches can be identified.

COLLECTIVE BEHAVIOR   This has been the dominant theoretical interpretation in American sociology and is best represented in the works of Herbert Blumer, Ralph Turner, L. M. Killian, and Neil Smelser.[7] The term "collective behavior" involves an unfortunate choice of words, since it is not at all synonymous with collective action. At the heart of this approach lies the distinction between "non-institutionalized" and "institutionalized" (or "routine") behavior. Whether one accepts the validity of the collective-behavior perspective depends primarily on whether one accepts the validity of this distinction. People are engaging in collective behavior, according to this perspective, when they collectively depart from or oppose some aspect of the prevailing institutional structure, that is, some established value, norm, and/or

[7] Herbert Blumer, "Collective Behavior" in A. M. Lee (ed.), *Principles of Sociology* (New York, 1951); Ralph Turner and L. M. Killian, *Collective Behavior* (Englewood Cliffs, N.J., 1957/72); and N. J. Smelser, *Theory of Collective Behavior* (New York, 1963).

leader that they formerly accepted, and when they search for or
advocate some alternative value, norm, and/or leader in its place.
In this sense collective behavior is less institutionalized than
routine behavior. True, it may eventually become "institutionalized" or "routinized," but then we would no longer call
it collective behavior. What distinguishes crowds, crazes, social
movements, and other forms of collective behavior from more ordinary social phenomena is that they are comparatively less institutionalized.[8]

Not surprisingly, many of those who have taken this line have
assumed that a precondition for collective behavior is a disrup-
tion of established institutions or a weakening of the integration
of people into established institutions. This assumption has often
been made at the psychological level, in which case one talks
about "alienation" or personal "maladjustment"; it has also been
made at the societal level, in which case one talks about "anomie"
or a decline in "social control." These "breakdown"[9] arguments
have explicitly and implicitly pervaded much of the sociological
literature, especially sociological writings on collective behavior.
The argument has been made most forcefully, however, in the
theory of mass society, particularly as it appears in William Kornhauser's *The Politics of Mass Society*. Kornhauser has argued that
the rise of mass movements is restrained by the integration of
people into social institutions, the most important of which are
"intermediate" institutions, such as community groups, occupational associations, religious institutions, and political parties.
Mass movements occur, Kornhauser claimed, in societies where
people are isolated and not well connected to social institutions;
and these movements attract persons "with the fewest social
ties."[10]

The approach I take in this study differs significantly from the
collective-behavior perspective. It gives much less attention to social psychological variables than does collective-behavior theory,
and much greater attention to social structure. Unlike collective-
behavior theory, it assumes that participants in social movements
are, on the average, acting no more emotionally and no less ra-

[8] For a very brief summary and interpretation of collective-behavior theory see
our "General Introduction" to Samuel Clark, J. P. Grayson, and L. M. Grayson
(eds.), *Prophecy and Protest: Social Movements in Twentieth-Century Canada*
(Toronto, 1975), pp. 1-7.

[9] Tilly, Tilly, and Tilly, *Rebellious Century*, pp. 4-6.

[10] William Kornhauser, *The Politics of Mass Society* (New York, 1959).

tionally than are participants in other kinds of behavior. It pays far more attention to conflicts of interest in society and to the social groups that underlie these conflicts, issues that are almost totally ignored in collective-behavior theory. And most of all, the approach taken here does not assume that those who join social movements are psychologically maladjusted or socially isolated. On the other hand, I shall suggest (in the concluding chapter) that an important lesson can still be learned from the collective-behavior perspective. There does seem to be a sense in which social disintegration is a precondition for social unrest.

DISCONTENT   This perspective comes the closest to the layman's common-sense explanation for social unrest. It seems almost painfully obvious that people will protest whenever their dissatisfaction with the government, or with some other aspect of existing social arrangements, reaches a peak. The sensible thing, therefore, is to direct one's research at explaining and predicting increases in discontent. This is precisely what a great many sociologists and social psychologists have done, with the result that it is now possible to find books on "why men rebel" that contribute primarily to our understanding of what makes them angry.[11] Indeed, the study of discontent has been going on so long, and has been pursued with such energy, that we can claim considerable sophistication in our understanding of it. The principal refinement that has been made is the realization that discontent is as much a function of people's expectations as of their objective situation. More precisely, discontent theory states that social dissatisfaction most often results from a discrepancy between what people believe they have a right to receive (expectations) and what they actually receive or anticipate receiving (achievements). This discrepancy, known as "relative deprivation," may occur in a number of ways. Both expectations and achievements may rise, but the former more rapidly than the latter. Expectations may remain constant, while achievements decline. Or expectations and achievements may rise together, but achievements may subsequently fall off while expectations remain high. The last-mentioned sequence is described by James Davies' well known "J-curve." Davies has argued that revolutions are most likely to occur when a prolonged period of objective economic and social development is followed by a sharp reversal. This reversal, even if it does not bring people

---

[11] See, in particular, T. R. Gurr, *Why Men Rebel* (Princeton, 1970); James C. Davies, *When Men Revolt and Why* (New York, 1970).

to their former low levels, can create tremendous dissatisfaction because the expectations acquired during the prosperity are disappointed.[12]

Despite its intuitive appeal, discontent theory does little to assist the present inquiry. None of its basic propositions helps to answer the major questions I have posed. It is true that the Land War broke out in the context of rising expectations among Irish farmers. In fact, the progress of social and economic conditions during the period immediately before the Land War conforms reasonably well to a J-curve, and so discontent theory does help us to understand what precipitated or "sparked" the Land War. One cannot, however, use the principles of the discontent approach to account for the particular character of the Land War or for the differences between the Land War and other cases of rural unrest in nineteenth-century Ireland, which are the paramount questions that must be answered in order to explain the movement.

Discontent theorists have always been rather mysterious about what it is they are trying to explain. The hypothesized causal factor, relative deprivation, has been thoroughly investigated and conceptualized. But the social phenomena that relative deprivation presumably causes has, almost without exception, been described vaguely or left as self-evident. By contrast, the theoretical perspective that has guided the present study demands that we describe and account for the major characteristics of the collective action in question. Writings in the discontent school have also, as a rule, focused on single cases of collective action and have normally been satisfied with analyzing the social conditions prevailing at the point in time that a rebellion breaks out. By contrast, in the present study, both collective action and the social conditions underlying it will be examined (albeit in a general way) over the entire nineteenth century.

MOBILIZATION   This third perspective says that social protest occurs when new political resources are being mobilized. Carried to the extreme, it insists that discontent is always present in sufficient intensity to cause rebellion, but only does so when the discontented are mobilized. Few of those who stress mobilization

---

[12] James C. Davies, "Toward a theory of revolution" in *American Sociological Review*, 27, no. 1 (Feb. 1962); and his "The J-curve of rising and declining satisfactions as a cause of some great revolutions and a contained rebellion" in H. D. Graham and T. R. Gurr (eds.), *The History of Violence in America* (New York, 1969).

have actually made the argument in this extreme form. They almost always allow that an increase in discontent can substantially
raise the probability of social unrest. Yet they frequently assert, to
quote Charles Tilly, that "men grow angry far more often than
they rebel."[13] If we want to explain why they sometimes rebel, we
need to examine how social groups acquire collective control over
their resources and how they are able, as a consequence, to challenge the power of established groups.[14] This approach obviously
questions the whole argument of the discontent approach. Less
obvious, but just as significant, is the fact that it also contradicts
many of the claims of breakdown theory. According to the mobilization perspective, one of the conditions that can facilitate the
mobilization of a social group is the organizational base provided
by strong institutional structures, including the very same intermediate structures that, in the view of mass-society theorists, are a
defense against social unrest. And mobilization theory emphati-
cally denies that those who participate in social movements tend
to be the most socially isolated or uprooted.[15]

It is from the mobilization perspective that the theoretical argument of this book is largely derived and to which it owes its
primary debt. There are, however, several points of disagreement
between the approach taken here and at least some of the writings
in the mobilization literature. The underlying assumption of
mobilization theory is that there are always categories of people
who share common grievances or discontents but have not yet
been mobilized. Social unrest erupts when one of these "latent"
groups, as they are termed, is mobilized and thus becomes a
"manifest" group.[16] Research usually begins with a specific latent

[13] Charles Tilly, "The changing place of collective violence" in Melvin Richter
(ed.), *Essays in Theory and History: An Approach to the Social Sciences* (Cambridge, Massachusetts, 1970), p. 144; see also David Snyder and Charles Tilly,
"Hardship and collective violence" in *American Sociological Review*, 37, no. 5
(Oct. 1972).

[14] William Gamson, *The Strategy of Social Protest* (Homewood, Illinois, 1975);
Oberschall, *Social Conflict and Social Movements*; and J. D. McCarthy and M. N.
Zald, "Resource mobilization and social movements" in *American Journal of
Sociology*, 82, no. 6 (May 1977). In addition to works by Tilly that have already
been cited, see his *From Mobilization to Revolution* (Reading, Massachusetts,
1978).

[15] See, in particular, Maurice Pinard, "Mass society and political movements: a
new formulation" in *American Journal of Sociology*, 73, no. 6 (May 1968); and
Oberschall, *Social Conflict and Social Movements*, especially pp. 102-45.

[16] This kind of argument appears explicitly in Dahrendorf, *Class and Class Con-*

group in mind, typically one that the investigator knows eventually did become manifest; some good examples are American blacks and women, both of which presumably became manifest groups in North America during the 1960s. The question for investigation is: How were these latent groups mobilized? How did they become manifest groups? This way of conceptualizing the problem can be useful, but there are several difficulties with it.

First, there is a tendency to disregard other social groups to which members of the latent group have belonged and to overlook the collective action in which they have been engaged as members of these other groups. The other collective action is either ignored or dismissed as failure, often being attributed to the inability of people—through lack of proper consciousness—to perceive their true interests. Thus, taking a mobilization perspective, one would dismiss as misdirected the collective action in which American blacks or women were involved before they became organized as blacks or as women. In the following pages, we want to avoid making judgments of this kind about rural collective action that pre-dated the Land War. This earlier collective action should be studied in its own right and explained in terms of the social groups that existed at the time and on which it was based.

Second, the presence of the latent group is frequently taken for granted in mobilization theory. The investigation usually begins with the assumption that there existed a group of people with shared discontents in the population and that what is problematic is how this group became mobilized.[17] But surely this latent group also requires explanation? *The mobilization approach has suffered from a lack of studies showing how and when, in specific cases, groups of people with shared discontents have evolved historically.* This failure is all the more surprising in view of the general recognition in sociology that latent groups, certainly social classes, are not invariable, but rather are products of particular social and economic systems. And yet many writers are quite willing to take latent groups as given when trying to explain social movements. Although I shall not be able to describe the historical development of all the social groups that come under discussion

flict in Industrial Society and in Oberschall, *Social Conflict and Social Movements*.

[17] Oberschall, *Social Conflict and Social Movements*, pp. 118-19; McCarthy and Zald, "Resource mobilization and social movements," p. 1236.

in this study, I shall trace with special care the evolution of the principal group whose shared discontents gave rise to the Land War.

And third, there has been an unfortunate tendency in much of the mobilization literature to equate the memberships of latent and manifest groups. Some writers use language which implies that latent groups themselves become transformed into manifest groups. This is often not the case. To begin with, and most obviously, not all members of the latent group necessarily become members of the manifest group. Even social groups whose members come to recognize their common interests and develop interlocking ties, may not become completely mobilized. As a rule, no more than a small portion of any social group (rarely more than 20 percent) actually joins a social movement. Moreover, those who do join may not be drawn from one latent group, but instead from several. Again, the situation varies, depending on the size and nature of the collective action in question. It is clear, nevertheless, that most social movements find support in more than one social group. In the present study a particular effort will be made to distinguish between those who take part in collective action and the social groups from which these participants are drawn.

Although too many writers to count have endeavored to define what is meant by "social category," "social group," and "collectivity," there remains much disagreement and confusion. The terms used here are (1) collectivity, (2) social group, and (3) active collectivity. By *collectivity* is meant any conceivable set of human beings regardless of whether they interact with one another or share common characteristics or interests. By *social group* is meant a collectivity whose members do tend to interact with one another and share common characteristics and interests; social groups are formed by the predominating lines of cleavage and integration in a society. And by *active collectivity* is meant those persons who, at a particular point in time, actually engage in collective action, that is, pursue a certain goal or set of goals. (The same meaning is intended whenever I use other adjectives implying activity, such as *challenging* collectivity or *political* collectivity.) An active collectivity is comparable to what other writers would call a manifest group so long as they are not referring to an entire social group. Empirically we may have difficulty drawing a sharp line between those who participate in a case of collective action and those who do not, since there are so many degrees and kinds of participation.[18] This methodological problem does not, however, allow us to equate entire social groups with active collectivities. Social groups are defined by social structure, while active collectivities are defined by specific cases of collective action. The best way to understand collective action, in my opinion, is to trace and analyze the evolution and dissolution of social groups in a society over time, and to explain how active collectivities emerge from these social groups.

The book is divided into three parts. Part A is concerned with social structure and collective action in the pre-famine period. It emphasizes class cleavages in the rural population and the strength of neighborhood and kinship ties. It also examines the nature of national and urban ties, as well as the importance of religion as a source of integration and cleavage. This discussion is followed by a chapter that seeks to demonstrate the effect of class cleavages on Irish rural collective action, but also the effect of strong neighborhood and kinship bonds. It then attempts to explain several national movements that emerged in Ireland during this period.

Part B describes post-famine social structure, calling attention to the development of a new social group in rural Ireland whose members—large and small farmers—shared common interests. I discuss the extent to which they were involved in national and urban interaction. I examine the social relationships between members of this group and those of the landed class. And finally, I consider the distribution of political power in this period, and trace the emergence of political collectivities representing the interests of farmers.

Part C analyzes the Land War. It describes how the economic depression of the late seventies affected farmers and how it prompted a large number of them to engage in political activity. It also describes how many clergymen, nationalist politicians and members of urban social groups were brought into the active collectivity. The discussion then turns to the way in which this new active collectivity, in order to achieve its goals, had to challenge the established holders of power. The final section indicates what subsequently happened to this challenging collectivity and what

[18] George Rudé, *The Crowd in History: A Study of Popular Disturbances in France and England, 1730-1848* (New York, 1964), p. 211.

its impact was on the distribution of power in Ireland. The under-lying argument of the book is that the causes of the Land War comprised essentially two social processes: first, the development of a particular social group whose members had a common set of interests, and second, the mobilization of many members of this group in defense of those interests.

Part A
Before the Famine

Two · **Social Structure**

Class

This chapter examines patterns of social relationships in rural Ireland before the Great Famine, beginning with patterns that emerged from the way economic resources were distributed, particularly the way land was controlled and occupied. The reason for looking at pre-famine social structure is twofold. First, we need to study it so that later in the book we can compare it with post-famine social structure and can thus appreciate the social changes that occurred before the Land War. Second, it is necessary to examine pre-famine social structure in order to understand pre-famine collective action.

LANDLORD AND TENANT

In nineteenth-century Ireland the occupation of agricultural land was separated from its ownership. Rarely did the occupier of a piece of ground hold it in fee; in the great majority of cases it was let to him by a landlord. The crucial social relationship in this land system was that between landlord and tenant. It was based on a mutual exchange of rewards or benefits so that, in many ways, it resembled what anthropologists would call a "patron-client" tie. This term refers to a relationship in which a person of higher socioeconomic status provides protection or benefits to a person of lower status, who reciprocates by offering general support or some kind of service.[1] The benefit most important to ten-

---

[1] The literature on patron-client ties is extensive. Some of the best-known works are George M. Foster, "The dyadic contract in Tzintzuntzan, II: patron-client relationship" in *American Anthropologist*, 65, no. 6 (Dec. 1963); Eric Wolf, "Kinship, friendship, and patron-client relations in complex societies" in Michael Banton (ed.), *The Social Anthropology of Complex Societies* (London, 1966); Alex Weingrod, "Patrons, patronage, and political parties" in *Comparative Studies in Society and History*, 10, no. 4 (July 1968); Robert Paine (ed.), *Patrons and Brokers in the East Arctic* (St. John's, Newfoundland, 1971); and James C. Scott, "Patron-client politics and political change in Southeast Asia" in *American Political Science Review*, 66, no. 1 (March 1972). The best summary of the literature can be found in Scott.

ants was land. Whether or not they accepted the legitimacy of the landlord's legal claim to the land, the facts remained that he controlled it and that they were able to occupy it only because he granted them permission to do so. The majority of Irish tenants held land either on a seasonal basis, a yearly basis, or as tenants at will, with the result that, legally at least, they had no long-term security. And even long-term leaseholders were faced with the prospect that they might eventually lose their holdings. Hence, though the landlord's power was often curtailed by legal requirements for ejectments, ultimately he decided who should occupy his land.

Besides allowing a tenant to occupy a holding, a landlord might supply other benefits. He might protect a tenant from outsiders, from outlaws, and even from the law itself. He would usually grant his tenants certain rights to commons, and also the right to cut turf (known as the right of turbary). A landlord might assist his tenants during hard times, and many landlords gave employment to persons living on their estates. Finally, a landlord could help a tenant to farm his holding or to improve it. In reality, Irish landlords had a reputation for providing few additional services. There was, nevertheless, an expectation that they should do more than just let land. Consequently, the extent to which they did so had a considerable effect on the nature of the relations that they enjoyed with their tenantry.

In return for providing a tenant with land (and for additional services if they were rendered), the landlord expected to receive a rent. In practice, this rent could take a variety of forms. It was common for rents to be paid not only in money, but also in labor and occasionally in kind. Even when rent was paid in money, there could be, in addition, labor duty or possibly a payment in kind, such as the occasional "duty fowl." Quite distinct from the payment of rent, an important service that could also be provided by tenants was political support for their landlord. In the nineteenth century political support customarily took the form of voting for the landlord's candidate in parliamentary elections.

The essence, then, of the landlord-tenant relationship was an exchange of benefits, the most important of which were land and rent. For how long had such a system prevailed in rural Ireland? How had it come to be established? According to one view, there was nothing like this system before the arrival of the Normans, since there was then no private property. Supposedly, in ancient

Gaelic Ireland land was held in common by a tribe; every member of the tribe was entitled to a share of the land; and a chief who acted as a trustee (rather than owner) allotted these shares, which were subject to periodic redistribution according to a mode of succession that resembled the English gavelkind. It is now known, however, especially for the period before and during the Viking invasions, that most land was actually owned by extended families. Within such families it was indeed held communally and redistributed periodically. Although these landowning families constituted a much larger proportion of the population than did landowners in the nineteenth century, they were nevertheless outnumbered by tenants, as well as by serfs, landless laborers, and slaves. Among themselves, many groups of tenants farmed land in common and redistributed it periodically in much the same way as did those who owned it. Yet communal sharing of land by tenants, so far as it existed, did not mean that land was owned by a tribe. Land was owned by landowning families, and what they did not use themselves, they let out as landlords to tenants in return for payments in kind or other services. They also let out livestock, particularly cattle, often in conjunction with the letting of land.[2]

The principal effect of the Anglo-Norman invasion and settlement of Ireland in the twelfth century was to introduce a variant of the English feudal system. The Normans never managed to conquer the entire island, with the result that two different systems of land tenure, indeed two different cultures, prevailed simultaneously in medieval Ireland, in some places fusing together, in other places remaining largely distinct. This mixture of systems persisted until the sixteenth and seventeenth centuries when England extended its control, and the country went through a vast and extremely complex transformation in the way it was governed and in the way its land was distributed. Large amounts of land

[2] This is, of course, an extremely complex subject about which any kind of generalization is hazardous. Recent accounts appear in Gearóid Mac Niocaill, *Ireland Before the Vikings* (Dublin, 1972), pp. 59-69; and Donncha Ó Corráin, *Ireland Before the Normans* (Dublin, 1972), pp. 42-74. The classic works are Eoin MacNeill, "Communal ownership in ancient Ireland" in *Irish Monthly*, 47 (Aug.-Sept. 1918); W. F. Butler, "Irish land tenures: Celtic and foreign" in *Studies*, 13, no. 52 (Dec. 1924); and Michael Duignan, "Irish agriculture in early historic times" in *Journal of the Royal Society of Antiquaries of Ireland*, series seven, 14, pt. 3 (Sept. 1944). See also W. E. Montgomery, *The History of Land Tenure in Ireland* (Cambridge, 1889), which is useful in many ways, though more ambiguous than the above works on the question of land ownership.

were lost by Gaelic chiefs and Anglo-Irish lords, and acquired by English or Scottish Protestants. In some cases concerted efforts were made to settle or "plant" English and Scottish colonists on confiscated land. The major confiscations occurred in the midlands and in Munster during the late sixteenth century, in Ulster during the early seventeenth century, and throughout the country (with the partial exception of Clare and Connaught) during the mid-seventeenth century. Finally, after the defeat of James II by William of Orange in 1690, Protestant control over the island was consolidated, and a series of "penal laws" were subsequently passed by the Irish parliament. These laws sought to limit the rights of Catholics in politics and land ownership, to restrict Catholic education, and to destroy the formal organization of the Catholic church by abolishing Catholic orders and expelling Catholic bishops.[3]

We do not yet know exactly what effect this upheaval had on the social structure. The most obvious consequence was a nearly complete transformation in the religious affiliation of landowners. It has been estimated that, as late as 1640, almost 60 percent of the land was still owned by Catholics. After the confiscations of the mid-seventeenth century, the proportion was cut to 22 percent, and after the Williamite confiscations it was reduced to 14 percent.[4] This meager number was diminished yet further in the eighteenth century by the operation of the penal laws, which stated that no Roman Catholic could purchase any interest in land or acquire land from a Protestant by inheritance or marriage. The laws also stipulated that leases granted to Catholics could not exceed thirty-one years, and that land could not be let to Catholics at a rent of less than two-thirds the annual value of the property. These letting restrictions were not generally enforced on small tenants, but were used to frustrate Catholic middlemen who leased tracts of land and sublet portions to smaller agriculturalists. The main intent of this legislation was not to oppress the Catholic masses, but rather to assure that few Catholics would remain either real owners of land or de facto owners through long leases at low rents.

On the other hand, there is no doubt that the confiscations and the penal laws established a religiously stratified social order in

---

[3] See Maureen Wall, The Penal Laws, 1691-1760 (Dublin, 1961/1967).

[4] E. M. Johnston, Ireland in the Eighteenth Century (Dublin, 1974), p. 13.

Ireland that put all Catholics, whatever their position in society, at a disadvantage relative to Protestants. In addition, there are some grounds for believing that the confiscations had an effect on the nature of the landlord-tenant relationship. Communal sharing of land among tenants disappeared in most parts of the country between the sixteenth and eighteenth centuries, presumably as a result of opposition on the part of the new landowners. It was also widely believed by contemporaries that the new owners were more ostentatious and materialistic than were the old ones, that the relations they established with their tenantry were more commercialized, and that they regarded their tenants primarily as a source of cash income.[5] It is extremely difficult, however, to distinguish between the effects of the confiscations and the consequences of other sources of change in this period, particularly economic factors. Further research is necessary to permit anything more than hypothetical conclusions.

In any event, whatever the impact of the confiscations on landlord-tenant relations, it was eventually to be overshadowed by the catastrophic results of population growth in the late eighteenth and early nineteenth centuries. Within the space of fifty years, from the 1790s to the 1840s, the population of Ireland rose from four to eight million. Irish historians do not yet agree on what caused this remarkable increase. One theory has it that the traditional balance between births and deaths, which kept population at low levels before 1750, was upset in the late eighteenth century by the concurrence of two developments: a shift from pasture to tillage, and the expansion of potato cultivation. These changes, it has been alleged, brought about a sharp decline in the average age at which people married. Presumably the reason was that the potato provided higher food yield per acre, and thereby offered young couples a means by which they could set up house at an early age while parents and younger siblings still remained on the family holding.[6] The shift to tillage had a compounding effect by reducing the capital necessary to begin farming and by increasing the demand for agricultural labor.[7] Young couples could establish themselves without expensive livestock, and could find

[5] Edward MacLysaght, *Irish Life in the Seventeenth Century* (New York, 1939/1969), pp. 112-13.

[6] K. H. Connell, *The Population of Ireland, 1750-1845* (Oxford, 1950).

[7] Raymond Crotty, *Irish Agricultural Production: Its Volume and Structure* (Cork, 1966), pp. 30-32.

room on part of the family holding, on reclaimed wasteland, or on land made available by farmers who were shifting from pasture to tillage and had land to let in return for labor. Earlier marriages, so the argument goes, meant more births, which thus set in motion an upward spiraling of population. This explanation has, however, been disputed by a number of scholars. One writer has argued that there was no decline in the average age of marriage and that the potato contributed to population growth not by encouraging earlier marriages, but rather by increasing the fecundity of women and by lowering the mortality rate.[8] It has also been suggested that the potato may not have been a significant causal factor at all. Elsewhere in Europe populations were increasing at the same time and almost at the same rate, even in places where the potato could not have been responsible. Moreover, there is some reason to believe that the dissemination of the potato in Ireland came after population expansion was well underway. It is possible that the death rate declined in the late eighteenth century for reasons independent of the potato and that the potato diet was primarily a consequence of population growth rather than a cause.[9]

The additional population was accommodated on the land by the subdivision of holdings. There were two ways in which this occurred. First, it resulted from the traditional practice in Ireland of dividing land among the children of the family. As the supply of land dwindled in the late eighteenth and early nineteenth centuries, the pressure to carve up the family holding in this manner became all the greater. Second, subdivision resulted from subletting. In the eighteenth century, landowners often leased large portions of their estates to Protestant gentlemen or wealthy Catholic farmers, thus sparing themselves the burden of managing them. Several legislative measures in the late eighteenth century further

[8] Michael Drake, "Marriage and population growth in Ireland, 1750-1845" in *Economic History Review*, second series, 16, no. 2 (1963); see also his "Population growth and the Irish economy" in L. M. Cullen (ed.), *The Formation of the Irish Economy* (Cork, 1969).

[9] See L. M. Cullen, "Irish history without the potato" in *Past and Present*, no. 40 (1968); and his *An Economic History of Ireland Since 1660* (London, 1972), p. 118. See also Drake, "Population growth and the Irish economy," p. 68. Further commentaries on the Connell thesis and its critics can be found in Joseph Lee, "Marriage and population in pre-famine Ireland" in *Economic History Review*, second series, 21, no. 2 (1968); and G.S.L. Tucker, "Irish fertility ratios before the Famine" in *Economic History Review*, second series, 23, no. 2 (1970).

encouraged landowners to grant long leases: first, the Catholic relief act of 1778, which allowed Catholics to take leases for any
fixed term up to 999 years or for any number of lives up to five;
and second, the Catholic relief act of 1793, which extended the
parliamentary franchise to Catholics, including Catholic tenants
with a lease of at least one life. Thereafter, in an effort to enhance
their political power, landowners began to grant even more
leases, which rarely contained any covenants against subletting.
As a result, more and more tenants became free to sublet land,
and, beginning in the 1790s, the entire middleman system in Ireland underwent a substantial change. The number of middlemen
increased and the typical middleman came to be, not a Protestant
gentleman, but a large (usually Catholic) farmer.[10] In this way agricultural holdings in Ireland were repeatedly subdivided, with
the result that by the second quarter of the nineteenth century the
great mass of Irish people pursued miserable lives on mere scraps
of land.

I shall indicate later that this population growth had significant
consequences for the class structure. Right now I am interested in
the effect that it had on the landlord-tenant relationship. Initially,
it provided advantages for the landlord because it magnified his
rewards from the land system. Population growth increased landlord income by generating competition for land and driving up
the value of rents.[11] It was often noted that farmers were able to
make more money by subletting their land than by farming it
themselves, and it was commonly believed that many graziers
made fortunes doing just that.[12] Landowners, perhaps, experienced less of a windfall from population growth, since so many of
them had tied up great portions of their estates in long leases at
fixed rents. Nevertheless, they could take advantage of rising rents
on holdings for which leases had expired, while enjoying unusually regular payment of rents on the remainder of the property.
Evidence collected from the records of individual estates shows
gross rents doubling, and in some cases tripling, between the

[10] James S. Donnelly, Jr., The Land and the People of Nineteenth-Century Cork:
The Rural Economy and the Land Question (London, 1975), pp. 9-12.

[11] Crotty, Irish Agricultural Production, pp. 33-4; see also David Large, "The
wealth of the greater Irish landowners, 1750-1815" in Irish Historical Studies, 15,
no. 57 (March 1966), p. 28.

[12] Isaac Weld, Statistical Survey of the County of Roscommon (Dublin, 1832),
p. 667.

mid-eighteenth century and the second decade of the nineteenth
century.[13]

Population growth, however, had positive consequences for
Irish landlords only so long as it was accompanied by economic
prosperity. High English demand for Irish agricultural exports
during the French Revolutionary and Napoleonic Wars maintained this prosperity until almost 1815.[14] But the close of the
Napoleonic Wars reversed the economic trend and initiated a
period of weak demand for agricultural produce, lower government expenditure, and a restriction of the money supply.
There began a long deflationary period, lasting until the mid-
1830s and drastically reducing economic returns to Irish agriculturalists. Actually the volume of agricultural exports continued to
rise. But prices fell, especially for corn, butter, and provisions,
which declined by a third or more between 1812-15 and the early
1830s.[15] To make matters worse, serious crop failures repeatedly
occurred in various districts, particularly in the west. And Irish
industry, which had gradually fallen into a precarious position as
a result of competition from much cheaper British goods, suffered further market losses when the remaining tariffs protecting
Irish goods from British competition were abolished in 1824.
Formerly, in the late eighteenth century, a significant proportion
of both the urban and the rural labor force had been engaged in
manufacturing, but this vital source of employment now declined
precisely when population growth was creating an even greater
need for it. The worst affected was the textile industry, in which
rural as well as urban people (including many farm families) had
been employed as domestic weavers. The major exception to this
general trend was in Ulster, where the linen industry recovered in
the late 1820s owing to the introduction of power-spinning. Yet
even here a serious loss of income was experienced by farm
families because spinning was no longer done in the home.[16]

As the economic situation deteriorated, it became more difficult
for tenants to pay their rents. Middlemen, now caught between

[13] Large, "The wealth of the greater Irish landowners," appendix.

[14] Cullen, An Economic History of Ireland, p. 100; Crotty, Irish Agricultural
Production, pp. 276-7, 282-5.

[15] Crotty, Irish Agricultural Production, p. 284.

[16] E.R.R. Green, "Industrial decline in the nineteenth century" in L. M. Cullen
(ed.), The Formation of the Irish Economy (Cork, 1969); see also Cullen, An Economic History of Ireland, pp. 105-8 and 119-20.

defaulting under-tenants and leases at fixed rents, found it hard to balance their accounts. Historians have been able to document a number of cases in which middlemen went bankrupt.[17] Land-owners also suffered losses as both middlemen and direct tenants began to accumulate arrears. One of the most striking examples was the Fitzwilliam estate in the counties of Wicklow, Waterford, and Kildare. This region was not especially hard hit by the economic depression or by crop failures, and yet arrears on the Fitzwilliam properties rose from just under £3,000 in 1814 to over £11,000 in 1818 and by 1826 to over £35,000, which was then almost exactly equivalent to a year's rent.[18] On the Queen's County estate of George Rutland, arrears already averaged 91 percent of the annual rent in the five-year period 1816-20. On this property they fell to an average of 73 percent in 1821-5, but on Rutland's Tipperary estate they rose from an average of 63 percent during 1816-20 to an average of 71 percent in 1821-5, while on his Cork property they rose from an average of 7 percent to an average of 28 percent over the same period. On the Earl of Leitrim's Mohill estate in County Leitrim, the average arrears due at each gale day increased from £259 in 1810-14, to £1,171 in 1815-19, and to £1,871 in 1820-4.[19]

A landlord faced with a tenant in arrears had two principal ways to force payment: he could seize the tenant's property or he could threaten him with ejectment. If rents were not paid, the law allowed a landlord to seize or "distrain" chattels that were not perishable and were capable of being restored. Most often live-stock belonging to the tenant would be taken and held at the ten-ant's expense. This method had certain advantages over eject-ments. No period of notice was required and no court order was necessary. On the other hand, distraining had its disadvantages. There was room for corruption on the part of drivers and pound-keepers who seized and held distrained property. Tenants could, and often did, hide livestock, boycott the sale of distrained goods, or even forcibly recover their property. After 1832, the law re-

[17] F.S.L. Lyons, "Vicissitudes of a middleman in County Leitrim, 1810-27" in *Irish Historical Studies*, 9, no. 35 (March 1955); see also Donnelly, *Cork*, pp. 49-50.

[18] Large, "The wealth of the greater Irish landowners," pp. 32-3.

[19] N.L.I., Rutland papers: Rentals of the Cork, Tipperary, Wicklow, and Queen's County properties (MSS 12769-78); Leitrim papers: Rentals of the Mohill estate, 1809-29 (MSS 12792-804). Averages are based on both the March and September gales.

quired that distraining be carried out by the sheriff, and other restrictions were placed on the practice. At the same time, ejectments were becoming easier and less costly. Before 1816 ejectment decrees could be obtained only in a superior court at a cost of £15, but legislation passed in that year enabled landlords to obtain decrees through a local civil-bill court at a cost of only £2.[20]

Ejectments had another advantage. If carried through, they rid the landlord of a weak tenant. This was an important consideration during a period in which landowners were generally making efforts to reform the management of their estates and to put them on a sounder economic footing. The most noticeable sign of this new approach was a growing reluctance on the part of owners to grant leases, particularly to middlemen. As revenues declined, they became increasingly distressed about how much of the rental was going to intermediaries.[21] In the post-war period a greater number of them began to take advantage of the expiration of leases to assume direct control over their properties.[22] In doing so, they inevitably had to confront the problem of subdivision of holdings. This had not been a source of great concern when arrears had been low, but after 1815, when rents became difficult to collect, most owners looked with horror on the great number of small landholders who inhabited their estates. In most cases, these small tenants were the ones responsible for unpaid rents, and no owner could seriously hope to maximize the economic return from his lands without disturbing them.

[20] 56 Geo. III, c. 88. See also Patrick Dardis, The Occupation of Land in Ireland in the First Half of the Nineteenth Century (Dublin, 1920), pp. 32-7.

[21] For instance, in 1832 it was estimated that the Earl of Essex could have collected £36,000 per annum from his estate in Roscommon if he had let it directly to the occupiers, whereas the rent he in fact received was only £16,000. See Weld, Statistical Survey of Roscommon, pp. 398 and 460. For other examples see the diary of Sir John Benn-Walsh, owner of some 11,000 acres in Kerry and Cork, who frequently referred to differences between the rent he collected from a middleman and what he could have obtained by letting directly to the occupiers. See James S. Donnelly, Jr. (ed.), "The journals of Sir John Benn-Walsh relating to the management of his Irish estates, 1823-64" in Cork Historical and Archaeological Society Journal, 79, no. 230 (1974) and 80, no. 231 (1975).

[22] O. Robinson, "The London companies as progressive landlords in nineteenth-century Ireland" in Economic History Review, 15 (1962-3); W. A. Maguire, The Downshire Estates in Ireland, 1801-1845 (Oxford, 1972), pp. 120 and 129; and Donnelly, Cork, pp. 50-53. W. H. Crawford argues that phasing out middlemen began in the late eighteenth century in Ulster. See his "Landlord-tenant relations in Ulster, 1609-1820" in Irish Economic and Social History, 2 (1975), pp. 13-14.

The courses of action that landowners followed varied greatly. At one extreme was the owner who conscientiously set about to reorganize his property. Such reorganization did not necessarily entail removing tenants completely, but it normally did require that large numbers of holders be relocated. In the late 1830s Lord Palmerston took advantage of the expiration of six leases to relocate 280 tenants on his estate in County Sligo.[23] The second Earl of Leitrim personally surveyed his Mohill property in 1839 and directed his land agent to break leases in order to rearrange holdings.[24] More than occasionally, landowners sought to evict small holders regardless of whether they were paying their rents, so that their lands could be consolidated to form larger farms. In 1843, for example, over 150 families were reportedly evicted from Lord Lorton's estate near Boyle to form six large holdings.[25] Most often, however, notices to quit fell on tenants who were heavily in arrears. The majority of owners adopted a policy of proceeding mainly against defaulting tenants, getting "rid of the poorest by degrees" and hoping that eventually they would weed out most of the "bad" tenants on their lands.[26]

Landowners were especially anxious to dislodge squatters who occupied land without official permission and frequently without paying rent. On the Farnham estates in County Cavan, plans were made in 1830 to clear large areas inhabited by "transient paupers."[27] Six hundred acres of land near Nenagh were originally let to three or four farmers, but were occupied almost entirely by "families of squatters" in 1843 when they were all served with notices to quit by the head landlord.[28] According to Isaac Weld, when the Coote Hall property in north Roscommon was purchased by Hugh Barton in the 1820s, it "had the reputation of being inhabited, at least in great part, by a lawless race." "Crimi-

[23] Dardis, *The Occupation of Land in Ireland in the First Half of the Nineteenth Century*, p. 103.

[24] N.L.I., Leitrim papers: Second Earl of Leitrim's directions, 1839 (MS 3829).

[25] *Dublin Evening Post*, 25 July 1843, p. 3. For other examples, see Samuel Nicholson, *Report upon the general state of agriculture in the district of the country adjoining the middle Shannon; comprising parts of the counties of Tipperary, Galway, Roscommon, Westmeath and King's County* (Dublin, 1841), pp. 34-5; Robinson, "The London companies," p. 12; and Donnelly, *Cork*, pp. 55-8.

[26] The language quoted is that of Sir John Benn-Walsh. See Donnelly, "Journals of Sir John Benn-Walsh," pp. 83 and 101.

[27] *A Statement of the Management of the Farnham Estates* (Dublin, 1830).

[28] *Dublin Evening Post*, 16 Sept. 1843, p. 3.

nals flying from other parts had here found a ready and secure asylum." The new owner removed all but the best tenants. "What became of the outcasts is not known;" observed Weld, "they had been expelled, and of course had to seek elsewhere for a new settlement."[29] Lord Leitrim faced a similar problem with laborers on his Mohill estate. "Some of the cottiers," he noted in 1839, "are sitting rent free. They should be ejected and put out immediately and let them make whatever bargain they please for a new house elsewhere."[30]

The unmistakable motivation underlying ejectments, as well as other steps landlords were taking in this period, was to prevent their revenues from shrinking. Post-war economic conditions made it necessary for them to manage their affairs more carefully in order to continue to receive the same level of economic returns that they had enjoyed in the earlier years of prosperity. The difficulties they faced were in no small way of their own making. They had run their estates poorly in the late eighteenth and early nineteenth centuries. Many proprietors had also accumulated enormous debts,[31] which often constituted the major reason they were so determined to maintain their incomes during the economic downturn. Yet their situation was also, of course, a product of demographic and economic forces over which they had no control, but with which they were forced to cope. By resisting demands for abatements, reducing the number of leases, taking legal action against tenants in arrears, and working to remove insolvent occupiers from their properties—by these and other methods many landlords tried to minimize their losses.

Inevitably, they did so at the expense of tenants. The economic downturn obviously meant a decrease in the rewards that tenants received from the land system. The deflation in agricultural prices fell heaviest upon their shoulders. Self-employed tenants engaged in commercialized agriculture now earned a lower return on their investments, while those who worked for them had to endure the consequences of a reduced demand for agricultural labor. Moreover, though agricultural prices were falling, many of the costs faced by tenants were not. The total amount of county cess

---

[29] Weld, *Statistical Survey of Roscommon*, pp. 247-51.

[30] N.L.I., Leitrim papers: Second Earl of Leitrim's directions, 1839 (MS 3829).

[31] See Large, "The wealth of the greater Irish landowners"; Maguire, *The Downshire Estates in Ireland*, pp. 65-106; and Maguire, "The 1822 settlement of the Donegall estates" in *Irish Economic and Social History*, 3 (1976).

levied in Ireland (an acreable charge) rose from less than £900,000
in the 1820s to over £1,100,000 in the 1840s.[32] Similarly, the tithes
that tenants were required to pay to the Protestant Church of Ireland were generally computed at acreable rates, and so did not
vary with the value of their output, though legislation passed in
the 1820s did reform the method of collection and bring tithes
more into line with post-war prices. And it is unlikely that rents
declined sufficiently to offset the fall in agricultural incomes. Indeed it is possible that rents in Ireland increased slightly between
1811 and 1843.[33]

By the 1820s the traditional exchange of benefits between landlords and tenants had become severely strained because both
sides were faced with actual or potential losses that could only be
minimized at the expense of the other.[34] Tenants could offset their
declining incomes only by reducing their rent payments; landlords could prevent their rental income from falling only by insisting that rents be paid and by removing tenants who defaulted.
On the one hand, landlords had legal resources that enabled them
to execute a number of changes in estate management to their advantage. On the other hand, tenants were far from powerless to
protect their interests. There were ways in which they could collectively resist landlord encroachments. To understand the form
this resistance took, however, the landlord-tenant relationship
must be viewed in the context of the rural class structure as a
whole. What were the major social classes in the rural society at
this time?

THE MAJOR CLASSES

At the top of the social ladder we can confidently place large
landed proprietors, numbering probably less than 10,000 even if

[32] Return of the total amount of county cess levied in each county, &c., in Ireland, in each year since 1824, H.C. 1839 (353), xlvii; Account of the total amount
levied for all purposes by grand juries in Ireland, and amount of repayments to
government, for the years 1843 to 1849, inclusive, H.C. 1850 (630), li.

[33] Crotty, Irish Agricultural Production, pp. 305-6.

[34] Here and elsewhere in this book (most of all in Chapters Five and Seven) the
reader may detect the influence of Barrington Moore Jr., Social Origins of Dictatorship and Democracy: Lord and Peasant in the Making of the Modern World (Boston, 1966), especially Chapter 9. Moore's explanation of peasant rebellion has recently been developed and expanded in James C. Scott, The Moral Economy of the
Peasant: Rebellion and Subsistence in Southeast Asia (New Haven, 1976). See in
particular Chapter 6.

all those with estates of over a hundred acres are included. They were very much aloof from the people who lived on the land they owned; perhaps more than half resided away from their properties. Those with aristocratic titles or conspicuously large amounts of land comprised an elite segment with special status, but the majority of them belonged to the same religious group and were tied together by interlocking social networks. Along with their control over the use of land, they had immense political power. They monopolized parliamentary representation and dominated the principal institutions of local government, most notably the local courts and the county grand juries.

So striking was the distinctiveness of this social group, and so enormous was its power, that it is tempting to think of pre-famine rural society as divided into two social classes consisting of those who owned the land and those who cultivated it. This picture of the class structure is indeed the one that most Irish people have been given. As historians have begun to discover, however, it is far from the truth. The social cleavage between owners and cultivators, while very real, was no greater than the cleavages that divided the cultivating class itself.

First, there were differences among cultivators in their relation to the land. Size of holdings varied greatly, between large farms of fifty, a hundred, or even several hundred acres, and small holdings of one, five, or ten acres; half the holdings in 1844 were under eleven acres.[35] A critical difference also obviously existed between those who occupied land and those who did not; in the early 1840s one-quarter of the adult male agricultural labor force may not have held land.[36] And perhaps the most important difference resulted from the practice of subletting. We have already seen that in the eighteenth century it was common for landowners to let their lands to middlemen. I indicated that in the early nineteenth century many proprietors tried to eliminate middlemen; they either refused to give leases or gave leases containing strict covenants against subletting.[37] It should not be assumed, however, that they succeeded in eliminating middlemen altogether, or even that the practice of subletting declined substantially in the first half of the nineteenth century. It is perhaps true

[35] See Table 2 in Chapter Four below.

[36] See Table 4 in Chapter Four below.

[37] James S. Donnelly, Jr., *Landlord and Tenant in Nineteenth-Century Ireland* (Dublin, 1973), pp. 22-3; and his *Cork*, pp. 59-62.

that there were now fewer "gentry-middlemen" than in the eighteenth century, that is, fewer land agents, lawyers, Protestant clergymen, or landowners' sons who made a comfortable living by leasing and then subletting large portions of estates. But this decline was certainly offset by an increase in the number of "farmer-middlemen." The growing population had to find land somewhere, whether by obtaining tenancies, squatting, or hiring land on a seasonal basis.

Of necessity, subletting in one form or another was still to be found in almost all parts of the country. One historian has cited a case in Fermanagh where seventy tenants who let land directly from the owner had 167 undertenants; and another source refers to a case where as many as five persons intervened between the head landlord and the occupier.[38] James Donnelly, in his study of social life in nineteenth-century Cork, makes mention of a 750-acre tract on the Rathcool property of Sir George Colthurst, which was sublet sometime before 1770 to a middleman, who then sublet it to two other tenants, who then further sublet the property so that when the original lease expired in 1845 there were over 300 inhabitants on the property.[39] Also in County Cork, eighty-eight holdings let directly from Viscount Midleton were occupied by no less than 494 tenants in 1839.[40] And a Trinity College survey conducted in 1843 returned a total of 12,529 tenants on lands owned by the College, of whom less 1 percent held directly from the College, while 45 percent held from a College lessee, and 52 percent held from still another middleman who was a tenant to a College lessee.[41]

It is no exaggeration to say that most landlords in pre-famine

[38] Harold T. Masterson, "Land-use patterns and farming practice in County Fermanagh, 1609-1845" in *Clogher Record*, 7, no. 1 (1969), p. 78; Dardis, *The Occupation of Land in Ireland in the First Half of the Nineteenth Century*, p. 43.

[39] Donnelly, *Cork*, p. 14.

[40] These eighty-eight holdings represent a sample of holdings in seventeen different townlands on the Midleton estate. P.R.O.I., Midleton papers: Descriptive report and survey, with maps, by Charles Bailey, Cheltenham, England, of the Irish estates of Viscount Midleton, 1839-40 (978/2/4/1). See Donnelly, *Cork*, pp. 13-14 for further illustrations of extensive subletting on the Midleton estate.

[41] T.C.D., Trinity College papers: Descriptive survey and valuation of the Trinity College estate, 1845 (MUN/V/78/46-61). The lands covered by this survey were situated in sixteen different counties and represented just over 195,000 acres, mostly in the southwest and northwest. Virtually all the land was let to "College lessees" on long leases of twenty-one years renewable yearly. For further explanation of this survey see F. J. Carney, "Pre-famine Irish population: the evidence

Ireland were not landowners; they were tenants with large holdings. The system was so complex that it was not unknown for two
people to be both landlord and tenant to one another.[42] The result
was obviously that many persons found it difficult to think of
themselves either as landlords or as tenants, because they were
both. It also meant that tensions which developed in landlord-
tenant relationships during this period put occupiers at odds not
only with owners, but also, in many cases, with other occupiers.
In fact, relationships between middlemen and their tenants were,
by reputation, far worse than those between landowners and their
tenants, primarily because subtenants enjoyed, as a rule, much
less security of tenure than did their landlords, and because middlemen ordinarily charged at least double the rent they paid
themselves and often considerably more.[43]

A second major source of cleavage in rural society resulted from
the fact that many cultivators worked for other cultivators. According to the 1841 census, 70 percent of the adult male agricultural labor force consisted of laborers. This figure includes many
adult farmers' sons working on the family farm, and I would estimate that excluding them would reduce the proportion comprised
by laborers to 56 percent.[44] This is still over half of the labor force.
Many laborers were landless, but most were *laborer-landholders*.
They had cabins and small potato gardens, and were often known

---

from the Trinity College estates" in *Irish Economic and Social History*, 2 (1975).
For an examination of landlord-tenant relationships on the estate during the last
half of the nineteenth century see W. J. Lowe, "Landlord and tenant on the estate of
Trinity College Dublin, 1851-1903" in *Hermathena*, no. 120 (Summer 1976).

[42] See a case before the Kilmacow Petty Sessions reported in *Kilkenny Journal*,
10 Nov. 1830, p. 4.

[43] Weld, *Statistical Survey of Roscommon*, p. 323; Dardis, *The Occupation of
Land in Ireland in the First Half of the Nineteenth Century*, pp. 42-3; Masterson,
"Land-use patterns in Fermanagh," p. 78. The Midleton estate survey also gives
numerous comparisons between rents paid by middlemen and the rents they
collected.

[44] This estimate is obtained by assuming that the ratio of adult farmers' sons to
farmers was the same in 1841 as it was in 1881 when farmers' sons were listed
separately. Making this assumption, I have estimated that there were 226,658 adult
farmers' sons in 1841, which represents 14 percent of the adult male agricultural
labor force. What I have called laborers includes "servants and laborers," "plow-
men" and "herds." By adult is meant fifteen years of age and over. The source is
*Report of the commissioners appointed to take the census of Ireland for the year
1841*, p. 440 [504], H.C. 1843, xxiv.

as "cottiers."[45] In addition, both landless workers and laborer-landholders frequently obtained land on a seasonal basis, a practice known as taking land in "conacre." Laborer-landholders might be forced to seek employment wherever they could find it, but they often worked for the same farmer from whom they obtained their small holdings. In such cases a landholder was usually bound to work for his landlord when called upon, and, in effect, paid his rent in labor. The farmer might keep a tally of wages owed to the laborer, and at the end of the season deduct the sum from the total rent that was due.[46] Or he might pay the laborer a reduced wage, but provide him with a cabin, garden, or rights to grazing and cutting turf, perhaps also making a separate bargain for potato ground.[47]

The rents charged by farmers were high. Cabins, gardens, and related privileges often cost nearly £2, though near towns as much as six guineas might be charged.[48] Rents for potato ground varied considerably from one district to another and depending on whether or not the farmer prepared the ground. Taking land in conacre was the most expensive; conacre rents usually ranged between £6 and £8 per acre, but they could go as high as £10 or even £12 per acre.[49] At the same time, wages were low. There was an over-supply of labor relative to the demand as a result of the massive growth in population, the industrial decline, and the efforts of farmers to economize in the face of lower prices. In most areas an unbound laborer could expect to earn no more than 4d. to 8d. per day for most of the year and no more than 10d. to 1s. 2d. during the harvest, or even less in some districts, particularly in Con-

[45] The usage of this term varied. It could also refer simply to a landholder with a very small holding, usually less than ten acres, or it could refer to the occupier of a cabin, without any consideration of his occupation or the character of his land holding. See M. R. Beames, "Cottiers and conacre in pre-famine Ireland" in *Journal of Peasant Studies*, 2, no. 3 (1975).

[46] Jasper W. Rogers, *The Potato Truck System of Ireland* (London, 1847), p. 4; Thomas P. O'Neill, "Rural life" in R. B. McDowell (ed.), *Social Life in Ireland, 1800-45* (Cork, 1957), p. 42.

[47] E.R.R. Green, "Agriculture" in R. Dudley Edwards and T. Desmond Williams (eds.), *The Great Famine* (Dublin, 1956), pp. 92-5; Donnelly, *Cork*, pp. 16-18; Nicholson, *Report upon the general state of agriculture*, p. 59.

[48] Green, "Agriculture," pp. 92-5; Donnelly, *Cork*, p. 17; Weld, *Statistical Survey of Roscommon*, p. 323.

[49] Donnelly, *Cork*, p. 20; Nicholson, *Report upon the general state of agriculture*, p. 57.

naught, where 8d. per day was the standard harvest wage.[50] Typically, the annual earnings of a laborer ranged from £5 to £10.[51]
Moreover, it was frequently claimed that farmers mistreated their
laborers. Farmers were sometimes brought by laborers before the
petty sessions for withholding wages, refusing to draw out manure or plow potato ground, failing to re-thatch cabins, and ille-
gally taking possession of potato gardens, dung, sheep, or pigs.[52]
Not surprisingly, the relations between farmers and laborers were
often bitter.

And finally, still another source of conflict among cultivators
came from differences in attitudes toward pasture farming. Grazing was generally preferred by large farmers, perhaps because in
most regions in Ireland the land is better suited to pasture than to
tillage. It is also possible that in the post-war period prices for tillage products fell more sharply than did prices for grassland products and that the latter recovered sooner.[53] If so, market conditions were pushing Irish agriculture in the direction of greater
pasture farming, while at the same time population expansion
was pushing it in the direction of increased tillage. Small farmers
and laborers depended on the preservation of tillage land to find a
place to grow their potatoes and for agricultural employment. The
widespread hostility among the poor against grazing and against
farmers who specialized in grazing indicates that these people
were well aware of the danger that pasture farming presented to
their interests.

To reiterate, any description of the class structure of pre-famine
Ireland would need to emphasize not only the cleavage between
owners and cultivators, but also divisions among cultivators
themselves. These divisions were intricate and cannot be easily
delineated. Realistically, we should think of the agrarian class
structure as formed by a gradation in levels of power and wealth,
from the landless laborer to the very large farmer, with infinite
distinctions in between. We should take into account differences
among farmers according to the size of their holdings, the terms of
their tenure, and whether or not they employed laborers; we

---

[50] Poor Inquiry (Ireland): appendix (D) containing baronial examinations relative to earnings of labourers, cottier tenants, employment of women and children,
expenditure; and supplement containing answers to questions 1 to 12 circulated
by the commissioners [36], H.C. 1836, xxxi; see also Donnelly, Cork, p. 21.
[51] Poor Inquiry: appendix (D).   [52] Donnelly, Cork, pp. 17-18.
[53] Crotty, Irish Agricultural Production, pp. 35-6, 287-93.

should also consider differences among laborers according to whether they had access to land, and if so whether on a permanent or seasonal basis, as well as whether they had regular or casual employment.

It is not impossible, however, to sort out some of this complexity and to divide cultivators into two or three broad categories. Some sources of cleavage had more effect on social behavior than others and can be used as the basis for arriving at several major divisions. We can identify three such cleavages, one of which was especially important.

The people themselves made a sharp distinction between those who held land and those who did not. However small a holding might be, possession of land placed an individual or a family in a position that was qualitatively different from the situation of a person without land, particularly if possession was long-term and relatively secure. Contemporaries also recognized the distinction between farmers and laborers. Farmers were occupiers whose produce was sufficient, in normal times, to feed their families, pay their rents, and make possible the purchase of at least some goods that were not produced in the home. Farmers spent the better part of their working days in self-employment; they were, in this sense, *independent landholders*. Laborers, on the other hand, were persons who had no land or not enough land to support themselves without working for someone else; they were, in the Marxist idiom, more "proletarianized" than farmers, a difference that carries great significance in almost any society. Yet both these cleavages were frequently obscured. There was often more in common between small farmers and laborers than between small farmers and large farmers. In life style and standard of living small farmers were ordinarily little better off than laborers. Small farmers did not, as a rule, employ laborers; on the contrary, some small farmers (and very often their sons) could be forced to engage in outside work. Some small farmers were, like laborer-landholders, subtenants to large farmers. And most small farmers shared with laborers an interest in preserving land for tillage. Similarly, there was often much in common between those who occupied land and those who did not. Indeed, in the Irish context, the term "landless" can be somewhat misleading, since many landless people depended for their livelihood on obtaining land in conacre. And those who were truly landless (mostly farm servants) were usually related by blood to small landholders.

The greatest cleavage among cultivators in pre-famine Ireland was between large farmers and the rest. Collectively we can refer to small farmers, laborer-landholders, and landless laborers as the *rural poor*. The boundary between this group and the large-farmer class was continuous rather than dichotomous, and hence cannot be specified precisely; whenever I refer to a specific acreage as the cut-off point (as I occasionally shall), I do so for analytical purposes only, and not because any precise acreage can be used to put people into one category or the other. In spite of these limitations, the classification serves to identify the most critical differences in interests within the cultivating population. Generally speaking, it was the large farmer who filled the unpopular roles of landlord, employer, and/or grazier. Large farmers comprised an elite group within the agricultural population, and the differences that separated them from the rest of the rural society were more important than sources of opposition among the rural poor themselves. They were greatly outnumbered. If we take twenty acres as the cut-off point for a small farmer, then roughly three-quarters of the adult male agricultural force belonged to the rural poor.[54]

Community

We have seen how people were set against some of their fellow citizens and united with others through patterns of inegalitarian relationships. To stop here, however, would be to provide an incomplete picture of the social structure. While class differences are often the most important divisions in a society, they are never the only divisions. Other sources of integration and cleavage exert pressures, either reinforcing or cross-cutting class divisions. Let us, then, try to identify the other critical integrative bonds and cleavages in pre-famine rural Ireland that, together with class cleavages, determined who was likely to engage in collective action with whom.

NEIGHBORHOOD AND KINSHIP

The emphasis that one must necessarily give to overpopulation at this time can obscure some noteworthy features of Irish rural

[54] See Table 4 in Chapter Four below. This figure is obtained by adding the total number of laborers to the number of farmers with twenty acres or less, and then assuming that at least half the farmers' sons were on holdings of twenty acres or less. Emmet Larkin uses thirty acres as his cut-off point. See Emmet Larkin,

settlement. An image has unfortunately developed of a densely populated country with people living almost on top of one another, particularly in western counties. There is an element of truth here, at least if one thinks in terms of the number of persons per acre of *arable* land, which is certainly the statistic to use for measuring the relation of population to economic resources. Prefamine Ireland was a wretchedly poor country because there were simply far too many souls for the amount of good agricultural land. Yet in another sense the population was thinly distributed. The number of persons per square mile of *total* area was not high by European standards. Moreover, in the very coastal districts that were so congested in economic terms, overall population density was comparatively low. The Irish county with the lowest number of persons per square mile in 1841 was Kerry, and the province with the lowest number was Connaught.[55] In many parts of Ireland, but especially in these western districts, great distances could separate people. What sorts or communal ties brought them together in regular social interaction?

Traditional settlement patterns in Ireland were characterized by a noteworthy lack of towns. The native ruler lived on a homestead (*baile*), rather than in a burgh. His subjects lived either on single homesteads, dispersed and separated from one another, or in clusters of homes comprising villages or hamlets. These hamlets were sometimes as large as thirty houses and were important socially, but they were small in comparison with English openfield villages and did not, as the English villages did, serve as religious, political, administrative, or trade centers for outlying populations. As we shall see, hamlets failed to survive the great land upheavals of the sixteenth and seventeenth centuries, except in the west. Yet the territorial units defined by homesteads and hamlets did endure, in part because they were adopted as the units of measurement for plotting plantation grants. Called townlands, they remained the basic units for describing neighborhoods in rural Ireland in the nineteenth century. Although the inhabitants were now dispersed on individual holdings, they still recognized a social affinity with other families residing in the same townland. Townlands continued to be salient social and economic entities. They remained the chief place-names in rural districts, where

---

"Church, state and nation in modern Ireland" in *American Historical Review*, 80, no. 5 (Dec. 1975).

[55] *Census of Ireland, 1841*, p. xiii.

they were invariably used by people as addresses, and indeed still are to this day.

Rural neighborhood ties have traditionally been strong in Ireland. One manifestation of this is the prevalence of agricultural cooperation, which is so firmly grounded in cultural tradition that terms with a Gaelic origin, such as *cooring*, are still used to refer to it. Ordinarily, *cooring* transpires among residents of the same or adjacent townlands, or else among people with recognized kinship ties. It often takes the form of lending a son or daughter to a relative or a neighbor for the day. In earlier times, it was also customary for a gathering, or *meitheal*, to plow or harvest together. Gatherings of this kind were discovered by Weld in his tour of County Roscommon in the 1830s:

> In certain districts of Roscommon, as in other places, where spade husbandry prevails, it is usual for people to exchange labour reciprocally, and to unite in considerable numbers in the fields of individuals in rotation, more especially for the purpose of planting or digging out potatoes. These congregations of workmen give vivacity to the labour, and are ordinarily scenes of much cheerfulness.[56]

One of the more elaborate examples that can be found was reported among farmers from contiguous townlands on the estate of the Earl of Arran shortly before the Famine. Here it was the practice to

> meet together on a certain day, and draw lots to see whose land will be first plowed, hay saved, or corn reaped, as the case may be—when they all assemble, with their respective workmen, and effect in one day what could not be done by the individual resources of a single holder in several weeks; they then proceed to the farm of the next highest drawer, and so on, until each person's business is complete. This plan was found on his lordship's estates in the west of Ireland to work beneficially for the farmer, as well as produce a community of interests amongst the most valuable portion of the great social family.[57]

Cooperation was often encouraged by the prevailing methods of husbandry. Plowing with the old Irish wooden plow, for instance,

[56] Weld, *Statistical Survey of Roscommon*, p. 660.

[57] *Irish Farmer's and Gardener's Magazine and Register of Rural Affairs*, Jan.-Dec. 1840.

took four to six horses hitched together. Yet even tasks requiring only one horse could necessitate agricultural cooperation, since most landholders could not afford their own horse. In the Curlew mountain district in northern Roscommon, it was common for several families to club together for the purchase of a horse in the spring, to lend it around, and then to sell it in the autumn.[58] Sharing horses was also practiced among farmers in the district surrounding the middle Shannon, though it reportedly resulted in some delays and disputes.[59]

These neighborhood ties usually overlapped with and were reinforced by bonds of kinship. As one might expect, the kinship group was traditionally the most important social unit in the society. In ancient Gaelic Ireland, it constituted the greater part of one's claims, obligations, and loyalties.[60] Conflicts between individuals usually took the form of clashes between kinship groups since kinsmen were expected to defend one another's interests and to accept responsibility for the consequences of one another's actions.[61] Family members were, in theory at least, entitled to shares in the land owned or held by the extended family or to a share of the produce of this land; and these shares were periodically redistributed at the extinction of each generation.[62] According to the records that have survived, descent was predominantly patrilineal, but there are some scholars who believe that bilateral descent may have been more common.[63] In either case, since claims to land were made on the basis of descent from a common ancestor who once held it, theoretically it was possible for a very large number of people to claim rights to the same piece of land.

In practice this did not happen, mainly because people did not keep track of all their ancestors. Nevertheless, the effect of this system was that the number of persons living in close proximity and sharing the same ancestral land could be very large. Over a

[58] Weld, *Statistical Survey of Roscommon*, p. 274.

[59] Nicholson, *Report upon the general state of agriculture*, p. 63.

[60] Mac Niocaill, *Ireland Before the Vikings*, p. 51.

[61] Ibid., pp. 51-4.

[62] Butler, "Irish land tenures," pp. 526-8; MacNeill, "Communal ownership in ancient Ireland."

[63] J. R. Fox, "Kinship and land tenure on Tory Island" in *Ulster Folklife*, 12 (1966). Fox believes that bilateral or "cognatic" descent on present-day Tory Island is a survival of what was once the prevailing pattern.

long period of time, it easily resulted in extensive fragmentation
of holdings. It could also result in large residential clusters since,
in many cases, conjugal families did not dwell on their allot-
ments, but lived with other members of their descent group, either
in the same house or more often in closely situated abodes. Residential clusters might include only one lineage, but they could,
especially if descent was reckoned bilaterally, include several
overlapping lineages. Hence, while some residential clusters were
small and resembled dispersed farmsteads held in severalty and
occupied by only one or two conjugal families, other clusters were
large and consisted of perhaps dozens of conjugal families loosely
connected through membership in the same descent group or
groups.[64] This type of nucleated settlement, or *clachan*, usually
consisted of ten to fifteen houses (occasionally as many as thirty),
grouped together in no organized pattern and sharing the surrounding land by a mode of landholding that has come to be
known as "rundale." Each house in a *clachan* normally had an
enclosed garden, but the principal farming area consisted of an
open infield, which would be divided into numerous minute and
unfenced holdings, with each conjugal family in the hamlet holding several plots in different locations. The infield was subject to
continuous cultivation, while beyond it lay an outfield, which
was used for pasturing livestock and which was cultivated only
occasionally.[65] This pattern had some obvious similarity to the
English openfield system, the major difference being that population clusters were generally smaller than English openfield
villages.[66]

The massive changes in landownership in the sixteenth and
seventeenth centuries had dramatic consequences for this traditional pattern. The new owners endeavored to destory the rundale
system of land holding and to replace it with consolidated farms,
whereby every tenant would have all his land in one place. English landlordism also tended to weaken the authority of the descent group over land. The periodic redistribution of holdings

[64] E. Estyn Evans, "Some survivals of the Irish openfield system" in *Geography*,
24 (1939), p. 28; E. Estyn Evans, *Irish Folkways* (London, 1957), p. 107; D.
McCourt, "The rundale system in Donegal: its distribution and decline" in
Donegal Annual, 3 (1955).

[65] Evans, *Folkways*, pp. 29-33.

[66] See George Homans, *English Villagers of the Thirteenth Century* (New York,
1941/1960), pp. 12-28.

among family members, which the English thought to be the same as their system of gavelkind, was made illegal under James I. The new landowners sought to replace the extended family by the conjugal family as the basic working unit, and they frequently refused to recognize more than one individual as the tenant on a holding. Whether through their efforts, or as a result of other forces that historians have yet to uncover, the hamlet-rundale system gradually gave way to dispersed single farmsteads in most parts of the country by the end of the eighteenth century.

Yet in some places the traditional settlement pattern survived. It was most likely to do so in those areas that had been subjected to relatively less intensive plantation and landlord supervision—mainly the northwest and west, and most especially County Donegal and the province of Connaught. Using ordnance survey maps, T. W. Freeman has been able to show that in the 1830s nucleated settlements constituted the prevailing pattern of population distribution in most of Donegal, in many parts of Mayo, Galway, and Roscommon, and in a few coastal areas in Clare and Kerry.[67] And a poor-law return of the mid-1840s showed very large numbers of joint tenancies in some western unions, such as Ballina where 69 percent of the land was held in common and Westport where the figure was 83 percent.[68]

It is not difficult to understand why nucleated settlements survived in at least some areas. As already suggested, they originally emerged whenever a large number of people claimed ancestral rights to the same piece of land. The Irish kinship system made this kind of thing likely and made the society vulnerable to an extensive fragmentation of holdings during periods of population expansion. The outcome of the massive growth in population that occurred during the late eighteenth and early nineteenth centuries was inevitably to increase the number of persons laying claims to the same land. The industrial decline and the post-war economic depression only increased this tendency by rendering the great majority of people too poor to meet their kinship obligations in any other way than by dividing up their holdings. A contemporary legal authority, arguing that pre-famine subdivision

[67] T. W. Freeman, Pre-Famine Ireland: A Study in Historical Geography (Manchester, 1957), p. 32.

[68] Appendix to minutes of evidence taken before Her Majesty's commissioners of inquiry into the state of law and practice in respect to the occupation of land in Ireland, pp. 280-88 [672], H.C. 1845, xxii.

was an outcome of the traditional kinship system, noted that even the tenant-at-will in Ireland believed that "his title is paramount to that of all others, and though according to existing law he holds from year to year, he may dispose of his land among his children and other members of his family as he pleases; this being the closest approximation to the Irish law of Gavelkind which the present circumstances admit of."[69] The unavoidable consequence was extensive subdivision of holdings in the pre-famine period, and the persistence of nucleated settlement in at least some areas.

This population growth created problems that may have weakened the social solidarity of hamlets. It could not help but add to congestion, which aggravated personal animosities and disputes over property as people had to cope with ever-more minute divisions of the infield.[70] Nevertheless, the western hamlet was a relatively well integrated communal structure in the pre-famine society. Much of the conflict noted by visitors was simply the unavoidable consequence of intense and regular social interaction. A hamlet was invariably a center of social activity— the locus of spinning parties, story-tellers, and fiddlers or pipers.[71] Underlying the apparent chaos that so impressed outsiders, there was often a highly structured social organization, usually corresponding to the kinship structure, with community leaders in many cases composed of a council of elders.[72] The solidarity of these communities is confirmed by the difficulties faced by landlords who wanted to get rid of them. In a well-known pamphlet, one such landlord recounted his efforts to break up hamlets in County Donegal. He was eventually successful, but only against great odds since "the pleasure people feel in assembling and chatting together, made them consider the removal of the houses, from the clusters or hamlets in which they were generally built to the

[69] Henry Kimmis, "An inquiry into those causes which have tended to produce the existing relation between proprietors and occupiers of land, and have affected the social condition of the people in the rural districts of Ireland" in *Proceedings of the Evening Meetings of the Royal Dublin Society* (May 1885), p. 352.

[70] Weld, *Statistical Survey of Roscommon*, p. 75; Lord George Hill, *Facts from Gweedore* (Dublin, 1845).

[71] Evans, *Folkways*, p. 32.

[72] Or it might be the custom, as it was in at least one large hamlet which was broken up about 1798, to elect a chief magistrate each year. Charles Coote, *Statistical Survey of the County of Monaghan* (Dublin, 1801), pp. 142-4; cited in Green, "Agriculture," p. 111.

separate farms, a great grievance.''[73]

In other parts of the country, strong kinship bonds survived, even if the hamlet-rundale settlement pattern did not. So did the traditional notion that all members of the extended family were entitled to a share in the produce of the land. There are two kinds of evidence for this. The first is the practice of subdividing holdings. Subdivision was by no means confined to western districts, though it was more advanced in the west than the east. In Leinster and east Munster, landowners had to fight as hard as did those in Connaught and west Munster to prevent their estates from being divided up. The second kind of evidence is the dowry system. The dowry was essentially a substitute for the inheritance of land, a way of meeting traditional kinship obligations without fragmenting the family holding. Thus, even if the land went to one son, there persisted the notion that it was held by the family and that all family members were entitled to some share in its fruits. Here we have the cultural basis for the Irish practice of withholding succession until provision was made for non-inheriting children—a practice that became more extensive after the Famine and resulted in late marriages and a low fertility rate. Yet the practice could also be found in the pre-famine period where two conditions obtained: (1) the pressures from landlords against subdivision were strong; and (2) there was sufficient movable capital, in the form of either money or livestock, that kinship obligations could be met without subdividing land. Both conditions were more often met in the east than in the west.[74]

[73] Hill, *Facts from Gweedore*. See also Weld, *Statistical Survey of Roscommon*, p. 473.

[74] Witnesses before the Devon commission revealed the lengths to which farmers might go to meet kinship obligations to children who did not inherit land. A middleman from Kilkenny indicated that his tenants, on farms of from thirty to forty acres, never gave fortunes to their children of less than £100. Another landlord referred to the case of a farmer with twenty-two acres, who gave £100 to each of his children on their marriage. The same witness replied to a general question on how children were provided for by noting that "their wish is to give their farms among their families, and when that is prevented, the son who gets the farm endeavours to pay certain portions to other members of his family, particularly to his sisters, varying in my neighbourhood from ten to a hundred pounds." Altogether, at least twenty-four witnesses before the Devon commission referred to this system of providing for children who did not inherit the family holding. See Crotty, *Irish Agricultural Production*, p. 58; Dardis, *The Occupation of Land in Ireland in the First Half of the Nineteenth Century*, pp. 81-2; and Donnelly, *Cork*, p. 221.

INTER-REGIONAL SOCIAL COMMUNICATION
AND POPULATION MOVEMENT

Neighborhood and kinship ties formed the basis of "primary" groups in pre-famine Ireland. Within such groups, social relations are durable and are characterized by personal and emotional involvement. In very small societies, virtually all social relations may be primary. But in most societies, including "peasant societies," people also have contact with those outside their primary groups, directly through face-to-face interaction, and perhaps also indirectly through various media of social communication. The remainder of this chapter is concerned with social interaction in pre-famine Ireland beyond the primary group. How frequently did people come into contact with those outside their neighborhood and kinship groups? What social bonds and cleavages emerged as a result?

Let us begin at the national level by examining the frequency of inter-regional social communication. The medium through which social communication takes place is, of course, language. Pre-famine Ireland was linguistically divided. Although English was the language of government and commerce, and was spoken by most people, roughly half the population spoke Irish.[75] No doubt many of these Irish speakers, probably the majority, could also converse in English, but far from all those who spoke English could read it. Until the 1830s, when the National schools were established, there was no publicly supported school system in Ireland. There were a variety of privately organized programs, some of which (such as the Kildare Place Society) received state grants. Yet most were regarded by Catholic religious leaders with suspicion, if not outright hostility, because they were managed primarily by Protestants. The most common form of education available to Catholics consisted of the so-called "hedge" schools, which were small local schools operated by self-employed and usually untrained schoolmasters. They struggled under poor conditions and met the needs, in a very limited way, of only a part of the rural population. According to the 1841 census, 53 percent of the population of Ireland five years of age or older admitted they could neither read nor write. In the province of Connaught the figure was 72 percent.[76]

[75] Gearóid Ó Tuathaigh, *Ireland Before the Famine, 1798-1848* (Dublin, 1972), pp. 157-9.
[76] *Census of Ireland, 1841*, p. 433.

This illiteracy was one of the reasons why there was little market in Ireland at this time for books and newspapers. Another reason was that printed matter was very expensive. Newspapers, in particular, were "beyond the reach of all but the well-to-do" as a result of stamp duties, which amounted to 2d. per issue until 1836 and 1d. per issue thereafter.[77] In 1830 sixty-six newspapers were being published in Ireland, which sold a total of approximately four million copies. In 1841 the figure reached eighty-one, with total sales of almost six million. If we assume that a regular newspaper purchaser would buy at least one paper per week, then in 1841 there were not many more than 100,000 regular purchasers in a country with a total population of more than eight million and a total adult male labor force of more than two million. (To the extent that those who bought newspapers did so more often than once a week, the figure would be even less than 100,000.)[78] This small market was heavily concentrated in eastern districts, especially in Dublin. In 1849 there were 101 newspapers being published in Ireland, twenty-eight of which were located in Dublin, and only fourteen in the entire province of Connaught.[79]

Virtually no railways were operating at this time, only several short lines running out of Belfast and Dublin. Roads, on the other hand, were numerous, partly as a result of the availability of cheap labor and partly as a result of the pressures that prevailed upon the government to give employment through public works. Public transportation was provided on these roads by mail coaches, which ran between major centers, and by coaches owned by an Italian immigrant named Bianconi, which serviced a wider area. By the 1840s Bianconi cars covered over 3,000 miles daily. Fares, it is true, were high, restricting the number of persons who could travel in this way. The Dublin-Belfast fare on the mail coach, for instance, was 15s. for an outside seat and 27s. 6d. for an inside seat, while Bianconi charged 1½d. per mile.[80] Moreover, as

[77] Brian Inglis, The Freedom of the Press in Ireland, 1784-1841 (London, 1954), pp. 233-4.

[78] The number of newpapers sold is based on the number of stamps issued. Obviously the number of regular purchasers is not the same thing as the number of regular readers, but even allowing for multiple readers it is evident that newspapers were reaching only a small portion of the population. The source is Thom's Irish Almanac and Official Directory (Dublin, 1850), p. 181.

[79] Ibid.

[80] K. B. Nowlan, "Travel" in R. B. McDowell (ed.), Social Life in Ireland, 1800-45 (Cork, 1957).

Freeman has shown, there was considerable regional variation in transportation services; both canal and road services declined sharply as one moved westward.[81]

Admittedly, in one sense at least, the pre-famine Irish population was highly mobile. It has been estimated that some 2 million emigrated to Britain or America between 1785 and 1845.[82] In addition, every spring, thousands of laborers, mostly from Connaught and Ulster, migrated to England and Scotland for harvest work. A head count made at the ports in the summer of 1841 recorded a total of some 58,000 seasonal migrants.[83] There was also considerable movement of laborers within the country. Contemporaries frequently made reference to large numbers of people leaving home either voluntarily or involuntarily to find employment or to beg in other regions. Some authorities felt that the movement of people was so great that it helped to spread disease. One report, published in 1821, stated that workers from Connaught usually migrated to Meath and Dublin; those from Clare went to the area around Kilkenny; while laborers from the poorer areas of County Londonderry found their way into Antrim and Down.[84]

Yet it is important to recognize that this population movement did not necessarily give rise to stable social relationships. Migrant laborers and mendicants were, as a rule, unpopular in Ireland, not only because they were thought to spread disease, but also because they competed with local men for work. More integrative kinds of population movement were lacking in comparison. Indeed, the population as a whole moved very little. When the 1841 census was taken, only 5 percent of those enumerated lived outside their county of birth, and more than half of these lived in a county adjoining the one in which they were born.[85] This is not surprising. The Irish countryman was by necessity attached to his holding, which he rarely gave up voluntarily; and ejectments were not so frequent that they could produce an inordinate amount

[81] Freeman, Pre-Famine Ireland, p. 112.

[82] K. H. Connell, "Population" in R. B. McDowell (ed.), Social Life in Ireland, 1800-45 (Cork, 1957), p. 80.

[83] Census of Ireland, 1841, pp. 450-51.

[84] F. Barker and J. Cheyne, An Account of the Rise, Progress and Decline of Fever Lately Epidemical in Ireland (Dublin, 1821), I, pp. 139-40; cited in Timothy P. O'Neill, "The state, poverty and distress in Ireland, 1815-45," unpublished Ph.D. thesis, University College Dublin, 1971, p. 51.

[85] Census of Ireland, 1841, pp. 446-7.

of population movement. Urban centers did provide economic opportunities for some migrants; 23 percent of those living outside their county of birth in 1841 resided in County Dublin, which was the largest recipient of migrants in the country. Dublin was not, however, sufficiently industrialized to absorb vast numbers of new residents, and other cities in Ireland were even less so. For the majority of people, it was the land on which they were born that gave them their livelihood.

TOWNS AND TRADE

Social ties over and above the primary group resulted less from inter-regional social communication and population movement than from the pull of towns, and from the trade that passed through towns. Invaders built the earliest urban settlements in Ireland, first the Danes, and then later the Normans. Very little of the native Celtic population lived in these towns, however, and much more significant were those introduced in the sixteenth and seventeenth centuries under the English plantations. Initially these towns were inhabited mostly by new English settlers, but in the course of the eighteenth century three things happened. First, some landowners built new towns, or redesigned existing ones to serve as trade and administrative centers for the tenantry on their estates.[86] Second, there was considerable growth in the number of Catholics living in towns and participating in trade.[87] And third, agriculture became much more commercialized,[88] with the result that trade and social intercourse between town and country increased.

By the early nineteenth century, Ireland had an active urban society, and one that was well integrated into the rural world that surrounded it. Population growth served to increase the size of urban centers, if not to make them prosperous, while commer-

[86] T. Jones Hughes, "The origin and growth of towns in Ireland" in University Review, 2, no. 7 (1960), pp. 12-13.

[87] Maureen MacGeehin, "The Catholics of the towns and the quarterage dispute in eighteenth-century Ireland" in Irish Historical Studies, 8, no. 30 (Sept. 1952); Maureen Wall, "The rise of a Catholic middle class in eighteenth-century Ireland" in Irish Historical Studies, 11, no. 42 (Sept. 1958).

[88] Crotty, Irish Agricultural Production, pp. 17-28. Perhaps the most impressive measure of the economic expansion that took place in Ireland during the eighteenth century was the remarkable growth in the supply of money, which rose three- to fourfold between the 1720s and the 1770s, and by 1797 had trebled again. See Cullen, An Economic History of Ireland, p. 95.

cialized agriculture gave rise to considerable trade between urban and rural areas. As several historians have argued, there was almost no part of Ireland divorced from the market economy in the first half of the nineteenth century. These historians challenge the alternative thesis put forward by Lynch and Vaizey that pre-famine Ireland was divided into two distinct and separate economic regions: a western subsistence economy and an eastern maritime economy.[89] They quite rightly point out that agricultural production for the market was to be found almost everywhere in the country, if for no other reason than because everywhere money was necessary to pay rents.[90] Even small towns in western districts were important centers for trade and social life. In his tour of County Roscommon in the early 1830s, Isaac Weld was impressed with the number of shops he found in several places he visited, particularly in Boyle and Athlone, but even in smaller towns such as Strokestown, where he commented on "the fondness for finery amongst the female peasantry, and the eagerness with which they survey it in the shops and windows." Even the rural poor frequently came to town—to drink, fight, play street games, watch executions, look for work, or beg. "I was assured that certain persons in high rank and station," wrote Weld, "were actually deterred from entering into the town of Boyle, except on urgent occasions, by crowds of beggars. . . . The shops also were infested, and through mistaken notions of charity, beggars were sometimes allowed to squat within them." Most of all, rural people visited towns to attend fairs and markets, which were great social events as well as occasions for economic exchange. Weld was astounded at the throngs of people at several of the markets he attended in County Roscommon, such as the market in Strokestown, which was so crowded that it was impossible to move a carriage up the main street.[91]

It is important, however, not to get carried away in efforts to correct the dual-economy thesis. First, though Lynch and Vaizey may have overstated variations from one part of the country to

[89] P. Lynch and J. Vaizey, *Guinness's Brewery in the Irish Economy, 1759-1876* (Cambridge, 1960).

[90] Crotty, *Irish Agricultural Production*, pp. 306-7; L. M. Cullen, "Problems in the interpretation and revision of eighteenth century Irish economic history" in *Transactions of the Royal Historical Society*, 5th series, 18 (1967); Joseph Lee, "The dual economy in Ireland, 1800-50" in *Historical Studies*, 8 (1971).

[91] Weld, *Statistical Survey of Roscommon*, pp. 199-200, 203-6, 324-6, 339, 401-3, 406-7, 470, 556-7.

another in the volume of trading and in the market orientation of agriculture, there was nevertheless substantial regional variation that should not be overlooked. Freeman has shown that the same kind of disparity that characterized transportation services also could be found in the distribution of inland trade: it was much greater in the east and the south, and much lower in western districts, such as Donegal, Connaught, Clare, and Kerry.[92] And the 1841 census shows that the percentage of the labor force employed in trade differed greatly from one province to another—only 1.6 percent in the province of Connaught as compared with 4.7 percent in Leinster and 3.2 percent in Munster.[93]

Second, though the market economy penetrated into almost every part of Ireland, not all social classes were equally integrated into this economy. In absolute terms there was a growth in the amount of trade carried on during the first half of the nineteenth century, but most of the increase was simply a function of population expansion. The *proportion* of the population engaged in extensive commercial transactions with townspeople was declining. By the 1840s *over half* of the agricultural holdings in Ireland were too small to provide their occupiers with more than a subsistence livelihood, and *over half* of the adult male agricultural labor force consisted of laborers. While the farmers for whom they worked were highly commercialized, these laborers themselves were not significantly involved in agricultural production for the market, at least not directly. Most of the produce from their small holdings (mainly potatoes) was used for home consumption. Any surplus was generally set aside to feed the pig, which was often the only item marketed by a small landholder (if he marketed anything at all), and was then the means by which he paid his rent. Those who had enough land to grow grain had a greater opportunity to become involved in market transactions, but usually on a meager scale. Pressures from land agents to pay rents typically forced them to sell their grain all at one time (when the market was glutted and prices were low), leaving little produce to market at any other time.[94] It was also possible for tenants to pay their rents in the form of agricultural produce.[95]

[92] Freeman, *Pre-Famine Ireland*, p. 117.

[93] *Census of Ireland, 1841*, p. xxii.

[94] Weld, *Statistical Survey of Roscommon*, pp. 655-6.

[95] Denis Browne, a landowner and member of parliament for County Mayo, permitted his tenants to pay their rents in grain. In 1816 he reportedly allowed

If laborers had little to sell, they had even less means to buy. The reason was simply that wages were so low and rents so high that hardly any income was left with which to make purchases. Indeed laborers were not always able to put their hands even on the money they did earn, since their rent (and perhaps the cost of their diet if it was provided) would be deducted from their wages before they were paid. Laborers might also, as already noted, accept a lower wage in return for a cabin and related privileges, thus in effect being paid in kind. Reports to the Poor Inquiry Commission of 1836 indicated that laborers' wages were paid in the form of land and provisions almost as often as they were paid in money.[96] Even unbound laborers were frequently paid at least partly in kind, in the form of conacre ground and/or provisions. Visiting Elphin at the height of the harvest, Weld found able-bodied men offering to work merely for their food.[97]

If purchases could be made, they usually consisted of tobacco, tea, and cotton clothing, the latter often secondhand and obtained at the stalls in the markets. Food was not, as a rule, purchased by small landholders. It has been estimated that between three and four million people in the country subsisted almost entirely on a diet of home-grown potatoes.[98] Tragically, when this means of livelihood failed, as it repeatedly did during the first half of the nineteenth century, people were left to starve even though food was available in the country. They had little cash with which to buy it.[99] "Money is, in truth, not to be found in almost any part of the country," declared one pamphleteer, "and its value is so little known or understood in consequence of its total disuse, that it is no uncommon thing for a peasant who becomes possessed of a bank note to pledge it at a pawnbroker's for so many shillings as he may want, and pay the interest on the loan."[100] Although Weld was impressed with the number of shops in Boyle, he also found shopkeepers complaining that the peasantry who frequented the

them 5s. on their rents for a quantity that would not have sold for 3s. 6d. on the open market. *Ennis Chronicle*, 20 Jan. 1816, p. 3.

[96] *Poor Inquiry: appendix (D).*

[97] Weld, *Statistical Survey of Roscommon*, p. 338.

[98] Thomas P. O'Neill, "Food problems during the great Irish Famine" in *Journal of the Royal Society of Antiquaries of Ireland*, 82 (1952), p. 100.

[99] Tavern committee, *Report of the committee for the relief of distressed districts in Ireland, appointed at a general meeting held at The City of London Tavern on 7th May, 1822* (London, 1822), pp. 11 and 73; Rogers, *The Potato Truck System*.

[100] Rogers, *The Potato Truck System*, p. 13.

town were poorer than formerly and did not have as much money to spend.[101] Weld attributed these complaints to increased competition resulting from a growth in the number of shops, but the weight of evidence suggests that shopkeepers were quite correct in their conviction that people were becoming poorer, and that their purchasing power was diminishing.

There was, in a very real sense, a dual economy in pre-famine Ireland. Great differences existed in the extent to which people were integrated into the national market. The duality, however, was not a simple one between a traditional subsistence economy and a more modern commercialized economy. Those who reject dual-economy theories of economic development have correctly insisted that the "underdeveloped" subsistence sector is usually not a survival of the pre-modern society.[102] For this reason, distinctions so often made between "traditional" and "modern" sectors can be misleading. In pre-famine Ireland, the massive and impoverished laboring population was largely a product of social changes occurring in the late eighteenth and early nineteenth centuries (population growth, industrial decline, and economic stagnation) rather than a residue of an earlier period. It may be possible to argue that this social group was traditional in cultural terms, but in structural terms it was not traditional at all. What can easily appear as a division between a modern sector and a traditional sector was in fact a class cleavage, which intensified enormously in the first half of the nineteenth century almost everywhere in the country. In both western and eastern counties, there could be found "strong" or "respectable" farmers heavily engaged in agricultural marketing and shop purchasing. Cooperative economic relationships with townspeople were most extensive among members of this class, and became steadily weaker as one moved down the social ladder. In so far as there was a regional duality in the economy, it resulted from the fact that the size of the large farmer class, and the size of the towns with which they traded, varied from one part of the country to another.

---

[101] Weld, *Statistical Survey of Roscommon*, p. 203.

[102] This is one of the best-known arguments of the dependency theory of economic development. For the classic statement, see André G. Frank, "The development of underdevelopment" in *Monthly Review*, 18, no. 4 (Sept. 1966). See also Rodolfo Stavenhagen, *Social Classes in Agrarian Societies* (New York, 1975), especially, pp. 8-13; and Stuart Holland, *Capital versus the Regions* (London, 1976).

Farmers who could trade with townspeople were most numerous
in the northeast, the east, and the south, and least numerous in the
northwest and the west. In Connaught the median size of holdings
in 1841 was under ten acres as compared with over seventeen
acres in both Leinster and Munster.[103] Regional variations in the
size of towns were just as pronounced; they too were relatively
small in Connaught, where 6 percent of the population lived in
towns of 2,000 or more persons as compared with 22 percent in
Leinster and 16 percent in Munster.[104]

Alongside this economic intercourse, and supported by it, was
a town-centered social life that attracted rural people of all social
classes. In this case, however, the nature of the town-country relationship was qualitatively different. It was personal and communal rather than economic and associational. Towns in the daily
lives of most people were primarily centers for interaction and
festivity, where they would find friends and excitement, and
where they often came when they had nothing else to do. Inevitably, this social life was segmented on the basis of social class. The
urban middle class, most especially the shopkeepers, had mixed
feelings about country people. On the one hand, they appreciated
the cooperative economic relationship that they had with farmers;
they also recognized the importance of town-centered social life
to the vitality of their communities. On the other hand, they had
considerable reservations about the contribution made by the
rural lower orders to this social life. The latter came to towns, not
to patronize businesses, but for other reasons, some of which
served to make them very unpopular with the urban middle class.
As we shall see in the following chapter, fairs were frequently
broken up by fights. And the drift of the rural poor into towns to
beg or to obtain relief was a constant source of complaint from
townspeople, who blamed not only the vagrants themselves, but
also the landlords who refused to support them. These complaints
became shrill after the introduction of the poor law in 1838, when
towns were forced to pay higher poor taxes than rural divisions
owing to the steady influx of paupers from the countryside.[105] For

[103] These data are based on the 1841 census rather than the poor-law return of
the mid-forties and they refer to holdings over two acres. They have been computed from grouped data and have been corrected for errors made by the census
takers. See note to Table 2 in Appendix A for a fuller explanation.
[104] Census of Ireland, 1841, pp. 432-7.
[105] William L. Feingold, "The Irish boards of poor law guardians, 1872-86: a

a number of reasons, therefore, town-country relations in pre-famine Ireland were characterized by sharp discontinuities and conflicts as well as close social and economic ties. It will help to keep this in mind as we turn to assess the role of the all-important religious structure, which constitutes the final pattern of social relationships to be discussed in this chapter.

RELIGION

It is hardly necessary to persuade the reader that a major source of cleavage in pre-famine Ireland was religion. Even those with the most superficial knowledge of the country are aware of the intensity of religious divisions in Ireland and of their deep historical roots. The religious struggles of the seventeenth century ultimately resulted in the defeat of Catholic interests and the evolution of a religiously stratified social order. The principal means of establishing this Protestant Ascendancy, as it was called, was the confiscation of land owned by Catholics and the enactment of a series of repressive penal laws. Though these laws were, for the most part, repealed in the late eighteenth century, the Protestant Ascendancy that they had served to establish remained entrenched, and constituted a source of resentment for Catholics, among whom the feeling was not uncommon, nor unjustified, that they suffered social disadvantages on account of their religious affiliation. The consequence was that Catholics felt a strong sense of shared interests and could easily think of themselves as one group in opposition to Protestants. Protestants, for their part, were divided into two major denominations: Presbyterians and members of the Church of Ireland. Within these denominational groups, and even between them, there also existed a sense of common interests, as well as a shared apprehension that the social advantages they enjoyed might be lost. What made the religious factor still more important, however, was that the members of each religious group were bound together not only by common interests, but also by communal ties. At various levels they formed communities through repeated social interaction with one another. Briefly I shall try to describe these groupings as they existed in the early nineteenth century, restricting my discussion to Catholic communities since they were more numerous, and since

revolution in local government," unpublished Ph.D. thesis, University of Chicago, 1974.

the collective action I shall examine in the following chapter was undertaken largely by Catholics.

The principal institutional basis of Catholic communal interaction was the parish. Parishes developed more slowly in Ireland than in other parts of Europe, and even when they became established in the twelfth century they were, as a rule, not centered in towns or large villages because settlements of this kind were too few. Towns that evolved in the seventeenth and eighteenth centuries still did not form the nuclei for Catholic parish organization because their development coincided with the rise of the Protestant Ascendancy. The religious edifices that were built in the new or expanding towns of the seventeenth and eighteenth centuries were not Catholic, but Protestant. It is true that, as the Catholic church reorganized in the late eighteenth and early nineteenth centuries, it sought to establish centers in towns and villages. Yet the vast majority of parishes remained rural. The distribution of Catholic chapels noted on the six-inch ordnance survey maps for County Roscommon illustrates the extent to which this was still true in the 1830s. Out of sixty-five chapels, only nine were located in towns or villages, eleven were located on the peripheries of towns or villages, while forty-five were located in the countryside, either standing alone or surrounded by only a few buildings.

What this tells us is that the local organization of the Catholic church did not depend for its strength on population concentrations. In so far as it integrated people, it did so independently of other potentially integrating structures, such as towns or villages. *The Catholic parish was an important social unit in its own right and served to bring people together who otherwise might not have engaged in regular social intercourse with one another.* We can safely assume that the chapel played a critical role in creating such communities. Sunday mass was a convenient time for people to get together, not only because they were assembled in one place, but also because Sunday was a day when they were free to spend time in socializing. It was common to hold public meetings and gatherings in the chapel or the chapel yard after Sunday mass, simply because no other place or time could have secured comparable attendance.[106]

[106] Mark Tierney, *Murroe and Boher: the History of an Irish Country Parish* (Dublin, 1966), p. 66. Samuel Nicholson discovered during his tour in the 1840s of the region surrounding the middle Shannon that rural inhabitants frequently held political discussions after mass in a location convenient to their place of worship. See Nicholson, *Report upon the general state of agriculture*, p. 59.

Data on church attendance, however, caution against exaggerating the extent to which the Catholic church brought people together, at least at the chapel door. Basing his calculations on a survey of public instruction carried out in 1834, David Miller has estimated that in most parts of the country only 30 to 60 percent of the population regularly attended mass, and in western districts only 20 to 40 percent.[107] Miller insists that these data are not indicative of a low level of religiosity in the society, but rather of the fact that other forms of religious activity besides attending mass were important to the people. He points to survivals of the pre-Christian Celtic religion, which he calls "customary practices," consisting of various types of gatherings such as celebrations at "holy wells," bonfires, festivals attached to local patron saints' days ("patterns"), wakes, and other folk customs. It was also common for Catholic religious services to be held in private homes. Not only were marriages generally conducted in this way, but priests also held "stations" in the houses of parishioners in order to hear confessions, say mass, and catechize children. Typically, every townland would be visited twice a year, and in large populous parishes over one hundred stations might be held annually.[108] Like customary practices, stations fulfilled both a religious and a social function. They were occasions, not only to hear confessions and say mass, but also to engage in social interaction, including great drinking and eating. It is probable that stations were but part of an extraordinary amount of visiting carried out by Catholic priests and curates, and that the social integration of parishes rested as much on clerical rounds as it did on church attendance. Writing to Daniel O'Connell in 1842, the Archbishop of Cashel called attention to the importance of this kind of clerical activity in a country where the population was so dispersed:

Your lordship is not ignorant of the nature and the difficulties of our Irish mission and of the laborious duties which almost incessantly occupy the time of our clergy from morning till night. You know that our people are not located in towns and villages, with a priest and a church at their very doors, as is the case in Catholic countries on the continent, but that on the contrary our rural parishes consist of a large population

[107] David W. Miller, "Irish Catholicism and the Great Famine" in *Journal of Social History*, 9, no. 1 (Fall 1975).

[108] J. A. Murphy, "The support of the Catholic clergy in Ireland, 1750-1850" in *Historical Studies*, 5 (1965), p. 111.

thinly scattered over an extensive district, and the priest as well as many of themselves residing two, three, and in some instances four miles or more from the chapel. He, perhaps without an assistant, has many duties, besides that of marriages, to perform; he has the sick to visit, the children to baptise, and, for more than half the year, he has the stations for confession to attend in the different districts of the parish.[109]

The picture we get of the Catholic church in the early nineteenth century is one in which a critical role was played by the parish priest and his curate. The strength of parishes as communal structures depended, more than anything else, on the capacity of the parish clergy to link together people attached to different townlands and kinship groups. How well did they perform this role?

One factor that limited their effectiveness was their lack of manpower. Although the Catholic clergy had continued to function throughout the eighteenth century, the penal laws had severely hampered their training and recruitment. It was hoped that the founding of the national seminary at Maynooth in 1795 would solve this problem, and there was an increase in the absolute number of priests during the early nineteenth century. Their numbers did not expand sufficiently, however, to match the growth in population. As a ratio of the population, the Catholic clergy declined in the pre-famine period, falling from one for every 2,100 Catholics in 1800 to one for every 3,000 in 1840.[110] The organizational weakness of the church resulting from the penal laws may also have been responsible for impropriety on the part of the clergy. As Emmet Larkin has shown, there was much concern in the pre-famine period over the moral failings of clergymen, the chief vices apparently consisting of drunkenness, women, and avarice.[111] Of these, it was the third that had the most serious adverse effect on priest-parishioner relationships; it was also, unfortunately, the most widespread. The problem was that the Catholic church in Ireland was not state-supported, but relied entirely on voluntary contributions. The revenue of parish priests and curates came almost exclusively from their parishioners, with

[109] Cashel Diocesan Archives, Slattery papers: Michael Slattery to Daniel O'Connell, 8 April 1842.

[110] Emmet Larkin, "The devotional revolution in Ireland, 1850-75" in *American Historical Review*, 77, no. 3 (June 1972).

[111] Ibid.

the result that an income which a priest considered moderate was often regarded as excessive by those who were expected to provide it.[112] Whereas land agents, for instance, ordinarily earned from £500 to £1,000 per year, the average annual income of a parish priest has been estimated at about £150 in the 1820s.[113] By contrast, the income of a laborer was usually less than £10 per year. As early as 1786, a bishop complained that one-third of the parishioners of his diocese "through inability or otherwise" seldom or never contributed one penny toward the subsistence of their parish priests.[114] The income of a priest thus depended very much on how energetic (or ruthless) he was in exacting his dues and perquisites.[115]

On the other hand, the voluntary system of support was partly responsible for the close bond between Catholic priests and the people. It gave parishioners a measure of control over their local priest, and forced him to pay close attention to their wishes. A Catholic clergyman was quite aware that if he disappointed the members of his parish "they will naturally disappoint him in their turn."[116] Writing in the 1860s, one curate recalled a parish priest who "seldom mixed with his flock, but left all the active duties of the parish to his curates." It was not long before "the revenue had fallen so low that it was insufficient to support him and his household."[117] A priest told de Tocqueville when he was touring the west of Ireland in 1835: "The day I received government money, the people would no longer regard me as their own. I for my part might be tempted to believe that I did not depend on them and one day perhaps we would regard each other as enemies."[118]

Most parishioners must have felt that, on the whole, the Catholic clergy were earning their money. Like the landlord-tenant relationship, the priest-parishioner relationship was one of patron and client. In addition to monetary levies, the priest exacted from his clients a modicum of piety and a minimum of respect for himself, in addition to a considerable measure of polit-

[112] Murphy, "The support of the Catholic clergy," p. 114.

[113] Ibid., p. 112.   [114] Ibid., p. 106.

[115] Again see Murphy and also Larkin, "The devotional revolution," for more extensive discussions of this subject.

[116] Cashel Diocesan Archives, Slattery papers: Michael Slattery to Daniel O'Connell, 8 April 1842.

[117] Cashel Diocesan Archives, Diary of Rev. James O'Carroll, C.C., Clonoulty, County Tipperary, p. 44.

[118] Alexis de Tocqueville, *Journeys to England and Ireland* (London, 1958), p.

ical support, as we shall see in the next chapter. Yet in return, he provided his clients with a wide range of benefits. And, if they compared what they received from their priest with what their landlord provided (in return for what was rendered to him), they had little reason to believe that the former was excessively rewarded. Most parish priests and curates performed a variety of social functions in addition to their specifically religious duties. In many cases this role was thrust upon a clergyman as one of the few educated persons willing to associate with the lower classes. In Ireland, wrote Gustave de Beaumont, "where all the superior and privileged classes are unpopular, the Catholic clergy is the only body more enlightened than the people, whose intelligence and power it gladly accepts."[119] A priest's temporal work might consist of seemingly unimpressive activities such as serving as a lost-and-found; it might also include eventful contributions such as founding schools and vocational centers, or helping renovate laborers' dwellings.[120] The parish priest was typically regarded as the "official organ" of his community, as well as a channel for transmitting information through the countryside.[121] And the clergy, both Catholic and Protestant, were the foremost organizers of poor relief at the local level. Virtually all relief committees included clergymen of one denomination or the other and usually both. Priests also raised money through Sunday collections, and they repeatedly petitioned the government to assist their communities. The Catholic orders were active as well, in nursing and charity, but their impact was mainly confined to the towns. In rural areas it was the secular clergy who played an invaluable role.[122]

CONCLUSIONS

The conclusions we come to about the shape of communities in Ireland during the early nineteenth century must necessarily be

---

172; quoted in Murphy, "The support of the Catholic clergy," p. 119.

[119] Gustave de Beaumont, *Ireland: Social, Political and Economic*, ed. W. C. Taylor (London, 1839), II, pp. 90-91.

[120] *Ennis Chronicle*, 4 May 1816, p. 3; *Waterford Mirror*, 18 Feb. 1824.

[121] Oliver MacDonagh points out that shipping agencies in their advertisements routinely asked priests to tell parishioners who had prepaid passages the dates on which their vessels would sail. See Oliver MacDonagh, "The Irish Catholic clergy and emigration during the Great Famine" in *Irish Historical Studies*, 5, no. 20 (Sept. 1947), p. 288.

[122] O'Neill, "The state, poverty and distress in Ireland," pp. 32, 262-80.

phrased in relative terms. In all but very small societies, there exist a great variety of social relationships emerging out of the multitudinous interactions of people with one another. We can therefore speak only in terms of relatively frequent or infrequent interaction. There were especially strong bonds of primary relations at the local level in pre-famine Ireland. Most people were identified by the immediate neighborhood in which they lived, which was usually defined by the townland. Overlapping with neighborhood was kinship, by far the most binding communal structure we have examined. In all parts of the country it formed the basis of intensive social interaction and a pattern of almost incontestable social obligations. In some districts, including over half of the province of Connaught, it was the foundation of cohesive nucleated settlements.

These local primary groups were not socially isolated. Rural-urban contacts, and to a lesser extent inter-regional intercourse, were sufficient to enable people to form relationships outside their immediate neighborhoods and family groups. There was, however, noticeable variation among rural classes in the nature of these relationships. For the rural poor, the most frequent contacts came as a result of migrating from one part of the country to another to beg or look for work, or as a result of regular trips into towns, in many cases for these same reasons, but often simply to enjoy the social life that was centered in towns. If stable relationships emerged they were largely personal and non-utilitarian. Farmers, on the other hand, especially large farmers, were able to develop better associational relationships outside their local primary groups. They were more directly involved in production for a national market and were extensively engaged in commercial transactions with middle-class traders in the towns. We can also assume that they enjoyed a higher rate of literacy than did the rural poor, and consequently that their level of awareness of developments in other parts of the country was greater.

Yet it is clear that in pre-famine Ireland the most powerful source of social integration beyond the local primary group was religion. Like the town, but even more so, the parish integrated people from various townlands and kinship groups into a larger communal structure. Religion also served to bridge class divisions within the two major religious groups. Common religion did not overcome these class divisions by any means, but it was the major force in the society that served to reduce them. Large landholders and small landholders could be found attending the same chapel, listening to the same priest, and sharing common interests on account of their religion. Religion brought people together in a way that no other structure did. It also, by the same token, set people of different religions apart.

Three · **Collective Action**

FATAL AFFRAY IN LEITRIM

We learn from a correspondent that an affray took place at Mohill, on Thursday night, between the Police and a party of "Molly Maguires." According to our informant, the parties fired on each other. One of the peasantry was shot through the heart, and others were wounded. The "Molly Maguires" retreated, but soon after returned, with a reinforcement, rescued the body of their deceased companion, and compelled the Police to fly.

LOYAL NATIONAL REPEAL ASSOCIATION

The weekly meeting of the Association was held yesterday in Conciliation Hall. Shortly after one o'clock, Mr. J. O'Connell, M.P. accompanied by the Head Pacificator and Captain Broderick, entered the Hall, and was received with loud cheers. The chair was taken by Mr. Law.

HOMICIDE AT BANTRY

On Friday and Saturday last the Coroner, F. Baldwin, Esq., held an inquest at the Court House, Bantry, on the body of John Murphy of Droumduff, who was killed in a faction fight between the Flynns and the Murphys who had assembled together at the annual pattern held at Lady's-well on the lands of Lisheens. The deceased, it appeared, was knocked down with the blow of a spade-tree given by a man named William Downey, and while down was struck with a stone on the chest by a woman named Margaret Flynn.

Three items appearing in the *Dublin Evening Post* during the summer of 1845;[1] three active collectivities among the thousands of active collectivities in the society. Taken literally, our theoreti-

[1] *Dublin Evening Post*, 3 June, 1845, p. 3; 19 Aug. 1845, p. 4; and 30 Aug. 1845, p. 3.

cal approach says we should analyze and explain them all. In fact
we cannot, and the best strategy is to focus on several major types
that seem to have been especially important to the people who
lived in pre-famine Ireland. Even this modest inquiry must necessarily be brief and far from comprehensive, since the main purpose of this book is to explain the land movement of 1879-82 and
we want to get on with the rest of our story. What I shall do in the
following pages is identify some of the more outstanding features
of several major types of pre-famine collective action, emphasiz-
ing those characteristics that make sense in terms of what we
have just learned about the prevailing social structure. Can we see
in this collective action any consequences of the social cleavages
and integrative bonds that were discussed in the preceding chapter?

Collective Violence

Pre-famine Ireland was a remarkably violent country. Nothing
could have been further from the peaceful peasant society of some
anthropological folklore. The violence was often inflicted by individuals on other individuals, but it was also very often committed by collectivities of people, acting together in gangs or
crowds, usually small in size, but sometimes numbering in the
hundreds and occasionally in the thousands. It was frequently
committed by secret societies which existed under various names,
such as the Whiteboys, Whitefeet, Thrashers, Rockites, Molly Maguires, Ribbonmen, Terry Alts, and many others. Organized rural
violence in Ireland can be traced back at least to the first half of the
eighteenth century, and perhaps farther. The late eighteenth and
early nineteenth centuries saw a sharp increase. The response of
the state provides some indication of the magnitude of the problem. A coercion statute was introduced in 1814, which had to be
renewed in 1817; and in 1822 a comprehensive insurrection act
was passed to control violence resulting in part from a disastrous
crop failure in 1821. A serious outbreak of violence in 1830-34
produced an unusually repressive coercion act in 1833, which
was re-enacted in 1834. Even during periods of less noteworthy
unrest, violence occurred so regularly that the government passed
or renewed, between 1800 and the Great Famine, no fewer than
thirty-five coercion acts designed to control lawlessness in Ire-

land, and in most cases specifically to control collective violence in rural areas.[2]

AGRARIAN VIOLENCE

THE STRUGGLE OVER LAND The distinctive features of the Irish rural economy at this time gave rise to patterns of popular violence that differed noticeably from those found in other countries. For example, in England and France, where both rural and urban people depended heavily on purchased food, the most common form of popular violence during the late eighteenth century (and, in some places, during the early part of the nineteenth century) was the "food riot," in which a crowd of persons reacted to a sudden rise in food prices by seizing produce, usually grain or flour, from a miller, merchant, or baker, and then selling it at a "just" price.[3] Although there were crowds that engaged in somewhat similar activities in Ireland (for instance, in the 1760s and again in the 1840s), food riots were much less common there than other forms of popular violence. As a rule, the Irish rural poor, in the eighteenth and early nineteenth centuries, were not heavily dependent on purchased food, and consequently, they did not suffer particular hardship when food prices rose. Rather they suffered the most hardship, frequently indescribable hardship, whenever their potato crop failed or whenever they could not obtain land. The great majority of rural inhabitants depended for their survival first and foremost on access to land.

Regulating the distribution of land constituted, therefore, the single greatest concern of participants in pre-famine popular violence. Even landless laborers could have an interest in land and the terms by which it was distributed. In the words of G. C. Lewis, the most authoritative contemporary commentator, "none but the very poorest of the Irish labourers are entirely without land, either permanently or as conacre," but even when participants in disturbances were completely landless, it did not follow, he insisted, that their object was not to regulate its distribution. "They act on the general impression, prevalent among their class, that land is necessary to the maintenance of a poor man's family; and though

---

[2] G. Locker Lampson, *A Consideration of the State of Ireland in the Nineteenth Century* (London, 1907), pp. 637-8.

[3] Rudé, *Crowd in History*; E. P. Thompson, "The moral economy of the English crowd in the eighteenth century" in *Past and Present*, no. 50 (Feb. 1971).

they may not have at present, yet they have a future interest in the matter; though they may not be personally concerned, yet their kinsmen and friends and fellows are concerned."[4]

Thus agrarian combinations repeatedly endeavored to protect tenants threatened with losing their holdings, and to dissuade tenants from competing for one another's land. The members of a Whiteboy band in 1762 swore an oath "to do all in our power to hinder anyone from taking the little concerns we held, when out of lease."[5] A notice posted in 1820 on a chapel wall at Kilconnell, County Galway, warned "no man to bid, propose or demand another's ground or land."[6] Inevitably, the victims of assault included landlords, land agents, bailiffs, and process servers. Just as often, however, the victims were tenants who had taken land from which the previous occupant had been evicted, generally denounced in this period as "land jobbers," but known in later years as "landgrabbers." According to one witness before a Commons committee in 1824, the usual target of agrarian crime was "the property of the landlord who had distrained or ejected a tenant, or the property of the tenant who had succeeded the former occupant."[7]

The normal pattern was that a landgrabber would be visited at night and warned to give up his land.[8] If the warning went unheeded, the consequences could be brutal. It is not hard to find reports in newspapers of landgrabbers who were beaten or murdered, or whose property was destroyed, their houses sometimes burnt to the ground.[9] Violence was also directed at preventing distraint or ejectments. In January 1816 three men and one woman were shot to death at Athlacca, County Limerick, when a consta-

---

[4] George C. Lewis, *On Local Disturbances in Ireland, and the Irish Church Question* (London, 1836), pp. 188-9.

[5] Maureen Wall, "The Whiteboys" in T. Desmond Williams (ed.), *Secret Societies in Ireland* (Dublin, 1973), p. 15.

[6] S.P.O., State of the country papers: 1820/2188/10. This notice is otherwise similar to the one I have reproduced later in this chapter.

[7] *First report from the select committee on districts of Ireland under the Insurrection Act*, p. 8, H.C. 1824 (372), viii.

[8] See extracts provided by Lewis of a police report listing outrages committed in 1834 in the Garrycastle district of King's County. The most common demand was that people give up their land. Lewis, *Local Disturbances*, pp. 230-31.

[9] For examples in the last half of 1829 see *Dublin Evening Post*, 21 July 1829, p. 2; 13 Aug. 1829, p. 4; 5 Sept. 1829, p. 2; 1 Oct. 1829, p. 3.

ble with a sergeant's guard was resisted in the execution of an ejectment decree "by a great number of country people armed with scythes, reaping hooks etc."[10] In May of the same year, an armed party broke into out-offices near Bunratty, County Clare, where livestock distrained for rent had been deposited, and carried away a large number of sheep.[11] In June 1829 a bailiff was stoned to death by a mob in County Limerick while trying to impound cattle.[12] In 1843 a number of cases were reported in Carlow and Tipperary of crowds of people trying to carry off distrained crops.[13] And in the same year the authorities expected such stout resistance to evictions near Woodford, County Galway, that they assembled a force of 300 of the 5th Fusiliers, a troop of the 4th Royal Irish dragoons from Athlone, a troop of the 10th Hussars from Limerick, and 200 police.[14]

Generally speaking, rural people engaged in violence of this kind in the name of traditional rights. Distraint, evictions, or increases in rents were considered violations of conventions. Opposition on the part of "progressive" landowners to subdivision interfered with the ancestral custom of partible inheritance. Even refusing to grant reductions in rent could be taken as a breach of custom; reductions were usually demanded by tenants as a form of assistance that tradition dictated they should receive during periods of economic distress. To deny any of these rights was often regarded as a violation of unwritten laws. Most agrarian combinations believed it was their duty to punish these and other "crimes," and in general to enforce the unofficial contract that existed between landlord and tenant.[15] The problem, as we know, was that as the population expanded and the state of the economy deteriorated in the first half of the nineteenth century, the implicit terms of this traditional contract were more and more often broken. The actions taken by some "improving" landlords could shock even the most hardened of government officials, and leave them wondering how they were expected to maintain order. Writing to Robert Peel on 12 October 1830, the chief secretary for Ireland, Henry Hardinge (not one especially noted for taking the side

---

[10] Ennis Chronicle, 31 Jan. 1816, p. 3.   [11] Ibid., 8 May 1816, p. 3.
[12] Dublin Evening Post, 16 June 1829, p. 3.
[13] Ibid., 16 Sept. 1843, p. 3.   [14] Ibid., 1 Aug. 1843, p. 4.
[15] M. R. Beames, "Peasant movements: Ireland 1785-95" in Journal of Peasant Studies, 2, no. 4 (1975).

of the masses), suggested that it was from the ranks of evicted tenants, thrown "in want and despair" upon the country, that violent combinations recruited their members. In another letter to Peel sent the following day, he elaborated further on the point, making no effort to conceal his moral indignation:

> When we know that a Protestant gentleman, a Sir Robert Hudson, ejected in the depth of winter 400 Catholics from his estate in [County Cavan], who retired into the mountains, having no means of lawful existence from the difficulty of obtaining work, whilst the farms were chiefly relet to Protestants, can we be surprised at the burnings of houses and the maiming of cattle in that neighbourhood? On Lord William Beresford's estate (a minor) in Wicklow, arrangements are making to eject about 500 Catholics under the Subletting Act. . . . The Archdeacon has successfully mediated for the present, but admitting the improvement of the estate, and the liberality and kindness with which the measure will be carried into execution in the spring, can it be matter of wonder, that young men, whose Fathers for two or three generations have lived on the Estate, and who have punctually paid their rents, should become Ribbon-men and outlaws? Whilst the popular discontent has such natural causes for indulging in vengeance and outrage, I do not expect any cessation of midnight hostilities.[16]

For generations, rural people in Ireland had used violence to defend their customary rights. During the pre-famine social and economic crisis, this tradition of popular violence became a desperate struggle to preserve the very means of their existence.

THE WAR AGAINST FARMERS   But were rural people all united in this struggle? The answer very clearly is that they were not. As much as agrarian violence was a war between tenants and landlords, it was also a war between the rural poor and large farmers.

There are three types of evidence that point to this conclusion. First, the participants in pre-famine collective violence were disproportionately drawn from the class of laborers and small farmers. Witnesses before parliamentary committees generally agreed that most activists were laborers. Some witnesses sug-

[16] McGill University Library, Hardinge papers: Hardinge to Sir Robert Peel, 12 Oct. 1830 and 13 Oct. 1830.

gested that small farmers, "although not themselves actually participators," were in sympathy with the violence because they "are of the opinion that but for those outrages their lands would be taken from them on the fall of their leases." It was also said that the better and middle ranks of farmers "have felt an interest in those disturbances, and that their immunity from the payment of rent during the disturbances was an advantage they felt they derived from them." But most witnesses asserted that only "the poorest description of farmers" or those of "the middling description" took part, and they almost all agreed that large farmers rarely committed outrages. The most repeatedly mentioned were "labourers" and others of "the very lowest class."[17]

Second, the demands made by violent combinations represented most of all the interests of the rural poor. The secret societies sought to enforce, as Lewis observed, "a code of unwritten law set by the class of cottiers and agricultural labourers."[18] The Whiteboy disturbances in the 1760s began with the purpose of leveling ditches erected by landlords and graziers around commons on which small landholders had formerly enjoyed grazing rights. Their objectives subsequently broadened to include the prevention of ejectment, but also to represent such grievances as low wages, unemployment, the price of conacre ground, and the tithing of potatoes, all of which were of concern primarily to laborers and small farmers.[19] As the size of the laboring class grew in the early nineteenth century, violence representing the interests of laborers became all the more common. One indication of this is the frequency with which it was directed against pasture farming. Gangs often "houghed" cattle, dug up grassland, or threatened herdsmen.[20] Transcribed on the following page is a notice posted in 1820 near Aughrim, County Galway, which warns all "herds" (i.e., herdsmen) to quit their employers, except

---

[17] Lewis, *Local Disturbances*, pp. 182-5.   [18] Ibid., pp. 233-4.

[19] Wall, "The Whiteboys." See also James S. Donnelly, Jr., "The Whiteboy movement, 1761-5" in *Irish Historical Studies*, 21, no. 81 (March 1978).

[20] See references to such activities in *Select committee on districts of Ireland under the Insurrection Act*, pp. 4-7; Peter Gorman, *A report of the proceedings under a special commission of Oyer and Terminer in the counties of Limerick and Clare in . . . 1831* (Limerick, 1831); and in newspaper reports in the *Dublin Evening Post*, 22 March 1827, p. 3; 3 April 1827, p. 6; 5 April 1827, p. 4; 6 Aug. 1829, p. 3; 5 Sept. 1829, p. 2; 3 March 1831, p. 3; 17 March 1831, p. 4; 7 April 1831, p. 3; 19 April 1831, p. 3; 2 June 1831, p. 2; and 19 Sept. 1833, p. 3.

Threatening notice posted on a tree in the neighborhood of Aughrim, County Galway, 1820.

NOTICE

This is to give notice to the public at large of
The different rates of Crops per acre &.&.&.

Beating ground best quality	£ 5.0.0
Oats soil first Crop	4.0.0
Do. . . . . second Crop	3.0.0
Do. . . . . third Crop	2.10.0
Medow per acre best quality	3.0.0
Second .... Do.	2.10.0
Third Do. .... Do.	1.10.-

CLERGYS FEES

For marriage	0.11.4½
For anointing in case of death	2.8½
For Churching and Babtizing	1.3
For Easter duty married Couples	1.1
For Single persons	0.6½

TYTHES

Tythes to be paid to the Minister at 6d per acre
[illegible] average for every acre tilled or untilled
No proctor to be allowed to View or Value same
No vestry money to be paid by Roman Catholic
But every profession to support and keep their own
House of worship in repair and no Collector to drive
Or Collect for same at their peril

Every Gentleman or a man of property will be allowed
To have herds but all other herds are hereby warned
Not to follow their Charge from the day they are
Apprized of same otherwise they will receive due
punishment for their disobedience
No Act of [illegible] to be done without first acquainting
The Captain of it

By Order of the gay boy   Jack late and Early

SOURCE: S.P.O., State of the country papers: 1820/2188/10

those employed by a "gentleman or a man of property." Rents in general came under attack, but a special emphasis was usually given to conacre rents and rents for sublet land. The notice we have here, for instance, systematically stipulates the rates that farmers could charge for different types of land let in conacre.[21] More demanding still was a notice posted in County Kildare in the 1820s warning farmers to return their undertenants to the head landlord at the same rates at which they held the land themselves.[22] In many cases outrages were also aimed at regulating wages and preventing employers from hiring strangers.[23]

Still a third type of evidence that can be cited is that farmers were disproportionately the victims of pre-famine violence. We must be careful not to make too much of this. Laborers were frequently assaulted for accepting low wages, taking work in place of local laborers, or other violations of regulations that were intended to protect the interests of their own class. Similarly, farmers were often attacked because they were undermining the interests of their class, for example, by paying high rents or by landgrabbing. In addition, however, farmers could be made to suffer for hiring strangers, refusing to turn up pasture, charging high rents to subtenants, failing to provide satisfactory accommodation, or paying low wages. During the first five months of 1846, six of the fifty-one recorded outrages in County Limerick were committed by farmers against landlords, ten by farmers against other farmers, three by laborers against landlords, four by laborers against other laborers, but no fewer than twenty-eight (over half) by laborers against farmers.[24]

OTHER COLLECTIVE VIOLENCE

Many visitors to pre-famine Ireland, seeking to correct its reputation for lawlessness, insisted that Irish crime was almost entirely a consequence of agrarian grievances and that no safer place could be found on earth for persons not connected with rents or eject-

[21] Similar tables of acceptable conacre rents can be found in other notices in the same file, including the Kilconnel notice cited above.

[22] Lewis, Local Disturbances, p. 221. The full text of this notice can also be found in Donnelly, Landlord and Tenant, p. 31. A portion of it is quoted in Joseph Lee, "The Ribbonmen" in T. Desmond Williams (ed.), Secret Societies of Ireland (Dublin, 1973), p. 29.

[23] Select committee on districts of Ireland under the Insurrection Act, p. 9; and Lewis, Local Disturbances, p. 102. For newspaper reports of attacks on laborers see Dublin Evening Post, 10 May 1827, p. 3 and 15 July 1845, p. 1.

[24] Lee, "The Ribbonmen," p. 29.

ments.[25] Unfortunately, it was not until 1844 that the Constabulary began to distinguish systematically between agrarian and non-agrarian outrages. Yet it is worth noting that in 1844-6 only 16 percent of the reported outrages were considered to be agrarian, and almost half of these were merely threatening letters or notices.[26] One must, of course, be careful with data of this kind. It is especially important not to make the distinction between agrarian and non-agrarian violence too rigid; and the level of agrarian violence in 1844-6 may have been below average.[27] The conclusion to be drawn from the Constabulary figures is, all the same, quite unmistakable: violent people were doing more than protecting tenants and laborers.

They robbed, raped, brawled, and murdered. They sometimes did these things as individuals, but often they did them in collectivities. Rural combinations, even those whose primary objective was to protect tenants and laborers, frequently engaged in other types of violence, particularly banditry and raids for arms. They also fought among themselves. In most parts of the country, but especially in Munster, it was common for feuds to develop between rural combinations, which were usually called "factions" whenever they fought against one another.

FACTIONS   Although feuding has a long history and can be found in many societies, it has received little attention from social scientists, with the notable exception of anthropologists.[28] The signifi-

---

[25] Nicholson, *Report upon the general state of agriculture*. See similar claims by visitors, including de Tocqueville, cited in Gale E. Christianson, "Secret societies and agrarian violence in Ireland, 1790-1840" in *Agricultural History*, 46, no. 4 (Oct. 1972), pp. 383-4.

[26] *Return of outrages reported to the Royal Irish Constabulary office from the 1st January 1844 to 31st December 1880* [C 2756], H.C. 1881, lxxvii.

[27] One could argue that the Constabulary's classification was biased and that crimes which the public would regard as agrarian in motivation were not treated as such by police. It would take, however, an enormous bias to alter the conclusion one would draw from these data; furthermore, at least one historian firmly believes that the Constabulary always exaggerated the proportion of crimes that were agrarian. See William Vaughan, "A study of landlord and tenant relations in Ireland between the famine and the Land War, 1850-78," unpublished Ph.D. thesis, Trinity College Dublin, 1974. A more serious objection to this finding is that the years 1844-6 may have been atypical of the pre-famine period. Certainly it has to be admitted that the proportion of violence that was agrarian must have been much higher during some of the great waves of unrest, such as 1821-4 and 1830-34. This should be kept in mind in interpreting these data.

[28] See, for example, Paul Stirling, "A death and a youth club: feuding in a Turkish village" in *Anthropological Quarterly*, 33 (1960); M.J.L. Hardy, *Blood Feuds*

cance of feuds, and perhaps the reason they have been generally ignored, is that they represent power struggles which are relatively independent of central authority structures. Feuds have most often appeared in areas where, for one reason or another, alternatives to central regimes have gained legitimacy and people have developed a tradition of self-help rather than reliance on bureaucratic judicial systems for protection and for the redress of wrongs. Such areas are usually, but not necessarily, geographically isolated and sparsely populated. Parts of the world best-known for feuds are Sicily, Corsica, the Balkans, and Appalachia in the southern United States.

No one knows when faction fighting started in Ireland, but accounts of fights can be found in late eighteenth-century newspapers, and the practice was extensive and well reported by the second decade of the nineteenth century. Some of the better-known feuds occurred between the Caravats and Shanavests, the Whitefeet and Blackfeet, the Gows and Poleens, and the Blackhens and Magpies. Yet feuds were too numerous for anyone to keep track of all the antagonists, and many fights occurred between locally known factions. The particular issues over which they fought varied greatly, but two common themes pervaded faction quarrels: first, the members of one party were often seeking revenge for a defeat, insult, or injury inflicted on them by the other party, or by a member of the other party; and second, each party was typically endeavoring to demonstrate its physical superiority over the other and thus establish its dominance within a certain territory.

By what criteria did people become identified with one faction or another? One basis was evidently place of residence. Occasionally factions would claim to represent large districts or regions, even provinces. In the early part of the century there were regular fights in the area surrounding the middle Shannon between Connaught men and Munster men. More often, however, factions recruited their supporters from particular baronies, parishes, or townlands, frequently using these territorial units or local landmarks for their names.[29] Not surprisingly, in western districts,

---

and the Payment of Blood Money in the Middle East (Leiden, 1963); E. M. Peters, "Some structural aspects of the feud among the camel-herding Bedouin of Cyrenaica" in Africa, 37, no. 3 (July 1967); and Jacob Black-Michaud, Cohesive Force: Feud in the Mediterranean and the Middle East (Oxford, 1975).

[29] Patrick O'Donnell, The Irish Faction Fighters of the 19th Century (Dublin, 1975), pp. 25-6.

hamlets could form the basis for uniting partisans. Hely Dutton, writing of Galway in 1824, attributed faction fighting in that part of the country to the social cohesiveness of the hamlet-rundale settlement pattern:

> Though latterly in most cases ruinous to the tenants in this county, yet [the rundale system] tends to encourage such strong attachments, generally strengthened by intermarriages, that though they may have some bickerings with each other, they will, *right* or *wrong*, keep their companions; this is frequently the source of much disturbance at fairs and any other public meeting.[30]

Lewis suggested that faction fighting was more prevalent in the west.[31] Actually, the data we have indicate that people on the west coast were no more inclined to engage in this kind of collective action than people elsewhere.[32] What may be true is that when faction fighting did occur in the west, the encounters were most often between members of rival hamlets. In any case, we can note in passing that the clustering of populations in hamlets could constitute a source of solidarity for the formation of agrarian societies or crowds resisting rent collections or evictions.[33]

Along with residence, the most common basis for collecting faction fighters was kinship. Many feuds had their origin in ancestral quarrels. The reason participants frequently gave for fighting was simply that their fathers and grandfathers had fought before them. Often factions were known by the surnames of their leaders or members. The "Cummins" and the "Darraghs" fought

---

[30] Hely Dutton, *A Statistical and Agricultural Survey of the County of Galway* (Dublin, 1824), p. 518. Quoted in Green, "Agriculture," p. 114.

[31] Lewis, *Local Disturbances*, p. 295.

[32] *A return of all crimes and outrages reported by the stipendiary magistrates and officers of police in Ireland . . . as having been perpetrated in their respective districts from the 1st January 1836 to the 12th December 1837 . . .*, H.C., 1837-8 (157), xlvi; *Outrages reported to the constabulary office, Dublin, as having occurred during January and February, 1837*, H.C. 1837-8 (214), xlvi.

[33] Opposition to the breakup of hamlets resulted, according to one observer writing in the mid-nineteenth century, from "the recollection of nights of social intercourse, of aid in sickness, of sympathy in joy and sorrow, of combined operations against bailiff and gauger." Quoted in Evans, *Folkways*, p. 32. Donnelly points out that the Whiteboy movement was especially strong in the upland and mountainous areas of Tipperary and Waterford (around the Galtees, Knockmealdowns, and Comeraghs) where joint tenancies were common. See his "Whiteboy movement."

in King's County; the "Gallaghers" and "McGettigans" in Donegal; the "Collinses" and "Macks" in Kerry, and so on. It is true that, even if it took a family name, a faction was not necessarily limited to persons within that family; nor did factions necessarily encompass entire kinship groups. What was invariably the case, however, was that *family loyalty was the strongest force drawing people to one side or another*. This was true even in the case of factions without kinship titles.

Normally, faction fights occurred when special events brought people from different districts or family groups together in one place. Thus most clashes broke out at fairs, markets, race-meetings, patterns or funerals, and sometimes even on Sundays after mass. For ten years Templemore in County Tipperary was "the scene on fair days, Sundays and at funerals of many a bloody faction fight," originating in a dispute near Roscrea between two neighbors.[34] "Patterns" (festivals for local patron saints) were frequently disrupted by drinking and battling; this was one of the reasons they were opposed by the Catholic clergy.[35] Sometimes faction fights would start with an argument among several individuals, which would escalate as friends and relatives of the contending parties joined in. Usually, however, the factions came to a fair or pattern with fighting on their minds. In November 1814 a man was killed at Nenagh, County Tipperary, "in a quarrel between two factions that assembled there to fight in consequence of a previous arrangement for that purpose."[36] In the following month "a considerable number of armed persons assembled at the fair of Montpelier to decide a quarrel between two factions. One of the parties did not appear; the other continued in possession of the town the whole of that day and night committing every sort of excess, firing shots, etc."[37] In 1825 a justice of the peace reported from Tipperary:

> This part of Ireland had been long agitated by the custom of forming factions to avenge private feuds at different fairs. But for the last four years the practice had been nearly discontinued. Since the beginning of this year the reorganizing of

[34] Cashel Diocesan Archives, Diary of Rev. James O'Carroll, p. 78.

[35] Weld, *Statistical Survey of Roscommon*, pp. 269-70; O'Donnell, *Irish Faction Fighters*, pp. 30-31.

[36] S.P.O., State of the country papers: James Ormsby to Chief Secretary, 1 Jan. 1815 (1815/1682/3).

[37] Ibid.

factions under their various denominations has been to an extent beyond calculation, and I have now to assure you that the entire of this county of Tipperary, the whole of Limerick, and parts of Cork, Kilkenny and Kerry are regularly enrolled under various well-known chiefs who send them, in large bodies, to every fair. . . . By examining the police reports, you will no doubt perceive that no fairday, holiday, funeral, and I may add, any day passes without the assembling of thousands, to the total cessation of all public business, and to which meetings *arms* in large quantities are beginning to be brought.[38]

SECTARIANISM   It is important not to overstate the impact of religion on rural violence. To do so can obscure a crucial difference between rural secret societies and some of the more plainly religious-based movements to be discussed in the second part of this chapter. The priority that rural people gave to economic interests and kinship loyalties put limits on the influence religion could have. Catholic landlords, farmers, or landgrabbers enjoyed no special immunity from attack; and Catholic factions fought against other Catholic factions.

Moreover, there was a noticeable lack of sympathy between the Catholic clergy and the violent collectivities. Most secret societies were hostile toward the clergy and some engaged in campaigns directed specifically at Catholic priests, or at least against clerical dues. The best-known and by far the most virulent anti-clerical campaign was conducted by the Rightboys in the 1780s.[39] In the first two decades of the nineteenth century, some agrarian combinations gave considerable attention to priests' dues. In Connaught, for example, the Thrashers (as well as other gangs who frequently assumed the same name) sought to regulate both tithes and payments to the Catholic clergy; they specified acceptable rates, and intimidated priests who tried to charge more or parishioners who tried to pay more.[40] Violent opposition to clerical dues became much less prominent in the 1820s and 1830s,

[38] S.P.O., State of the country papers: James Roe, J.P. to Henry Goulburn, 6 Oct. 1825 (1825/2731/4).

[39] James S. Donnelly, Jr., "The Rightboy movement, 1785-8" in *Studia Hibernica*, nos. 17-18 (1977-8); Lewis, *Local Disturbances*, pp. 27-8; R. E. Burns, "Parsons, priests and the people: the rise of Irish anticlericalism, 1785-1789" in *Church History*, 31, no. 2 (June 1962).

[40] Lewis, *Local Disturbances*, pp. 40-42; William Ridgeway, *A report of the proceedings of a special commission of Oyer and Terminer, and Gaol Delivery for the*

perhaps as a result of the emergence of religious-based national movements. Nevertheless, there remained a noticeable lack of respect for the clergy on the part of the violent societies.

Most Catholic clergymen, for their part, had little use for the violent combinations. There were several reasons. First, the clergy found this violence morally offensive. Second, their parishioners included many of the victims of violence as well as those who engaged in it. And third, the clergy were usually opposed to any oath-bound association claiming the allegiance of members of their flock. As a result, they frequently denounced rural violence and those who committed it.[41]

Yet, in spite of this antipathy between the Catholic clergy and the violent societies, pre-famine violence was hardly free of religious influence. The extensive communal ties Catholics shared with one another, and the enormous divisions that existed between Catholics and Protestants, made it most unlikely that people of different religious affiliations would join together in collective action. As a rule, collectivities engaging in violence, like most other active collectivities in pre-famine Ireland, were religiously homogeneous. This inevitably had an effect on their aims and activities. Religion often increased the intensity of particular struggles. Were landlord, farmer, or landgrabber a Protestant, this fact was usually noted and served to reinforce hostility against him. Almost invariably, any landlord who installed Protestant tenants in place of Catholics (or in some other way laid himself open to a charge of religious persecution) evoked great indignation, which could generate unusually vigorous opposition.[42] And not surprisingly, the religious cleavage added fuel to the unpopularity of tithes, which Catholic as well as Protestant tenants were forced to pay to the Church of Ireland. Resistance to the collection of tithes was as determined as resistance to the collection of rents, even though the financial burden represented by rents was far greater. Tithes were a major target of the Whiteboys in Munster during the

---

counties of Sligo, Mayo, Leitrim, Longford and Cavan in the month of December 1806 (Dublin, 1807) pp. 9, 17, 134, and 149. See also the acceptable rates for clerical fees in the threatening notice reporduced earlier in this chapter. Similar tables can be found in other notices in the same file.

[41] Donnelly, "Rightboy movement"; Burns, "Parsons, priests and the people"; Lewis, Local Disturbances, pp. 30-31. and W. G. Broehl, The Molly Maguires (Cambridge, Massachusetts, 1965), pp. 32-3.

[42] For example, a crowd said to number 5,000 persons was prepared to resist evictions in County Tipperary in 1843 apparently because the local Catholic clergyman was among those to be ejected. See Dublin Evening Post, 12 Aug. 1843, p. 4.

1760s and 1770s, as well as of the Rightboys during the mid-1780s. They continued to occupy the attention of secret societies in the early nineteenth century, most notably in the 1830s during what is known as the Tithe War, but earlier as well, particularly during the great wave of violence of the early 1820s. The unrest of the early 1820s was characterized by particularly vicious sectarianism. Anti-Protestant sentiment found expression in threatening notices, and in attacks on Protestants and their churches, partly inspired by the prophecies of Pastorini, who had predicted that Protestantism would be extinguished forever in 1825.

Religious cleavage also gave rise to a number of unreservedly sectarian combinations. Sectarian fighting could be found in most parts of the country, but it was especially common and brutal in Ulster and in the counties bordering on Ulster. Here a war between Catholics and Protestants raged on and off throughout the first half of the nineteenth century. Most of the sectarian combinations could, directly or indirectly, trace their history to the religious conflicts of the late seventeen hundreds. During the 1780s and 1790s a noticeable transformation occurred in the character of collective violence in Ulster. Both agrarian societies and feuding factions became more denominational. As early as 1784 bands of Protestants engaged in daybreak raids on the homes of Catholics for the purpose of seizing arms; and by the late 1780s most encounters between hostile factions at fairs and cockfights were actually encounters between Catholics and Protestants.[43] Combinations formed by Catholics to fight against Protestants became collectively known as the Defenders, which soon evolved into an extensive movement. By 1790 they embraced the counties of Tyrone, Armagh, Down, Monaghan, Cavan, Louth, and Meath.[44] In some of these counties, such as Meath, the Defenders were concerned principally with rents and tithes, but in the border counties, where large numbers of both Catholics and Protestants resided, their objective was primarily the protection of the former and the intimidation of the latter. During the early 1790s the Defender movement continued to expand, and eventually the strength of Catholic organizations in the border counties exceeded that of Protestant groups, until Protestants were prompted in 1795 to form their own defense organization, the Orange Order,

[43] Hereward Senior, *Orangeism in Ireland and Britain, 1795-1836* (London, 1966), pp. 7-12.
[44] Ibid., p. 12.

which grew considerably in power in the succeeding years. During 1796-7 Protestants gained the upper hand in Ulster by conducting raids on the homes of Catholics (forcing an estimated 700 families to flee the province) and by filling the ranks of a new yeomanry force established by the government in 1796.[45] Alarm among Catholics over this awesome Orange movement provided, in turn, a stimulus for further growth in the number of Defender societies. Fear of Orangemen also promoted support in southern rural areas for a movement led by republican revolutionaries known as the United Irishmen. In 1798 the United Irishmen made preparations for a general uprising which resulted in several abortive revolts, the largest being an insurrection in Wexford. The Wexford rebellion was supported by a substantial number of rural people and included some vicious sectarian assaults on Protestants.

In the following decade the Orange movement consolidated its power, and the functions of the Defenders were taken over by societies of so-called Ribbonmen which operated in Ulster, in the northern counties of Leinster, and in parts of Connaught. These or smaller bands of Catholics and Protestants participated in regular attacks on each others' homes or meeting places, and clashed at fairs. In May 1815 it was reported from County Londonderry that large bodies of Ribbonmen roamed the countryside and sought to provoke fights "upon the slightest quarrel in any fair or market."[46] In August of the same year, an estimated 1,500 Ribbonmen tried to storm a public house in Londonderry where Freemasons and Orangemen customarily met.[47] A few weeks later the Chief Secretary's office was warned that "the party spirit, which so unfortunately exists amongst the lower orders, is gaining ground. It is positively reported from a most respectable quarter that both Protestants and Catholics are unlawfully putting down their names to resolutions, binding themselves to attend at different fairs and markets, for the avowed purpose of fighting."[48] On 12 June 1823 a riot broke out at a fair at Maghera in County Londonderry that fol-

[45] In addition to Senior's account, a useful analysis of the social basis of the Orange movement is found in Peter Gibbon, The Origins of Ulster Unionism: The Formation of Popular Protestant Politics and Ideology in Nineteenth-Century Ireland (Manchester, 1975), pp. 22-43.

[46] S.P.O., State of the country papers: John Hill to E. Littlehales, 17 May 1815 (1815/1711/14).

[47] Drogheda Journal, 7 Aug. 1815.

[48] S.P.O., State of the country papers: Thomas Burnet to Chief Secretary, 27 Aug. 1815 (1815/1682/41).

lowed a common pattern. Yeomen, some of whom were Orangemen, were driven into the local barracks where they collected
arms and fired on their pursuers, wounding a score and killing
several.[49] The Orange movement was especially active in the late
1820s and early 1830s when Protestant fears were raised by the
growth of national movements representing Catholic interests. Although the Order as such was legally dissolved between 1825 and
1828, combinations composed of Orangemen (both violent and
non-violent) were active during the Emancipation campaign and
subsequently during the Tithe War. Orange processions, which
were unusually large and militant at this time, frequently clashed
with Ribbonmen, most often in County Cavan, but also in County
Down. Similarly, during the Repeal movement of the early 1840s,
Orangemen were active in disrupting political meetings and ter-
rorizing Catholics in the border counties.

LEVEL OF ORGANIZATION

Many students of social conflict would be inclined to refer to the
violence that we have been discussing as "turmoil" or "primitive
protest." They would regard it as the incipient and less effective
form of a collective struggle that could become better organized
only at a later historical stage. Although they might have little
sympathy for the class that ruled pre-famine Ireland, they would
share their view that the violence was chaotic. This ruling class,
of course, generally regarded violence as a threat to the social order, serving no legitimate purpose, and often no other purpose
than the amusement of the "ruffians" who engaged in it. People
fought, it was repeatedly said, just for the sheer love of fighting.
Even observers sympathetic to the hardships endured by the rural
population often regretted the apparent aimlessness and selfish-
ness of the violence. Lewis, for instance, remarked that it often
stemmed from personal quarrels, even when it was done in the
name of a land code. He also deplored the close tie between agrarian violence and banditry. "Any persons engaged in a lawless
course of life," he lamented, "are likely to take part in Whiteboy
disturbances when they have once begun." "Anybody . . . who

---

[49] Senior, *Orangeism*, p. 205. See also William Carleton, "The party fight and
funeral" in his *Traits and Stories of the Irish Peasantry* (London, 1867). Though
presented as fiction, the fight described by Carleton was undoubtedly based on a
real case.

wishes to resist the law may, if he is inclined, make use of the services of the Whiteboys.''[50] And faction fighting, Lewis suggested, represented a failure of the Irish peasantry to rise above kinship loyalties to class loyalties.[51]

To say this is to make some valid points about the nature of pre-famine collective violence, but it is also to judge the violent collectivities by standards different from those by which they would have judged themselves. Faction fights, superficially so chaotic, were in fact well organized in their own terms. Factions typically had recognized leaders, who commanded unswerving obedience from a large following. It would actually be difficult in the modern world to find examples of violent conflict as institutionalized as Irish faction fighting. Fights were remarkably predictable. With almost monotonous regularity, they broke out during the late hours of fairs, at patterns, or after funerals; usually they had been pre-arranged. Many observers remarked on the familiar routines that participants followed and the well-recognized norms that told people what to do and on what signal they should start fighting. (Many fights did not begin until the leaders of opposing factions had finished an elaborate taunting ritual known as the "wheel.") From the viewpoint of the higher social classes, faction fighting was disorganized and chaotic. For those engaging in this violence, there was nothing chaotic about what they were doing at all. And should the arm of the state try to impose its notion of order on them by breaking up a fight, the feuding factions often united and turned on the police.[52]

Similarly, one could hardly claim that agrarian combinations were poorly organized. The very term "secret society," which has so often been applied to them, is indicative of how sophisticated their organization could be. Members were usually bound together by oaths and subject to the strict authority of leaders.[53] They were well organized to avoid legal prosecution. They met in

[50] Lewis, Local Disturbances, pp. 119-20, 184-5, 279-81. The term "Whiteboys" was frequently used in the early nineteenth century to refer not to the Whiteboys of the 1760s, but to agrarian combinations in general. It is in this sense that Lewis is using the term here.

[51] Ibid., p. 223.

[52] For examples, see Kilkenny Journal, 19 May 1838, p. 3; Dublin Evening Post, 3 Aug. 1843, p. 3; 17 June 1845, p. 2; and O'Donnell, Irish Faction Fighters, passim.

[53] So far as is known, the first to use oaths extensively were the Whiteboys of the 1760s. See Donnelly, "Whiteboy movement" and Wall, "The Whiteboys," both of whom make this point.

secrecy and ordinarily carried out their attacks at night, especially during the long nights of winter, though distress among the peasantry was usually greatest in June and July when the previous potato crop was exhausted. And they sometimes recruited persons from other districts to commit crimes, thus making it extremely difficult for law-enforcement authorities to track them down.[54] They were engaged in a constant battle with the state for the allegiance and obedience of the people in their district and for other kinds of resources that they needed to maintain themselves and their organizations. It is in these terms, I suggest, that we can understand the frequency with which they practiced banditry and raids for arms.

There is more truth to the argument that these organizations did not usually extend much beyond one locality. Even this statement ignores the fact that some combinations evolved into large regional movements. The Whiteboy campaign of 1761-6 branched out from its stronghold in south Tipperary into parts of Limerick, Waterford, and Cork. During the mid-1870s the Rightboys made themselves felt in all six counties in Munster, four counties in Leinster (King's, Queen's, Kilkenny and Wexford), and one in Connaught (Galway). The Defenders, as already noted, spread initially through the border counties, and then subsequently across the midlands, eventually joining forces with the United Irishmen in a rebellion that sought (albeit unsuccessfully) to encompass the entire country. In 1813-16 the Caravats stretched over a wide area covering Waterford, Tipperary, Limerick, and Clare in Munster, and Westmeath, Longford, and east Galway in the midlands. The Rockite movement of 1821-4 extended through most of Munster, including the counties of Cork, Limerick, Kerry, Tipperary, and Clare. And the Terry Alts covered large parts of Clare, Galway, Westmeath, and Limerick in the years 1829-31.[55]

It is true, however, that even these comparatively large agrarian movements were not nationally directed or organized. A partial exception was the Defender movement, but it became national only in so far as it was transformed from an agrarian/sectarian society into a revolutionary movement. The others were all very clearly identified with a specific part of the country. Moreover,

[54] Christianson, "Secret societies and agrarian violence in Ireland," pp. 376-7; Broehl, Molly Maguires, p. 48.

[55] See Donnelly, "Whiteboy movement" and his "Rightboy movement." I have also drawn heavily on conversations with Donnelly in my efforts to trace the areas embraced by the regional movements.

taken as a whole, most of the rural violence that occurred in the pre-famine period (certainly most of the violence committed during years between major outbursts) was perpetrated by combinations which were not part of any large regional movement and which drew their members from restricted areas—in most instances, from the same barony, parish, or townland. Ties of neighborhood and kinship usually helped to unite members of these combinations. Most factions were based primarily on such ties, and most agrarian societies were based at least partially on them. Indeed some agrarian societies were indistinguishable from local factions and fought against one another as well as seeking to regulate the distribution of land. It is true that the aims, codes, and techniques of these agrarian societies could extend over large areas, even if the combinations themselves did not. This is another reason why one must be very careful in characterizing them as local. But their organizational structure—invariably strong within specific localities—was generally weak or nonexistent over large areas; and there was rarely any formal means for coordinating activities. In 1816 the Lord Lieutenant reported:

> I could not ascertain that the various combinations which existed in different parts of the country, proposed to themselves any definite object of a political nature, nor was there any evidence at all conclusive, that they acted under the immediate guidance of leaders of weight, either in point of talents or property, and that although there had appeared symptoms of concert and co-operation in some parts, I had no reason to believe that there was any general understanding between combinations existing in different counties.[56]

Writing in the 1830s, Lewis argued that the agrarian societies were not centrally directed. Referring to efforts by the Ribbon society to transform local combinations into Ribbon branches, Lewis admitted that "the rural population of Munster and Connaught are constantly in a state in which they are liable to be practised upon by such agents," but he insisted "that scarcely any influence of this kind is *in fact* exercised, that the objects of the Whiteboys are exclusively local, and that, if any attempts have been made to engraft more general views, they have proved fruitless."[57] In 1839

[56] Christianson, "Secret societies and agrarian violence in Ireland," p. 382.

[57] Lewis, *Local Disturbances*, p. 163. Again Lewis is using the term "Whiteboys" in its general sense.

the Under Secretary for Ireland asserted that if local combinations were to endeavor to combine for more general purpose "they would fall instantly to pieces like a Rope of Sand."[58]

It is important, however, to avoid an implication of failure when one calls attention to this localism. It is easy to assume that the violent collectivities should have engaged in a coordinated struggle or that they were trying to do so but failed. In particular, it is tempting to suppose that pre-famine collective violence was effective only when it united large numbers of persons on a class basis, and that whenever people became involved in kinship feuds or other local disputes they were not promoting their true interests. Yet in making such judgments we would be imposing our notions as to the most important social group in the rural society. We would be giving second place to other structures, besides class, that shaped the composition and objectives of many violent collectivities. Too often students of social unrest have underestimated the capacity of peasants for independent collective action because they have dismissed the violence in which many peasants have engaged as "disorganized," "spontaneous," or "amorphous" when in fact it was well organized, but on some basis other than social class. If some rural combinations in pre-famine Ireland did not achieve class unity and instead became entangled in faction fights or other local disputes, the reason was that these combinations were formed on the basis of personal ties and animosities as well as on the basis of common class position. Settling old scores, taking sides in personal quarrels, and establishing their power over a limited area was not failure from their point of view. *For many of the violent collectivities, these were the things they were trying to do.* Likewise, and more obviously, if some rural combinations became involved in religious conflicts, it was because the religious structure, as well as the class structure, was a major source of integration and cleavage in the society.

National Movements

Three national movements emerged in Ireland during the 1830s and 1840s that conform more closely to our "modern" notions of effective collective action. How did these movements develop? On what social structures were they based?

[58] Broehl, *Molly Maguires*, p. 37.

The Emancipation campaign is the most famous national movement in the pre-famine period. Its leadership came largely from
the Catholic middle class—Catholic lawyers, journalists, merchants, shopkeepers, comparatively large farmers, and what
Catholic landowners there were. Since Chapter Two was concerned almost exclusively with rural social structure, it is now
necessary to say a few words about urban social structure, and
specifically about the position of the Catholic urban middle class.

During the eighteenth century Catholics had made gradual but
significant social and economic advances in towns and cities. The
penal laws imposed restrictions on them with respect to both
owning land and engaging in business, but restrictions on business activities were apparently much less effectively enforced.
Even in the early eighteenth century, Catholics were heavily engaged in trade in the towns. Although they operated under severe
disabilities and were forced to pay fees ("quarterage") to Prot-
estant-controlled guilds, in which they were not allowed membership and from which they obtained only limited benefits,[59]
they were, nevertheless, the principal traders in the country. They
even possessed some measure of political power and ultimately
succeeded in preventing guilds from collecting fees and harassing
their operations.[60] Their position was strengthened in the late
eighteenth century by the repeal of most of the penal laws, including the removal in 1793 of religion as a barrier to voting, to sitting
on grand juries, and to holding certain political offices. By the
1820s Catholics had acquired considerable wealth in trade and
commerce. They were also, though to a much lesser extent, to be
found among owners of landed estates. Yet they still could not
hold high judicial and political posts, including seats in parliament. The removal of these remaining exclusions was generally
referred to as "Emancipation."

The movement by which Emancipation was won emerged as a
result of a significant change in the nature of Catholic lay leadership. The chief lay spokesmen for Catholic political interests in
the late eighteenth century had come from the very small and almost powerless Catholic landed gentry. Toward the close of the
century their claim to represent Catholics was challenged by a
politically active group consisting mostly of Catholics engaged

[59] MacGeehin, "The Catholics of the towns."
[60] Ibid. See also Wall, "The rise of a Catholic middle class."

either in the professions or in trade. The influence of this group
grew steadily in the first two decades of the nineteenth century.
Eventually, under the leadership of Daniel O'Connell, a new organization, called the Catholic Association, was founded in 1823
to represent Catholic interests.[61] In the following year this body
began a campaign to mobilize the rural population. There were
two main ways in which O'Connell and his associates utilized
rural support. Both depended on the cooperation of the Catholic
clergy.

First, they sought to use the rural population as a financial resource. It is a testimony to O'Connell's ingenuity and skill as a
political leader that he was able to accomplish a feat of this kind
in a society in which the majority of the people were so impoverished. In February 1824 he restructured the Catholic Association to include not only those who could afford membership
dues of a guinea a year, but also "associates" who were encouraged to join at a cost of a penny a month. The plan was to establish
in every parish in Ireland a committee headed by the parish priest,
who would forward the "Catholic rent," as it was called, to the
secretary of the Catholic Association and would also post the
names of subscribers in or as near as possible to the Catholic
chapel. Several Catholic bishops assisted by providing lists of
priests and their addresses. In this way the Association was able
to organize committees in a great number of parishes. Most were
directed by parish priests, while the "collectors" whom the clergy
supervised were usually shopkeepers and farmers. By March 1825
the Catholic Association had collected over £19,000, and by the
end of 1828 over £51,000.[62]

Second, O'Connell and his associates, again in conjunction
with the Catholic clergy, made use of the rural population as a
source of electoral support. For this purpose they were able to
mobilize the votes of the so-called "forty-shilling freeholders," an
important section of the electorate that included not only owner-
occupiers, but also tenants who held their land on lease for a term

[61] The social group that the Catholic Association most clearly represented is reflected in the composition of its original sixty-two members, of whom thirty-one
were lawyers, eleven were merchants, three were newspaper editors, and one was
a surgeon. Another ten were landed gentlemen, five were members of the aristoc-
racy, and one was a Carmelite friar. See James Reynolds, *The Catholic Emancipation Crisis in Ireland, 1823-1829* (New Haven, 1954), p. 31.

[62] Reynolds, *Catholic Emancipation Crisis*, p. 62.

of a life or lives and were willing to swear that their farms were worth at least forty shillings more than the rent reserved in their leases. Since 1793 Catholic as well as Protestant forty-shilling freeholders had enjoyed the right to vote in parliamentary elections. For roughly the first thirty years landlords were, by and large, able to control this vote. But in 1826 they were given some reason for concern. In the general election of that year, a local committee of the Catholic Association in County Waterford launched an extremely well organized campaign in support of Villiers Stuart, a close ally of O'Connell and an advocate of Catholic Emancipation. This committee provided each priest in the constituency with a list of electors in his parish. The priest was expected to arrange for voters to be canvassed and persuaded to support Stuart. In the eight days before the election, a team of speakers, lay and clerical, toured the chapels and addressed the congregations after mass. And during the voting the clergy accompanied their parishioners to the polls and superintended them as they exercised their franchise.[63] The result was the success of the Emancipationist candidate against the powerful Beresford interest, which had controlled the seat for generations. Subsequently, similar revolts occurred in Westmeath, Monaghan, and Louth. Then, in 1828, again using the clergy to organize voters, the Catholic Association successfully elected a Catholic, in the person of O'Connell, in a by-election in County Clare. It was evident that, if organized to vote in unison, forty-shilling freeholders could be persuaded to defy their landlords. It was therefore possible that the government would soon be faced with an embarrassing number of elected candidates who could not take their seats in parliament because they were Catholics. More disturbing still, there was good reason to believe that without some form of appeasement the Emancipation movement might soon go out of control and could even become violent if not checked. For these reasons and others, the government decided that the religious qualification for membership in parliament had outlived its usefulness. In the following year it was abolished.[64]

The Emancipation campaign stirred the hearts of almost all Irish Catholics. Even the rural poor felt grievances as Catholics,

[63] J. H. Whyte, "The influence of the Catholic clergy on elections in nineteenth-century Ireland" in *English Historical Review*, 75, no. 295 (April 1960), p. 241.

[64] 10 Geo. IV, c. 7. See also Reynolds, *Catholic Emancipation Crisis*, especially chapters 7, 8 and 9.

and could identify their interests with Emancipation. Nevertheless, the extent to which the movement mobilized the rural population was limited in a number of important respects. For one
thing, its strength was not well distributed regionally, not even in
the Catholic part of Ireland. It was strongest in those areas that
were most urbanized, where inter-regional social communication
was most advanced, and where there was comparatively less rural
poverty. Catholic rent committees were busiest and most successful in Leinster and east Munster, while much less active in western counties (with perhaps the exception of O'Connell's home
county of Kerry).[65] Similarly, the electoral support for the Emancipation campaign came from a comparatively small segment of
the population. Although the forty-shilling freeholders represented a decisive portion of the total electorate, they comprised a
very minor portion of the total number of landholders, probably in
the neighborhood of 10 percent. And even these freeholders did
not control the Emancipation movement. That control lay with
members of the Catholic urban middle class and the Catholic
clergy. They were the ones who had the most to gain from Emancipation, particularly the lawyers who dominated the Catholic
Association. Though rural people were led to expect much, the
benefits they actually derived were primarily emotional and vicar-
ious. Indeed, it is difficult to draw any great distinction between
the manner in which priests marched forty-shilling freeholders to
the polls during the Emancipation campaign and the manner in
which landlords had marched them to the polls over the preceding thirty years. The Emancipation campaign gave the forty-
shilling freeholders hardly more political experience than they
already had. At most it taught them that, if united, they could ignore their landlords' wishes with relative impunity. Yet this lesson was to become immediately meaningless as a result of an act
of parliament that laid bare the irony of the Emancipation campaign. Emancipation was accompanied, with surprisingly little
opposition from the Catholic Association, by legislation that
raised the property qualification for the county franchise to ten

---

[65] In 1827, for example, the Catholic Association reported rent receipts totaling
close to £1,300 from Leinster (particularly Dublin, Meath, and Louth), approximately £1,200 from Munster (mostly from Cork, Tipperary, and Waterford), but
little more than £200 from Connaught (mainly Galway and Mayo) and £200 from
Ulster. *Connaught Telegraph*, 3 March 1828, p. 3. See also Reynolds, *Catholic
Emancipation Crisis*, pp. 62-3.

pounds, thus disenfranchising most of the people who had defied their landlords to win it.[66]

THE TITHE WAR

The "Tithe War" was a national movement that broke out in Ireland shortly after Emancipation. It sought to abolish tithes that tenants had to pay to the established church. By the eighteenth century tithes were levied throughout the country on Catholic as well as Protestant tenants, and collection was plagued by fraud and by inconsistencies in value.[67] Opposition to the payment of tithes began long before the Tithe War. As already noted, it was a grievance repeatedly expressed by rural secret societies in the late eighteenth and early nineteenth centuries. In 1823 and 1824 significant reforms were enacted in parliament reducing the average cost of tithes and making their collection, at least within the same district, more consistent. Nevertheless, in late 1830 a national movement emerged against tithes. Why did such a movement appear at this time?

Two reasons stand out. The most obvious is the organizational base provided by the Emancipation campaign, which successfully mobilized a great number of Catholics and gave them a taste for political agitation. Though the Catholic Association was outlawed at the same time as Emancipation was granted, many of the groups organized during the Emancipation campaign did not break up when their immediate objective had been achieved. On the contrary, their success strengthened their resolve to work together, encouraging them to regard Emancipation as the first step in an assault on the Protestant Ascendancy.

Secondly, there was a shift in the source of opposition to tithes. The Tithe Composition Act of 1823 decreed that special vestries

[66] The franchise was extended soon afterwards by the Reform Act of 1832, but it remained much more restricted than before 1829, and the size of the electorate actually declined during the following two decades. See K. T. Hoppen. "Politics, the law and the nature of the Irish electorate 1832-1850" in *English Historical Review*, 92, no. 365 (Oct. 1977). Hoppen also shows that the wealth of county electors varied greatly (many voters had holdings under ten acres), but that the overall mean was very high at forty statute acres. Little is known about the social composition of the electorate in the counties between 1793 and 1829, but what is known would suggest that it was extremely diverse as well.

[67] Patrick O'Donoghue, "Causes of opposition to tithes, 1830-38" in *Studia Hibernica*, no. 5 (1965), pp. 7-8; Angus Macintyre, *The Liberator: Daniel O'Connell and the Irish Party, 1830-1847* (New York, 1965), pp. 169-73.

should negotiate a composition for tithes, fixing their value for every holder in a parish for a specified period. Legislation in the following year abolished the previous exemption of grassland and its produce from tithes, an exemption that had been introduced in 1735 and had spared many large farmers either entirely or partially the obligation of payment. These legislative measures reduced the burden of tithes for small landholders engaged in tillage farming, but they increased the burden for large farmers. The burden became steadily heavier in the late 1820s as the value of tithes remained fixed under new agreements while agricultural prices declined. Before the reforms of 1823-4, only part of the farmer population had been strongly opposed to tithes; after these reforms, farmers drawn from all classes, including even many Protestant farmers, were now in opposition.[68] One of the more politically active large farmers, Patrick Lalor of Queen's County, later maintained that only the lowest class of landholders, having an acre or two of tillage, benefited from the reforms, while the farmer of ten acres was no better or worse off than before.[69] Large farmers, in contrast, had more to complain of than in earlier years. "In composition parishes," writes one historian, "a new class of farmer, the wealthy grazier and large farmer, was frequently added to the ranks of tithe opponents, and the legion of small farmers and cottiers had now more powerful allies and leaders, and some from the established church itself."[70]

Like the Emancipation campaign, the Tithe War was organized at the local level with the help of the Catholic clergy. Priests were generally willing to support an anti-tithe effort for the same reason that they had been willing to support the Emancipation campaign. Most were in sympathy with any movement, at least any non-violent movement, that would help undermine the established Protestant church. The beginning of the Tithe War can be traced to demands for a reduction in the tithe composition organized by a local priest in October 1830 in a parish near the Kilkenny-Carlow border. As the agitation spread to other districts, it was promoted by Catholic clergymen, most notably in the counties of Carlow, Wicklow, Tipperary, Westmeath, and Kildare. Although some priests would have nothing to do with the movement, in almost every county where it took hold at least a few Catholic clergymen lent a hand and assisted with local organiza-

[68] Macintyre, The Liberator, pp. 177-8.
[69] O'Donoghue, "Causes of opposition to tithes," p. 19.   [70] Ibid., p. 16.

tion. When anti-tithe meetings were held throughout the country in the spring and summer of 1832 priests were to be found on nearly every platform.[71] The movement was also supported by several Catholic bishops.[72]

During the Tithe War there were numerous clashes involving crowds, usually as they tried to obstruct the serving of processes, the valuation of tithes, or the sale of distrained livestock. Agrarian secret societies continued to engage in their varied forms of violence, and, not surprisingly, they continued to include the abolition of tithes as one of their demands. Coincident with the rise of the national anti-tithe movement, there emerged three more localized movements: the Tommy Downshires in the counties of Down and Armagh, the Whitefeet in Queen's, Carlow, and Kilkenny, and the Terry Alts in Clare, Galway, Westmeath, and Limerick. Their methods were more violent and their aims broader, but they were similarly committed to the abolition of tithes. And in many other districts, there were increases in the number of threatening notices forbidding the payment of tithes. These were the only years during the pre-famine period when rural violence corresponded in a substantial way with a national movement. It was no accident that such a correspondence occurred in this connection. Opposition to tithes was an interest that the rural lower classes had in common with large farmers, an interest that was also shared by the Catholic church. Still, their interests were far from identical. For small farmers and laborers, tithes were merely one of many payments they had to meet, including payments to the very groups leading the anti-tithe movement. Thus the violent combinations frequently lumped demands for the abolition of tithes together with demands for reductions in the rents they paid to large farmers. The hostility between rural secret societies, on the one hand, and large farmers and priests, on the other, insured that the Tithe War would be fought on two levels. Although some links no doubt existed, historians are agreed that, on the whole, there was little direct connection between the anti-tithe movement and the anti-tithe activities of the agrarian societies.[73]

[71] Patrick O'Donoghue, "Opposition to tithe payments in 1830-31" in *Studia Hibernica*, no. 6 (1966), pp. 89-90.

[72] Ibid., pp. 76-84.

[73] Macintyre, *The Liberator*, pp. 178-80; O'Donoghue, "Opposition to tithe payments," pp. 91-4. My friend James Donnelly, on the other hand, does not agree.

At the local level, the anti-tithe movement was often well organized. Neighborhood efforts were directed primarily at obstructing distraint of livestock. One common practice was for tenants to hide livestock or to drive them onto one another's land where they could not be touched because the law allowed distraint only on the premises of the defaulter. Attempts were also made to obstruct the sale of distrained goods and to establish funds to compensate those whose livestock had been seized.[74]

Beyond the local level, however, the organization of the anti-tithe agitation was weak. It was certainly national in scope. It spread through most of the country and focused its demands directly on the state that ruled over the entire nation. Yet there never emerged a national headquarters to coordinate it. Most directly, the reason was that any combination advocating that people refuse to pay tithes was subject to prosecution. Even strong supporters of the movement, such as the *Kilkenny Journal*, insisted that for this reason the resistance to tithes "must be given by individuals only, as any coalition between farmers would subject them to prosecutions for combinations to defraud the clergyman."[75] This difficulty was partly overcome by holding meetings under the guise of hurling matches,[76] or by criticizing tithes at meetings of a new movement that O'Connell was trying to organize for the repeal of the Act of Union. O'Connell's new movement was built on the network of local organizations established by the Catholic Association during the Emancipation campaign. Many of the farmers who were active in the Tithe War had previously been active in the Emancipation campaign and were also participating in the new Repeal movement.[77] It was this network of relationships that gave the anti-tithe movement a minimum of national organizational structure. Yet O'Connell's organization was itself operating under severe legal harassment.[78] More important, though O'Connell frequently denounced tithes in speeches and made clear his basic sympathy for the movement, he was unwilling to provide any direct leadership. For him the abolition of tithes was but one of a number of reforms that he advocated and included in the demands of the Repeal movement.

[74] O'Donoghue, "Opposition to tithe payments," pp. 69-74.
[75] *Kilkenny Journal*, 9 June 1832, p. 2.
[76] O'Donoghue, "Opposition to tithe payments," p. 70.
[77] O'Donoghue, "Causes of opposition to tithes," pp. 20-21, 27.
[78] Macintyre, *The Liberator*, p. 23.

The anti-tithe agitation drew its earliest and strongest support from those areas where inter-regional intercourse and urbanization were most developed, and where large farmers were relatively numerous, most notably the four Leinster counties of Carlow, Kilkenny, Queen's, and Wexford. In late 1831 it took hold in several other Leinster counties, such as Kildare, Meath, Wicklow, Westmeath, and King's, and in one Munster county, Tipperary.[79] In 1832 it spread throughout Munster and into some parts of Connaught, but it was always much weaker and less effective in the west than in Leinster and east Munster.

Nevertheless, the movement succeeded in making tithes a leading political issue in the 1830s. In 1832, and again in 1833, legislation was passed that sought to dampen the unrest, while at the same time meet the obligation felt by the government to protect the interests of those to whom tithes were paid. Finally, in 1838 the Tithe Commutation Act converted tithes into rent-charges, which meant that landowners were obliged to collect tithes as part of their rent, but were permitted to retain 25 percent as compensation for their trouble. They were not, however, permitted to subsume tithes under rents in the case of holdings held at will or from year to year. It is very possible that many landlords also reduced the charge or did not impose it on their remaining tenants. In any case, little was heard of the issue after 1838.

THE REPEAL MOVEMENT

The objective of this movement was the repeal of the Act of Union of 1800, which had abolished the Irish parliament and had given Ireland representation in the British parliament. It drew its support almost entirely from Catholics. Although there had been no clear-cut division between the two major religious groups over the passage of the Act of Union, such a division subsequently emerged as most Protestants came to see the British parliament as their only defense against the Catholic majority in Ireland, and as most Catholics came to see this parliament as the chief obstacle to the exercise of their majority power. In 1830 O'Connell formally launched a Society for the Repeal of the Union, but throughout the following decade he actually tried to operate within parliament to obtain a number of specific reforms relating to Ireland. It was not until 1841, after he had become discouraged with this

[79] O'Donoghue, "Opposition to tithe payments," pp. 75, 79-80.

policy and when his own party suffered a serious defeat at the polls, that he began to organize a determined Repeal campaign. He founded a new political body called the Repeal Association, reinstated the earlier "Catholic rent" in the form of a "Repeal rent," and established Repeal wardens whose job it was to organize branches of the Repeal Association in all parts of the country.

Again local organization depended, in large measure, on the Catholic clergy. Despite instructions from bishops that they should restrict their political activities,[80] many priests had continued to play an energetic political role after the Emancipation campaign and during most of the 1830s. The bishops did not prevent priests in many areas from assisting in the anti-tithe agitation and helping to collect a tribute to O'Connell.[81] Nor did they stop many local priests from engaging in election activity. In the election of 1832, for example, a parish priest in County Wicklow provided 350 of his parishioners with transportation at his own expense to enable them to register as voters. In the same election, the Catholic clergy assisted in the registration of voters on the Marquess of Bath's estate in County Monaghan. In County Limerick priests were active in political canvassing, even speaking at several public meetings.[82] And a parish priest in Kildare collected money with which voters had been bribed in the Conservative interest, but which he turned over to the National Rent Fund.[83]

The clergy became even more active in the 1840s when views among church leaders changed and strong sentiment developed in favor of clerical participation in politics, and more specifically in the new repeal movement that O'Connell was organizing. Eventually, sixteen of twenty-seven Catholic bishops joined the Repeal Association.[84] Under the leadership of John MacHale, archbishop of Tuam, the clergy in Connaught were largely responsible for the support the movement received in that province.

[80] Whyte, "The influence of the Catholic clergy on elections." See also J. F. Broderick, *The Holy See and the Irish Movement for the Repeal of the Union with England, 1829-47* (Rome, 1951), pp. 46-9; and Oliver MacDonagh, "The politicization of the Irish Catholic bishops, 1800-1850" in *Historical Journal*, 18, no. 1 (1975).

[81] Macintyre, *The Liberator*, p. 112.

[82] Whyte, "The influence of the Catholic clergy on elections."

[83] Macintyre, *The Liberator*, p. 113. Still more illustrations of clerical political activity in the 1830s are provided by Macintyre.

[84] Larkin, "Church, state and nation," p. 1249.

Subscriptions to the Repeal Association came from the lower
clergy in Connaught and many other districts.[85] And, typically,
the lower clergy were essential for the local organization of the
movement, assisting Repeal wardens and organizing public demonstrations.[86] As O'Connell admitted, "I could do nothing without them." Or as a hostile observer wrote, the "priests are the
agents of the agitation. . . . They circulate petitions that peasants
sign without knowledge of their contents. . . . By their means the
wardens and the collectors are appointed and excited to act; and
by their exhortations the masses are congregated to hear the ora-
tions of the 'travelling apostles of repeal.' "[87]

How widespread was the Repeal agitation? O'Connell claimed
that the Association had wardens in every parish, and that the
rural population was being drawn into the movement, even in
Connaught, which "for the first time had become perfectly en-
livened."[88] On the other hand, in the movement's newspaper, one
finds reports from wardens coming mainly from Munster (especially Cork) and Leinster (especially south Leinster), while it is
possible to find only a few references to Repeal activity in Connaught.[89] There was also a rural-urban difference, at least in the
social composition of the most active membership. This statement
is corroborated by some very interesting statistical evidence. In
1849, several years after the movement had collapsed, an effort
was made to enlist support for a national conference from those
who had formerly been active for Repeal. Although conducted at a
later point in time, this requisition provides some useful information on the social background of active nationalists in the 1840s.
An occupational breakdown of those who signed the requisition
is given in Table 1. It shows a marked over-representation (con-
sidering their numbers in the society) of professionals and "merchants, traders and artisans," while there is a marked under-
representation of "landholders and farmers." This urban bias did
not escape the attention of contemporaries. "The very bone and
muscle of the movement," the Nation remarked in 1846, consisted
of "gentlemen of education and rank, professional persons of

[85] Broderick, The Holy See, p. 158.   [86] Ibid., passim.
[87] Irish Landlords, Rents and Tenures . . . by an Irish Roman Catholic Landowner (London, 1843), p. 31.
[88] Kevin B. Nowlan, The Politics of Repeal: A Study in the Relations between
Great Britain and Ireland, 1841-50 (London, 1965) pp. 37 and 39.
[89] See Nation, Nov. 1842-March 1843.

TABLE 1· Occupations of persons who signed a requisition for the
Irish Alliance conference held in Dublin, 20 November 1849

OCCUPATIONS	PERCENTAGE OF TOTAL
Dignitaries of the Catholic church	3.8
Curates	5.2
Regular clergy	1.0
Magistrates, land proprietors, corporators, and poor-law guardians	5.6
Members of the learned professions	9.4
Landholders and farmers	32.8
Merchants, traders, and artisans	42.2
Total number	2,132

NOTE: This list does not, of course, represent an accurate occupational
breakdown of persons sympathetic to the nationalist cause. What it likely does
show is a fairly representative sample of those who were regarded as instrumental
for the organization of a political movement. The source is *Nation* 24 Nov. 1849,
pp. 196-7.

every kind . . . [and] intelligent tradesmen."[90] Later the *Nation*
looked back on the Repeal movement and compared the role of
farmers in this political struggle with their role in the Tithe War:

> Since 1832, when the farmers of the South rose to a man
> against the tithe system, they have not entered, as a class, into
> any political movement. [During the Repeal movement] they
> swelled the tremendous chorus of the monster meetings at
> the call of O'Connell; and if he had lifted the green banner
> multitudes of them would have shouldered muskets for love
> of the old leader. . . . But the cry did not burst from their ranks
> spontaneously, as it burst from the students, traders, and me-
> chanics. . . . It was not as the tithe campaign their own proper
> work which they knew and accepted instinctively.[91]

As this passage suggests, the principal way in which the Repeal
movement did mobilize rural support was through large public
demonstrations or "monster meetings." Better than any other
political movement in nineteenth-century Ireland, the Repeal agitation demonstrated the effective use that could be made of the
custom of the rural Irish to gather in towns for special occasions.

[90] Ibid., 10 Oct. 1846, p. 9.   [91] Ibid., 12 Jan. 1850, p. 312.

During the years 1842-3, and again in 1845, great meetings were held in the towns of every province (except Ulster), drawing audiences of tens of thousands. As one historian writes, the atmosphere at these meetings "was a mixture of fair, football game and evangelical revival." Large crowds paraded from long distances, marshaled by Repeal wardens or priests, and often accompanied by their local Temperance Band.[92] The political limitations of these meetings should not, it is true, be overlooked. They did not entail much active participation for many more than the few people who organized them; in fact, as a very consequence of their size, only a minority of the audience could hear what the speakers were saying. Despite the presence of all classes in the audience, the meetings had a tone of social exclusiveness about them; the platforms were generally filled with local landowners who sympathized with the Repeal movement.[93] And they were not uniformly distributed throughout the country. There were fewer meetings in Connaught than in Leinster or Munster, and the rate of attendance (proportional to population) was apparently much lower in Connaught.[94]

Still, the Repeal meetings were a remarkable achievement in mass political mobilization. In 1843 alone, there were thirty-two meetings with audiences estimated at over 100,000 persons: thirteen in Leinster, eleven in Munster, seven in Connaught, and one in Ulster.[95] They converted a movement that would otherwise have been mostly middle-class and urban into a mass movement. Their importance is revealed perhaps best of all by the response they provoked from the government, a response that may have contributed to the collapse of the agitation but also indicates the threat that monster meetings posed to the established order. Few things worried the Irish administration more than the collective power represented by these meetings, and throughout 1843 authorities in Dublin and London watched them closely. During the summer troops were sent to increase Irish garrisons. Finally, in October, a scheduled meeting at Clontarf, County Dublin, was

---

[92] Ó Tuathaigh, *Ireland Before the Famine*, p. 189.

[93] For examples, see a meeting in Kildare reported in the *Nation*, 13 May 1843, p. 486; a meeting in Galway, *Nation*, 3 June 1843, p. 534; and a meeting in Roscommon, *Nation*, 26 Aug. 1843, p. 734.

[94] K. T. Hoppen, "Landlords, society and electoral politics in mid-nineteenth-century Ireland" in *Past and Present*, no. 75 (May 1977), p. 65.

[95] Ruth Dudley Edwards, *An Atlas of Irish History* (London, 1973), p. 98.

prohibited by the Lord Lieutenant, and subsequently the government arrested the leaders of the movement, including O'Connell.[96] O'Connell's influence in Irish politics never fully recovered
from the Clontarf fiasco. The Repeal movement as such persisted
until 1846, when it eventually collapsed, seemingly no closer to
its goal than when it had started. Yet in the course of its stormy
career, it had perfected a method of political agitation that would
be used repeatedly in later years. Collective action in the form of
large public demonstrations came to be used with great effectiveness by groups challenging established power in post-famine Ireland, though they never again reached the size or enthusiasm of
the monster meetings for Repeal.

CONCLUSIONS

We can now make some brief observations on the character of
these movements and compare them with pre-famine collective
violence. First, in very general terms, it can be said that they were
more supra-local than were the violent combinations. This is true
even if we are comparing these three pre-famine movements with
large regional movements such as the Caravats and the Terry Alts;
it is obviously true if the comparison is with the typical violent
faction or agrarian band. Support for the Emancipation campaign,
the anti-tithe movement, and the Repeal movement extended over
a large part of the country. People living in different counties and
even provinces participated in what they regarded as the same
collective struggle; and in two of the movements—the Emancipation campaign and the Repeal movement—central bodies were
formed to coordinate their activities. Moreover, the area over
which people sought to achieve their objectives was the entire
country. They tried to challenge their adversaries at the national
level, and consequently directed much of their efforts at the state
apparatus that ruled over the nation. Concretely, they sought to
change the laws that governed the country.

   It follows that, for these national movements, neither the active
collectivities, nor the social groups from which these collectivities were drawn, can be defined in territorial terms. There were
certainly pronounced and noteworthy regional variations in their
strength. Yet people were not recruited into these movements on
the basis of regional or subregional loyalities, and they did not

---

[96] Nowlan, *Politics of Repeal*, pp. 55-6.

think of themselves as representing a particular region or subregion. They claimed to represent the interests of all Ireland. Though this was pretentious, it was true that they drew their support from broad social groups whose members were not confined to any one locality, but were to be found, in varying numerical strength, almost everywhere in the country.

All three movements were successful in mobilizing rural support, but there were noticeable differences among them in this regard. The Emancipation campaign and the Repeal movement received the bulk of their leadership from the urban middle class; members of this class were especially active supporters of these two movements; and the goals of the Emancipation campaign and the Repeal movement more clearly reflected the interests of this class than the interests of the rural population. The Tithe War, in contrast, was essentially a rural movement. Many of its leaders and most of its active supporters were from rural areas, and it plainly represented agrarian interests. As we can appreciate fully only after we have looked at post-famine collective action, the Tithe War is historically of considerable significance because it marked the beginning of the gradual evolution in Ireland of national collective action primarily by and for farmers.

This point brings us to the second major difference between these movements and pre-famine collective violence. Whereas the violent combinations drew mainly from the class of small farmers and laborers, the national movements drew their support as much from the large-farmer class as from the rural poor. Indeed it is very possible that support for the national movements came disproportionately from large farmers. It was at least the case that these movements were stronger in those parts of the country where large farmers were relatively numerous. These were the regions where social communication and urbanization were comparatively more developed and where the social basis for organizing national collective action was therefore more solid. Although O'Connell had useful personal contacts and considerable charismatic appeal in many western districts, his political machine was centered in Dublin, and it was most effective in those counties, all in Leinster, that lay within easy traveling distance of the city. This region, writes one historian, "was the most sensitive, perhaps the most politically conscious part of Ireland, a direct consequence of the area's proximity to the capital whose numerous and politically committed newspapers reported its politics with an accuracy which was never bestowed on the politically stable northern area or on the often confused situations in western constituencies."[97]

Rural support for these movements was not, however, limited exclusively to large farmers or to eastern parts of the country. It is apparent that the Repeal meetings were successful in the west as well as in the east, and that they were built primarily on the class of small farmers and laborers. Similarly, the Tithe War mobilized great numbers of small farmers, and the Emancipation campaign enjoyed widespread sympathy from the rural lower classes. This mass popularity can be explained in a number of ways, depending on which struggle is being discussed. But the explanation that is common to all three movements is that the rural poor gave their support because they belonged to the same religious group as did those who were leading these movements. All three were, in some sense, Catholic movements. This is not to deny that Protestants could be found among those who took part in them, but the great majority of supporters were Catholics, and the goals of the movements more closely reflected the interests of Catholics than the interests of Protestants. This was most obviously and explicitly true of the Emancipation campaign and the Tithe War, but even Repeal had become a Catholic demand well before the 1840s.

Although the intensity of religious cleavage in pre-famine Ireland may have been unusual, the critical unifying role played by religion in promoting and supporting national collective action does have parallels in other societies. Especially where local communal structures coexist with national/urban structures, it has often been found that collective action has a religious basis. Common religion can build on the organizational frameworks provided by local communal groups, while at the same time transcending these local groups and welding together people with otherwise diversified loyalties. When religion performs this function, it often (though not necessarily) has a millenarian character, in which case members of separate communal groups are drawn together by a common expectation of deliverance in the near future.[98]

No social structure could generate a more broadly based sense of solidarity in pre-famine Ireland than could religion. We can

[97] Macintyre, The Liberator, p. 72.

[98] Peter Worsley, The Trumpet Shall Sound: A Study of "Cargo" Cults in Melanesia (New York, 1968), pp. 227-8, 236-7.

note in passing that two other supra-local movements that emerged in the pre-famine period had religious foundations: the "Second Reformation," a proselytizing movement aimed at winning converts to the Protestant faith; and the Total Abstinence Society, a temperance movement led by a Capuchin friar and drawing a large number of adherents from the Catholic population. This temperance movement had some striking millenarian features, at least in its promises of the potential dawn of a new era. And one historian has argued that the same can be said of lower-class support for the Emancipation campaign. Gearóid Ó Tuathaigh points out that prophecies of deliverance from Protestant domination were prominent in the rich oral tradition of the Catholic peasantry. Just before the Emancipation campaign such prophecies had played a part in the violent agrarian upheavals of 1821-4. "In due course," writes Ó Tuathaigh, "O'Connell inherited the mantle of deliverer and the winning of emancipation became for many of the peasantry the pursuit of the millennium."[99]

Yet millenarianism was only a secondary characteristic of pre-famine social movements. The religion on which these movements were built was not cultic, but instead highly institutionalized and solidly based on a traditional formal organization. Indeed, religion could overcome communal and class divisions in the society in a way that no other structure could, precisely because, through this traditional formal organization, it brought people with different class, neighborhood, and kinship ties together in regular social interaction. The leading figure in this network was the local clergyman. There has, it is true, been a tendency to overstate the social bond between the Catholic priest and his parishioners in early nineteenth-century Ireland. Their interests were not entirely in harmony and their relationship was hardly free of conflict. Yet underneath the exaggerated stereotype is an element of truth without which the stereotype would never have emerged. Whatever their failings, the priests occupied the central role in the most important social group in the society beyond the kinship group. It is therefore not surprising that all three national movements we have examined depended heavily on the clergy, at least in rural areas, for grass-roots collective organization. One reason local Catholic clergymen were able to perform this function was that they belonged to a church that was itself

[99] Ó Tuathaigh, *Ireland Before the Famine*, p. 67.

trying to challenge established authority and whose leaders, by comparison with those in other European countries, were inclined to engage in radical political activity. Yet the local Catholic clergy were not led into politics by the bishops; if anything, it was the other way around.[100] The parish priest was unavoidably involved in collective action with his parishioners because he was a vital part of the social organization on which this collective action was based.

[100] MacDonagh, "The politicization of the Irish Catholic bishops."

Part B
After the Famine

Four · **Structural Change**

Post-Famine Social Transformation

The focus of our inquiry now moves forward in time to the years between the Famine and the Land War. In a study that seeks to demonstrate the impact of changes in social structure on collective action, the present chapter forms a critical part of the whole because it describes how the social structure changed in rural Ireland during the decades that preceded the Land War. Essentially the objective is to identify new lines of cleavage and integration that will later help to explain differences between pre-famine collective action and the agrarian upheaval of 1879-82.

POPULATION AND ECONOMY

We begin with some underlying demographic and economic transformations that proved to have immense consequences: a decline in population resulting primarily from the Great Famine; and a change in land use stemming partly from the population decline and partly from the movement of agricultural prices.

The demographic impact of the Famine was most striking. Through death and emigration the population was cut by one-fifth between 1841 and 1851, falling from over 8 million to approximately 6.5 million. After 1851 it continued to decline, though less rapidly than during the late 1840s. Emigration, together with a lower fertility rate in some regions, reduced the population by 12 percent between 1851 and 1861, 7 percent between 1861 and 1871, and 4 percent between 1871 and 1881, when it stood at just over 5 million. Closely related to this fall in population was an increase in the average size of landholdings. Median size of holdings over one acre increased from 10.8 acres in 1844 to 15.6 acres in 1851 and 18.5 acres in 1876. Table 2 shows that the rate of increase was lowest in Ulster and Leinster, and highest in Munster and Connaught, though in 1876 farms in Connaught were still smaller on the average than in any other province.

The agricultural changes resulting from a shift in prices occurred more gradually. Prices for almost all agricultural products rose in the post-famine period, but those rising most sharply were for store cattle, eggs, mutton, and beef, while those rising least

TABLE 2 · Median size of holdings of over two acres for 1841 and of over one acre for 1844, 1851 and 1876 by province

	1841 (estimated)	1844	1851	1876
Leinster	17.7	—	16.5	20.2
Munster	17.8	—	26.3	30.3
Ulster	13.3	—	13.9	15.1
Connaught	9.8	—	13.1	14.1
Ireland	12.8	10.8	15.6	18.5

NOTE: The sources are *Census of Ireland, 1841*, pp. 454-5; *Appendix to minutes of evidence taken before Her Majesty's commissioners of inquiry into the state of law and practice in respect to the occupation of land in Ireland*, p. 288; *The census of Ireland for the year 1851*, pt. ii: *Returns of agricultural produce in 1851*, p. xxviii [1589], H.C. 1852-3, xciii; and *The agricultural statistics of Ireland for the year 1876*, p. 6 [C 1749], H.C. 1877, lxxxv. For an explanation of the data in this table and how they were calculated see Appendix A.

were for wheat, barley, and oats.[1] As already suggested in Chapter Two, this relative gain in prices for livestock over tillage produce may have begun before the Famine. In any event, a pronounced shift in prices certainly did occur after it, primarily as a consequence of improved methods of transportation and greater competition in the grain market from American agriculture, but also as a result of higher standards of living in England which made possible a greater volume of meat consumption. In addition, the Famine made more land available for pasture in Ireland by reducing population.

Unfortunately, good statistical information on land use did not become available until 1851. Already in that year 68 percent of the farm land in use was devoted to grass and meadow; by 1876 the figure had risen to 79 percent. Perhaps more indicative of the magnitude of the change was the growth in the number of cattle and sheep. Between 1847 and 1876, cattle increased by almost 60 percent, from about 2.5 million in 1847 to over 4 million in 1876, while sheep rose by 83 percent, from roughly 2.2 million in 1847 to about 4 million in 1876.[2]

In the post-famine period Irish agriculture became overwhelm-

[1] Thomas Barrington, "A review of Irish agricultural prices" in *Journal of the Statistical and Social Inquiry Society of Ireland*, 15 (1927), pp. 251-2.

[2] By "land in use" I mean the total area under grass or crops, thus excluding woods, plantations, fallow, bog, wasteland, water, etc. The sources are *Census of*

ingly pastoral. Livestock now outranked all other sectors of the
rural economy and left almost no part of it untouched. Although
large landholders were, in general, more deeply involved in the
livestock trade than were small ones, this trade was by no means
restricted to an elite class of graziers. Taken as a group, even those
with holdings of only 5 to 15 acres used almost half of their land
for pasture (not including meadow) in 1871; and those with 15 to
30 acres used more than half of their land for pasture (not including meadow).[3] If we look at regional variations, we find that animal production was important in small-farm as well as in large-
farm areas. A partial exception was Ulster, where tillage farming
remained more important despite an increase in animal production. But the shift to pasture was pronounced in small-farm districts in the west, such as in Kerry, Clare, and many parts of Connaught. In Connaught no less than 84 percent of the farm land in
use was allocated to grass or meadow by 1876, more than in Leinster, where the percentage was 80, and almost as much as in Munster, where the figure was 85.[4] The reason was simply that most of
the land in Connaught was unsuitable for tillage but could be
used for rough pasture. Table 3 gives the percentage increases in
acreage devoted to crops, grass, and wasteland in each province
between 1851 and 1876. It indicates that the rate of change in the
way land was used was lowest in Ulster and greatest in Munster.
Farmers in Munster expanded their grassland at a faster rate than
did those of any other province because they substantially reduced both the number of acres under crops and the number of
acres of wasteland. Farmers in Leinster expanded their grassland
partly by making better use of wasteland, but primarily by cutting
back on the number of acres under crops. Farmers in Connaught,
on the other hand, expanded their grassland almost entirely by
reducing the number of acres of wasteland. Thus, strictly speaking, it is not accurate to talk about a *shift* from tillage to pasture in
Connaught after the Famine. What transpired, at least between
1851 and 1876, was really an increase in the number of acres

Ireland for the year 1851: agricultural produce, pp. xxvii and xxxvii; and *Agricultural statistics of Ireland for the year 1876*, pp. 31, 52, and 55.

[3] In 1871 grass alone (not including meadow) covered 30 percent of the total
acreage in use occupied by holders of 1-5 acres, 48 percent of the total acreage in
use occupied by holders of 5-15 acres, and 54 percent of the total acreage in use
occupied by holders of 15-30 acres. See *The agricultural statistics of Ireland for
the year 1871*, p. xiii [C 762], H.C. 1873, lxix.

[4] *Agricultural statistics of Ireland for the year 1876*, pp. 31 and 52.

TABLE 3 · Percentage increases in number of acres of land devoted
to various uses, 1851-76, by province

	CROPS	GRASS	WASTE
Leinster	−18.6	22.2	−11.3
Munster	−16.5	25.7	−27.0
Ulster	− 2.7	7.0	− 5.2
Connaught	− 2.9	24.8	−21.9
Ireland	−11.1	20.1	−17.9

NOTE: The total decline in wasteland may not have been as great as these figures
suggest, since the standards of classification of wasteland changed between 1851
and 1876. But there is no reason to believe that this error in the data seriously
distorts comparisons among provinces. Better data would no doubt still show a
greater decline in wasteland in Munster and Connaught than in Leinster or Ulster.
The sources are *Census of Ireland for the year 1851: agricultural produce,*
p. xxviii; *Agricultural statistics of Ireland for the year 1876,* p. 52.

under grass achieved primarily by converting formerly unused
land into rough pasture.

I would suggest, therefore, that the development of the livestock economy represented *in relative terms* an even greater boon
to farmers in the west than to those in most other parts of the
country. One must be careful not to exaggerate post-famine economic advancement in western districts. Later in this chapter I
shall indicate that severe poverty persisted in Connaught for
many years after the Famine. It is true, nevertheless, that livestock
production offered comparative advantages to western farmers by
enabling them to make better use of their meager resources than
they could in an economy based on commercial crops. Though
holdings remained small in Connaught, and though most of the
land was poor, it was still possible for western farmers to enjoy
benefits from the livestock trade. In addition to raising pigs and
poultry (which was common even before the Famine), they could
participate in the livestock economy in two principal ways. First,
they could take advantage of rising prices for young cattle by becoming cattle breeders. Small farmers were able to maintain a few
cows, which they could not only milk, but also use to produce
calves. Though generally unable to fatten store cattle on their own
farms, they could sell calves to large farmers, most of whom
needed to buy calves in order to replenish their stocks. To this
day, one of the most noticeable features of Irish agriculture is this
reciprocal relationship between large and small farmers. Al-

though the practice actually began before the Famine, it was during the period from the 1850s to the 1870s that the system became firmly established. Primarily as a result of this system, small farmers in Connaught became actively involved in the cattle trade, and the number of cattle in Connaught rose by 82 percent between 1847 and 1876.[5]

The second way small farmers in Connaught participated in the livestock economy was by raising sheep. Sheep could be grazed on poorer land than cattle and were therefore comparatively suitable for conditions in Connaught. The sheep population in Connaught almost doubled between 1847 and 1876, most of this expansion occurring in Galway, Mayo, and Roscommon.[6] These counties, along with the Leinster counties of King's, Kildare, and Wicklow, were the leading sheep-producing districts in the country. Typically, sheep were bred and reared by western farmers until they were two or three years old, then sold to eastern, midland, or southern graziers, either for breeding purposes or to be fattened off. The biggest center of the sheep trade was the Ballinasloe fair, where the average price of first-class wethers rose by more than 50 percent between the 1840s and the 1870s, and the average price of first-class ewes by almost 80 percent.[7] The great bulk of Irish sheep was shipped live to Britain. The average annual number going there rose from less than 300,000 in the period 1846-55 to almost 700,000 in the period 1866-75.[8]

This growth in the livestock economy was largely responsible for the post-famine rise in agricultural income. Unfortunately, serious methodological problems have plagued the calculation of Irish agricultural production for this period, and the data now assembled are inconclusive. According to tentative figures provided by Cormac Ó Gráda, the gross value added in Irish agriculture rose from an annual figure of about £39 million in the early 1840s to £43 million in 1854 and roughly £50 million in 1876.[9] Since the human population was at the same time contracting, the per

[5] *Census of Ireland for the year 1851: agricultural produce*, p. xxxvii; *Agricultural statistics of Ireland for the year 1876*, p. 55.

[6] Ibid. See Appendix A for an explanation of why I have chosen 1847 as the base year for these livestock figures.

[7] *Thom's*, 1849, p. 173; *Thom's*, 1856, p. 491; *Thom's*, 1882, pp. 693-4. The percentages given here are based on the means for the years 1842-9 and 1870-79.

[8] *Thom's*, 1851, p. 232; *Thom's*, 1857, p. 543; *Thom's*, 1872, p. 842; *Thom's*, 1877, p. 679.

[9] Cormac Ó Gráda, "On some aspects of productivity change in Irish agriculture, 1845-1926." Paper presented at the Seventh International Economic History Con-

capita income of persons employed in agriculture must have risen
at an even faster rate. After one deducts for estimated landlord income, Ó Gráda's figures imply that annual per capita agricultural
income rose from less than £20 in the early 1840s to £25 in 1854
and £36 in 1876.[10] Purchasing power, it is true, did not advance as
much as these figures would suggest, since prices also rose,
perhaps as much as 20 to 30 percent. Nevertheless, it is clear that
the post-famine period saw a significant increase in the average
purchasing power of rural people.

Ideally we would like to have comparative estimates of the receipts and expenditures of rural families. The only estimates that I
could find were for so-called "congested districts," that is, districts with unusually small holdings and poor land. The information was collected in the 1890s by inspectors for the Congested
Districts Board for eighty-four such districts, most of them in
Connaught, but including some in Kerry, Cork, Clare, and
Donegal.[11] The estimates given by these inspectors suggest that
even people with miserably small holdings relied heavily on cash
income from the livestock trade. The estimate by an inspector of
the typical income of a family in his district from the sale of agricultural produce was, in most cases, far more than the estimate
that he gave of the value of home-grown food consumed, and in
some cases, several times the estimated value of home-grown
food. And, in virtually all estimates, *over half of the income from
agricultural produce came from selling livestock*. If this were true
of small landholders in congested districts, it must have been
doubly true for those with larger holdings.

THE AGRICULTURAL CLASSES

The above-mentioned changes in population and economy had an
enormous impact on rural class structure. First, there was a substantial decline in the practice of subletting land. I do not mean to
imply that subletting disappeared entirely; yet it was definitely

gress, Edinburgh, Aug. 1978. His estimate for 1876 is taken from Barbara L. Solow,
The Land Question and the Irish Economy, 1870-1903 (Cambridge, Massachusetts,
1971), p. 171.

[10] Ó Gráda, "Productivity change in Irish agriculture." Ó Gráda does not actually give an estimate for the early 1840s, but it seems reasonable to assume that it
was less than £20.

[11] T.C.D., Congested Districts Board: Base line reports of inspectors for the Congested Districts Board, 1892-8.

much less prevalent after the Famine than it had been before. Extensive clearances were carried out during the Famine, and it is almost certain that the victims of the crowbar were disproportionately subtenants. Even after the Famine, subletting probably continued to decline, since the smaller population and the shift to livestock production meant that large landholders were under less pressure to sublet land to small holders and at the same time were less willing to do so. These are extremely difficult changes to document, since there were no published statistics on subletting. Nevertheless, a comparison of a sample of townlands on the Trinity College estates in the early 1840s with the same townlands around the year 1880 illustrates the general trend. In thirty-six townlands the proportion of tenants holding directly either from the College or from a College lessee rose from 22 to 60 percent, while the proportion who held from a middleman (who let from a College lessee) fell from 78 to 40 percent.[12]

The second major change in the class structure was a marked decline in the number of laborers. This change is also difficult to document, in this case owing to ambiguities and modifications over time in the definitions given to occupational categories in the censuses. Table 4 represents the best estimates I can provide of the relative size of each social class in 1841 and 1881. It shows that the percentage of the adult male agricultural labor force comprised by laborers fell from an estimated 56 percent in 1841 to 38 percent in 1881, while the percentage comprised by farmers and farmers' sons rose from an estimated 42 percent in 1841 to 60 percent in 1881. In other words, within the space of forty years the social composition of the rural society was transformed from one in which laborers were in the majority to one in which farmers were in the majority. This transformation was not limited to prosperous regions. Indeed, if one were to construct a similar table for Connaught alone, it would show an even greater shift. In Connaught farmers and farmers' sons rose from an estimated 38 percent of the adult male agricultural labor force in 1841 to about 74 percent in 1881.[13]

[12] The data for the early 1840s come from the Trinity College survey and the data for c. 1880 from the Land Valuation Office, Land Valuation Records. The sample included nineteen townlands in Kerry, three in Limerick, five in Tipperary, and nine in Longford. Altogether there were 3,319 tenants in the sample for the early 1840s and 2,075 in the sample for c. 1880.

[13] Census of Ireland, 1841, p. 430; Census of Ireland, 1881: pt. i . . . vol. iv. Province of Connaught, p. 623 [C 3268], H.C. 1882, lxxix.

TABLE 4 · Estimates of relative size of agricultural classes, 1841 and 1881

	ESTIMATED PERCENTAGE OF ADULT MALE AGRICULTURAL LABOR FORCE	
AGRICULTURAL CLASS	1841	1881
Farmers and farmers' sons	42	60
Farmers: over 50 acres	4	9
Farmers: 21-50 acres	9	14
Farmers: 20 acres or less	15	17
Farmers' sons	14	20
Laborers	56	38
Laborer-landholders	30	12
Landless laborers	26	26
Other	2	3
Total number of adult males in agricultural labor force	1,604,034	970,835

NOTE: The sources are *Census of Ireland, 1841*, p. 440; *Appendix to minutes of evidence taken before Her Majesty's commissioners of inquiry into the state of law and practice in respect to the occupation of land in Ireland*, p. 288 (which gives the poor-law return to the number and size of holdings in 1844); and *Census of Ireland 1881: General report*, pp. 108 and 199 [C 3365], H.C. 1882, lxxvi. See Appendix A for an explanation of how these estimates were calculated.

It may be possible to contest some of the assumptions I have made in order to arrive at these estimates. In particular, one might dispute the estimate given here of the number of farmers' sons in 1841 and the number of laborers in both 1841 and 1881, especially landless laborers in 1881. (See Appendix A.) It is also important to understand that, for both 1841 and 1881, the category "landless laborer" includes many of those who occupied cabins on large holdings or who took land in conacre. Under the category "laborer-landholder," what I have tried to estimate is the number of laborers who separately occupied a holding that was recognized and included in the official enumerations of all agricultural holdings. Making different assumptions, or using a different definition of laborer-landholder, one might not find, as I have, that the decline in laborers occurred mainly among laborer-landholders, while landless laborers held steady as a proportion of the work force.

Still, these data strongly suggest that landholding by laborers declined during and after the Famine. While such a finding is in some ways surprising, it does make sense in view of the clearances that occurred during the Famine and the lower rate of subletting after it. It is also consistent with observations made by numerous contemporaries. Several poor-law inspectors reporting on the condition of laborers in 1870 noted that it was no longer the general practice for farmers to engage laborers by granting them small plots of land. As a rule, farmers preferred to employ servant boys for constant work and to rely for hands during the heavy season on casual workers who lived in villages or on the fringes of towns.[14] One inspector wrote in his report that, in addition to the uncertainties of casual employment, "the want of suitable habitations for themselves and their families" was the main source of discontent among laborers. "I have heard from those well qualified to give an opinion on this question," he went on to say, "that the want of even a small portion of land—say a garden for potatoes—is much felt, and renders them dissatisfied with their present position."[15] Another inspector, exaggerating the comforts of pre-famine laborers, may nevertheless have identified accurately the important transformation that had occurred in the situation of agricultural workers:

> Previous to the famine the labourer enjoyed his cabin, attached to some farm, with rood, or half acre, or acre of land, and facilities for obtaining con-acre land to sow a crop of potatoes. He was able to rear his pig and keep fowl. . . . The social changes and custom of the last twenty years render it most difficult for a labourer to get an allotment of land. Landlords' views are generally opposed to it; and let it be viewed as it may, the fact remains, that you cannot convince an Irishman that he is better off as a daily labourer, even with fair wages, than he would be with the possession of a bit of land.[16]

If landholding by laborers did indeed become less common after the Famine, it was a development of some importance. Before the

[14] *Reports from the poor law inspectors on the wages of agricultural labourers in Ireland*, pp. 25, 27-8 [C 35], H.C. 1870, xiv.

[15] Ibid., p. 32.   [16] Ibid., pp. 29-30.

Famine, the most effective class alliance within the rural population was the alliance between laborers and small farmers. This union was based on a number of social factors, but most of all on the common interests they shared as tenants. In so far as the laboring population became landless in the post-famine period, a common interest between laborers and small farmers must have diminished.

In more general terms, the transition I am describing resembles the well-known final stage of rural proletarianization, in which agricultural workers are "reduced" to pure wage laborers. In post-famine Ireland this historical process was obscured by the much more noticeable strengthening of the family farm as the dominant agricultural unit. The laboring class, meanwhile, diminished greatly in size and lost much of the significance it had possessed in the pre-famine period. Yet noteworthy qualitative as well as quantitative changes were taking place at this time among Irish rural laborers. Whether or not they less often held land after the Famine, it is clear that wages became more important to them than land as a source of livelihood. The greater emphasis on livestock production must have curtailed the demand for agricultural work. Under most circumstances, wages would have declined in consequence, but in post-famine Ireland they did not. The substantial growth in returns for agricultural produce, together with the reduction in the supply of workers, caused wages to advance. During the winter months there was generally an oversupply of agricultural labor, and many workers went unemployed for most of the winter. During the summer months, on the other hand, especially during the turf-cutting and harvest season, there was often a shortage of labor. This was the time of year when Irish farmers most needed hands and also the time when many laborers went to England and Scotland to work on the harvests. In some western districts, such as west Galway, almost no able-bodied workers remained during the months of June, July, and August. Between the early 1840s and the late 1860s, wages in most places rose by at least 50 percent, and in some places doubled. Before the Famine, a laborer usually earned 4d. to 8d. per day, but in the late 1860s he could make 1s. to 1s. 7d. per day. Before the Famine, harvest work generally yielded 8d. to 1s. 2d. per day, but in the 1860s it was frequently worth 1s. 3d. to 2s. per day.[17]

[17] *Return of the average weekly earnings of agricultural labourers in Ireland for*

This increase in average wages for agricultural work served to moderate the level of conflict between laborers and the large farmers who employed them, but it did not eliminate this conflict altogether. The loss of potato ground, the unwillingness of many farmers to provide satisfactory housing for workers, and the failure of most farmers to give steady employment—all contributed toward maintaining a good measure of hostility. In addition, laborers were often unhappy with the high rents they had to pay for potato ground when they could get it, with the increasing use of machinery by farmers, and most of all, with their wages, which were still low compared to what they could earn by going to England for the harvests.[18] Inevitably, relationships between farmers and laborers were often strained and sometimes openly antagonistic. Farmers contributed no more to the support of those they hired than was necessary to persuade them to work; and laborers, in most cases enjoying only casual employment, had no permanent stake in the prosperity of their employers' farms. "There is little community of feeling between the labourer and the farmer," wrote a poor-law inspector in 1870. "A struggle appears to be always maintained between them as regards wages, and whilst the farmer sacrifices nothing to the comfort of his workman, the latter gives no more of his labour than he can help to his employer, and has little regard for his property or his interests."[19]

In addition to their economic antagonism, there also existed a wide social gulf between farmers and laborers. Few social links cemented the two groups—few kinship ties, for example, that might have helped to offset their economic differences. This becomes apparent from an examination of patterns of marriage and occupational mobility. The data in Table 5 are taken from all marriages registered in the superintendent-registrar district of Roscommon between 1864 and 1880. The major class cleavages in the society emerge very clearly from these figures. The occupational groups with the lowest intermarriage rates with farmers were

---

the last six months previous to the 1st day of January 1861, H.C. 1862 (2), lx. See also Reports from the poor law inspectors on the wages of agricultural labourers in Ireland.

[18] For more extensive discussions of the contentious issues between farmers and laborers, see P. G. Lane, "The general impact of the Encumbered Estates Act of 1849 on Counties Galway and Mayo" in Journal of the Galway Archaeological and Historical Society, 33 (1972-3), pp. 51-8; and Donnelly, Cork, pp. 239-41.

[19] Reports from the poor law inspectors on the wages of agricultural labourers in Ireland, p. 21.

TABLE 5 · Percentage of brides and grooms who married children of farmers, classified according to occupation of father, for marriages registered in Roscommon, 1864-80

OCCUPATION OF FATHER	PERCENTAGE OF GROOMS WHO MARRIED FARMERS' DAUGHTERS	TOTAL NUMBER OF GROOMS	PERCENTAGE OF BRIDES WHO MARRIED FARMERS' SONS	TOTAL NUMBER OF BRIDES
Farmers	87.4	1187	85.5	1213
Herdsmen	56.4	55	70.6	61
Laborers	13.5	334	8.0	336
Traders and business proprietors	63.4	41	51.4	37
Artisans and non-farm laborers	43.5	115	43.0	79
Civil service and defense	50.0	10	38.9	18
Domestics	37.5	8	80.0	10
Gentry	9.1	11	40.0	10
Other	38.5	39	44.4	36
All occupations	67.4	1800	65.9	1800

NOTE: If the occupation of either father was not given, the marriage was omitted from the sample. The boundaries of the Roscommon registrar district conformed to those of the Roscommon poor-law union, though marriages taking place in two neighboring unions (Glenamaddy and Mount Bellew) were also registered in the Roscommon district. The source was Custom House, Registry of births, deaths, and marriages. The basis for the occupational classification is given in Appendix B.

those highest and those lowest in the social ladder, i.e., gentry and laborers. An exception can be found in the case of one low-status group, namely herdsmen, who had a comparatively high intermarriage rate with farmers. But laborers, who were much more numerous, were infrequently linked to farmers through marriage: only 13.5 percent of the sons of laborers married farmers' daughters and only 8 percent of the daughters of laborers married farmers' sons. Table 6 uses the same marriage data for a different purpose. Here the rate of mobility from farming to other occupational categories is obtained by calculating the percentage of grooms in each category whose fathers were farmers. Except for the gentry, the lowest percentages were among herdsmen (16.4)

TABLE 6 · Percentage of grooms whose fathers were farmers, classified according to occupation of groom, for marriages registered in Roscommon, 1864-80

OCCUPATION OF GROOM	PERCENTAGE WHOSE FATHERS WERE FARMERS	TOTAL NUMBER OF GROOMS
Farmers	95.8	974
Herdsmen	16.4	67
Laborers	19.9	388
Traders and business proprietors	40.0	75
Artisans and non-farm laborers	25.0	136
Civil service and defense	54.9	51
Domestics	34.3	35
Gentry	0.0	10
Other	39.4	33
All occupations	64.3	1769

NOTE: The total number of marriages is less in this table than in Table 5 because there were some marriages for which groom's occupation was not given. The source is the same as Table 5.

and laborers (19.9). One should not overlook the fact that some farmers and many farmers' sons frequently engaged in periodic work away from the family farm, including large numbers who still migrated to England and Scotland, especially from the west, to obtain employment during the harvests.[20] Workers of this kind do not show up in Table 6, however, most likely because they were not regarded as laborers by occupation and were carefully distinguished from permanent agricultural workers.

In contrast with the cleavage between laborers and farmers, the social cleavage between small and large farmers seems to have diminished in the post-famine period. It is essential not to overstate this point. Vast differences in the size of holdings, and consequently in status, interests, and life style, still remained among

[20] A return for 1880 shows that the majority of migratory laborers were not landholders, but it would be a mistake to take this to mean that they were not related to farmers. See Report and tables relating to Irish migratory labourers for 1880, p. 11 [C 2809], H.C. 1881, xciii.

farmers. As later events were to show, small farmers recognized the benefit that would accrue to them if large landholdings were broken up, while large farmers were quite aware of this danger and the threat that it represented to their interests. On the other hand, there are two good reasons for believing that the differences in the interests of these groups were narrowing in the years after the Famine. First, they were no longer divided in their respective orientations toward pasture farming. Both large and small farmers were now engaged in a common economic system based on live-stock raising, and a reciprocal relationship involving the sale of livestock by small farmers to large ones was an integral part of this economy. Second, with the decline in subletting, small farmers were less likely to be tenants of large farmers and were less likely to come into conflict with them for this reason. In the post-famine period, the vast majority of farmers shared a common position in the land system. They were tenants of landowners.

This would not have been the case if there had been more farmers who owned their land. The existence of a substantial number of owner-occupiers would have split the farmer population, since tenant-occupiers and owner-occupiers, though sharing other common concerns, would not have shared the same opposition to the existing system of property rights. This fact was well recognized and was often used as an argument in favor of land purchase legislation.[21]

Yet one of the most striking features of the Irish land system in the nineteenth century was the very small number of owner-occupiers. In 1870 only 3 percent of all agricultural holdings were occupied by proprietors in fee.[22] Legislation that sought to increase this proportion in the post-famine period had little impact. The Incumbered Estates Act of 1849 and the Landed Estates Act of 1858 were designed to facilitate the sale of estates that had gone bankrupt during the Great Famine. While nothing in these acts

[21] Report from the select committee on Irish Land Act, 1870; together with the proceedings of the committee, minutes of evidence and appendix, p. xx, H.C. 1878 (249), xv; Report of her majesty's commissioners of inquiry into the working of the Landlord and Tenant (Ireland) Act, 1870, and the acts amending the same, p. 16 [C 2779], H.C. 1881, xviii (hereafter cited as Bessborough commission).

[22] Return showing the number of agricultural holdings in Ireland and the tenure by which they are held by the occupiers, pp. 16-17 [C 32], H.C. 1870, lvi. An additional 2.8 percent held their land on leases for terms exceeding ninety-nine years, for lives renewable forever, or in perpetuity. To treat these occupiers as effective owners of their holdings would raise the proportion to 5.8 percent.

prevented tenants from buying their holdings, no special facilities were afforded to enable them to do so. A series of clauses included in the Land Act of 1870 were intended to remedy this deficiency.[23] Known as the "Bright clauses" after John Bright, the English Liberal who was primarily responsible for their inclusion, they empowered the Landed Estates Court (the court entrusted with carrying out the provisions of the Landed Estates Act) to make arrangements for the sale of holdings to occupying tenants if both the owner and the tenant were agreeable. The Bright clauses also empowered the Board of Works to lend tenants up to two-thirds of the purchase price at an annuity of 5 percent repayable over thirty-five years.

The Bright clauses were almost a complete failure. There were a number of reasons, but the main one was simply that landlords and tenants found it difficult to arrive at mutually satisfactory terms. Most landlords insisted on at least twenty-five years' purchase (i.e., a purchase price equal to twenty-five times the annual rent), which presented a tenant with the prospect of paying out the equivalent of more than eight years' rent as down payment, then making substantial annuity payments for the next thirty-five years. Few tenants were willing or able to take advantage of such an opportunity, and few did. Only 605 occupiers purchased their holdings through the Landed Estates Court by the end of 1876, and three-quarters of these sales were in the province of Ulster.[24] A far larger number of peasant proprietorships (some 4,000 by 1877) were created by the commission entrusted with disposing of Church of Ireland property after the Disestablishment Act of 1869. Again, however, the majority of sales took place in Ulster; and they were also limited to tenants occupying land that formerly belonged to the Church of Ireland. Together the two acts added less than 1 percent to the total number of agricultural occupiers in Ireland who owned their holdings. They did almost nothing to divide farmers into owners and tenants.

To sum up, and to describe what happened in very broad terms, before the Famine the rural class structure consisted of three groups: (1) landowners, (2) large farmers, and (3) small farmers and laborers. The largest of the three was the third. Indeed, labor-

[23] 33 and 34 Vict., c. 46: clauses 32-41, 44-56.

[24] Report from the select committee on Irish Land Act, 1870; together with the proceedings of the committee, minutes of evidence, and appendix, p. 239, H.C. 1877 (328), xii.

ers alone comprised a majority of the agricultural labor force. After the Famine, in contrast, laborers were in the minority, and it is likely that proportionately fewer of the laborers who remained were landholders. One thing is certain: they depended more heavily than did their pre-famine counterparts on wages for their livelihood. The interests of these laborers diverged sharply from those of farmers.

Farmers, for their part, were not so clearly split into two groups as they had been before the Famine. Although there were important differences among them in terms of the size of holdings, the distinction between large, rent-receiving farmers and small, rent-paying farmers had clearly diminished. They were now, in most cases, simply tenants who had no undertenants and whose landlords were landowners. Furthermore, whereas before the Famine small and large farmers differed in their respective orientations toward pasture farming, after the Famine the great majority of tenant farmers depended on livestock for the bulk of their income. In the post-famine period, then, the rural class structure still consisted of three groups, but the groups were now: (1) landowners, (2) tenant farmers, and (3) laborers. The largest group was the second.

Town and Country

INTER-REGIONAL SOCIAL COMMUNICATION

The social transformation discussed in the preceding section was accompanied by important changes in the locus and range of daily social interaction. Post-famine rural society was characterized by increased interaction beyond the primary group, both within the rural population, and between rural and urban elements. This social interaction was facilitated and broadened by some significant changes in the communicative media. One of the most dramatic developments of the post-famine period occurred with respect to both spoken and written language. To all extents and purposes, Ireland ceased to be a linguistically divided country. Primarily as a result of the selective impact of the Famine, the proportion of the population who spoke Irish fell from about half in 1841 to less than a quarter in 1851. Subsequently, it continued to decline and amounted to only one-seventh by 1891. At the same time, the percentage who could read English rose dramatically. Again this was primarily a result of the decline in population, which affected most of all the illiterate, but it was also a result of the National school system established in the 1830s. Between 1841 and 1881 the number of persons five years of age or older who were returned in the census as unable to read or write fell from 53 percent to 25 percent; in Connaught it fell from 72 percent to 38 percent.[25] One important concomitant of greater English literacy was an increase in the number of newspapers. In the country as a whole, the number rose from 73 in 1849 to 122 in 1879; in Connaught it rose from 14 to 18.[26] These figures are remarkable in view of the simultaneous decline in the size of the population, and they indicate a substantial growth in the proportion of people exposed to the mass media.

Methods of transportation also improved. In the 1840s there were only a few railway lines extending out of Dublin and Belfast; by the 1870s the basic network of Irish railways was complete. Although railway development was certainly more advanced in relatively populous regions, it nevertheless succeeded in opening up remote parts of the country. By 1859 a main line of the Midland Great Western Railway had been built from Dublin to Galway. In the early 1860s the same company acquired a branch through Roscommon to Castlerea, and by the 1870s lines had been completed all the way to Westport and Ballina, linking these remote towns to Dublin in a day's journey. Also by the 1870s, lines reached Kerry through branches of the Great Southern and Western railway, and into Clare through a branch of the Waterford and Limerick railway, which also extended as far as Tuam in County Galway. During the 1860s the railway companies also began to erect telegraph lines that afforded a rapid means of communication not only to businesses, but also to politicians and newspapers.

Special fourth-class rail fares were available to take harvest laborers to Dublin on their way to England, but even the cost of third-class rail travel was less than that of coach travel. As a result, the number of third-class railway passengers rose steadily in the post-famine period, constituting 51 percent of all passengers in 1861, 60 percent in 1871 and 65 percent in 1876. Consistently, total receipts from passenger traffic exceeded total receipts from

[25] Census of Ireland, 1841, p. 433; Census of Ireland, 1881: General report, p. 343.
[26] Thom's, 1850, p. 181; Thom's, 1880, pp. 1022, 1292.

goods traffic.[27] Railways were used even to carry passengers to fairs and races. The railway companies often ran special trains for such purposes, and in local newspapers one can repeatedly find advertisements soliciting business of this kind.

On the other hand, the cost of railway transportation was still high enough that long trips constituted a major expenditure for most rural people, and were beyond the means of many. Generally, 1d. per mile was charged for third-class travel, and so the cost of a return trip to Dublin from most places in Connaught exceeded £1, which was about what a laborer might hope to earn in two weeks. It is important not to draw unwarranted conclusions from the very high volume of passenger traffic on Irish railways. A large portion of this passenger traffic was conveyed on short lines emanating from major urban centers. In 1873-8, for example, the Belfast and County Down line, the Belfast, Holywood, and Bangor line, and the Dublin, Wicklow, and Wexford line together ran on only 9 percent of the track of Irish railways, carried only 9 percent of the merchandise and minerals—but were responsible for 33 percent of all passengers.[28] By contrast, the major cross-national lines, the Midland Great Western Railway and the Great Southern and Western Railway, together ran on 41 percent of the track of Irish railways and transported 30 percent of the merchandise and minerals—but carried only 19 percent of all passengers.[29] These cross-national lines did enable some rural people to make long trips. For example, they greatly facilitated the movement of migratory agricultural workers.[30] In general, however, the significance of the cross-national lines lay in the merchandise and livestock they carried, and in the convenience they afforded to people who wanted to visit remote districts. Merchandise could now be shipped to most places. And businessmen, commercial agents, lecturers, religious leaders, professionals, and politicians could now visit almost all parts of the country with relative ease.

It is not at all clear that the Irish were geographically much more mobile after the Famine than before. The most frequent kind of geographical mobility was still permanent and seasonal migration out of the country. Internal migration, in contrast, remained low. The number of people residing outside their county of birth rose from 5 percent of the population in 1841 to only 10 percent in

---

[27] Thom's, 1879, p. 709.   [28] Ibid., pp. 707-8.

[29] Ibid.

[30] Cormac Ó Gráda, "Seasonal migration and post-famine adjustment in the west of Ireland" in *Studia Hibernica*, no. 13 (1973), pp. 52-4.

1881.[31] Although inter-regional social communication was certainly greater in the post-famine period, it is evident that most of this communication did not result directly from the movement of rural people themselves, but must have taken place through newspapers and through various kinds of intermediaries. It is to the foremost intermediaries that we shall now turn our attention.

SHOPKEEPERS AND PUBLICANS

During the post-famine period, a number of factors combined to produce a substantial alteration in the consumption patterns of the rural population. I have already noted the increase in cash receipts from Irish agriculture and the rise in laborers' wages. These developments could explain the growth in consumption of some items, particularly tobacco and tea. The annual average quantity of tobacco imported for home consumption rose from .6 pounds per capita in the late 1830s to 1.2 pounds per capita in the early 1860s, while tea rose from .5 pounds to 2.2 pounds over the same period.[32] Although whisky consumption declined, beer consumption rose, especially beer that was not locally produced. In 1855 Guinness's Irish trade beyond Dublin consisted of 17,000 hogsheads (or about 21 percent of total sales); by 1880 this country trade had risen to 230,000 hogsheads (or about 40 percent of total sales).[33] Furthermore, the tendency for English manufactured goods to displace Irish manufactured goods, already noticeable in the pre-famine period, was accelerated after the Famine by the building of Irish railways. By the 1860s home-made clothing had been largely replaced by English cotton products. Henry Coulter, a correspondent for *Saunders' News-Letter*, who visited Mayo in the early 1860s, was struck by the fact that even laborers generally took "their wages to the shops to buy, instead of manufacturing themselves." "You will rarely see," he lamented, "a suit of home manufacture worn by any of the peasantry, either male or female, particularly the latter, who spend their earnings in the neighbouring towns in the purchase of cotton dresses and striped petticoats, and have got quite out of the system of making their own clothing."[34] Perhaps the most remarkable development of all was the

[31] *Census of Ireland, 1841*, pp. 446-9; *Census of Ireland, 1881: General report*, p. 266.

[32] Thom's, 1868, p. 770.

[33] Lynch and Vaizey, *Guinness's Brewery*, p. 201.

[34] Henry Coulter, *The West of Ireland: Its Existing Condition and Prospects* (Dublin, 1862), p. 191.

greater quantity of shop-purchased food. Such purchases included more than just tea, sugar, and spices. The increase in the
cash resources of the rural population, the repeal of the Corn Laws
in 1846, and the decline in potato production—all combined to
effect a significant change in the diet of laborers and small
farmers. Potatoes were now supplemented by imported wheat,
used to make wheat bread, and by imported Indian meal, used
with milk to make "stirabout." Between the early 1860s and the
late 1870s, the quantity of wheat imported through the port of
Cork tripled and the quantity of Indian corn increased more than
fivefold.[35]

The extent of shop purchasing, even by the poorest members of
the rural population, can be illustrated by referring again to the
reports of inspectors for the Congested Districts Board in the
1890s. Most inspectors found that people relied heavily on shops
for such goods as fertilizers, flour, Indian meal, tea, sugar, bacon,
and tobacco. Clothing was usually bought in local shops, except
for underclothing and socks, which were generally made in the
home, and work clothes, which were often obtained by seasonal
laborers when they were in England. Almost always, the estimates
given by inspectors of the value of shop purchases made by a family greatly exceeded their estimated rent. Indeed, purchases of
clothing alone often equaled rent. The largest category of expenditure was invariably food, which typically ranged from £15 to £30
for a year and was usually about the same as the estimated value
of home-grown food consumed. In other words, purchased food
constituted (in terms of value) about half of all food consumed. As
a rule, the consumption of purchased food was heaviest in the
spring and summer after the former year's supply of home-grown
food had been exhausted but before the next harvest.[36]

One of the most important consequences of this greater shop
purchasing was a growth in the prosperity of the small-business
class, particularly shopkeepers and publicans. Some indication of
this prosperity is afforded by looking at the number of persons
employed in shops and public houses. Unfortunately, the 1841
and 1881 censuses did not provide comprehensive categories that
are directly comparable. It is nevertheless clear that these occupational groups increased in proportion to the size of the popula-

[35] Donnelly, Cork, p. 245.
[36] T.C.D., Congested Districts Board: Base line reports.

tion. There are several ways in which we can demonstrate this, no one of which is satisfactory by itself. First, we can compare the number of persons returned as "shopkeepers" or "dealers" in each census. In absolute numbers, people in these categories diminished from some 32,000 in 1841 to some 24,000 in 1881, but in proportion to the population they rose from 39 to 47 per 10,000 persons. This category does not, however, include anything like the total number of shopkeepers, and it includes no publicans. Publicans and their employees fell into a "food and lodgings" category, which also included people who owned or worked in

TABLE 7 · Number per 10,000 in total population for selected non-agricultural occupational categories in 1841 and 1881 by province

	"SHOPKEEPERS" AND "DEALERS"	"FOOD AND LODGINGS"	SAMPLE OF TRADERS	SAMPLE OF ARTISANS
Leinster				
1841	57	88	18	138
1881	69	189	83	151
Munster				
1841	45	57	10	98
1881	77	136	53	137
Ulster				
1841	26	56	10	446
1881	36	122	51	377
Connaught				
1841	26	34	4	103
1881	44	57	23	109
Ireland				
1841	39	61	11	210
1881	47	132	55	218

NOTE: The "food and lodgings" category was not referred to as such in the 1841 census. It was a subcategory within a larger classification called "ministering to food." The sources are *Census of Ireland, 1841*, pp. 152, 262, 364, 430 and 440; *Census of Ireland, 1881*: pt. i . . . vol. i, *Province of Leinster*, p. 1191 [C 3042], H.C. 1881, xcvii; *Census of Ireland, 1881*: pt. i . . . vol. ii, *Province of Munster*, p. 1002 [C 3148], H.C.1882, lxxvii; *Census of Ireland, 1881*: pt. i . . . vol. iii, *Province of Ulster*, p. 972 [C 3204], H.C. 1882, lxxviii; *Census of Ireland, 1881*: pt. i . . . vol. iv, *Province of Connaught*, p. 623; *Census of Ireland, 1881*: pt. ii, *General report*, p. 108.

shops that sold food or alcoholic beverages. The number in this category rose from almost 50,000 in 1841 to more than 68,000 in 1881, or from 61 to 132 per 10,000 in the total population. Still another method is to select a sample of trading occupations for which roughly equivalent categories can be found in both censuses. The sample that I selected consisted of twelve trading occupations held by 9,001 persons in 1841 and by 28,272 in 1881, or 11 per 10,000 in 1841 and 55 per 10,000 in 1881. For purposes of comparison, I also selected a sample of artisan occupations for which roughly equivalent categories could be found in both censuses. They rose in proportion to the population much less than did the trading occupations. My sample consisted of thirty-two artisan occupations held by 171,723 persons in 1841 and by 112,991 in 1881, or 210 per 10,000 in 1841 and 218 per 10,000 in 1881. As shown in Table 7, all four provinces experienced substantial increases in the proportion of persons engaged in the trading occupations, while a substantial increase in artisans as a proportion of the population occurred only in Munster and to a lesser extent in Leinster.

The significance of this small-business class lies in the special role that many of its members came to play in agrarian communities. By no means an inconsequential social group even before the Famine, in the post-famine period their importance was enhanced still further and they came to rival landowners and clergymen as wielders of local power and patronage. They often enjoyed a social relationship with rural people that was comparable even to that of the parish priest.

First, there were strong kinship ties between this social group and the farming population. This can be illustrated by referring again to patterns of marriage and occupational mobility in the Roscommon registrar district. A second glance at Table 5 reveals that, in comparison with other occupational categories, a high proportion (51.4 percent) of the daughters of traders and business proprietors married farmers' sons, and an even higher proportion (63.4 percent) of the sons of traders and business proprietors married farmers' daughters. Similarly, Table 6 shows that a comparatively large percentage of traders and business proprietors were farmers' sons. Indeed, no less than 40 percent of the traders and business proprietors who married in Roscommon between 1864 and 1880 were from farm families.

Along with kinship ties, there was also a cooperative economic relationship between shopkeepers and farmers, one that went far beyond the simple retailer-customer arrangement. This relationship often developed into a patron-client tie, which could link the two parties together in a powerful, and sometimes almost inescapable, bond.[37] In order to understand the dynamics of this relationship, it is essential to recognize that the increase in purchasing power enjoyed by the rural population after the Famine did not mean that farmers always had money in their pockets. On the contrary, most farmers, especially small farmers, were desperately short of cash for most of the year. Money was tied up in livestock, to a lesser extent in crops, artificial fertilizers, and imported guano, and not infrequently in expensive dowries. Many small farmers also lacked cash because they had insufficient land for their livestock and were forced to use purchased feed.[38] They depended, therefore, upon loans or credit to make ends meet. The actual amount of cash required was not very great, typically less than £10. On the other hand, they needed loans for relatively long periods. For the purchase of seeds, manures, and feed, a loan of less than six months was useless. To buy livestock and agricultural implements or to hold livestock over for another season, a loan of at least one year was usually necessary. For any permanent improvements a farmer might want to make to his holding or to his buildings, an even longer loan was required.[39]

One possible way for a farmer to obtain cash was to borrow from the joint-stock banks. But the banks preferred short-term loans with a fixed date of repayment. Their loans were typically for three to four months or, in exceptional cases, eight to twelve months. And the banks were also unfavorably disposed toward small loans since the administrative costs were proportionately higher. Statistics from the Bank of Ireland published by a report on agricultural credit in 1914 showed that only 25 percent of its

[37] For a suggestive analysis of the role of shopkeepers and publicans as patrons in Ireland, see Peter Gibbon and M. D. Higgins, "Patronage, tradition and modernisation: the case of the Irish 'Gombeenman' " in Economic and Social Review, 6, no. 1 (Oct. 1974). But see also Liam Kennedy, "A sceptical view on the reincarnation of the Irish 'Gombeenman' " in Economic and Social Review, 8, no. 3 (April 1977); and Peter Gibbon and M. D. Higgins, "The Irish Gombeenman: reincarnation or rehabilitation?" in Economic and Social Review, 8, no. 4 (July 1977).
[38] Report of the departmental committee on agricultural credit in Ireland, pp. 73-4 [Cd 7375], H.C. 1914, xiii.
[39] Ibid., pp. 23-4.

loans (by branches outside Dublin, Belfast, and Cork) were to farmers, and only 10 percent were for less than £10.[40]

Although large farmers often borrowed from the banks, the principal source of credit for small farmers was the small-business class. Shopkeepers were willing to lend modest amounts for long periods, with a flexible date of repayment. And whereas banks would not make loans to small farmers without several sureties (usually a shopkeeper or a large farmer), shopkeepers gave credit to small farmers on the strength of their social relationship. W.J.D. Walker of the Congested Districts Board told the departmental committee reporting on agricultural credit in 1914: "The people are very honest, and the grocer knows these people, and lends to them when no bank would touch them, because there is nothing in the house to seize."[41] Of course, the credit that a shopkeeper would give a farmer was not unlimited. Typically he provided it only in the form of goods purchased at his shop. Credit was not, however, restricted to fertilizers and feeding stuffs. It was usually given for a wide range of items, including food, and especially flour and Indian meal.

Inevitably, the credit system gave rise to conflict between shop-keepers and farmers. The terms of credit were sometimes high, even if interest as such was not charged. Shopkeepers invariably put a higher price on goods bought on credit, or, in the language that they preferred, they generally offered discounts if payments were made in cash. The difference between the two prices was normally 10 to 20 percent.[42] In addition, on an overdue account, a farmer might be charged interest of 6 to 10 percent on top of the credit price.[43] If an account still went unpaid, a shopkeeper might sue a farmer in the civil-bill court to recover his money, or force the farmer to sign a bill of sale for the property on his farm or for

[40] Ibid., pp. 24-6.   [41] Ibid., p. 76.

[42] Ibid., p. 74. See also Kennedy, "A sceptical view on the reincarnation of the Irish 'Gombeenman.' " Kennedy has calculated that in roughly one-quarter of the congested districts, the average interest rate, as reported by the inspectors in the 1890s, was 10 percent or less, while in more than half of the districts, it was under 15 percent. But Kennedy also notes that, according to contemporaries, excessive interest rates were less common in the 1890s than in earlier decades. It may be assumed, therefore, that in the 1870s interest rates were often as high as 20 percent.

[43] Report on agricultural credit, p. 71; T.C.D., Congested Districts Board: Base line reports, p. 307; T. A. Finlay, "The usurer in Ireland" in New Ireland Review, 1, no. 5 (July 1894), pp. 313-14.

his interest in the farm.[44] Rarely did matters come to such ex-
tremes, but even the most amicable credit relations between a
shopkeeper and a farmer gave the former considerable power over
the latter. By getting into debt, a farmer became bound to a shopkeeper, unable to shop for the best bargain or to question the price
or quality of the goods his creditor was offering.[45] "The people
generally," reported an inspector for the Congested Districts
Board in the 1890s, "deal with the same shopkeeper year after
year, keeping a running account."[46] "If the trader suspects his
customer of distributing his patronage with others," explained
another inspector, "he usually presses for payment of his account,
and by this means is able to keep his customers and charge them
his own prices."[47] The farmer, declared still a third inspector, is
"hardly ever out of the shopkeeper's power."[48] Usually customers
had to make at least one cash payment a year, but they were rarely
able to clear the debt entirely, and this payment merely permitted
them to make further purchases on credit.[49]

On the other hand, if customers were bound to their shopkeepers, so too were shopkeepers bound to their customers. To fore-
close on a farmer meant losing him as a customer, and perhaps
many of his kin and friends as well. Consequently, the amount of
credit given, especially in hard times, was liberal, sometimes "beyond all conception."[50] In an effort to maintain their clientele,
shopkeepers were known to advance credit for years without
payment and even to write debts off if customers could not afford
to pay.[51] Though some shopkeepers became professional moneylenders (known as "gombeen men"), the majority gave credit
simply because it was the only possible way to sell their goods to
a population that lacked cash. Shopkeepers usually preferred to
deal in cash for a number of reasons: the limited terms that they
could get from wholesale merchants, the very high risk that they
would not be repaid by their customers, and the bad name that
they could acquire if they pressed for payment. As a rule, they ac-

---

[44] Finlay, "The usurer in Ireland," p. 314.
[45] Report on agricultural credit, pp. 69, 71, and 73.
[46] T.C.D., Congested Districts Board: Base line reports, p. 381.
[47] Ibid., p. 400.
[48] Ibid., p. 320.
[49] Ibid., p. 400.
[50] Ibid., p. 381.
[51] Report on agricultural credit, p. 76; See also "Correspondence" in New Ireland Review, 1, no. 6 (Aug. 1894), pp. 398-9.

cepted credit only because their customers would otherwise have taken their business elsewhere.[52]

We should not allow the strain that unavoidably arose between shopkeepers and farmers over credit to obscure the essentially cooperative and interdependent nature of their relationship. By encouraging a particular set of farmers to patronize a particular shopkeeper, the credit system contributed to a mutual bond between them. The shopkeeper depended on his customers for business, and the farmer depended on his shopkeeper for goods and for credit. Though the terms of credit may have been high, they were often unrecognized because they were incorporated as part of the price of goods. Moreover, the shopkeepers' terms were no more (usually less) than the terms offered by other sources of credit that were available to the small farmer, such as professional moneylenders, trust auctions, and pawnbrokers.[53]

Yet the close relationship that a shopkeeper usually had with farmers did not mean that he was in reality one of them. Their ties could not erase the differences that distinguished the two occupational groups—differences that were a function of their divergent modes of livelihood and patterns of daily activities. Indeed, the very social bond that linked the shopkeeper to his customers served to distinguish him from them. He had a much wider circle of friends than they did. Notwithstanding the tendency of the credit system to limit the scope of any one shopkeeper's clientele, his customers were generally large in number, and with almost all he could claim personal acquaintance. Thus he was the center or "star" in a sociogram of human relationships, and in this way he acquired a position of considerable influence in the community. He was a source of information, both a receiver and transmitter of news ranging from trivial gossip to matters of social and political import.

This special position may have been enhanced by another difference between the shopkeeper and the farmer. It is possible that the former was more *cosmopolitan* than the latter, that is, that he had greater contact with people beyond his own community. The shopkeeper's economic role was not merely to handle the exchange of goods within the local community, but also to receive and distribute goods from other places. To do so effectively, he

[52] Report on agricultural credit, p. 72.

[53] For discussions of these and other sources of credit see ibid., pp. 51-65; and W. Neilson Hancock, The Usury Laws and the Trade of Lending Money to the Poor in Ireland (Dublin, 1850).

had to keep himself informed of developments outside of his area. The ordering and receiving of goods brought him into contact with sales representatives and commercial agents located in other parts of the country, sometimes in neighboring towns, but also from as far away as Dublin. It is also likely that the shop-keeper's business compelled him to make at least occasional trips to other towns or to major urban centers. It is not unreasonable to suppose that trade with the larger society broadened the horizons of those who handled that trade.

An investigator studying people who lived a hundred years ago searches in vain for a good measure of cosmopolitanism. We cannot take a survey of attitudes, nor can we determine the scope of informal networks. We cannot even count the number of trips that people made beyond their locality. We can, however, get some indication of the cosmopolitanism of different groups by once again examining their marriage patterns. The sample utilized here is the same as that employed in Tables 5 and 6, except that this time subsamples are used for two of the occupational groups.

TABLE 8 · Percentage of brides marrying someone living outside their poor-law union for marriages registered in Roscommon, distinguished according to occupation of bride's father, 1864-80

OCCUPATION OF FATHER	PERCENTAGE OF BRIDES MARRYING SOMEONE LIVING OUTSIDE THEIR POOR-LAW UNION	TOTAL NUMBER OF BRIDES
Farmers	28.8	66
Laborers	10.0	30
Traders and business proprietors	43.8	32
Artisans and non-farm laborers	20.0	40
Civil service and defense	35.7	14
Gentry	30.0	10

NOTE: The source is the same as for Tables 5 and 6. Figures for daughters of farmers and for daughters of laborers are based on subsamples taken from marriages in 1866 and 1872 only. As a result, the totals for these groups differ from those given in Table 5. Totals for other groups also differ, as some brides could be included in Table 5 but not in this table because I was unable to establish their place of residence. See Appendix A for further discussion of these data.

Table 8 gives the percentage of brides marrying someone living outside their district of residence, distinguished according to father's occupation, for six occupational groups. It is convenient, and also appropriate, to define their district as the poor-law union in which they resided, since the poor-law union consisted of the major town plus its surrounding area. Some idea of the size of this district may be obtained by noting that the Roscommon union, in which most of the sample resided, had a population of some 22,500 persons in 1871 and covered roughly a circular area with a diameter of 12 to 14 miles. Table 8 shows that the brides least likely to marry someone from outside their union were daughters of laborers and those most likely to marry outside were daughters of traders and business proprietors. Farmers' daughters and artisans' daughters fell in between, with the former marrying out more often than the latter, but still much less often than the daughters of traders and business proprietors. Admittedly, it is not entirely clear what we are entitled to conclude from these data with respect to cosmopolitanism. That a group of people frequently married outside their district does not tell us how often they made trips elsewhere or how broad their social orientation was. Still, in most societies marriage patterns tend to conform to the boundaries of social relationships. Nor are we far wrong in using marriages of daughters to tell us something about the social contacts of fathers. In Ireland during this period fathers had a strong hand in their daughters' marriages, not only among farmers but among traders as well. Until better data become available, we may take these Roscommon marriage patterns as furnishing limited evidence to support the assertion that traders had broader social networks than did farmers.

TOWNS

Most shopkeepers and publicans lived in towns, and the relationships that developed between these small businessmen and rural people were actually part of a more general transition in the nature of Irish communal structures in the post-famine period. The town became the center of the local community to an extent that it had never been before. This did not happen because towns grew larger. It is true that the proportion of the population living in centers of 2,000 or more persons rose from 14 percent in 1841 to 24 percent in 1881. Yet more careful examination suggests that most of this "urbanization" was probably a consequence of differential rates of decline between urban and rural areas during the

Famine, as evidenced by the fact that most of it occurred between 1841 and 1851 when the percentage stood at 23. Furthermore, in Connaught the increase in the proportion of the population living in towns of 2,000 or more was minimal, rising from 6 to only 8 percent over the entire interval between 1841 and 1881. Since we have a special interest in Connaught, this finding is important in itself, but in addition it suggests that it was the growth of cities and large towns, not towns in general, that was responsible for the urbanization that occurred in the country as a whole.

The unimpressive rate of urban growth from 1841 to 1881 should occasion no surprise. There was little economic base on which large urban centers could be built. Except in the northeast, no industrial expansion occurred in Ireland during the post-famine period. On the contrary, as I have already noted, in most of the country the strength of manufacturing continued to decline after the Famine as it fell victim to English competition. Large cities such as Dublin, Cork, and Belfast were able to hold their own, but most of the other towns lost whatever status they had formerly enjoyed as viable economic entities in their own right. They became appendages to the farming population; and their main function was now to serve its needs. What this meant, strangely enough, was that the importance of towns for rural people became greater as the vitality of these towns actually declined. Most were now primarily agrarian-service towns, especially those in Connaught, where they had always been small and had never performed a significant manufacturing function.

Towns were partly saved by the fact that, if they declined, villages and hamlets declined even more. The tremendous fall in population during the Famine meant a reduction in the size of most towns. But for many villages and hamlets it meant extinction. In both 1841 and 1881, census commissioners considered a village or town to be any nucleated settlement containing twenty or more inhabited houses, which normally meant a population of 100 or more persons. In 1841 there were twenty-eight such settlements either within or bordering on the County of Roscommon, of which eleven could be called towns since they had populations of 500 or more persons. In 1881 eight of these eleven towns (though reduced in size) still had 500 or more persons. In contrast, villages numbered seventeen in 1841, but only seven of these even appeared in the 1881 census.[54] Most of these villages, of

---

[54] *Census of Ireland, 1841*, pp. 406-9; *Census of Ireland, 1881: Province of Con-*

course, did not entirely disappear; they simply became insignifi-
cantly small and did not qualify as villages by the criteria
employed in the census. Many hamlets, on the other hand, did actually disappear. As noted in Chapter Two hamlets before the
Famine were to be found mainly in Connaught, where they were
important centers of social and sometimes economic interaction.
After the Famine they were no longer numerous even in Connaught.

Thus the towns that survived the Famine became the focus for
social and economic intercourse that formerly had been more dispersed. The reports of inspectors for the Congested Districts
Board, for instance, indicate that even small farmers went to
towns to make purchases. In the case of Islandeady, which "is
central between [the towns of] Westport, Newport and Castlebar,"
an inspector reported that "food and other supplies were obtained
at those places." The same inspector noted that people in the district surrounding the town of Louisburgh "are remarkably well
dressed, principally in shop goods purchased from traders in
Westport and Louisburgh."[55] According to another inspector, the
people in the Glenamaddy district in County Galway "buy their
purchased food and other supplies from the fair towns."[56] Of
course, there were shopkeepers in small villages and even at
crossroads, but "they are usually dealt with only when the town
supplies run short."[57] In remote districts, these village shopkeepers served the important functions of collecting eggs from the
small farmers and providing people with goods needed during
the middle of the week. But the inspectors were unanimous in
stating that, except in extremely remote areas, business went primarily to shopkeepers in towns, not villages.

The consequence was that Irish towns presented an odd mixture of prosperity and decay. Small, often poor, having few if any
manufacturing enterprises, they were nevertheless vital economic
centers. Describing the Clare town of Scariff in the early 1860s,
Henry Coulter remarked that he had "never seen more wretched-
looking hovels than those which are clustered together on the
outskirts of the town." Yet he also found that Scariff "affords a

naught, pp. 430-72. Altogether there were ten villages in 1881: the seven villages
that survived plus the three towns that became villages.

[55] T.C.D., Congested Districts Board: Base line reports, pp. 362 and 377.

[56] Ibid., p. 572.

[57] Ibid., p. 399.

striking illustration of the prosperous state of the country for some years past."

> The population of Scariff has suffered great diminution since the famine year; but the town, which in 1846 had only one little shop of the meanest description, now contains several thriving and wealthy shopkeepers, who have set up establishments and made their fortunes within a period of ten or twelve years. One of these enterprising traders possesses a very large concern, a sort of general miscellaneous "store", containing all kinds and descriptions of goods, not omitting crinoline, hoops, and other articles of fashionable female attire for the farmers' wives and daughters. The proprietor of this shop is worth several thousand pounds, all realized within a few years in a poor-looking little town—a conclusive proof that the farmers of the surrounding districts had plenty of money to spend.[58]

And of the town of Ballinrobe in County Mayo, Coulter wrote: "Some twenty years ago, Ballinrobe did not contain a decent shop; now it has a good many large establishments, evincing by their thriving and prosperous appearance that there is an active and profitable trade carried on here."[59]

Along with their shops, towns were centers of communication, transportation, and local government. Newspaper offices were invariably located in towns, and, of course, so were railway stations. The constabulary, courts, jails, infirmaries, registrars and poor-law boards were also centered in towns. A visitor to County Galway in the late 1880s described the small town of Clonbur, "which in Lancashire would be an insignificant village, but here is called a town, and is the headquarters of the magistracy and constabulary of the district."[60] Not least in importance, fairs and markets were usually held in towns. Fairs were used by peddlers to hawk their goods and by farmers to dispose of all varieties of agricultural produce. As a rule, grain and eggs were taken directly to merchants; and pigs and poultry, though commonly sold at fairs, were usually relegated to a place of lesser importance, and at some fairs were assigned a separate day. The biggest traffic was in cattle and sheep, which were sold to dealers from Belfast, Dublin,

[58] Coulter, *The West of Ireland*, pp. 30-31.
[59] Ibid., p. 165.
[60] W. A. Abram, *Irish People at Home* (London, 1890), p. 60.

and England, to local cattle and sheep jobbers, and among farmers themselves.

The success of a fair depended in large measure on its ability to attract buyers from other districts. Only fairs held in towns were able to do so because only they could be large enough to make it worthwhile for outsiders to attend. True, some villages occasionally held fairs, usually so that farmers in the immediate vicinity could exchange livestock with one another, or so that local livestock dealers could buy stock, which they would then sell at a fair in one of the towns. During the post-famine period, however, village fairs became less common. There was, in fact, a tendency for fairs to become concentrated, and for certain towns to evolve as fair towns and to hold a large number of fairs each year. In Connaught the number of places holding six or more fairs a year increased from 33 to 44 between 1850 and 1880, while the number of places holding less than six fairs a year declined from 161 to 85.[61] It is difficult to exaggerate the advantages derived by those towns that managed to become centers for fairs. They were significant social occasions when many people would go to town just to meet friends. From early in the morning the main street of the town would be thronged with people and livestock—groups chatting, farmers haggling, entertainers performing, peddlers hawking, children playing, and animals bellowing. Shopkeepers and publicans could do more business during a good fair day than over an entire week. Indeed, many farmers settled or partly settled their accounts with shopkeepers on fair days. Despite the disorder and filth created by the crowds, it is not at all surprising that towns competed so energetically for fairs. They formed the very hub of the post-famine livestock economy.[62]

The Persistence of Social Discontinuities

Most of the developments with which we have been concerned in this chapter had the effect of increasing the economic and cultural integration of Irish society. They promoted social intercourse

[61] Thom's, 1850, p. 488; Thom's, 1880, p. 35.

[62] For discussions of the social significance of Irish fairs in reference to later periods, see C. M. Arensberg and S. T. Kimball, Family and Community in Ireland (Cambridge, Massachusetts, 1940), pp. 297-305; T. W. Freeman, Ireland, A General and Regional Geography (London, 1950), p. 149; and J. P. Haughton, "The livestock fair in relation to Irish country towns" in Irish Geography, 3, no. 2 (1955).

among various regions and reduced the social isolation characteristic of some areas before the Famine. As I have repeatedly stressed, most of these developments were not restricted to eastern or northeastern parts of the country, but also affected western districts, even many of the coastal counties. In order to appreciate the consequences of this integration, however, it is also necessary to understand that it did not eliminate regional differences. What was, in fact, most significant about post-famine national integration in Ireland was that it embraced not only regions that were or became much alike, but also regions that were and remained very different. There is nothing contradictory about this statement. When I use the term national integration I am talking about the extent to which people in different regions are voluntarily or involuntarily linked together by social or economic interaction and interdependence. They need not be homogenized.[63]

RURAL POVERTY

Along with religious differences, the most important social differences that remained in late nineteenth-century Ireland were economic. This was true even though national integration had advanced perhaps furthest in the economic sphere as a result of the expansion of the livestock economy. Yet precisely because the livestock economy was now so widespread, it came to embrace extremely diverse regions, including parts of the country characterized by severe poverty. The livestock trade was itself healthy during most of the period 1854-76, but many farmers who participated in it were desperately poor. In fact, some of the districts in Ireland with the largest percentages of land devoted to raising livestock were also the most impoverished. These districts included the counties of Clare, Kerry, and west Cork in the province of Munster, and virtually all of the province of Connaught.

Connaught, indeed, can serve as a convenient statistical unit for illustrating this admixture of livestock and poverty in the west. As we have seen, proportionately more land was devoted to pasture and meadow in Connaught than in either Leinster or Ulster. The rate of growth in the cattle and sheep population from the pre-famine period was at least as great in Connaught as in the country

[63] Indeed, the dependency theory of economic development would argue that homogenization in dependent countries such as Ireland is extremely unlikely. See Frank, "The development of underdevelopment"; and Stavenhagen, *Social Classes in Agrarian Societies*.

as a whole, and the increase in the proportion of the agricultural labor force made up of farmers was greater. By the 1870s these farmers were an integral part of a cash livestock economy and their purchasing power had substantially increased. But they were still poor.

One reason was the inferior quality of the land from which they sought to gain a livelihood. The mean valuation per acre of agricultural land was only 7s. in Connaught, while in Leinster it was 14s.[64] Large areas in the west consisted of barren mountain and bog, almost unusable for agricultural purposes. Even much of the land that could be used was of inferior quality, severely restricting production. We have already noted that farmers in Connaught were forced to specialize in certain kinds of livestock raising (pigs, young cattle, and sheep) for this reason.[65] One might expect, given the greater amount of useless or inferior land, that holdings would have been larger in the west than in other regions. Though some of the largest holdings in the country were indeed to be found in remote western districts (where they usually consisted of immense mountain tracts), on the average holdings were *smaller* in Connaught than in most other parts of the country. As shown above in Table 2, the median size of holdings was 14.1 acres in Connaught in 1876, as compared with 20.2 acres in Leinster, 30.3 acres in Munster, and 15.1 acres in Ulster. While it is true that the rate of increase in the size of holdings between 1841 and 1876 was greater in Connaught than in Ulster or Leinster, this consolidation in Connaught occurred almost entirely during the Famine. After the Famine, that is from 1851 to 1876, median size of holdings advanced less in Connaught than in any other province.

A similar pattern can be observed with respect to population. Between 1841 and 1851 the population of Connaught fell at a faster rate than did that of any other province, by some 29 percent as compared with a national rate of 20 percent. In the period 1851-81, however, it fell by only 19 percent, while the total population in the country fell by 21 percent. The difference after 1851

[64] In Munster it was 10s. and in Ulster it was 12s. See *Census of Ireland, 1881: General report*, pp. 165-6.

[65] In 1876, for instance, the ratio of the sheep population to the cattle population was 1.82 in Connaught as compared with .97 in the country as a whole. See *Agricultural statistics of Ireland for the year 1876*, p. 55.

did not stem from lower rates of emigration from the west; indeed it is possible that the rate of emigration was higher out of poorer western districts than out of wealthier eastern districts.[66] What kept the population from declining quite as rapidly in the west as elsewhere was the continuing high rate of natural increase. Everywhere in Ireland marriages were later and the number was lower after the Famine, but more so in the eastern half of the country than in the west. In Connaught and west Munster, the marriage rate in the 1860s and 1870s actually differed little from the pre-famine rate.[67] The consequence was that usable farm land in Connaught, despite its inferior quality, had to support more people per acre than did farm land in Leinster or east Munster.

It may never be possible to determine exactly how poor people were in post-famine Connaught. Standards of living are always difficult for historians to assess. The available evidence suggests that poverty remained extensive, notwithstanding considerable advances made during the post-famine period. Irish historians have typically used the quality of housing to measure standards of living for the last half of the nineteenth century. The census commissioners made a distinction between four classes of houses on the basis of the number of rooms and windows and the quality of building materials. The worst were third and fourth-class houses, which declined sharply as a proportion of all homes between 1841 and 1881 in almost every region, partly because some better homes were built, but primarily because so many miserable cabins fell vacant during and after the Famine. It is true that, by this measure, poverty declined considerably in post-famine Connaught. By the same measure, however, it was still much greater than in most other areas. In 1841 third and fourth-class houses comprised no less than 90 percent of all homes in rural areas of Connaught; by 1881 the number had fallen to 68 percent. But in rural Leinster the corresponding statistic for 1881 was 47 percent.[68]

[66] Cormac Ó Gráda, "Some aspects of nineteenth-century Irish emigration" in L. M. Cullen and T. C. Smout (eds.), *Comparative Aspects of Scottish and Irish Economic and Social History 1600-1900* (Edinburgh, 1977).

[67] S. H. Cousens, "The regional variations in population changes in Ireland, 1861-1881" in *Economic History Review*, second series, 17, no. 2 (Dec. 1964).

[68] Houses placed in the fourth category were miserable one-room mud cabins with no more than one front window, but even the majority of third-class houses were small one- or two-room cabins with no more than a couple of front windows.

Another indication of enduring poverty was the number of seasonal migrants. Migration to England and Scotland to work on the
harvests did not decline after the Famine. It actually increased,
perhaps from as low as 60,000 in the 1840s to as high as 100,000
in the 1860s. It fell sharply after 1870, but in 1880 it was still
38,000 by one estimate.[69] The highest rates of migration were
from western counties, particularly from Donegal and the counties of Connaught, above all County Mayo, which alone accounted
for 45 percent of all seasonal migrants in 1880.[70] Even in the
1890s, reports from inspectors for the Congested Districts Board
indicate that returns from migratory labor represented one-quarter
to one-third of the total income of families in normal circumstances, and that sending a man to England each year was necessary for many families to meet their cash expenditures. For some,
seasonal migration was the only way they could pay the rent.[71]
This was especially true in Connaught, where a comparatively
large proportion of those who made the trip were landholders.[72]
Seasonal migration constituted an essential part of the western
economy until the 1870s, when it began to decline (though by no
means disappeared), not because the need for it in the west was
diminishing, but primarily because the demand for such labor in
England was shrinking.[73]

Finally, poverty in post-famine Connaught was manifested in
the continued dependence of rural people on the potato. Potato
production in Ireland varied independently of other kinds of tillage agriculture. It was not uncommon for potatoes to be grown in
relatively large quantities in areas that otherwise had little tillage.
Indeed, as a rule, the proportion of tilled ground allocated to

---

See *Census of Ireland, 1881: General report*, pp. 7 and 400; *Census of Ireland,
1881: Province of Connaught*, p. 619; and *Census of Ireland, 1881: Province of
Leinster*, pp. 1185-6.

[69] These figures must be treated with considerable caution. See Ó Gráda, "Seasonal migration," pp. 52, 54, and 56-7. The estimate for 1880 is taken by Ó Gráda
from J. E. Handley, *The Irish in Modern Scotland* (Cork, 1947), p. 171.

[70] *The agricultural statistics of Ireland for the year 1880*, p. 7 [C 2932], H.C.
1881, xciii. This figure is based on the Constabulary return, which, as Ó Gráda
points out, probably underestimates the number of migrants. But there is no reason
to believe that it seriously distorts regional variations.

[71] Ó Gráda, "Seasonal migration," pp. 60-2.

[72] Even in Connaught, the majority were not landholders. See above, note 20.

[73] Ó Gráda, "Seasonal migration."

potatoes was greatest in regions where the total tillage area was comparatively small. Thus 42 percent of the tillage land in Connaught and 29 percent of the tillage land in Munster were devoted to potatoes in 1881, as compared with 25 percent in Ulster and 20 percent in Leinster.[74] For the year 1876, potato production per capita in Connaught was roughly one and a quarter times that of Ulster, one and three quarter times that of Munster, and twice that of Leinster.[75] The reports of inspectors for the Congested Districts Board in the 1890s do indicate, as noted above, that people frequently resorted to shop-purchased food in the west. The reports also demonstrate, however, that the potato remained the staple of the small farmer's diet. From August until the spring months it was often taken at all three daily meals, and almost always it formed the basis of at least two of them. It was only when the potatoes were exhausted during the spring and summer months that corn meal became predominant.[76]

We can approach the subject of regional economic disparities more systematically by undertaking a "factor analysis" of major economic variables. A factor analysis is a statistical technique that facilitates the examination of a large number of variables at once by extracting from them several underlying dimensions. On the basis of the intercorrelations among a set of variables, factor analysis reduces them to a smaller number of "factors" which are easier to comprehend.[77] The variables that I have selected for investigation are thirteen economic characteristics of Irish counties, including not only agricultural characteristics (e.g., the percentage of land devoted to pasture), but also measures of poverty (e.g., the quality of houses) and aspects of land tenure (e.g., the size of estates and the percentage of tenants with leases). County Dublin was excluded since it was predominantly urban; there were, consequently, thirty-one units analyzed. It became clear from this analysis that the variables could be reduced to two basic dimensions. There were only two factors with high loadings that ex-

[74] Census of Ireland, 1881: General report, p. 216.

[75] Agricultural statistics of Ireland for the year 1876, p. 33.

[76] T.C.D., Congested Districts Board: Base line reports, pp. 388, 394, 581, 602, and 614.

[77] Several possible types of factor analysis could have been employed. I adopted the most common, namely a principal factors solution with successive iterations to improve the communality of estimates.

plained more than 10 percent of the total variance. These two factors were then rotated using a varimax rotation procedure that yielded orthogonal (i.e., uncorrelated) factors. The correlations between our variables and the two rotated factors are shown in Table 9.

The next step in any factor analysis is to ask whether or not the factors are meaningful. In this case, the appropriate question is whether they make sense in terms of what we already know about post-famine economic structure, and in particular, are they meaningful in relation to the preceding discussion of regional disparities? The answer is that they do make sense and actually support the argument presented above. Let us first consider the loadings on Factor I. The highest is for the ratio of pasture to land under crops; it has a coefficient of .94. Also high on Factor I are other measures of the way in which agricultural land was used, namely, the percentage of tillage land under potatoes (Variable 4) and the ratio of sheep to cattle (Variable 6). Consistent with what I have said above, all three of these land-use variables have positive loadings, indicating a tendency for them to vary directly with one another. That is, the same parts of the country tended to have a large number of acres allocated to pasture relative to the number of acres under crops, to have comparatively large amounts of tillage land under potatoes, and to have a large number of sheep relative to the number of cattle. Several other loadings on this factor are also consistent with the preceding argument: the strong negative coefficient for agricultural valuation per acre (Variable 3), and the reasonably strong positive coefficients for measures of poverty, namely, average class of houses (Variable 5) and the number of migratory laborers (Variable 10). Factor I identifies very clearly the admixture of livestock and poverty that I have emphasized. But more especially, with the high loading for the potato/tillage variable, it demonstrates the important covariation of livestock and subsistence tillage.

Less predictable is the extremely high loading on Factor I for median size of landed properties (Variable 2). In interpreting this finding we should note that none of the other variables that relate to the land system have high loadings on Factor I; here I am referring to Variables 7, 8, and 11. Under these circumstances, it seems ill-advised to argue that Factor I is tapping some fundamental variation in the operation of the land system. The more obvious and much simpler explanation for the high loading of estate median is

TABLE 9 · Rotated factor loadings for economic characteristics of counties (N = 31)

ECONOMIC VARIABLES	FACTOR I	FACTOR II
1. Ratio of pasture to land under crops in 1881	.94	.10
2. Median size of landed properties in 1876 (properties of over one acre)	.92	−.05
3. Agricultural valuation per acre in 1881	−.72	.35
4. Percentage of tillage land under potatoes in 1881	.66	−.48
5. Average class of houses in 1881	.64	−.11
6. Ratio of number of sheep to number of cattle in 1881	.45	.23
7. Percentage of tenants who had leases in 1870	−.17	−.12
8. Percentage of land owned by absentee proprietors in 1870 (properties of 100 or more acres)	.03	−.59
9. Median size of holdings of over one acre in 1881	.24	.62
10. Number of migratory laborers per capita in 1881	.44	−.63
11. Percentage of occupiers who held in fee in 1870	.34	.78
12. Ratio of number of farmers and farmers' sons to number of laborers in 1881	.23	−.88
13. Agricultural valuation per holding in 1881	−.16	.89

NOTE: These variables are self-explanatory, except perhaps Variable 5. It is a class-point average based on the ordinal scale used in the census for rating houses. There were four classes, and I assigned each class a value. This was done in such a way that counties with inferior houses had high scores on Variable 5. The sources for all variables are given in Appendix C.

that estates were generally larger where the land was of poorer quality. It is, I submit, the character of the land and the consequent use to which it was put that is the underlying dimension identified by Factor I. We can call it the "pasture and subsistence-tillage factor."

Factor II also makes substantive sense. It measures the size of agricultural enterprises. The highest loading is for agricultural valuation per holding (Variable 13), and most of the other high loadings are for variables that one would expect to correlate with farm size. For example, we would expect and we indeed find a high positive loading for median size of holdings based on acreage (Variable 9). It also makes sense that there should be negative loadings for Variables 4, 10, and 12; that is, where farms were large we find proportionately less potato cultivation, a smaller number of migratory laborers, and fewer farmers relative to laborers. On the basis of these loadings, we can call this the "large-farm factor." One would not necessarily predict some of the other loadings that are obtained, but they are interesting and not inexplicable. There is a high positive loading for percentage of occupiers who held land in fee (Variable 11) and a high negative loading for percentage of land owned by absentees (Variable 8). These coefficients suggest that an important connection may have existed between the size of agricultural enterprises and certain features of the land system.

The discussion thus far has focused entirely on the factor loadings. These are the correlations between our variables and the factors. One can also use the factors as the basis for constructing new variables. The most straightforward way of doing this is to compute "factor scores," which will indicate the degree to which each county is high or low on a factor. In Figure 1 scores on Factor I are illustrated by dividing the counties of Ireland into five groups according to their scores on this factor; Figure 2 provides the same information for Factor II. Roughly speaking, the counties that are high on the pasture and subsistence-tillage factor are in the western part of the country and to a lesser extent in the southwest and the midlands; those lowest on this factor are in the southeast and especially in the northeast. In the case of Factor II, the division is between the northwest and the southeast. Counties with the highest scores (i.e., the largest farms) are in the southern part of the country, and in the east as far north as County Louth; those with the lowest scores are in the north and the west.[78] One should keep in mind that the two factors were rotated orthogonally so that they would not correlate with one another. Nevertheless, in certain parts of the country a very strong *inverse* relationship can be found. We should pay attention, in particular, to those counties that are high or very high on Factor I, and at the same time, medium, low, or very low on Factor II. In these areas, livestock and subsistence tillage coexisted with comparatively small farms. There were, to be precise, seven districts that had this special combination of economic characteristics: all five counties in Connaught, plus Clare and Kerry. These counties comprised a distinct economic region in Ireland where livestock was bred and reared for the market on poor land and small holdings.

CONCLUSIONS

The period of Irish history between the Famine and the Land War saw the crystallization of two distinct social classes in rural Ireland. The one consisted of commercialized farmers; the other, of wage laborers. This is a common path for rural societies to take. It is the course that has been followed by almost all western European countries. And yet we are still a long way from understanding it. There remain a number of unanswered questions that relate not only to why it happened, but also to how—what were the critical stages in the process and in what order did these stages occur?

In the case of Ireland, the process was not a simple one. It did not take place through a direct transition from a society composed of self-sufficient peasants to one made up of commodity producers and wage laborers. It was instead a two-stage process, and in the first stage commercialized farmers seemed to be retreating rather than advancing. During the late eighteenth and early nineteenth centuries, the structure of the rural society underwent massive changes. Agriculture became more commercialized and the population expanded at an excessive rate. Yet the demographic growth

[78] One of the difficulties with this kind of analysis is that we are ignoring regional variations *within* counties. This is most serious for several large counties, particularly Cork and Galway. West Cork, for example, is economically more like Kerry and Clare than like east Cork, and yet it appears in Figure 2 as "very high" on the large-farm factor. Similarly, it is misleading to portray west Galway as "medium" on the large-farm factor; this area is much like Mayo in this regard.

FIGURE 1 · County Scores on Factor I: Pasture and Subsistence-Tillage

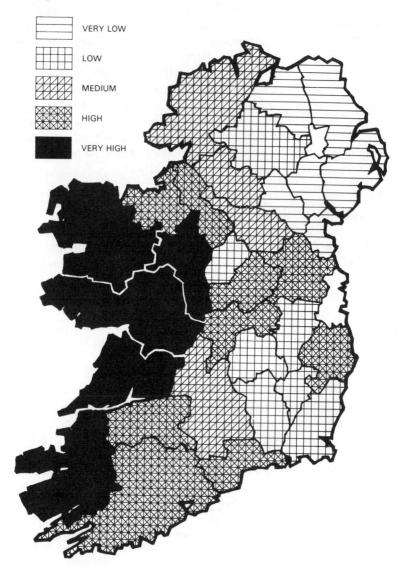

FIGURE 2 • County Scores on Factor II: Large-Farm

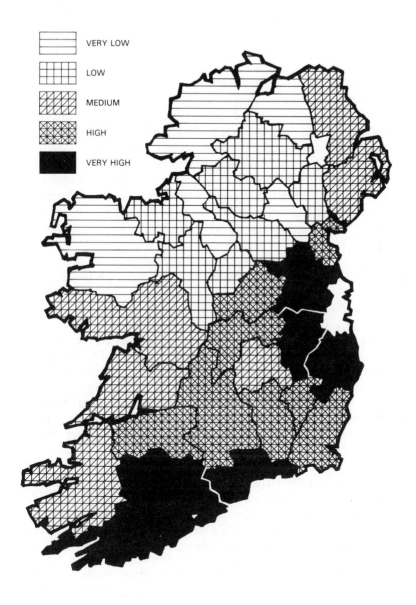

involved mostly an increase in the number of rural laborers, while farmers engaged in business enterprises actually declined as a proportion of the rural population. The majority of these laborers were not personally involved in much marketing of agricultural produce. Nor were they, on the other hand, true wage laborers. Their livelihood came mostly from small subsistence holdings or from potato ground taken seasonally.

Antecedents of the second stage in the social tranformation of rural Ireland can be detected in the pre-famine period, but it essentially occurred during and after the Great Famine, when population decline (together with significant changes in the agricultural economy) transformed the rural class structure. Migration out of the country fed the laboring classes of England and elsewhere. Within Ireland, the size of the laboring class decreased drastically; per capita earnings from wage labor rose substantially; and there may have been a decline in the proportion of laborers who farmed for themselves. Most important, the numerically largest social group in the rural population now consisted of farmers who were directly engaged in market transactions.

This new social group had three especially important characteristics. First, it consisted of landholders who varied greatly in the size of their agricultural enterprises. The polarization of the rural society into commodity producers and wage laborers did not mean the disappearance of small farmers. In spite of increased agricultural commercialization, "middle peasants," as they are often called, survived in Ireland during the last half of the nineteenth century, and indeed well into the twentieth. The persistence of this particular class of peasant, though perhaps more striking in Ireland than elsewhere, was not unique. A similar pattern could be found in other European countries at this time. Much to the dismay of contemporary Marxists,[79] large capitalist farms failed to replace small family farms during the late nineteenth century in western Europe as economic theory had predicted they would. Generally speaking, capitalism did not separate rural society into a simple dichotomy between a stratum of large commercialized farmers, on the one hand, and one of landless laborers, on the

[79] Karl Kautsky, Die Agrarfrage (Stuttgart, 1899); compare Harriet Friedmann, "World market, state, and family farm: the social bases of household production in the era of wage labor" in Comparative Studies in Society and History, 20, no. 4 (Oct. 1978).

other. Often between the class of wage laborers and that of large-scale commodity producers, there remained a class of small-scale producers, who in some places, such as Ireland, were still exceedingly poor and continued to rely on subsistence tillage for a major part of their livelihood.

The second important feature of this new social group was the extent to which its members enjoyed close ties with the urban society and a relatively high level of national integration. It is necessary to be careful in making this point. Before the Famine there was considerable inter-regional social communication and also a national agricultural economy. Pre-famine society had its towns, its shopkeepers, its fairs, and active trading between these towns and better-off sectors of the rural population. Yet, as argued in Chapter Two, for a large segment of the rural population ties with national and urban structures were still weak, especially in comparison with ties based on other social structures such as townland, kinship, and parish. The latter structures did not collapse in the post-famine period, but they now coexisted with stronger national and urban structures. Taking into consideration not only the participation of a larger proportion of the rural population in agricultural marketing and the increased trade between town and country, but also the decline in the number of Irish-speaking people, the increase in literacy, the growth in the number of newspapers, and the considerable improvement in modes of transportation, it is not necessary to exaggerate the social isolation of rural people before the Famine to arrive at the conclusion that the farmers of post-famine Ireland were more integrated into national and urban structures than could be claimed for the bulk of the rural population in the pre-famine period. With reference to other societies, a development of this kind has sometimes been called "social mobilization" and regarded as significant because it weakens the control of traditional or regional social units and increases the control of modern, national units defined in larger ethnic or territorial terms.[80] Students of social mobilization have emphasized that the consequences of this process can vary greatly depending on whether or not the "nation" into which people are mobilized happens to coincide with the boundaries of the state that rules over that nation. In Ireland, of course, the two did not

[80] See in particular, Karl W. Deutsch, "Social mobilization and political development" in *American Political Science Review*, 55 (Sept. 1971).

coincide, and the ultimate consequence was nothing less than the dismemberment of the existing political order.

And finally, the third most important characteristic of the new social group that emerged in post-famine Ireland was the fact that it consisted entirely of farmers who, though engaged in essentially autonomous commodity production, still did not own the land they used and therefore were not wholly free entrepreneurs. Moreover, it was their dependent status as tenants, more than any other single factor, that united the members of this social group and gave them a common interest. We should, therefore, turn our attention to the relationships between these farmers and the elite that owned the land they occupied.

Five · The Land System

The Landlord-Tenant Relationship

ACCOMMODATION

Why the late nineteenth century saw a mass uprising against Irish landlordism is not immediately obvious. Indeed the period that led up to the revolt was characterized by comparative order and tranquillity. The strains that had plagued the system in the pre-famine period had noticeably subsided. And, relatively speaking, an era of conflict had given way to an era of accommodation between Irish landlords and their tenants.

Perhaps the most important factor in the post-famine accommodation was that rents did not advance at the same rate as did agricultural prices. Whereas prices for the major agricultural products rose an average of some 50 percent between the early 1840s and the early 1870s,[1] total rents fell from an estimated £12 million in the early 1840s to about £8.5 million in the early 1850s, and then returned to £12 million by the late 1860s.[2] These general figures obviously ignore variations among estates and regions, as well as abrupt increases in rents and yearly fluctuations in prices. Nevertheless, it is clear that, on the whole, the gains that tenants derived from the rise in prices after the Famine were not simultaneously extracted from them by higher rents.

This in turn meant that tenants more often paid their rents on time. Heavy arrears, which could be found on so many estates before the Famine, were comparatively rare in the post-famine period. We are still in need of more data on this subject, but the conclusion that can be drawn from the information now available is that arrears rose sharply during the Famine and remained high in the early 1850s, but then declined quickly, rising again only for a brief period in the early 1860s. Out of eight landowners whose es-

[1] Barrington, "A review of Irish agricultural prices," pp. 251-2.

[2] Cormac Ó Gráda, "Agricultural head rents, pre-famine and post-famine" in *Economic and Social Review*, 5, no. 3 (April 1974). These figures are consistent with estimates provided by Barbara Solow, who suggests that rents reached £12 million by the late 1860s or very early 1870s. See Solow, *The Land Question and the Irish Economy*, p. 62.

tates were studied by William Vaughan, only two had arrears that averaged more than 30 percent of the annual rent for the period 1866-75.[3] On the Ranelagh estate of the Incorporated Society in Roscommon, arrears averaged 18 percent of the annual rental from 1851-60, 16 percent from 1861-70, and 24 percent from 1871-77, though on this same estate arrears had averaged 54 percent of the annual rental from 1832-37 and 29 percent from 1842-50.[4] The arrears on the Mote estate of Lord Crofton in County Roscommon were 28 percent of the annual rental in 1852, 22 percent in 1855, 17 percent in 1862, but never more than 6 percent in any year from 1863 through 1878.[5] On the County Leitrim estates of the Earls of Leitrim, arrears constituted more than 50 percent of the annual rental in every year from 1845 to 1853, but in the period 1855-73 they were only once greater than 20 percent and in only four years were they greater than 10 percent.[6]

Logically, one would expect the eviction rate to be lower after the Famine as a result of this decline in arrears, and also as a result of the Famine clearances and the smaller size of the laboring class. Unfortunately, post-famine and pre-famine eviction rates cannot be compared since we have no reliable data on the number of evictions before the Famine. We do know, however, that evictions were infrequent after the Famine. The mean annual number of evictions without readmission reported by the Constabulary declined from more than 7,000 in the period 1849-55 to just over 700 in 1856-60, rose to more than 1,000 in 1861-65, and then fell again

[3] Vaughan, "Landlord and tenant relations," p. 88. The estates studied by Vaughan included those of the Earl of Erne in Donegal and Mayo, the Earl of Gosford in Armagh, the Hall family in Armagh and Down, the Baron of Inchiquin in Clare, Francis Blake Knox and Edward Ernest Knox in Roscommon, the Duke of Manchester in Armagh, and H. G. Murray Stewart in Donegal.

[4] T.C.D., Incorporated Society papers: Rentals of the Ranelagh estate, 1832-81 (IS/5562). The estate was owned by the Incorporated Society for Promoting Protestant (English) Schools in Ireland. Averages are based on both the May and November gales.

[5] N.L.I., Crofton papers: Rentals of the Mote estate, County Roscommon, 1852-81 (MSS 5632-3, 4074-94). Figures are based on the May gale only.

[6] N.L.I., Leitrim papers: Rentals of the Mohill, Manor Hamilton, and Newtown Gore estates, 1845-80 (Packing Crate 156). Data for 1849, 1854, 1860, and 1870 are missing, so those years may be exceptions to the generalizations made above. The total rents due were unknown for 1847, 1850, 1852, 1855, 1858, 1861, 1863, and 1871, so I have had to estimate them in order to compute arrears as a percentage of annual rent. Figures are based on the May gale only.

to less than 500 in both 1866-70 and 1871-75.[7] The extremely high number of evictions between 1849 and 1855 affords striking evidence of the reality of the clearances that occurred during and immediately after the Famine. But in subsequent years the number of evictions was remarkably low, at least on the basis of these Constabulary returns. Barbara Solow calculates that the overall rate from 1855 to 1880 was less than 3 percent.[8] Of course, a gross figure of this kind can be misleading, since the distribution of evictions was not uniform. In varying degrees, they tended to be concentrated in certain places and at certain times; and such concentrations could generate fierce resentment and antagonisms even though the overall rate was low.

Nevertheless, taken together the indicators we have (rents, arrears, and evictions) do strongly suggest that landlord-tenant relations improved greatly in the decades that preceded the Land War. This is not to deny that numerous clashes occurred, but it is to say that such clashes were much less common and the hostility generally less intense than had been the case before the Famine. Not surprisingly, many landowners appeared optimistic about the future of the land system, and there is little evidence that they thought it was in any great jeopardy. Indeed, there was a greater inclination to invest in land than at any time since the Napoleonic Wars, as reflected in the number of sales that passed through the Incumbered Estates Court (and later the Landed Estates Court) and the favorable prices that were obtained for land after the initial market glut of the early 1850s. Yet in the 1880s the land system came under the most serious attack in its history. By the turn of the century it was facing extinction. As we shall see, this reversal was precipitated by an agricultural depression beginning in the late 1870s, which introduced another period of serious strain in landlord-tenant relationships. And yet the speed with which eco-

[7] Return by provinces and counties (compiled from returns made to the Inspector General, Royal Irish Constabulary), of cases of evictions which have come to the knowledge of the Constabulary in each of the years from 1849 to 1880 (inclusive), p. 3, H.C. 1881 (185), lxxvii.

[8] Solow, The Land Question and the Irish Economy, pp. 56-7. Altogether the Constabulary reported some 20,000 evictions of families without readmission from 1855 to 1880, but this figure includes those readmitted as caretakers from 1870 to 1880, which Dr. Solow estimates to be about 2,200. If we deduct these 2,200 readmissions from the total, we are left with just under 18,000 evictions, or less than 3 percent of the number of agricultural holdings.

nomic adversity renewed hostilities indicates that, underlying the apparent harmony that prevailed during most of the 1860s and 1870s, there remained a basic weakness in the Irish landlord-tenant relationship.

THE WEAKNESS OF THE SOCIAL BOND

Perhaps the most common explanation that has been given for this weakness is that landlords and tenants in Ireland were divided by race and religion. Writing in the post-famine period, an Irish nationalist argued that the land system would have worked if these differences had not existed. The problem was that the soil had been "given over to be owned by men of one nation and creed, and tilled by men of another race and faith," and that "lord and peasant represented conqueror and conquered."[9] This view overstates the religious homogeneity of both the landowning class and the tenant population. It also underestimates the complexity of the land system. Before the Famine, the great majority of landlords were actually Catholic, if we include, as we should, landlords who did not own land but leased it and then sublet.

Nonetheless, the race and religion explanation contains a certain element of truth. The religious cleavage was, without question, a powerful uniting and dividing force in Irish society. We have already seen how it operated in the pre-famine period to integrate the rural population into social groups that provided the foundations for various forms of collective action. Moreover, the assertion that the majority of landowners in Ireland were Protestant is not a myth; it is an historical fact. There was some increase in the number of Catholic owners in the post-famine period as a result of transfers of land under the Incumbered Estates Act, but only a minority (40 percent) of those returned as landowners in the census of 1871 were of the Catholic religion;[10] and it is well known that Catholic-owned estates were generally smaller than those owned by Protestants. Both Protestant and Catholic proprie-

---

[9] A. M. Sullivan, New Ireland, Political Sketches and Personal Reminiscences of Thirty Years of Irish Public Life (London, 1882), pp. 145-6.

[10] Census of Ireland, 1871: part iii, General report, p. 83 [C 1377], H.C. 1876, lxxxi. This percentage is based on an occupational return. It includes only about one-third of all owners of land, since most owners were listed under other occupations that they pursued. It must therefore be treated with some caution, and we cannot assume that it is representative of all landowners.

tors were socially removed from the rural population by virtue of the higher rank they held and the social circles in which they interacted, but the separation was much greater for Protestant owners as a result of their social exclusiveness, their interlocking friendship networks, and their pronounced tendency to marry within their own group.[11] In addition, and most important for our purposes, the decline in subletting that occurred during and after the Famine probably meant that the proportion of tenants who let directly from a Protestant owner was greater in the post-famine period than was the case before the Famine. This would mean that the percentage of landlords who were Protestant rose even though the percentage of landowners who were Protestant declined. In this rather curious way, class cleavage in nineteenth-century rural Ireland came to coincide more closely with religious cleavage.

The second most common explanation given for the basic weakness in the Irish landlord-tenant relationship has been that many landlords were absentee. Again, care must be taken to avoid some of the myths that have persisted about Irish landlordism. It is simply not true that most of the land in Ireland was owned by persons living outside the country. It had been claimed that over one-third of the landowners in Ireland were absentee in 1830, and that £4 million of the £12 million Irish annual rental was then remitted to absentees. But even this estimate is probably exaggerated, since it represents only a rough guess made by parties who had an interest in demonstrating that absenteeism was widespread and economically damaging to Ireland.[12] Table 10 gives the most accurate data available on the residences of landowners of 100 acres or more. It shows that 13.3 percent of the owners lived outside Ireland in 1870; the estates owned by these absentees covered 23.5 percent of the land; and their land valuation represented 22.3 percent of the total valuation. Clearly, if by absenteeism one means living outside Ireland, then the problem was not critical in 1870. On the other hand, if one includes among absentees all those living away from land they owned, then the

[11] L. P. Curtis, Jr., "The Anglo-Irish predicament" in *Twentieth Century Studies* (Nov. 1970), pp. 42-3.

[12] This estimate can be found in Michael Staunton, *Reasons for a Repeal of the Legislative Union between Great Britain and Ireland* (Dublin, 1845). Lee suggests a figure of £2 million. See Joseph Lee, "Capital in the Irish economy" in L. M. Cullen (ed.), *The Formation of the Irish Economy* (Cork, 1969), pp. 58-9.

TABLE 10 · Absenteeism 1870: Percentage of landed proprietors, acreage of land, and valuation of land distinguished according to residence of proprietor for proprietors with 100 or more acres in 1870

CLASSIFICATION OF PROPRIETORS	PERCENTAGE OF PROPRIETORS	PERCENTAGE OF LAND	PERCENTAGE OF VALUATION
Resident in Ireland	85.5	73.4	75.3
Resident on or near the property	45.8	46.3	49.2
Resident usually elsewhere in Ireland and occasionally on the property	3.1	4.4	3.9
Resident elsewhere in Ireland	36.6	22.7	22.2
Resident out of Ireland	13.3	23.5	22.3
Resident usually out of Ireland but occasionally on the property	1.5	7.1	6.3
Rarely or never resident in Ireland	11.8	16.4	16.0
Public or charitable institutions or public companies	1.3	3.0	2.5
Total number	12,215	19,194,001 acres	£9,591,661

NOTE: The table does not include all landed property in Ireland. It excludes proprietors owning less than 100 acres, all land in cities, towns, and townships, and all properties not ascertained. The data were collected by poor-law inspectors. The source is *Return for 1870 of number of landed proprietors in each county*, p. 8, H.C. 1872 (167), xlvii.

problem appears more serious. Only 45.8 percent of the land-owners in Table 10, with land valued at 49.2 percent of the total valuation, regularly lived on or near their properties.

One cannot assume, of course, that resident landlords had better relations with their tenantry, or even that absenteeism had much effect one way or the other on landlord-tenant relationships. A closely associated factor, which may have made more of a difference, was size of estate. Many Irish properties were extremely large. The Incumbered Estates Act broke up some, but it had only a minor effect on the overall distribution. In 1876 no less than 78 percent of the land was owned by proprietors with estates of 1,000 acres or more, and 48 percent by proprietors with estates of 5,000 acres or more.[13]

What were the effects of this concentration of ownership? On the one hand, large landowners more often had the resources to manage their lands well, grant reductions in rent during hard times, and invest in improvements. Although there was certainly no necessary relationship between estate size and improvements, it is true that the best-known improving landowners had very large properties.[14] In addition, large landowners may have awed their tenantry more and commanded a greater amount of deference.

Yet, as I shall suggest in a moment, we cannot assume that the sort of improvements that Irish landowners preferred to make necessarily engendered better landlord-tenant relations. And expressions of deference could go hand in hand with a willingness to challenge a landlord's property rights. In 1878, just before the Land War, Lord Clanmorris (owner of over 17,000 acres in Galway and Mayo) received an address and presentation from his tenantry on the occasion of his marriage, while at the same time he was having considerable difficulty collecting his rents.[15] Moreover, though large landowners may have had more resources with which to run their estates, they also faced much greater logistical problems as a result of the sheer number of tenants they managed. Agents for the Skinners' Company had to cope with some 1,200 tenants on their estate in Londonderry; the Duke of Abercorn had over 1,000 tenants on his properties in Donegal and Tyrone; Lord Sligo had 1,600 tenants on his estate in Mayo; the Knox estates in Mayo altogether had just over 1,000 tenants; and Lord Dillon reportedly had some 4,000 tenants in Mayo and Roscommon.[16] It is also possible that large estates strengthened solidarity among

[13] Summary of the returns of owners of land in Ireland, showing, with respect to each county, the number of owners below an acre, and in classes up to 100,000 acres and upwards, with the aggregate acreage and valuation of each class, p. 25, H.C. 1876 (422), lxxx.

[14] Donnelly, Landlord and Tenant, p. 57.

[15] Finlay Dun, Landlords and Tenants in Ireland (London, 1881), p. 213.

[16] Ibid., pp. 116, 138-9, 201, 231, 236-7.

farmers. In those areas where estates were especially large, the common interests that farmers would feel as tenants could be reinforced by the fact that they were tenants of the same landlord, to whom they all paid rents and on whom they all depended for possession of their holdings.

Finally, the fact that much of the land in Ireland was taken up by very large estates meant, quite simply, that landowners constituted a smaller social group than would otherwise have been the case. If, for instance, all properties of 1,000 acres or more had been divided up into properties of 500 acres, there would have been over 42,000 estate owners in Ireland as compared with the 14,500 there actually were.[17] It is possible that a greater number of small proprietors would have bolstered the ranks of the landed class, giving it greater strength by augmenting the presence of landowners in a wide variety of social institutions at both the national and local level. A hypothetical proposition of this kind is, of course, difficult to test, but the issue should not be avoided on that account. The relationship between estate size and landlord-tenant relations is an important question for which we need some answers, if for no other reason than because regional differences in the distribution of large estates correlated with some significant variations in Irish agriculture. Specifically, as we just discovered in the preceding chapter, the largest estates were to be found in the poorest parts of the country.[18] Whatever effect large properties had on landlord-tenant relations, it was compounded by economic factors.

These sources of cleavage—racial and religious differences, absenteeism, and perhaps the size of estates—might not have imperiled the land system in any significant way if there had been cooperative economic relationships between landlords and tenants. If the two parties had frequently engaged in joint economic endeavors to their mutual benefit, particularly if landlords had more often assisted tenants in making improvements to their holdings, a stronger tie based on reciprocal interdependence

[17] *Summary of the returns of owners of land*, p. 25. By estate owner I here mean a proprietor with 100 acres or more. The return of 1876 was more complete than the return of 1870 on which Table 10 is based. This accounts for the difference in the total number of proprietors with 100 acres or more. In both returns, proprietors with land in more than one county were counted more than once. Consequently, the figure of 14,500 given in the return of 1876 must have slightly overstated the number of owners.

[18] See above, pp. 144-6.

might have emerged. Cooperative endeavors of this kind were not, however, the rule. True, they were probably more common in the post-famine period than they had been before the Famine, primarily as a result of the Land Improvement Acts, which empowered the Board of Works to make loans to landowners to enable them to improve their estates.[19] In an effort to provide relief works during the Famine, landed proprietors borrowed over £800,000 in the years 1847-9. In the ten-year period from 1850 to 1859 approximately £750,000 was borrowed, in the 1860s approximately £500,000, and then in the 1870s more than £1 million.[20] Much of this money was taken in the form of loans secured by landlords for tenants who then assumed responsibility for the interest and repayment. One historian suggests, however, that even if we include these loans along with rough estimates of other forms of investment, the total represents only 3 to 4 percent of the gross rental in this period.[21] Estate records that have been analyzed suggest a slightly higher rate of expenditure on improvements, but still typically less than 10 percent of the gross rental.[22] Moreover, by "improvements" what was often meant was renovation and beautification of the demesne. Improvements could also include the building of roads, afforestation, arterial drainage and other projects too costly for tenants to undertake. Occasionally, proprietors cooperated with tenants in erecting buildings, in undertaking ordinary drainage, and in building fences. Often the landlord would provide materials, such as timber or slate for buildings, while the tenant provided the labor. Yet these practices were by no means universal.

[19] The first act was passed in 1847. See 10 and 11 Vict., c. 32. This measure was amended in 1850 to permit loans for constructing farm buildings, in 1860 to permit loans for constructing laborers' dwellings, and in 1866 to permit loans for planting for shelter. See 13 and 14 Vict., c. 31; 23 Vict., c. 19; and 29 and 30 Vict., c. 40.

[20] Cormac Ó Gráda, "The investment behaviour of Irish landlords, 1850-1875" in Agricultural History Review, 23, pt. ii (1975).

[21] Ibid. Ó Gráda arrives at this figure by taking the total of about £3 million borrowed from the Board of Works between the Famine and the late 1870s, adding to this £500,000 as a rough estimate of the amount spent on arterial drainage, and then assuming, for the sake of discussion, that at the most another £3.5 million could have been spent in other ways. This gives a total of £7 to £8 million, which represents only 3 to 4 percent of his minimum estimate of total rents (£250 million).

[22] See ibid. where fifteen estates are examined and see also Vaughan, "Landlord and tenant relations," p. 109, where nine estates are examined.

The investment behavior of Irish landlords is not at all mystifying. By the 1860s landowners could usually obtain between twenty and thirty years' purchase for their estates. If an estate was worth, say, twenty-five years' purchase, the annual rental would represent 4 percent of the value of the investment. Even if an owner made few improvements, his profit would be substantially less than 4 percent after taxes, salaries, and other estate costs had been met. By contrast, a relatively safe investment, such as Government and India stock, paid interest rates of between 3 and 5 percent annually, and higher rates could be obtained on other kinds of investment that entailed no greater risk than did Irish rents. When it is furthermore considered that many Irish landlords were still burdened by excessive debts, it is small wonder that they did not invest very much in their estates.[23]

The low level of landlord investment was also a function of certain features of Irish agriculture. Tenants, it should be noted, were equally reluctant to invest in their holdings. The popular explanation for this has been that they lacked the security necessary to induce them to do so. But a number of historians have recently challenged this assumption. They have pointed out that the overwhelming majority of tenants enjoyed de facto if not legal security of tenure, and that tenants were not putting their money into improving their holdings primarily because they were instead buying livestock, which brought larger and more immediate returns in the post-famine period.[24] A tenant might also, of course, be interested in improving his home, or, in some cases, might want to build out-offices or fences. But landlords were, as a rule, willing to help only large tenants make physical improvements on their farms. The presence of a great number of small tenants on most estates made it difficult for landlords to finance buildings and other similar improvements for all of them. More than that, landlords had a prejudice against providing assistance of this kind to small farmers.[25] What typified the most conscientious landlord in Ireland was not an inclination to assist small farmers in making

[23] See Vaughan, "Landlord and tenant relations," pp. 124-8 for a discussion of landlord debts in this period.

[24] Crotty, Irish Agricultural Production; Vaughan, "Landlord and tenant relations," pp. 117, 315-16; Solow, The Land Question and the Irish Economy, pp. 51-88; Donnelly, Landlord and Tenant, pp. 59-60.

[25] Reports from poor law inspectors as to the existing relations between landlord and tenant in respect to improvements on farms, drainage, reclamation of land, fencing, planting etc. . . . , pp. 20, 33-5 [C 31], H.C. 1870, xiv.

physical improvements, but rather a desire to enlarge farms and to consolidate scattered holdings into single units. And yet this sort of improvement, far from endearing a landlord to his tenants, generally created ill-feeling. Finlay Dun described the efforts of Sir Arthur Guinness, first Baron Ardilaun, to square holdings on his estate in Galway:

> Lord Ardilaun has encountered the same difficulties as other landlords who have endeavoured to increase the size of their smaller holdings and provide better dwellings for their people. Those bought out of small farms, miserably inadequate to provide a livelihood, talk as if they had been dispossessed of a magnificent inheritance without requital.[26]

In fact, not much consolidation occurred in the post-famine period. But when it did, it revealed all too clearly one of the major difficulties with the Irish landlord-tenant relationship: the most conscientious and improving landlord was often the most unpopular. "It is a very curious thing," an agricultural expert told the Bessborough commission in 1880, "that what the people call a good landlord is a man who lets them alone."[27]

Perhaps the best example of what people thought was a "bad" landlord is the notorious third Earl of Leitrim, who owned approximately 76,000 acres of land in the counties of Donegal and Leitrim. His improvements included extensive efforts to square holdings by giving more land to favored tenants, moving others, and ejecting some altogether. Although it was customary for him to compensate those who were ejected, a feeling of intense hostility developed against the man among his tenants, reinforced by his abrasive personality, his determination to enforce the rules of the estate, and rumors that he had taken advantage of a tenant's daughter.[28] On 2 April 1878, while some eighty evictions were reportedly being carried out on his lands, Lord Leitrim, his clerk, and his driver were slain on a deserted road in the north of County Donegal.

There remains much that can be debated about the investment behavior of Irish landlords in the post-famine period. Yet none of this debate will, I believe, invalidate the point being made here,

[26] Dun, Landlords and Tenants in Ireland, p. 248.

[27] Quoted in Solow, The Land Question and the Irish Economy, p. 81.

[28] See Vaughan, "Landlord and tenant relations," pp. 219-20; and Annual Register, 1879, pp. 35-6.

which is simply that landlord investment was not a major source of strength for the land system. True enough, the notion that Irish landlords never invested in their estates is plainly false. On the other hand, it is also clear that such cooperation between landlords and tenants as did occur was insufficient to function as an integrative mechanism. Whatever held the system together, it was obviously not landlord-tenant economic cooperation. Nor was it any sort of strong social attachment of the kind that might have evolved out of common culture or intensive social interaction. What, then, was the basis of the land system? What enabled Irish landlordism, despite these fundamental weaknesses, to survive as long as it did?

Landlord Control over the Use of Land

The cohesion of the Irish land system depended primarily on the power that landlords exercised over tenants. There was, first of all, the immense political power wielded by landlords in both national politics and local government. The second source of power was the legal control landlords had over land and the terms by which members of the rural population were able to obtain it. These two sources of power were very much interwoven and served to reinforce one another, but for the sake of convenience I shall treat them separately. The political power of landlords will be examined in the following chapter. My concern here is with their legal control over land.

NON-CONTRACTUAL PRIVILEGES

"I now send you a list of applicants for grazing in Tully," wrote G. F. Stewart, land agent to the fourth Earl of Leitrim, in a letter addressed to his lordship in April 1879. "The only competition seems to be between Moloney and Wm. Spolton for nos. 6 and 7. Moloney had them last year and though his offer is less than Spolton's, I think it would be hard to pass him over. He has always behaved very well and obediently. Thomas Lipsey has asked for field no. 2, but I don't think he deserves it or anything else from you, and as Johnston is out in the cold you might let him have that field."[29] In numerous ways, some subtle, some not so subtle, Irish

[29] N.L.I., Leitrim papers: Letter book of G. F. Stewart: Stewart to Lord Leitrim, 22 April 1879. The ownership of the Leitrim properties was in dispute at this time. See Appendix A for an explanation.

landlords and their agents used their legal control over land to induce tenants to be "good" tenants—to pay their rents, look after their holdings, obey the rules of the estate, and in some cases, to vote for the landlord's candidate in elections. Concretely, their power took the form of conferring what I shall call *non-contractual privileges*, that is, privileges that landlords were not legally required to grant, but nevertheless did grant, at least partly in order to maintain tenant compliance and to reward good tenants. The conventional portrait of Irish landlords as harsh and demanding is not only inaccurate; it also prevents our understanding how tenants were bound to the land system. As a rule, Irish landlords were indulgent, not because they were a particularly magnanimous lot, but because indulgence was one of the major cornerstones on which the land system rested.

We can begin with a few illustrations of miscellaneous noncontractual privileges. On most estates, tenants were prohibited (either by the terms of their leases or by estate rules) from subdividing, subletting, building, or turning up pasture, at least without permission from the landlord or his agent. Granting such permission, or ignoring violations of these rules, was one kind of privilege that a landlord might confer on all or some of his tenants. In the pre-famine period, landlords frequently ignored much of the subdivision that occurred on their properties. After the Famine, they were generally less lenient, but if a farm was sufficiently large, or if the tenant had been cooperative in the past, or if he made some commitment for the future, the privilege of subdividing was occasionally granted.[30] Another privilege was to allow tenants reductions in their rents or to permit them to fall into arrears during hard times. In 1839 the second Earl of Leitrim instructed the agent for his Mohill estate to threaten all tenants with demands for arrears, with the withdrawal of abatements, or simply with the loss of any "indulgence" should they fail to improve their holdings.[31] Even after the Famine, abatements or arrears were commonly permitted whenever tenants were either individually or collectively experiencing economic difficulties. Although rents were now generally paid on time, arrears could be found in varying degrees on almost all estates, and in at least some cases, they were accumulated with the permission of the

[30] Donnelly, *Cork*, p. 163.
[31] N.L.I., Leitrim papers: Second Earl of Leitrim's directions.

owner or his agent because the tenant was for some reason unable to pay. A similar privilege was the six-month credit (or "hanging gale" as it was often called), which was given to tenants on most estates. This was, in a sense, the landlord's equivalent to the credit granted by shopkeepers, and it served much the same purpose. It was especially useful to incoming tenants, who were thereby given time to raise livestock and reap a harvest before making their first payment. It was, however, the subject of great controversy, since it augmented the landlord's power over his tenants. Throughout the nineteenth century, critics of the six-month credit reiterated Wakefield's denunciation when in 1811 he referred to the hanging gale as "one of the great levers of oppression by which the lower classes are kept in a kind of perpetual bondage, for as every family almost holds some portion of land, and owes half a year's rent, which a landlord can exact in a moment; this debt hangs over their heads like a load, and keeps them in a continual state of anxiety and terror."[32]

Let us now turn to the three paramount privileges that served to bind tenants to the land system: permission to sell, moderate rents, and undisturbed occupancy.

PERMISSION TO SELL   This refers to the practice of allowing a tenant to sell the "interest" in his holding to another tenant when he quit the farm voluntarily or involuntarily. The sale of holdings is most often associated with the province of Ulster, where it was generally regarded not as a privilege, but instead as a customary right known either as "tenant right" or as the "Ulster custom." In the remainder of the country, however, it was a privilege, which, though common, was not universally granted. On those southern estates where sales were permitted, tenants were almost always required to obtain permission in each individual case. The sale was usually closely supervised by the landlord or his agent; ceilings were often placed on the amounts that could be paid; and tenants were typically not allowed to advertise their farms in the press.[33] Most important, the landlord or his agent normally insisted on the right to accept or reject a prospective purchaser, and it was not unusual for them to restrict the acceptable purchasers to

[32] Edward Wakefield, *An Account of Ireland, Statistical and Political*, I (London, 1812), p. 244.

[33] Donnelly, *Cork*, pp. 210-13; Vaughan, "Landlord and tenant relations," pp. 273-4.

those who were already tenants on the estate, to adjoining tenants, or to some other specified tenant.[34] Although a number of considerations could persuade a landlord to place such restrictions on a sale, even the least vindictive owner would be more likely to do so if the outgoing tenant had been uncooperative. To deny the right of sale altogether, or to place a limit on the amount that could be paid, could mean a serious financial loss to a tenant; but even restricting the acceptable purchasers could sharply reduce the value of the sale by limiting the number of bidders. It gave a tenant good reason to avoid incurring his landlord's displeasure.

MODERATE RENTS   The majority of Irish tenants enjoyed the privilege of occupying their holdings at a moderate rent. There were no legal obstacles to prevent a landlord from raising a tenant's rent when the term of his tenancy expired, which, for most Irish tenants, was every year.[35] Technically, a landlord could have forced a tenant either to pay whatever rent an outside tenant might be willing to offer for his holding, or to allow the outside tenant to take his place. Yet it is now well known, from estimates that have been made of the rate of increase in rents during the post-famine period, that landlords did not generally do this. The practice of auctioning a holding off to the highest bidder was known as "canting." According to some contemporary observers, it was common in the pre-famine period, though the moral indignation that it could provoke suggests that, even then, it was the exception rather than the rule. Moreover, when it did occur, canting was normally used for letting vacated holdings rather than for raising the rent on an incumbent. After the Famine, canting was not the typical method of letting even vacant farms, primarily because landlords found that the tenants whom they acquired in this manner were not usually the best tenants, but rather the most irresponsible.[36] The truly outstanding feature of Irish rents was that landlords did not routinely increase them in response to increases in the value of land or agricultural prices. Instead they preferred, if the holding were occupied by a "good" tenant, to leave the rent unchanged over a long period of time. It is possible to find

[34] Donnelly, Cork, pp. 213-15.

[35] A return of 1870 indicated that 77 percent of all agricultural holdings were occupied by tenants-at-will. See Return showing the number of agricultural holdings in Ireland and the tenure by which they are held by the occupiers, pp. 16-17.

[36] Donnelly, Cork, pp. 189-93.

numerous examples of estates where rents were not raised significantly for ten, twenty, or even thirty years at a stretch.[37] Most tenants, therefore, lived with the knowledge that the rent they paid was less than their landlord could have charged.

UNDISTURBED OCCUPANCY   This was by far the most important non-contractual privilege that landlords granted their tenants. Until 1870 the law placed almost no restriction on the rights of landlords to evict tenants when the term of their tenure expired, save that the landlord had to give the tenant a half-year's notice to quit and had to obtain an ejectment decree in court in order to have the tenant forcibly removed by the civil authorities. Even after 1870, though they had to bear some costs in order to do so, landlords were still legally free to evict tenants. And yet, as we have seen, the rate of eviction was low. In the twenty-five years from 1855 to 1880 it was less than 3 percent. Though legally vulnerable to eviction, the vast majority of tenants enjoyed continuous occupancy. This was the privilege that landlords used more than any other to persuade them to cooperate and to obey the rules of the estate.

More than occasionally, the right of the landlord to evict was not left implicit, but was directly asserted in order to control tenants. The most common way of doing this was by making effective use of notices to quit, ejectment processes, or even ejectment decrees. In the years 1866-70, the number of civil-bill ejectments sought in court was seven times the number of families evicted (without readmission) according to the Constabulary returns; and the number of civil-bill ejectment decrees obtained by landlords was five times the reported number of evictions.[38] We have no statistics on notices to quit, but they were certainly even more numerous. Obviously, landlords found it either advantageous or necessary to threaten tenants with ejectment far more often than they found it necessary to put them out.

The threat of eviction was naturally a common method of forcing tenants to pay rents or to accept increases in rents. The agent for the Dungannon school estates in County Tyrone liked to have notices to quit ready in advance for each gale day.[39] J. P. Mc-

[37] Ibid.

[38] *Abstract return of the number of civil bill ejectment processes entered, heard and decided in each of the years 1866-73*, H.C. 1875 (260), lxii; *Return of evictions from 1849 to 1880*, p. 3.

[39] Vaughan, "Landlord and tenant relations," p. 174.

Extract from testimony before the Bessborough commission of Alexander Kirkpatrick, land agent to Lord Portarlington, 9 September 1880

Q: Have you had any ejectments for non-payment of rent?

A: Oh, I have had ejectments for non-payment of rent—that is, I have sent notice to the solicitor to serve ejectments for non-payment of rent but then they would all be settled.

Q: Within the last three years have you had any?

A: I had. My practice was that I gave the people up to the 1st of December to pay the March rents, there having been always a hanging half-year gale on the property. Then if they did not pay them by the first Friday in December, I would send their names to the solicitor to serve ejectment processes for the January sessions.

Q: That is, except they came in, I suppose, and gave you good reasons?

A: In every case, they came in and gave me good reasons, and paid up, and in no case did it proceed to going with the sheriff.

SOURCE: Bessborough commission, vol. ii: *Digest of evidence; minutes of evidence*, pt. i, pp. 138-9 [C 2779-I], H.C. 1881, xviii.

Geough Bond automatically served notices to quit on all his tenants when he purchased an estate in Armagh in 1869, and again on all his tenants in 1872 when he notified them of an increase in their rents.[40] Alexander Kirkpatrick, land agent to Lord Portarlington, frequently resorted to ejectment notices to collect rents. His considered opinion was that "if you don't serve people with notices sometimes they will do nothing."[41]

Such a handy instrument had numerous other applications as well. Although one poor-law inspector reported in 1870 that notices to quit were no longer "used, as formerly, as an engine to keep tenants up to the mark," several other inspectors claimed that they were still issued for such purposes as settling disputes among tenants, preventing tenants from leaving their farms to work on the harvests in England, forcing them to sign special

[40] *Kilkenny Journal*, 10 Jan. 1872, p. 4.
[41] Bessborough commission, vol. ii, p. 138.

agreements, or simply for "misconduct."[42] In his study of land-lord-tenant relations in the post-famine period, William Vaughan cites cases of landlords serving notices to quit (or securing eject-ment decrees) in order to curb subdivision, force tenants to make improvements, discourage trespass on meadows, bogs, or game preserves, and prevent poaching or squatting.[43] On the Fitz-william estates an annual average of eighty notices to quit were served on tenants for such activities as dividing without consent, encouraging lodgers, subletting, accepting squatters, bad farming, non-residence, and in the case of one tenant, for beating his wife.[44] Land agents often found that the most effective way of set-tling family disputes over land was to serve notices to quit or to obtain ejectment decrees against all parties concerned.[45] And it was even known for landlords or agents to use their right of ejectment to protect themselves or their families from attack. In one remarkable example, a Leitrim landowner, Colonel J. J. White, upon receiving a threatening letter in January of 1862, immedi-ately assembled all his tenants and "addressed them at some length, saying that he had made his will, leaving all his property to his eldest son, and that should his death be caused by violence that he . . . directed that all his tenantry should be removed from the property."[46]

We should not assume from these examples that most tenants were routinely presented with notices to quit or subjected to ver-bal threats of eviction. On the contrary, though such practices must be given attention because they help us understand how the landlord's right to evict could be used, they were not typical. If a landlord had to serve notice against a tenant, it meant that his im-plicit powers had broken down. "Good" tenants did not need to be reminded that the possession of their farms and other privi-leges were theirs at the sufferance of their landlord. And most landlords were very careful not to offend good tenants by bran-dishing their powers unnecessarily. Contrary to popular mythol-ogy, landlords and tenants in nineteenth-century Ireland were not

[42] *Reports of poor law inspectors as to the existing relations between landlord and tenant*, pp. 14, 22, 40-42.

[43] Vaughan, "Landlord and tenant relations," pp. 177-8.

[44] Ibid., p. 180.

[45] For examples, see ibid., p. 179; and T.C.D., Trinity College papers: J. E. Butler to bursar, 1 March 1888 (MUN/P/3/124).

[46] S.P.O., Chief Secretary's Office, Registered Papers: Jeremiah Browne, Sub-inspector for Drumkeeran, to Inspector General, 9 Jan. 1862 (1880/12174).

always engaged in bitter fights. Particularly during the post-famine accommodation, many tenants got along well with their landlord and regarded him as the basis of their economic security. They did so, I submit, primarily as a result of the non-contractual privileges he granted them.

THE LAND ACTS

Once we recognize the function of non-contractual privileges in the operation of the land system, we are in a much better position to understand reactions to several post-famine statutes affecting the occupation of agricultural land in Ireland. During the period in which we are interested, the legislative measures that caused the greatest controversy among landlords and tenants were the Incumbered Estates Act of 1849 and the Land Act of 1870.

THE REACTION OF TENANTS TO THE INCUMBERED ESTATES ACT This act established the Incumbered Estates Court (Landed Estates Court after 1858) with the power to order the sale of an estate at the request of an owner or creditor, notwithstanding statutes, settlements, deeds, or covenants to the contrary.[47] The main purpose of the act was to free for sale the properties of bankrupt landlords, but it was also expected that the land system would thereby benefit from an influx of capital. Many of the existing owners seemed far too burdened with debts and settlements to manage their estates properly, and it was hoped that new owners would have more money to invest. Some members of the government even anticipated that many buyers would be English or Scottish. It was also thought that the greater security of title that the act gave to new owners would result in greater security of title to occupiers. And, in general, it was hoped that a new breed of landlords would arrive who would make greater efforts to improve their estates and cooperate with their tenants.[48]

As it turned out, about one-quarter of the land in the country

[47] 12 and 13 Vict., c. 77. This act became law on 28 July 1849. An earlier act, passed in 1848, enabled persons to petition the Court of Chancery for sales of estates, but few petitions were presented (11 and 12 Vict., c. 48). Subsequent acts amended the law of 1849, the most important of which was an act passed in 1858. It extended the powers of the Incumbered Estates Court and changed its name to Landed Estates Court (21 and 22 Vict., c. 72).

[48] For a discussion and analysis of the thinking that lay behind the passage of these acts, see P. G. Lane, "The Encumbered Estates Court, Ireland, 1848-1849" in *Economic and Social Review*, 3, no. 3 (April 1972).

changed hands during the thirty years in which the act was in effect, with the result that existing owners remained in possession
of the majority of estates. Moreover, most purchasers under the act
were not English or Scottish; they were Irish. And far from setting
an example of good landlord-tenant relations, they quickly acquired a reputation for treating their tenants harshly. The usual
explanation for the unpopularity of these new owners was that
they came from a bourgeois class with comparatively mercenary
values, and, further, that they had insufficient financial resources
to enable them to treat tenants leniently. They were, so it has been
claimed, mostly shopkeepers, businessmen, attorneys, and "gombeen men," determined to raise their social standing and to make
a good investment by buying a little land. According to one
statement of this view, the purchasers "are chiefly mercantile men
who saved money in trade, and invest it at a safe percentage. They
import what the country people call 'the ledger and day-book
principle' into the management of their purchases, which contrasts unfavourably with the more elastic system of the old owners."[49] Yet this view plainly exaggerates the non-mercenary
values of the old owners, as well as their financial resources.
Moreover, research recently carried out in County Cork suggests
that most of the new owners were of the gentry class.[50] What,
then, explains their unpopularity?

My suggestion would be that the whole issue of the social characteristics of purchasers has been a red herring. What was important about those who bought land under the Incumbered Estates
Act was not their social background, but simply the fact that they
were new owners. The transfer of ownership of an estate, regardless of who bought it, presented tenants with the danger that the
non-contractual privileges they had enjoyed in the past would not
be respected by the new owner. One of the major purposes of
the Incumbered Estates Court was to establish once and for all
the rights of owners and to provide purchasers with a clear title.
Those legal or customary rights that tenants could demonstrate
before the Court were (at least theoretically) protected,[51] but
otherwise tenants were left to the mercy of the new owner. In 1851
several members of parliament introduced in the House of Commons a bill designed to empower the Court to grant leases to

[49] Sullivan, *New Ireland*, p. 142.   [50] Donnelly, *Cork*, p. 131.
[51] See 12 and 13 Vict., c. 77, clause xxiii; and *General rules and orders of the
Landed Estates Court*, p. 3, H.C. 1859 (83—sess. 1), xxii.

tenants-at-will; they claimed that "great hardship and inconven-
ience have arisen by reason of the uncertainty and insecurity of
the tenure of persons holding and occupying land" that was being
sold under the act of 1849.[52] This bill was never enacted. On the
other hand, in 1853 the original act was amended to permit the
Incumbered Estates Court to include rent arrears in the sale of an
estate, thus ensuring that a new owner would have a strong incen-
tive to collect debts that his predecessor had permitted.[53]

It may be true that "new" owners treated tenants more harshly
than did "old" owners. They may have been more anxious to consolidate holdings or to raise rents, though we still lack the kind of
systematic information we need on this question.[54] Even if this
were true, however, we could explain it without assuming that
the new owners were an unusually heartless or mercenary group.
It was easy enough for a new owner to think that the estate he
bought belonged to him, as it was when he inspected it and as it
had been described in the advertisement of sale. He would be
more likely than the previous owner to ignore non-contractual
privileges traditionally granted to tenants, including the privilege
of undisturbed occupancy. He might not realize until after he had
purchased the estate that his tenants would claim much of what
he thought belonged to him as the fruit of *their* improvements,
and that they would resent any efforts he might make to charge a
rent more closely reflecting the value of the farms. And he might
well have taken literally the claims frequently made in advertisements of estates that "a very large increase can be had upon the
rental" when leases expired.[55] Tenants, for their part, could
hardly be expected to view a prospective sale with anything but
alarm, at least if the sale was accompanied by advertisements of
this kind, as they usually were. The anxiety felt by so many is well
illustrated by a case appearing before the Castlerea quarter ses-

[52] *A bill to encourage and facilitate the granting of leases on encumbered estates
in Ireland*, H.C. 1851 (109), iii.

[53] 16 and 17 Vict., c. 64, clause ix. The same provision was included in the act
that established the Landed Estates Court in 1858. See 21 and 22 Vict., c. 72, clause
lviii.

[54] Some detailed research has been done for Galway and Mayo. See Lane, "General impact of the Encumbered Estates Act on Galway and Mayo."

[55] P.R.O.I., O'Brien rentals: Estates of the Duke of Leinster, Kildare (vol. 76, ID/
24/20), p. 3. The Bessborough commissioners referred to the consequences of the
routine inclusion of such claims in advertisements. See Bessborough commission,
vol. i, p. 6.

sions in 1872. A tenant from Ballycummin, County Roscommon, became concerned when he discovered that the estate on which his holding was situated was being sold through the Landed Estates Court and that the advertisement indicated that his rent could be increased by one-half on the expiration of his lease. The tenant went to court to register the value of improvements that he had made on the property "so that intending purchasers could see that at the expiration of his lease the claimant would at least be entitled to that sum." The lawyer for the landlord tried to persuade the court that the tenant was unduly alarmed; he noted that the statement in the advertisement was not placed there by the authority of the Landed Estates Court, but was merely "one of those puffs usually attached to such sales."[56] Needless to say, assurances of this kind neither convinced tenants that their rent would not be raised, nor dissuaded new owners from putting the increases that they had been promised into effect.

No doubt, many purchasers were aware in advance of the non-contractual privileges granted on the estate they were buying; and many more accepted them in time to prevent a serious rift with their tenants. Yet the unfavorable reputation of the new owners, as a group, was primarily the result of the failure of some of them to abide by customs that had long prevailed on their properties. This argument is, of course, not inconsistent with the possibility that purchasers under the Incumbered Estates Act did indeed hold more mercenary values than old owners, though no convincing evidence has yet been presented to demonstrate that such was generally the case. Whether or not they were more mercenary, however, the mere fact that they were new owners would have made them less likely to respect traditions of non-contractual privileges.

THE REACTION OF LANDLORDS TO THE LAND ACT OF 1870[57]   In order to understand why landlords reacted as they did to this law, it is necessary to appreciate how the act of 1870 differed from previous legislation affecting landlord-tenant relations in Ireland. The two most recent statutes, passed in 1860, had served primarily to protect property rights. The first, known as the Cardwell Act, entitled tenants to compensation for certain types of improvements carried out at their own expense, but only if these improvements had been made with the consent of the landlord.[58]

[56] *Roscommon Journal*, 19 Oct. 1872, p. 2.
[57] 33 and 34 Vict., c. 46.   [58] 23 and 24 Vict., c. 153.

The second, known as the Deasy Act, was a more comprehensive measure which sought to bring together all existing legislation bearing on landlord-tenant relations.[59] It reaffirmed existing procedures by which landlords could evict tenants when tenancies expired or before such time if they were not paying their rents.[60] It also sought to protect landlords from any customary rights to which tenants might lay claim. It explicitly denied legal status to non-contractual agreements between landlords and tenants, thus assuring landlords of the legal authority to grant or to refuse non-contractual privileges at their pleasure. "The relation of landlord and tenant," the act stated, "shall be deemed to be founded on the express or implied contract of the parties, and not upon tenure or service." The act not only guaranteed landlords the right to deny a new term of occupancy to any tenant whose term had expired, but also contained provisions clarifying the owner's right to control subletting, mining, quarrying, turf cutting, soil burning, or tree cutting on his estate.

The purpose of the Land Act of 1870 was altogether different. Rather than deny the customary rights of tenants, the English Liberals who drew up this statute sought to give these rights legal protection. Gladstone wanted to legalize Ulster tenant right throughout Ireland, but opposition within his own government was too strong.[61] In the bill that was presented to the House and that eventually became law, tenant right was deemed legal and enforceable in the civil-bill courts in the province of Ulster and in other parts of the country where a usage prevailed that corresponded to the Ulster custom. Where tenant right did not prevail, the act sought to provide equivalent protection to tenants. It did so by enabling a tenant who had been evicted (and who was not in arrears) to collect, through the civil-bill court, compensation from his landlord for "disturbance" and for the value of improvements made by the tenant or by his predecessors in title. The act also enabled a tenant evicted for non-payment of rent to collect compensation for certain kinds of improvements, and it decreed that, un-

[59] 23 and 24 Vict., c. 154.

[60] The procedures governing evictions were almost identical in the Deasy Act to those in the Civil Bill Act of 1851 (14 and 15 Vict., c. 57), save that the Deasy Act permitted landlords to take action against tenants in a civil-bill court if the rent did not exceed £100, whereas in the Act of 1851 the limit had been £50, and previous to that it had been £20.

[61] E. D. Steele, *Irish Land and British Politics: Tenant-Right and Nationality* (London, 1974), especially Chapter 6.

less evidence existed to the contrary, all improvements should be assumed to have been made by the tenant.[62]

The authors of the Land Act of 1870 were perfectly aware that most tenants in Ireland enjoyed *de facto* security of tenure as well as other related privileges. Yet they insisted that these privileges required legal protection to safeguard the interests of tenants whose landlords denied them. Supporters of the act argued that legislation making legal what most landlords were doing anyway could not do these landlords any harm. Landlords were still free to raise rents. Since most evictions were for non-payment of rent, in most cases landlords would be required to compensate only for improvements; and they could usually deduct a large portion of this compensation from the arrears due. Furthermore, the act could not harm good landlords because compensation of any kind had to be paid only when a tenant was actually evicted. Since they rarely resorted to eviction, the majority of landlords had nothing to fear. Nevertheless, the act raised a chorus of protest from the landed class. Landlords claimed that it seriously threatened their financial interests and made it difficult for them to manage their estates. Why?

The explanation for this outcry lies in the way that landlords used their power of eviction. As we have seen, the low rate of eviction does not reflect the use that landlords made of the threat of it to control the behavior of tenants. What landlords feared was that the Land Act would take this power away from them because tenants would now be able to call their bluff and force them to carry out the eviction at considerable cost. Under the new act, tenants were able to counter the threat of ejectment with the threat of extensive claims for compensation. Many landlords and agents argued that, as a result of the act, they were no longer able to make improvements on their estates or to grant certain kinds of customary privileges (such as permission to build, abatements for making improvements, the right to sell the interest in a holding, or allowance to use land temporarily), since they might subsequently be forced to pay for these indulgences.[63]

---

[62] In the case of evictions for non-payment of rent on holdings whose annual rent did not exceed £15, if the civil-bill court found the rent to be exorbitant, it could treat the eviction as a disturbance and require the landlord to compensate the tenant for this disturbance as well as for improvements.

[63] *Report from the select committee of the House of Lords on the Landlord and Tenant (Ireland) Act, 1870; together with the proceedings of the committee, min-*

How did landlords, in fact, respond to the Land Act of 1870? Loans granted by the Board of Works under the Land Improvement Acts rose from about £500,000 in the 1860s to over £1 million in the 1870s, suggesting that they invested more rather than less in their estates after 1870.[64] It is unlikely that they did so *because* of the Land Act, but the act obviously did little to discourage investment. On the other hand, it does seem that many owners became much more strict about sales on their estates in order to protect themselves from incurring heavy compensation for purchase premiums.[65] And it is almost certain that they began to grant more leases. They did so for two reasons. First, the provisions of the Land Act of 1870 made it possible for some leaseholders to contract out of any benefits under the act.[66] Second, landlords could include in leases provisions that strengthened estate rules against activities for which they might later have to pay compensation; they could insert clauses prohibiting the sale of a holding or restricting the construction of buildings or other expensive improvements. The most famous leases granted in this period were those used on the estates of the Duke of Leinster. They contained the usual covenants with respect to crop rotation, maintenance, and succession, but they also required tenants to relinquish claims to compensation, either for disturbance or for improvements, except for improvements made with the written consent of the lessor.[67] The "Leinster lease" became, in common

---

utes of evidence, appendix, and index, pp. 57-9, 114-15, 145-6, H.L. 1872 (403), xi. Similar statements were made before the Bessborough commission. Solow notes that the index to the Bessborough commission lists thirty-three witnesses who said that the Land Act had discouraged landlord improvements as against three or four who said it had no effect. See Solow, *The Land Question and the Irish Economy*, p. 86, note 48.

[64] James S. Donnelly, Jr., review of *The Land Question and the Irish Economy, 1870-1903* by Barbara L. Solow in *Studia Hibernica*, no. 13 (1973), p. 187.

[65] Donnelly, *Cork*, pp. 215-16.

[66] Tenants whose holdings were valued at £50 or more could contract in writing not to make any claim for compensation under the act. Furthermore, all tenants who held a lease for a term of thirty-one years or longer could not claim any compensation for disturbance, and could claim compensation for improvements only if it was allowed in the lease—with the exception of compensation for permanent buildings, reclamation of wasteland, and unexhausted manures or tillage.

[67] Dun, *Landlords and Tenants in Ireland*, pp. 26-7; Bessborough commission, vol. ii, pp. 46-7. Leases for tenants whose valuation was under £50 contained a clause by which the tenant agreed not to make a claim to compensation for any goodwill payment that he had paid on coming into the holding. Leases for tenants

parlance, a term that designated any lease seeking to contract tenants out of the Land Act of 1870.

Whether as a consequence of these precautions, or because such precautions were unnecessary, the Land Act of 1870 did landlords very little damage. True enough, tenants sometimes used the act to strengthen their bargaining position. When a landlord employed the threat of ejectment to force a tenant to abide by the rules of the estate or to accept an increase in rent, some tenants used the threat of heavy compensation for disturbance or improvements to force the landlord to moderate his demands. In most such struggles, the tenant was no more interested in actually receiving compensation than was the landlord in actually evicting the tenant. Both were simply using their respective rights before the court to bargain with the other. Consequently, over half of the claims entered into court under the Land Act between 1870 and 1878 were settled without a court decision.[68] Typical was the case of a tenant who sought to register improvements at the Athlone quarter sessions in October of 1872 in order to satisfy his landlord that he had "a just claim for a renewal of his lease on reasonable terms"; the tenant eventually received a new lease for thirty-one years.[69] Yet the number of tenants who tried to use the act in this way was small. From its enactment in August 1870 until the end of 1875, less than 4,000 claims for compensation were entered into court by tenants, far fewer than the number of civil-bill ejectment processes entered by landlords, which rose from roughly 17,000 for the period 1866-70 to roughly 25,000 for the period 1871-5. The number of decrees for compensation obtained by tenants was only about 1,000 by the end of 1875, while the number of civil-bill eviction decrees obtained by landlords was over 8,000 for the years 1871-3 alone.[70] Clearly landlords

whose valuation was £50 or more did not contain this clause, but instead contained a clause by which the tenant agreed not to make any claim to compensation under the provisions of the Land Act either for disturbance or for improvements, except improvements made with the written consent of the lessor. It was alleged before the Bessborough commission that, in contravention of the Land Act, the second kind of lease was being forced on tenants whose valuation was under £50.

[68] Statistical summaries of proceedings under the Land Act of 1870 were published yearly in Thom's.

[69] Roscommon Journal, 26 Oct. 1872, p. 2.

[70] I have taken the number of claims and the number of decrees for compensation from yearly tables in Thom's. For the years 1866-73, I obtained the number of civil-bill ejectment processes and eviction decrees from Abstract return of the

were still able to use the threat of ejectment against their tenants after 1870 as they had done before.

There were probably three reasons for this. First, some tenants may have been unaware of the rights granted to them by the act. Second, even if aware of these rights, many would have been unable to bear the legal costs of taking advantage of them. And third, tenants were usually so afraid of eviction that, with or without compensation, they were prepared to come to terms with their landlord in order to prevent it. This third reason was by far the most important. Taking a landlord to court was a dangerous way in which to bargain with him. In order to take advantage of the Land Act the tenant "is forced to begin by a surrender of the only thing for which he really cares," remarked the Bessborough commissioners in 1881. In the same year Finlay Dun summarized the effect of the Land Act of 1870 by noting that, to establish his claims, the tenant is "driven to appeal to a law court, to stand forth in antagonism to his landlord, and thus usually to destroy his chance of retaining his holding. Rather than thus run the risk of being removed, he submits to almost any advance of rent or to other arrangements detrimental to his interests."[71] Although the Land Act of 1870 may have effected substantial changes in how estates were managed, particularly in the care that landlords took to protect their property rights through leases, it cannot be argued that it did, in fact, weaken these rights.

THE VULNERABILITY OF THE LAND SYSTEM

Yet the position of Irish landlords was by no means secure. Any institution whose integration relies on non-contractual privileges faces an inherent danger: even though they are not legally entitled to them, those who receive these privileges may eventually expect them as their due. Since Irish landlords usually granted non-contractual privileges continuously over long periods of time, many tenants inevitably came to regard them as customary rights.

number of civil bill ejectment processes, 1866-73. The number of civil-bill ejectment processes is also given each year in the judicial statistics. Although the two sources rarely agree on the exact number of processes, the discrepancies are not great and do not affect our conclusions. Therefore, for the years 1874-5, I have used the number of civil-bill ejectment processes as given in Judicial statistics of Ireland for the year 1875: part ii, common law; equity; civil and canon law, p. 78 [C 1563], H.C. 1876, lxxix.

[71] Bessborough commission, vol. i, p. 7; Dun, Landlords and Tenants in Ireland, p. 4.

For example, tenants now and then claimed customary rights to bogs, rough pastures, and even game preserves. A celebrated case in point was the resistance of tenants in Gweedore, County Donegal, to the letting of mountain pastures on which they had traditionally been allowed to graze their livestock.[72] Cases can also be cited of tenants resenting penalties imposed by landlords for trespass in game preserves, and even instances where tenants tried to deny landlords the right to let bogs or to use game preserves.[73] Claims to game preserves were unusual, however, since most landlords were careful to guard rights of this kind. On the other hand, by leaving rents unchanged for years, sometimes decades, many landlords encouraged the assumption that rents should be low, and should not reflect the real letting value of the land. Similarly, many tenants expected to receive an abatement in their rent when they were having serious trouble making ends meet. And the general practice of leaving the same family in possession of a farm for generations almost inevitably led them to assume that undisturbed occupancy was a customary right rather than a privilege. Many Irish tenants came to believe that they had traditional claims to their holdings. This was especially true in Ulster, where, as we have seen, tenants took it for granted that they would be able to sell their holdings, and landlords usually found themselves powerless to prevent it. Elsewhere in the country, free sale had not become a customary right. Payments to an outgoing tenant were often made secretly, but premiums were generally low by comparison with those in Ulster; and in most places tenants could not openly assert the right to sell. All the same, there was a conviction, even among tenants in the South, that they had proprietary rights to their holdings. For this reason, tenants-at-will were frequently less than enthusiastic about obtaining leases, regarding them as "not a lengthening of the legal yearly tenancy, but a shortening of the continuous traditional tenancy."[74] If they gave up their holdings, they certainly expected some compensation, either from the incoming tenant or from the landlord or from both. Even before the Land Act of 1870, land-

---

[72] Report from the select committee appointed to inquire into the destitution alleged to exist in the Gweedore and Cloughaneely district in the county of Donegal . . . , H.C. 1857-58 (412), xiii.

[73] Report from the select committee of the House of Lords on the Landlord and Tenant (Ireland) Act, 1870, pp. 48, 50, 95, 150, and 153.

[74] Bessborough commission, vol. i, p. 6.

lords often felt obliged to pay outgoing tenants; they typically gave them at least a few pounds to leave quietly, and occasionally they made sizable payments as compensation for improvements.[75] Most revealing of all, it was nearly a universal practice in the South, as well as in the North, for tenants to bequeath their land to members of their families. It was also common for them to put their farms up as security for loans. Landholders in the South may not have enjoyed tenant right, but they frequently behaved as though they did.[76]

Legally landlords still had the upper hand; and on this account the privileges that they granted were still privileges. There were, however, other sources of power available to tenants. If landlords could punish "bad" tenants by withdrawing or threatening to withdraw privileges, tenants could punish "bad" landlords by breaking estate rules, not paying their rents on time, or in other ways being uncooperative. They might also, and in the pre-famine period frequently did, form combinations to resist demands made by their landlords and to enforce what they regarded as their rights. To the extent that a landlord feared these tenant powers, he did not grant privileges voluntarily, but instead because he was forced to do so. The major weakness in the Irish land system lay in the fact that the chief means by which landlords were able to persuade tenants to cooperate was by awarding them non-contractual privileges. Whenever landlords became unable or unwilling to grant these privileges, the integration of tenants into the land system invariably weakened.

[75] There was considerable variation in the poor-law inspectors' reports of 1870. They indicated that in some areas compensation was paid, while in others it was not. See *Reports from poor law inspectors as to the existing relations between landlord and tenant.*

[76] Steele, *Irish Land and British Politics*, especially pp. 7-10.

Six · **Politics Before the Storm**

The Ascendancy

We now broaden the discussion from one very specific sphere of power to the distribution of power in the larger political system. At this time political power in Ireland was heavily concentrated in the hands of a comparatively small social group. The historical basis for this concentration was set in the seventeenth and eighteenth centuries with the establishment of the Protestant Ascendancy. In the nineteenth century new groups emerged to challenge this elite and were able to win a considerable share of its power. They did not, however, displace it. The political elite in Ireland in the mid-nineteenth century was remarkably similar to the political elite of the eighteenth century. Two continuing social characteristics, in particular, stand out.

First, the political elite was still disproportionately, if no longer exclusively, made up of Protestants. The population of the country was roughly three-quarters Catholic, and yet many of the top positions in the government were held more often by Protestants than by Catholics. The highest official ranks were those of lord lieutenant and chief secretary, both of which were typically filled by Englishmen, and at no time in the nineteenth century was either one occupied by a Catholic. The office of under-secretary could be held by a Catholic (and was held by a Catholic from 1869 to 1882), but other high positions in the civil service and the judiciary were most frequently held by Protestants. In the Constabulary, for example, as late as the year 1880 both the inspector-general and the deputy inspector-general were Protestant, and altogether over three-quarters of the upper ranks (as compared with hardly more than one-quarter of the lower ranks) were filled by Protestants.[1] Catholics had been legally entitled to hold higher offices in the judiciary only since 1829, and so they were, not surprisingly, still greatly under-represented in these po-

---

[1] *Return showing the number of officers, and constables, in the Royal Irish Constabulary on 1st day January 1880, distinguishing Protestants and Roman Catholics*, H.C. 1880 (256), lix. I have classified as upper ranks subinspectors and above, while lower ranks consisted of head constables and below.

sitions in the 1860s and 1870s. But the same under-representation could also be found in lower-level courts. Most of the justices who sat on local courts were Protestant; in 1886 three-quarters of the commissions of the peace in Ireland were still held by Protestants.[2] And Protestants were overwhelmingly represented in the British parliament. Virtually all of the non-Irish M.P.s were, of course, Protestant, but even Irish representation was for a long time dominated by Protestants. Sixty-eight of the 105 Irish members elected to the House of Commons in 1868 were Protestants as compared to thirty-seven Catholics.[3]

Second, a disproportionate number of persons in the political elite belonged to the landed class. The lord lieutenant was invariably a landowner, and the chief secretary was usually a landowner or related to a landowner. Most of the under-secretaries appointed during the nineteenth century were sons of landowners, of clergymen, or of officers in the army or navy; and the same may have been true of most of those appointed to other high-level civil service positions. In the British parliament the landed interest was represented both by peers in the House of Lords and by members of the British and Irish propertied classes who sat in the House of Commons. Indeed, until 1885 landowners continued to be elected to the Commons in greater numbers than were commercial men and manufacturers.[4] Landowners exercised an inordinate amount of influence over Irish representation. They acquired this influence in a number of ways: by using their prestige to promote favored candidates, by providing candidates with financial assistance, and especially by telling their tenants how to vote. Ironically, the enfranchisement of Catholics in 1793 did not weaken their political power but actually increased it by transforming the electorate into one composed predominantly of tenants whose votes they could often control. In the first two decades of the nineteenth century landlord electoral power reached its

[2] Return for each county, city and borough in Ireland, giving names of the persons holding the commission of the peace . . . , p. 132, H.C. 1886 (20—sess. 2), liii.

[3] David Thornley, Isaac Butt and Home Rule (London, 1964), p. 210. As Thornley shows, the proportion of Protestants dropped in the election of 1874 when fifty-four Protestants and forty-eight Catholics were elected. Given that Protestants comprised only one-quarter of the population, this is still a remarkable over-representation.

[4] H. J. Hanham, Elections and Party Management: Politics in the Time of Disraeli and Gladstone (London, 1959), p. xvii; cited in Steele, Irish Land and British Politics, p. 43.

peak. One historian claims that during these years there were only six county contests in which voters showed any sign of disobedience to their landlords' instructions.[5]

It has been argued that this influence over the votes of tenants can be explained only partly by landlord intimidation. Several historians assert that it was also a result of what they call "loyalty" or "deference."[6] While this conclusion may, strictly speaking, be correct, we must be careful not to beg the essential question. Why were most tenants loyal? Although it is possible to cite examples of close relations between individual landlords and tenants, if the argument of the preceding chapter is correct, neither strong social attachments nor economic cooperation were sufficiently common to account for this loyalty, if indeed loyalty is the right word. Rather the explanation lies in the non-contractual privileges or favors that landlords and their agents generally granted tenants. Thus the many instances of blatant intimidation one can cite[7] represented merely those cases where landlords or agents were forced to invoke a power that normally operated implicitly and operated most effectively when it was left implicit. Probably the great majority of landlords did little more than make their political wishes clearly known to their tenants, most often in the form of a printed circular, but perhaps also through personal visits to tenants. The basis of their electoral influence, however, was still essentially the same as it was in cases of vulgar intimidation. An illustrative instance is provided by a letter cited by K. T. Hoppen in which a bailiff is given instructions to canvass tenants on an estate in County Wexford during the general election of

[5] J. H. Whyte, "Landlord influence at elections in Ireland, 1760-1885" in *English Historical Review*, 80, no. 317 (Oct. 1965), p. 743. The contests listed by Whyte are: Wexford in 1806, Leitrim in 1812, Wexford and Leitrim in 1818, Sligo in 1822, and Dublin in 1823. Another authority, however, lists six elections between 1807 and 1818 in which the organization of voters by Catholic leaders was "decisive." See P. J. Jupp, "Irish parliamentary elections and the influence of the Catholic vote, 1801-20" in *Historical Journal*, 10, no. 2 (1967), pp. 186-7. Jupp also argues that in many other contests the organized "Catholic vote" had an effect even though it may not have determined the outcome.

[6] Ibid.

[7] See Whyte, "Landlord influence at elections in Ireland," pp. 742-4 and 748-9; J. H. Whyte, *The Independent Irish Party, 1850-9* (Oxford, 1958), pp. 63-82; Macintyre, *The Liberator*, p. 100; Dardis, *The Occupation of Land in Ireland*, p. 3; Thomas P. O'Neill, "From famine to near famine, 1845-1879" in *Studia Hibernica*, no. 1 (1961), pp. 165-6; and Hoppen, "Landlords, society and electoral politics," pp. 85-7.

1859. This particular letter was written by a land agent. He included some notices to be delivered to tenants asking them "to give me one vote for my friend Mr. George," and he instructed the bailiff to "tell each man that if he won't give Mr. George one vote, at least, he must stay at home." If any tenant "comes in and votes entirely against my friend Mr. George, he may expect no favour from me. . . . If I have time I will go to each man myself before the election."[8]

The power that landlords or their agents enjoyed over the votes of tenants was repeatedly challenged throughout the nineteenth century, even in the early decades of the century when this power was so overwhelming.[9] The most serious rivals were Catholic priests, whose influence had become sufficient in the 1820s that they were able, working in conjunction with O'Connell's Catholic Association, to inflict some serious defeats on the Ascendancy interest. The Emancipation campaign marked the beginning of a significant clerical role in parliamentary politics. Yet it did not mark the collapse of landlord power. For at least forty years after Emancipation, the landowning class continued to exercise as much control over the rural electorate as did the Catholic clergy, and sometimes more control. Their power was not undermined—not directly at least—by the Irish Reform Act of 1850, which more than doubled the size of the county electorate. Eventually, as we shall see, these new voters were mobilized against landowners and became the means by which their parliamentary power was destroyed. In the short run, however, the act may actually have increased their power by providing them with more votes that they could command. In any event, the immediate post-famine period witnessed a resurgence of landlord electoral power.[10] In both borough and county constituencies, local issues and in-fighting once again came to assume more importance than national issues or party allegiances; and few electoral contests could claim to be much more than power struggles among local magnates.[11] In these petty encounters, regardless of the outcome,

[8] Hoppen, "Landlords, society and electoral politics," p. 79.

[9] See Jupp, "Parliamentary elections."

[10] Hoppen, "Landlords, society and electoral politics"; and his "Tories, Catholics and the general election of 1859" in *Historical Journal*, 13, no. 1 (1970).

[11] K. T. Hoppen, "National politics and local realities in mid-nineteenth century Ireland" in A. Cosgrave and D. Macartney (eds.), *Studies in Irish History Presented to R. Dudley Edwards* (Naas, 1979).

parliamentary representation remained largely in the hands of
landed proprietors. However bitterly they might fight among
themselves, they were almost unanimous in their reluctance to
support candidates who failed to qualify for membership in their
class.[12] The result was that as late as 1868, seventy-three of the
105 Irish representatives in the House of Commons were from the
landowning class.[13]

LOCAL GOVERNMENT

This parliamentary power was reinforced by an even greater control over local government. The highest administrative offices in
the counties (the lieutenant, high sheriff, and deputy lieutenant)
were invariably held by landowners. And any lower-level position that was thought to confer status or power was, in most cases,
filled by a landowner or someone closely related to a landowner.
The majority of other offices were held by persons friendly to the
landed interest.

The principal governing body in every county was a non-
elected "grand jury," whose main function was to finance and
supervise public works. As grand juries were composed almost
entirely of landowners, the landed class enjoyed maximum power
over the choice of public works to be carried out and the distribution of local patronage. Grand juries had a longstanding reputation for corruption. Jury members were at one time accused of
using their powers for such purposes as providing employment
for tenants whom they favored, enabling defaulting tenants to liq-
uidate arrears, or assisting tenants in distress.[14]

Serious criminal cases were tried at the assizes by public juries
presided over by justices of the higher courts. This served to limit
the power of local landowners over the judicial process, but considerable control still remained. The grand juries were entrusted
with deciding which cases should be sent for trial at the assizes.
Moreover, not all criminal cases were heard at the assizes. Some
were heard at the quarter sessions where landowning influence
was strong. The justices of the peace or magistrates who sat at the
quarter sessions, and also at the petty sessions, were mostly land-

[12] Hoppen, "Landlords, society and electoral politics," p. 73.

[13] Thornley, *Isaac Butt*, p. 207.

[14] Thomas Rice, *An inquiry into the effects of the Irish grand jury laws, as affecting the industry, the improvement and the moral character of the people of England* [should read *Ireland*] (London, 1815), pp. 22-3, 83.

Observations on the workings of local courts by an Irish barrister

Every prisoner put forward for his trial at Quarter Sessions is known to some one or more of the court, perhaps a tenant to some one of them. He is a man of either good or bad character, and may have been undeservedly represented to some one or more of the gentry in his neighbourhood as being a far different description of person from what he really is. If in the opinion of some of the assembled magistrates he is an orderly well-conducted individual, it will be very hard to convict him; while, on the other hand, if he be a wild and troublesome character, half the amount of evidence which will fail to convict in the former case will secure a verdict of guilty against him in the latter. . . . [He] is put forward, and some such whispered observations as the following pass on the bench:—"That is a bad boy; he is from my neighbourhood, and I hear very bad accounts of him; in fact he is a positive nuisance, and my bailiff tells me that some saplings of mine that were stolen must have been taken by him. I know myself he is always trespassing." Or, on the other hand:—"That poor fellow is a tenant of mine, a very regular kind of man, and I hear this whole thing is a charge trumped up against him, because he is going to get some land from me, out of which I had to turn a lot of idle ruffians who never would pay a halfpenny rent."

SOURCE: P. J. McKenna, "On the criminal jurisdiction of courts of quarter sessions in Ireland" in *Journal of the Dublin Statistical Society* (April 1856), pp. 278-9.

owners, sons of landowners, or land agents. They were appointed by the chancellor of Ireland on the recommendation of the lieutenant of the county. They were not required to possess any legal training. And they generally, so it was often charged, allowed personal biases and motives to influence their judgments. It was not unknown for suspects in criminal trials or litigants in civil suits to approach local magistrates and endeavor to persuade them to appear in court on the day of their case to represent their interests. "When I first went to Ireland," one landlord told a House of Lords committee in 1881, "I had the greatest difficulty to prevent people from coming and begging me to listen to their cases before the Petty Sessions."[15]

During the first half of the nineteenth century, local government and judicial administration in Ireland underwent reform and centralization. In 1836 taxpayers were given some measure of control over grand-jury spending through the introduction of special presentment sessions at which proposals for public works were openly discussed before being submitted to the grand jury. More important still, in 1831 a central Board of Works was set up and entrusted with funds to make loans to grand juries or to private individuals for public works, and even to carry out public works itself. Gradually the Board of Works took on more of the functions that had been performed exclusively by grand juries and it became a signficant element, not just in public administration, but in the entire Irish economy.[16]

Other local courts also underwent changes. An act of 1787 had empowered the lord lieutenant to appoint barristers in disturbed areas who were to assist magistrates at the quarter sessions. In the following decade assistant barristers could be appointed in every county and were given jurisdiction over civil-bill suits involving less than £20. In the subsequent period their jurisdiction was extended and their influence over the magistrates with whom they sat at the criminal quarter sessions was increased.[17] These assistant barristers were trained legal men with a mandatory six (later ten) years' standing in the profession. They were less often from the landed class than were magistrates, and were, presumably, committed to universal legal norms. Another important development began in 1814 when the lord lieutenant was given the right to appoint special "stipendiary magistrates" (or "resident magistrates" as they later came to be called) in disturbed areas. In 1822 he was empowered to name them in any area where local magistrates requested one; further changes in the appointment of stipendiary magistrates were made in the 1830s and in the late 1850s. By 1860 there were seventy-two stipendiary magistrates in the country, operating under strict central control from Dublin.[18]

One of the most urgent questions that needs to be answered by

[15] Irish Magistrate, *The Irish Magistracy* (Dublin, 1885), pp. 14-15.

[16] Ó Tuathaigh, *Ireland Before the Famine*, pp. 95-7.

[17] In 1858 the title of this office was changed to chairman of the quarter sessions and in 1877 to county court judge.

[18] R. B. McDowell, *The Irish Administration, 1801-1914* (London, 1964), p. 115.

Irish historians is what effect these changes in government administration had on the political strength of the landed class. There
can be no doubt that the steady transfer of power to the growing
government bureaucracy in Dublin Castle undermined their position to a considerable extent, but until a thorough analysis is
completed we cannot confidently say by how much. Since members of the grand juries continued to be selected by the high sheriff
from £50 freeholders or £100 leaseholders, it was almost impossible to challenge the elitist composition of this, the major institution in local government. The introduction of presentment sessions must certainly have trimmed the power of these jurors to
some degree, but it did not undermine their control. The presentment sessions only initiated proposals for projects; final approval
and funding still lay with the grand juries. Moreover, for two very
good reasons, the presentment sessions themselves were not independent of landed influence. First, they consisted of cesspayers
chosen by lot from a list nominated by the grand jury; second, any
justice of the peace in the barony had the right to attend, and in
fact most sessions were controlled by these justices. The Board of
Works undoubtedly weakened the autonomy of grand juries, but
it may at the same time have increased their local power by providing them with more money to spend. We can be sure, at least,
that the Land Improvement Act of 1847 increased the local power
of the landed class by authorizing the Board of Works to make extensive loans to landowners, but not tenants.[19]

The introduction of assistant barristers surely curtailed landed
power over local courts, especially in the civil-bill courts, where
assistant barristers sat alone. These were important tribunals in
the rural society because they had charge over most disputes between landlords and tenants, including claims under the Land
Act of 1870. We should not conclude, however, that assistant barristers (or "chairmen" as they were often called) destroyed landed
power in the local administration of justice. First, we have no reason to assume that the assistant barristers were completely free of
landed influence, professional men though they were. Second,
their powers were circumvented in a number of ways. Justices of
the peace still ran the petty sessions, and the assistant barristers
were still outnumbered at the criminal quarter sessions where
they served merely as chairmen with no more formal authority

[19] See note 19 in Chapter Five above.

than was possessed by any of the sitting justices.[20] These magistrates continued to be drawn primarily from the landed class. As late as 1886 no fewer than two-thirds of the justices of the peace in Ireland were either landed proprietors or land agents, and less than one-tenth were farmers.[21] It is true that stipendiary magistrates were required to attend petty sessions, but this did not necessarily represent a threat to landed interests. The social background of stipendiary magistrates is one of the many areas in which we need more information. It is highly likely, however, that most were relatives of landowners. We do know that many were ex-army officers or ex-magistrates. In 1860 some two dozen of the seventy-two stipendiary magistrates were former justices of the peace.[22]

The way in which the landed class was able to maintain its power despite the reform and centralization of government administration is also well illustrated by their domination of local poor-law boards. These "boards of guardians" were set up to administer the Irish poor law of 1838. Since they were more closely connected to the central administration and met more regularly than did the grand juries, they gradually came to assume a variety of functions, and their importance in the local community expanded accordingly. In 1848 they were given responsibility for assisting evicted tenants to emigrate; and in 1851 they were assigned the large job of administering local dispensaries. They also became responsible for apprenticing workhouse boys to the navy and merchant marine, placing illegitimate and orphaned children with foster parents, administering sanitation regulations and facilities, providing lists of names of persons eligible for jury duty and for the parliamentary franchise, and other diverse functions.[23] During the last half of the nineteenth century, the proportion of the total local government budget spent by the guardians increased almost steadily. In 1890 expenditures by poor-law boards represented about 36 percent of the total local government revenue in that year, as compared with 39 percent for the grand juries and 25 percent for the municipal and lower authorities.[24]

[20] McKenna, "Courts of quarter sessions," pp. 279-83.

[21] Return of the persons holding the commission of the peace, p. 132.

[22] McDowell, The Irish Administration, p. 115.

[23] Such as dog-catching, cattle inspection, and vaccination. See Feingold, "Boards of guardians," p. 18. See also his "The tenants' movement to capture the Irish poor law boards, 1877-1886" in Albion, 7, no. 3 (Fall 1975), p. 219.

[24] Feingold, "Tenants' movement," p. 219.

Initially, most landowners were opposed to the poor law, mainly because it meant they would have to pay poor taxes or "rates," but perhaps also because they thought it would undermine the local power they derived from their role in providing relief. Yet it was not long before they realized that the poor law put into their hands vastly more power over the disbursement of relief funds. There were essentially two reasons why landowners were able to control poor-law boards. First, one-half of the members of each board (before 1847, one-quarter) were *ex officios* appointed from among the justices of the peace holding land within the union. Second, landowners were in an advantageous position to influence the outcome of the election of the remaining board members. Every ratepayer whose holding was valued at over £4 was entitled to vote in poor-law elections, but the franchise was not distributed on a "one man one vote" principle. For various reasons landowners had no difficulty cumulating the maximum of eighteen votes allowed to any one person, while the majority of tenants possessed but one vote.[25] Furthermore, owners but not tenants were permitted to vote by proxy, a provision that not only enabled them to exercise their franchise while absent from the union, but also enabled them to concentrate their votes on selected contests by granting all their proxy votes to one individual.[26] Finally, the system of open voting papers (whereby ballots were available for everyone's inspection) meant that tenants could please or displease their landlord with the way they voted. And on some estates the landlord and his agent expected tenants to vote according to their instructions. In early March of 1879, for example, the fourth Earl of Leitrim received a letter from his agent, Stewart, who was greatly troubled about the forthcoming poor-law elections. Many of the tenants, Stewart explained, were complaining that one of the poor-law guardians had not attended to his duties, and consequently a rival candidate had been nominated. "But," Stewart quickly added, "I still think you should have been consulted as to his successor." And on the same day he sent the following instructions to the bailiff:

[25] Ibid., pp. 26-7. Vote entitlement increased for owners and occupiers according to the value of their holdings or properties, with six votes accorded to those holding or owning land valued at over £200. This provision in itself gave landowners a greater number of votes per person than it gave tenants, since few tenants had land valued at more than £200 while most landowners did. Furthermore, any ratepayer who both occupied and owned a holding could cumulate votes on the basis of that holding as both occupier and owner.

[26] Ibid., pp. 27, 56-7.

I am sure Lord Leitrim would not wish that any change should be made in the Poor Law Guardians for Newtown-Gore E.D. without his knowledge and approval, and I therefore wish you to let it be known among all tenants who have votes that I wish them to support Mr Roycroft. You may say at the same time that if they consider Mr Roycroft does not sufficiently attend to his duties Lord Leitrim will reconsider the matter before the election next year.[27]

How typical this kind of pressure was we do not know, but allegations of such interference in poor-law elections were numerous.[28]

The assignment of half the seats on boards to the ex *officio* guardians and the influence that landowners exerted over the election of the remainder meant that the landowning class virtually controlled the activities of these boards. Though there were some serious weaknesses in this control—indeed, it would eventually prove to be one of the most vulnerable of all their sources of power—until 1880 they remained firmly in command. Boards were made up mostly of landowners, their relatives, land agents, and "reliable" tenants. This landed control is reflected in the social composition of the officers that the guardians chose to manage their business, that is, the chairmen, vice-chairmen, and deputy vice-chairmen. In 1877 no fewer than 69 percent of the 489 officers of poor-law boards in Ireland were landowners; and an additional 19 percent, though not landowners, were justices of the peace, meaning that they were most likely related to landowners. Looking at the chairmanships alone, a remarkable 99 percent were held by landowners or justices of the peace.[29]

Their almost total domination over a comparatively minor political institution such as the local poor-law board gives us some indication of the extent of the political power possessed by the landed class on the eve of the Land War. Few political realms could be found in post-famine Ireland where their interests were not represented. Admittedly, a gradual weakening of their position could be observed over the course of the century. Nevertheless—until the Land War itself—the decline was slow and limited.

[27] N.L.I., Leitrim papers: Letter book of G. F. Stewart: Stewart to Lord Leitrim, 7 March 1879; Stewart to William Gibson, 7 March 1879.

[28] Feingold, "Boards of guardians," pp. 28, 59-60, 105. See also *Reports from poor law inspectors as to the existing relations between landlord and tenant*, p. 41.

[29] Feingold, "Boards of guardians," pp. 39-40.

They remained strongest in local government; still well entrenched in the central administration; and until the late 1860s, almost in command of parliamentary representation at Westminster. Their political power, it should be noted, was in no small way dependent on their economic power, that is, on their control over land. At the same time, however, it was by means of their political power that landowners protected the property rights on which their economic power rested. Indeed, the very existence of landlordism in nineteenth-century Ireland can only be understood by recognizing the enormous political power that landowners, and more specifically Protestant landowners, possessed and used to maintain their control over the land. What this concentration of political power also meant, of course, was that any other collectivity interested in expanding its power within the polity was by necessity forced to challenge theirs. In the post-famine period four significant political rivals can be identified.

Challenging Collectivities

THE CATHOLIC CLERGY

The most powerful rival was the Catholic clergy. Although their political strength had been all but destroyed during the seventeenth and eighteenth centuries, in the nineteenth century they gradually managed to acquire greater influence. They were instrumental in the success of the Emancipation campaign in the 1820s; they were active in the Tithe War of the 1830s; and they played a major role in the local organization of the Repeal movement in the 1840s. From the 1820s on, the Catholic clergy exercised a considerable, though fluctuating, influence over parliamentary elections and became a major contender for power in Irish politics.

The last half of the nineteenth century saw an almost steady strengthening of the Irish Catholic church as a religious institution. This happened for a number of reasons, but two factors in particular stand out: an increase in the per capita number of priests; and an improvement in clerical discipline. The priest-to-people ratio rose from one for every 3,000 persons in 1840 to one for every 1,250 persons in 1870.[30] The reform in clerical discipline began with the appointment of Paul Cullen as archbishop of

[30] Larkin, "The devotional revolution," pp. 626, 644.

Armagh in 1850, and with the National Synod of Thurles in the same year. The Synod was concerned with the proper administration of the sacraments and with regulating more closely the lives of the clergy. Priests were exhorted to administer the sacraments more often and only in church, and to lead lives that would serve as an example to parishioners.[31] Cullen had been sent from Rome with a specific mandate to restore ecclesiastical discipline in the Catholic church in Ireland. In 1852 he was appointed archbishop of Dublin, and during the next twenty years he presided over an impressive period of church reform. There was a noticeable improvement in the administration of the sacraments; most bishops with local ties were replaced by strangers to their dioceses; church attendance rose; and participation in devotional exercises became more common.[32]

At the same time, priests continued to perform the critical temporal functions that they had for so long performed in the local community. One might suppose that this temporal role would have diminished in importance as the century progressed, since the state was becoming more active in education and poor relief. This did not happen to any great extent. First, there remained a large number of functions that the clergy could perform that were still not being met by the state, ranging from settling family quarrels to organizing community activities. In addition, the clergy were often able to acquire a significant measure of influence and control over state programs, particularly at the local level. For example, though legally prohibited from holding the office of poor-law guardian, parish priests were invariably (in Catholic areas) appointed to the salaried position of workhouse chaplain and were normally on the executives of local relief committees on which the guardians depended for knowledge of distress in their districts. Furthermore, the parish priest was typically chaplain of the infirmary, the lunatic asylum, and barracks. He was also, as a rule, the manager of the national school in his parish. Though officially non-denominational, the state schools in nineteenth-century Ireland were in fact almost completely denominational. In 1867 more than 70 percent of the national schools were under Catholic control, and no less than 85 percent of the patrons of these Catholic schools were clergymen.[33]

[31] Ibid., pp. 639-40.   [32] Ibid., pp. 644-8.

[33] *Royal commission of inquiry into primary education (Ireland)*, vol. i, pt. i, *Report of commissioners*, p. 235 [C 6], H.C. 1870, xxviii; see also Donald H. Aken-

In view of this strengthening of the Catholic church as a religious institution and the continued importance of priests as leaders in their local communities, it is not surprising that the Catholic clergy also continued to play an influential role in parliamentary politics. They took part in elections so openly and so effectively that they were time and again accused of having improperly interfered in politics. In the last half of the nineteenth century, nine such accusations were successful to the point of unseating the elected member on whose behalf the clergy had supposedly interfered.[34] Almost always, priests, were accused of "spiritual intimidation." Cases were cited where recalcitrant voters were insulted from the altar, driven from the chapel, prevented from giving the customary Christmas or Easter offerings, or threatened with exclusion from the sacraments or even with eternal punishment.[35] J. H. Whyte has argued, however, that cases of this kind were far from common, and that in reality the priests exercised little spiritual influence over the politics of their parishioners. He says that spiritual threats were rare and usually resented when they were made, with the result that they were ineffective. Instead, the influence of the clergy derived largely from their capacity to provide the rural population with a means of organization.[36] Whyte asserts that during elections the clergy were crucial in helping with the selection of candidates, made candidates known to electors, assembled meetings for candidates (often after Mass), and brought voters to the polls, frequently making arrangements for transportation and accommodation.[37]

It is important for our purposes to understand that the political resources of the Catholic clergy were normally reserved for the purposes of the Church itself. Indeed, the political assistance offered by the clergy to their parishioners was primarily a means of ensuring that the latter would support clerical interests. Most clergymen remained aloof from political activities having "radical" implications, though there was, of course, enormous variation in this regard (including regional variation), and many exceptions to this rule could be found. Often these exceptions came

son, *The Irish Education Experiment: The National System of Education in the Nineteenth Century* (London, 1970), p. 215.

[34] Whyte, "The influence of the Catholic clergy on elections," p. 243.

[35] Ibid.

[36] Ibid., pp. 247-9. See also Whyte, *The Independent Irish Party*, pp. 63-81.

[37] Whyte, "The influence of the Catholic clergy on elections," pp. 249-51.

from the ranks of Catholic curates, who were younger and bore less responsibility for the moral tranquillity of the parish than did parish priests.

Yet the Church as a whole played a restricted political role during the 1850s and 1860s. In 1853, under the leadership of Paul Cullen, the hierarchy met in a National Council and outlined new rules governing the participation of the clergy in politics.[38] For at least twenty years, Cullen exerted a powerful restraining influence over the clergy. This does not mean that priests dropped out of politics altogether. Cullen held very strong sympathies in favor of both self-government and agrarian reform, and he allowed priests to pursue their political convictions so long as they did so with moderation.[39] Furthermore, the clergy continued, throughout the Cullen period, to engage in political activity in order to advance the interests of the Church. In 1864 Cullen himself joined with other Catholic leaders in the formation of a political group called the National Association. This body, however, never established any local organizations and operated largely as a pressure group seeking to influence politicians, particularly to win concessions from Gladstone and the English Liberals, to whom it promised support in return for a Liberal commitment to disestablishment of the Church of Ireland, land reform, and denominational education. But it was disestablishment that was given the greatest attention by the Church.[40]

Cullen's influence did not extend equally to all parts of the country, and the place where his control was weakest was the province of Connaught. There his efforts to bring the Catholic church under stricter discipline were vigorously resisted by John MacHale, archbishop of Tuam. It should also be pointed out that Cullen's restrictions on clerical political activity became less rigid in the 1870s. The reasons for this change were complex and cannot be properly treated in this study. The immediate cause was the collapse of the clerical alliance with English Liberals as a result of Gladstone's failure to satisfy the Irish Catholic church on the education question. When Cullen's interest in parliamentary political maneuvers waned in the early seventies, the lower clergy were at greater liberty to engage in politics on their own. They did

[38] Ibid., p. 246.

[39] E. D. Steele, "Cardinal Cullen and Irish nationality" in *Irish Historical Studies*, 19, no. 75 (March 1975).

[40] Thornley, *Isaac Butt*, pp. 28-9, 37-45.

so in large numbers, especially from 1873 on, when many threw their support behind the Home Rule movement. Yet this renewed participation could be deceiving. Although Cullen died in 1878, there remained inherent institutional restrictions under which the clergy took part in politics. The clergy were always restrained by the priorities and interests of the organization to which they belonged.

CONSERVATIVE NATIONALISM

In the decades prior to the Land War it is possible to distinguish between two rival factions within the nationalist movement: a conservative or constitutionalist faction and an extremist or physical-force faction. Both have considerable relevance to our inquiry in view of the role they eventually played in the Land War.

The conservative faction acquired its largest following during the 1870s in what was known as the "Home Rule" movement. This movement began in May 1870 when the Home Government Association (H.G.A.) was formed at a meeting in Bilton's Hotel in Dublin. The remarkable feature of this founding meeting was that it was attended by a number of influential Protestants.[41] Their interest in the nationalist cause at this time can be explained as a consequence of the alliance between Catholic leaders and the English Liberal Party, which made many Protestants lose confidence in the British government's determination to protect their dominant position in Irish society. It is true that the strength of Protestants in the H.G.A. was never again as pronounced as at the founding meeting. Almost immediately, Catholics took over as the majority. Nevertheless, the H.G.A. continued to seek Protestant backing and it remained in many ways an elitist clique, what one historian has described as "a little pretentious and pompous, over preoccupied with the running of its little Dublin club."[42] The H.G.A. encouraged the formation of regional branches, but it refused to grant them any official status, and partly as a result of that, only about nine were in fact organized.[43] It avoided commitments to popular causes, such as denominational education or land reform, hoping to maintain, if not increase, the support it en-

41 Ibid., pp. 92-3.   42 Ibid., p. 108.
43 L. J. McCaffrey, "Irish Federalism in the 1870's: a study in conservative nationalism" in Transactions of the American Philosophical Society, new series, 52, pt. 6 (1962), p. 10.

joyed from the Protestant Ascendancy. It advocated an extremely limited form of national independence, and proposed a federal system with an imperial parliament at Westminster. Consistent with such a program, many members of the Home Government Association did not call themselves nationalists, preferring instead to be called "Federalists."

The Federalists could not, however, completely isolate themselves from the mainstream of public opinion. Limited though their objectives were, they could not hope to bring any changes about by keeping the H.G.A. an exclusive club. Support from the Catholic community was crucial to promoting their cause, since even in their wildest dreams they could not expect sufficient political and financial backing from the Protestant establishment. The problem was that Catholic support could not be obtained without at least verbal commitment to Catholic interests, while any such commitment would inevitably alienate the Protestants. Repeatedly in the years 1871-3, Isaac Butt, the president of the H.G.A., took positions that further eroded his already meager Protestant support.[44] By 1874 the movement had virtually lost whatever backing it had enjoyed from the Protestant establishment. The last straw came with the collapse of the Catholic-Liberal alliance. In February 1873 Gladstone introduced a university bill whose provisions failed to meet Catholic demands for the endowment of denominational institutions. At last, the once strong Liberal alliance fell to pieces. The ensuing year saw Irish representatives in the House of Commons join with the Tories to defeat the government. Back in Ireland, former supporters of the Liberal alliance began to look more favorably on Home Rule, and many even enlisted in the Home Rule movement. In November 1873 the Home Government Association was reorganized at a Catholic-dominated conference and replaced by a new association called the Home Rule League.

The new movement achieved only limited success in the following years. Many of its members remained hesitant to take up popular causes. There lingered among at least some the desire to appeal to Protestant interests—to try to remake the Home Rule movement into the kind of gentlemen's club that it had been for a fleeting moment in Bilton's Hotel on the day it was founded in 1870. An effort continued to be made to put nationalism into a form acceptable to the Protestant elite. The movement also lacked

<hr/>

[44] Thornley, *Isaac Butt*, pp. 123-4.

a grass-roots political organization, and therefore possessed neither the means to mobilize the electorate to vote as the League wished, nor the power to nominate and promote candidates of its choice. Within three months of the League's founding parliament was dissolved, and the League faced a general election in which it had to rely, for the most part, on candidates selected in the traditional manner. In the absence of a Home Rule political machine, local election organization remained under the control of the clergy and the landowning class. As a result, a diverse group of Home Rule M.P.s were elected, including not only Catholics and tenant-right advocates, but also Protestants and landowners. They could be persuaded to work in concert on the issue of Home Rule, but there was no consensus to act as a bloc on any other issue.

It would be a mistake, however, to evaluate the Home Rule movement entirely in terms of the progress it made in achieving concrete objectives. While in these terms it was a failure, in other ways it was extremely successful. Not since the days of O'Connell had popular support for nationalism been raised to the levels reached during the 1870s. In fact, the Home Rule movement demonstrated, even more effectively than had O'Connell, that nationalism could be used to win votes in parliamentary elections. Candidates pledged to Home Rule won nine of fourteen by-elections between 1870 and 1874, and fifty-nine members of parliament were elected in 1874 who were nominally Home Rulers.[45] Some of these men even won their seats without clerical support. In 1871 John Martin, a veteran nationalist and opponent of the Liberal alliance, defeated a Liberal candidate in County Meath who had the endorsement of the Catholic clergy. In the following year a Protestant Home Ruler, R. P. Blennerhassett, was chosen for County Kerry in opposition to the candidate selected by the Bishop of Kerry. In the election of 1874 most Home Rule candidates enjoyed clerical support, but W. H. O'Sullivan was elected for County Limerick despite strong opposition from the clergy; and Nicholas Ennis was successful in Meath even though he was not the clergy's first choice.[46] Similarly, the electoral influence of the landed class was showing new signs of weakness. In 1874 fewer landed proprietors were sent to represent Ireland in the House of Commons than ever before. Their number fell from seventy-three in 1868 to fifty-two in 1874.[47]

[45] Ibid., pp. 113, 207. [46] Ibid., pp. 190-4.
[47] Ibid., p. 207. These figures include sons of landowners.

None of this indicates a fundamental shift in political power, but it does suggest that the Irish electorate was becoming less stable and more fluid. The control that landowners and the Catholic clergy had enjoyed over elections was no longer secure. Unfortunately, it is not easy to specify the reasons for this instability because there exist several possibilities. Most obvious, but somewhat dubious and certainly difficult to document, is the argument that the Land Act of 1870 made tenants less indebted to their landlords for security of tenure. A second conceivable factor was the Ballot Act of 1872, under which the old system of open elections was replaced by a secret ballot. The importance of this reform can easily be exaggerated. Even with secret ballots, there were ways of determining how a man voted and certainly there were ways of determining how most tenants on a particular estate voted. Still, the opportunities for intimidation on the part of landlords were no doubt restricted by the Ballot Act; and it was now a little more awkward for a voter to curry his landlord's favor by publicly declaring support for his candidate.[48] Likewise, a man's vote could now more easily be concealed from his priest. And since the act raised the average number of polling stations in an Irish parliamentary county from four to twenty, it may also have diminished the importance of the clergy in organizing voters to go to the polls.[49] Probably the most important factor, however, was the intense popularity of Home Rule. Quite simply, the Home Rule movement gave voters a cause they wanted to support and were usually willing to support when given the opportunity. It upset the stability of Irish electoral politics by making self-government the issue of the 1874 election. Although the party that was elected was conservative and ineffective, it was evident that the movement had struck a responsive chord in Irish public opinion. Clearly, there existed a substantial public with strong nationalist feeling, willing to defy landlords (and even priests, if necessary) in order to demonstrate their support for self-government. It was an immense source of political power still to be tapped.

EXTREMIST NATIONALISM

The extremist faction in the nationalist movement consisted of the Fenian association, also known as the Irish Republican Brother-

[48] Whyte, "Landlord influence at elections in Ireland," p. 755.
[49] Whyte, "The influence of the Catholic clergy on elections," p. 255.

hood (I.R.B.). Fenianism was organized in the late fifties as an underground movement committed to achieving national independence through the violent overthrow of the existing government. It represented yet another resurgence of a long tradition of revolutionary nationalism in Ireland. Unsuccessful rebellions had been staged in 1798 by the United Irishmen and in 1848 by a faction within the Repeal movement known as the Young Irelanders. These revolts provided inspiration for the Fenians, a few of whom had participated in the Rebellion of 1848. The Fenians, however, repudiated and were in turn scorned by the majority of Young Irelanders, who were by this time engaged in less daring forms of nationalist politics. From the very beginning the movement had strong connections with Irishmen in America.

Although some Fenian leaders were Protestant, most were Catholic; the majority belonged to the urban middle class.[50] But they did not recruit their support from this class. Their approach to nationalism was too extreme and too dangerous for any substantial number of middle-class Catholics to accept. Nor, in the early years at least, did they obtain much support from the farming population. They encountered great difficulty establishing contacts with potential recruits within rural areas, perhaps because most of them came from urban centers. The problem was that few individuals in the Fenian network were well enough known in rural communities that they could inspire the trust necessary to persuade people to join an underground organization. Agrarian secret societies, which they had great hopes of taking over, were not nearly as numerous as they had been twenty years earlier; and those that could be located were not especially

[50] The founders of the Fenian movement were John O'Mahony and James Stephens. O'Mahony came from a Catholic landowning family in Cork; Stephens was a non-practicing Catholic and by occupation a civil engineer. The principal Fenian intellectuals in the early sixties were John O'Leary, Charles Kickham, and T. C. Luby. All three were from relatively comfortable families and were university-educated; O'Leary and Kickham were sons of prosperous Catholic shopkeepers and Luby was the son of a Church of England clergyman who married a Catholic. On the other hand, O'Donovan Rossa, who founded the Phoenix Society in 1856, though a shopkeeper when his association merged with Stephens' movement, began as a shop assistant. And John Nolan, who was responsible for Fenian organization in Ulster, and Edward Duffy, who was responsible for Connaught, were both shop assistants. Particulars on the backgrounds of Fenians can be found in T. W. Moody (ed.), *The Fenian Movement* (Cork, 1968); John Devoy, *Recollections of an Irish Rebel* (New York, 1929); and William O'Brien and Desmond Ryan (eds.), *Devoy's Post Bag, 1871-1928*, 2 vols. (Dublin, 1948).

receptive to Fenian advances. Although some links between Ribbonism and Fenianism were established, on the whole this tenuous alliance was not a source of many recruits. John O'Leary remarks several times in his memoirs that it was easier "to make a rebel of an Orangeman than of a Ribbonman."[51]

In addition, and more fundamentally, the Fenians failed to attract rural support because they were ideologically committed to pure nationalism and were generally unwilling to make concessions to any other objectives. They insisted that independence must precede social reforms, because they were sure that nothing good could be expected from the government at Westminster. According to T. C. Luby, an early Fenian, independence had to be obtained at all hazards. "Any plan short of this for bettering the condition of Ireland," he wrote in 1863, "commences work at the wrong end. . . . Special efforts to remove special grievances are at best palliatives. . . . Let national independence once be reached through manhood's road, the only way it can be reached, and all other blessings will follow." What this meant for the farmer, said Luby, was that "the true land-measure, the establishment of a peasant proprietorship, can only be got from an Irish legislature."[52] Behind this reasoning lay a determination to avoid a program that would alienate any segment of the society, even landowners or others whose interests were tied to the existing land system. Fenians hoped that the nationalist cause would win the support of all classes and were consequently unwilling to make special appeals to any social group. They specifically rejected the notion that nationalists should give foremost place to the land question, insisting that tenant right was no more important than anyone else's right.[53]

The principal source of recruitment for the Fenian movement was the urban lower class. Table 11 gives an occupational breakdown of a sample of Fenians taken from an index kept by the government between 1866 and 1871. This index was constructed from police reports on the activities of suspected members of the organization. The most striking finding is the overwhelming number of artisans and non-farm laborers, who make up 44.7 per-

[51] John O'Leary, Recollections of Fenians and Fenianism (London, 1896), I, p. 111; II, p. 27.

[52] Quoted in T. W. Moody, "The Fenian movement in Irish history" in T. W. Moody (ed.), The Fenian Movement, p. 105.

[53] O'Leary, Recollections of Fenians, I, pp. 37-8, II, p. 142.

TABLE 11 · Occupations of a sample of suspected Fenians, 1866-71

OCCUPATIONS	PERCENTAGE OF SUSPECTS
Agricultural sector	21.2
Farmers	6.4
Farmers' sons	2.1
General laborers	10.6
Other agricultural	2.1
Commercial and industrial sector	66.0
Traders and business proprietors	8.5
Shopworkers and clerks	9.2
Innkeepers and publicans	3.6
Artisans and non-farm laborers	44.7
Professional sector	6.4
Clergy	2.1
Teachers	1.4
Newspaper editors and correspondents	2.1
Subordinate professional service	0.7
Civil service and defense sector	3.6
Domestic sector	2.8
Number of suspects	141

NOTE: The source is S.P.O., Fenianism, Index to Names, 1866-71. I have included in my sample only suspects residing in Ireland. The occupational classification is described in Appendix B.

cent of the suspects. The agricultural sector is poorly represented. Even if we were to assume that all the general laborers were farm workers (which is unlikely), agricultural laborers would still fall far below what could be expected in view of their number in the labor force. And farmers, with a larger number of persons to draw upon than any other occupational category, comprise only 6.4 percent of the suspects, or 8.5 percent if we include farmers' sons. One could raise some methodological objections to these data. The size of the sample is small, and a government index of political suspects no doubt contains serious biases. Yet it hardly seems possible, whatever the biases, that they could account for the tremendous over-representation of artisans in the sample. Nor could they account for the under-representation of farmers. Plainly, in the late sixties, the Fenian movement flourished principally among the urban lower class and attracted few supporters among the farming population.

The movement was strongest in large urban centers, particularly in Dublin and Cork, but also in many of the larger towns in Leinster and Munster. It made little headway in Ulster, except in such predominantly Catholic counties as Monaghan, where most recruits were persons of low social standing, including some small farmers, but primarily laborers, shop assistants, and artisans.[54] It was comparatively weak in western districts, and what strength it did have appears to have been, again, mainly in the towns.[55]

The farming population played almost no part in the abortive Fenian revolt of 1867. Disturbances occurred in Dublin, Tipperary, Limerick, and Cork, and there was some very minor activity in Louth, Waterford, and Clare. Farmers were involved in some of these places, but the total number was very small. In Connaught there was no rising at all. During the 1860s farmers made almost no contribution to Fenianism, and Fenianism had almost no immediate impact on the political mobilization of farmers.

Yet the farming population did not remain totally unaffected by Fenianism. Like the Home Rule movement, Fenianism cannot be fairly evaluated without taking into account its impact on public opinion. The Fenians did not recruit any significant number of farmers, but they did manage to arouse considerable public sympathy in many places, including many rural areas. The first event to stir up emotions was the funeral of T. B. MacManus, a veteran of the 1848 rebellion, whose body was returned from America in 1861 to be buried in Dublin. More sensational still was the suppression of the Fenian newspaper, the arrest of several key Fenian leaders, and the dramatic escape of the founder of the movement in 1865. Although the rebellion of 1867 was a failure as an insurrection, the trials that followed left an impression in the minds of many people that it had been carried out by sincere and dedicated, if very foolish men. And the execution in the same year of

[54] Breandán Mac Giolla Choille, "Fenians, Rice and Ribbonmen in County Monaghan, 1864-67" in Clogher Record, 6, no. 2 (1967).

[55] For Kerry, see Seán Ó Lúing, "Aspects of the Fenian rising in Kerry, 1867: I. The rising and its background" in Journal of the Kerry Archaeological and Historical Society, 1, no. 3 (1970), pp. 137-8; and for Connaught see Mark Ryan's autobiography, Fenian Memories (Dublin, 1945), especially pp. 31-7.

three members of the organization for accidentally killing a policeman during a successful rescue of a Fenian prisoner in Manchester generated so much public feeling that to this day the three are known to every Irishman as the "Manchester Martyrs." By 1868, for all their failures, the Fenians had become popular heroes in Ireland. A campaign was launched to appeal to the government to grant them political amnesty. The movement did not enjoy mass participation, but was regarded sympathetically by most people, even by a large number of Catholic clergymen.[56]

Moreover, Fenianism did not die in the 1860s. Unlike the Young Irelanders, who went their separate ways after the failure of 1848, the Fenian movement survived the rebellion of 1867. Subsequently, during what is usually known as "reorganized" Fenianism, it continued to thrive outside Ireland, especially in England and the United States.[57] Even within Ireland, much of the network that Fenians had built up in the cities and towns survived and may even have expanded into areas where Fenianism had formerly met with little success, including the province of Connaught. There is not the evidence one would like to have, but there are some indications that the movement was now making better progress in the west. It was during this period that Mark Ryan was active in Connaught and that George Henry Moore, an old nationalist parliamentarian, became once more involved in politics, apparently acquiring an affiliation with the Fenians at the same time.[58] John Devoy asserted in his recollections that reorganized Fenianism was "best" in Mayo,[59] but we need not go this far to allow for the possibility that Fenianism may have overcome some of the regional disparities that characterized it during the sixties. The most concrete evidence of Fenian progress in Connaught was the successful election in 1874 of a member of the Fenian Supreme Council, John O'Connor Power, as M.P. for County Mayo. Power was not elected as a Fenian, nor was he universally trusted by other Fenians. Yet he was reportedly assisted in his campaign by a group within the Fenian movement, indicating that a Fenian organization of some form must have existed in that part of the country in 1874.[60]

---

[56] Thomás Ó Fiaich, "The clergy and Fenianism, 1860-70" in Irish Ecclesiastical Record, 109 (Feb. 1968), pp. 94-9.

[57] Thomas N. Brown, Irish-American Nationalism (New York, 1966).

[58] Thornley, Isaac Butt, pp. 89-90.

[59] Devoy, Recollections, p. 33.   [60] Ryan, Fenian Memories, pp. 44-5.

Finally, and absolutely critical for our understanding of the Land War, there eventually occurred a significant change in the attitude of a substantial number of Fenians toward both constitutional agitation and the land question. Although this reorientation has itself been carefully studied by historians, its origins have not been explored. One factor that will almost certainly form part of the explanation was the transformation that took place in the social composition of Fenian leadership. As we have seen, notwithstanding the middle-class backgrounds of its founders, the Fenian movement had recruited its rank and file from the lower classes. If the movement had been short-lived, this might not have had any noteworthy consequences. However, because Fenianism survived its initial failure, it was inevitable that over time these lower-class recruits would become leaders of the movement. The most influential Fenian to fit this pattern was John Devoy. His father was a poor farmer who had moved to Dublin and had gone through several laboring jobs before becoming a clerk.[61] Devoy joined the Fenian movement in 1861 and was an active member during the 1860s, though it is significant that O'Leary insists in his memoirs that Devoy played no prominent part at that time.[62] By the 1870s, however, Devoy was a well-known Fenian chief, at the head of the principal American Fenian organization (the Clan na Gael), and perhaps the most powerful Fenian in America, where he lived in exile. Another example is John O'Connor Power, just mentioned; a laborer's son, he joined the movement in the 1860s and rose to become a member of the Supreme Council and an M.P. in the 1870s. The best-known example, however, and from the standpoint of the Land War the most important, was Michael Davitt. Son of an evicted Mayo tenant, raised in working-class Lancashire, victim of an industrial accident in his teens resulting in the loss of an arm, Davitt has become a major Irish folk hero, and his humble background remains an emotional part of the nationalist history of Ireland. Though active in the movement in the late 1860s, he did not become a prominent Fenian until after his release from prison in 1877. Ultimately, his influence on the Fenian movement was comparable to the influence of Devoy. His contribution to the Land War exceeds that of any other single man.

[61] Devoy, *Recollections*, pp. 377-9.
[62] O'Leary, *Recollections of Fenians*, I, p. 141.

What was different about these new leaders—perhaps as a result of their lower-class backgrounds—was that they were less dogmatically committed to pure nationalism and less opposed to constitutional activity than the early Fenian leaders had been. Originally accepting the standard Fenian position, these new men more easily became discouraged when it produced no tangible results. Gradually, a growing number of Fenians began to question the wisdom of underground political activity and started to consider other possible strategies. One factor that influenced their thinking was the electoral support that the Home Rule movement had been enjoying, and the fact that Fenianism itself had shown signs that it could command support at the polls.[63] Consequently, some extremists began to flirt with constitutionalist politics. As early as 1873 several Fenians joined the Home Rule movement, and a commitment may even have been made by the Fenian leadership to support Butt for a limited period.[64] The Supreme Council withdrew its endorsement of Home Rule in 1876, but the idea of cooperating with the constitutionalists did not die then. On the contrary, it was at this very time that the eventual basis for such an alliance was emerging within the Home Rule movement. One of the principal objections that Fenians had always made to constitutional agitation was that to work within the British parliament was to accept the legitimacy of that institution. In the late 1870s, however, there appeared in parliament a small band of Irish M.P.s who undertook a systematic and intentional campaign to discredit the House of Commons by obstructing its business. Among their number were two Fenians, John O'Connor Power and Joseph Biggar. And many others in the Fenian movement saw this obstruction of parliament as the next best thing to repudiating it. The acknowledged leader of this band of rebellious M.P.s was, curiously enough, a Protestant landowner.

Charles Stewart Parnell was first elected to parliament for Meath in 1875 as a member of Isaac Butt's Home Rule party. He very quickly found himself siding with those in the party who

---

[63] In 1869 O'Donovan Rossa was elected to parliament for County Tipperary. And in 1875 John Mitchel, whose political experience included activity both as a Young Irelander and as a Fenian, was returned twice for County Tipperary, being unseated on both occasions because he was an undischarged felon.

[64] Thornley, *Isaac Butt*, pp. 161-2; T. W. Moody and Leon Ó Broin, "The I.R.B. supreme council, 1868-78" in *Irish Historical Studies*, 19, no. 75 (March 1975).

were frustrated by its ineffectiveness under Butt's leadership,[65] and he soon became convinced of the need to broaden the party's base of support. Even more than the Fenians, Parnell appreciated the power that nationalism had over a large number of voters. He saw no reason why a nationalist party should not be able to establish its own electoral apparatus and develop its own loyal constituency, with less dependence on traditional political organizations. One might go further and specify how Parnell planned to use the farming population to establish this political structure, but we have no evidence that what he did in the 1880s was in his mind in the late 1870s. Indeed, there is good reason to believe that as late as the autumn of 1878 he was still not conscious of the enormous political force that lay behind the land question.[66] Yet his disappointment with Butt's movement must have led him, even at this stage, to reject one of its basic goals, namely, the attempt to form an alliance between the Catholic middle class and the landed gentry. Although himself a landowner, Parnell could only have despaired at the apathy and infidelity of landowners in the Home Rule party.

Whatever his long-run objectives might have been, in the short run Parnell's strategy was to dislodge Butt as leader of the party and to promote his own reputation among the electorate. He did so by pressing Irish demands vigorously in the House of Commons and by obstructing government bills. He did not initiate the Irish obstruction campaign, but he quickly became recognized as its most effective practitioner. Together with a handful of colleagues, Parnell interrupted the business of the House with motions to report progress or motions that the speaker leave the chair and the House adjourn, or with amendment after amendment to bills. This aggressive approach to parliamentary representation met with a favorable response in Ireland and served to enhance Parnell's political popularity, while at the same time it undermined Butt's position as head of the party, since Butt refused to be associated with such antics. Formal leadership of the Home Rule party was not assumed by Parnell until later, but he had the allegiance of a group of active members and was a popular political figure by 1878.

In 1877 some Fenians suggested to Devoy the possibility of

[65] For a discussion of the weaknesses and ineffectiveness of the party, see Thornley, *Isaac Butt*, pp. 233-4, 275, and 284.

[66] F.S.L. Lyons, *Charles Stewart Parnell* (Oxford, 1977), pp. 84-5, 87.

forming an alliance with Parnell. In the same year the Home Rule Confederation of Great Britain, which included a significant Fenian element, indicated their preference for Parnell over Butt by electing him president of their body. In early 1878 discussions were held between Parnell and a group of Fenians, including representatives of both the American Clan na Gael and the Fenian Supreme Council.[67] And in October 1878, when Parnell was reelected president of the Home Rule Confederation of Great Britain, Devoy sent him a telegram proposing that the physical-force and constitutionalist factions of the nationalist movement should combine efforts. Five conditions were set by Devoy for this alliance—which he dubbed the "New Departure"—one of which was that the new movement take up "vigorous agitation of the land question on the basis of a peasant proprietary, while accepting concessions tending to abolish arbitrary eviction." This reference to the land question was no more than part of a larger package, and the package itself was no more than a proposal. Parnell later claimed that he did not receive Devoy's telegram. Whether or not this is true, the available evidence indicates that he made no formal commitment in 1878.[68] Nevertheless, the offer to operate in the open and to cooperate with constitutionalists contrasted sharply with the hard line taken by Fenians in the 1860s, as did also the new willingness to include the land question as a short-term goal in the Fenian platform. By itself, the New Departure would likely have been forgotten. By itself, the reorientation spearheaded by Parnell would probably have generated a more active Home Rule party, but certainly not a mass movement. And yet ultimately these nationalist reorientations came to have immense significance for the course of Irish history. They acquired their importance, it will be seen, in connection with developments that were taking place at the same time in still a fourth challenging collectivity that was trying to assert itself in the post-famine period.

THE AGRARIAN CHALLENGE

The transformation that occurred in the rural class structure during and after the Famine had a very noticeable effect on agrarian

[67] T. W. Moody, "The new departure in Irish politics, 1878-9" in H. A. Cronne, T. W. Moody, and D. B. Quinn (eds.), *Essays in British and Irish History in Honour of James Eadie Todd* (London, 1949), pp. 311-12.

[68] Ibid.

collective action. As the proportion of the population consisting of agricultural laborers declined, so did collective action by and for laborers. Combinations were occasionally formed among agricultural workers to represent their interests against farmers, but such activity was generally sporadic and certainly much less common than before the Famine. Serious disturbances broke out in August 1858 mostly in County Kilkenny, but also in Tipperary, Waterford, and King's. The main grievances were low wages, unemployment, and the use by farmers and landowners of reaping and threshing machines, and of scythes instead of sickles. Bands of men broke machines and refused to work for less than a specified wage, usually 3s. a day for reaping.[69] There were also reports of active combinations of laborers in Galway and Mayo in the late 1850s and early 1860s.[70] Perhaps the largest laborer movement in this period appeared in County Cork in the early 1870s. A laborers' club had been formed at Kanturk late in 1869, apparently the first organization of its kind in Ireland, and in the following July crowds of agricultural workers broke or threatened to break mowing machines in nearby districts.[71] In 1873 the National Agricultural Labourers' Union of England sent representatives to help organize an Irish affiliate. A branch was formed in Kanturk in August and remained active for perhaps five or six years. However, its impact was confined largely to the Kanturk area and to some other parts of Munster, and it did not succeed in organizing a significant number of workers, nor did it obtain any noticeable improvement in their conditions.[72]

Agrarian violence, for which laborers had been primarily responsible before the Famine and which had served in no small way to protect their interests, subsided after the Famine. Unfortunately, statistics on agrarian as distinct from other types of violence were not collected before 1844. But even the figures for 1844-5 tell us something. These two years were not especially noted for agrarian unrest. Indeed, the level of violence during

[69] J. W. Boyle, "The rural labourer" in *Threshold*, 3, no. 1 (Spring 1959). I have also had the benefit of personal communications with Professor Boyle. His information comes mainly from newspaper clippings in the Larcom papers (N.L.I.).

[70] See Lane, "General impact of the Encumbered Estates Act on Galway and Mayo," pp. 55-6.

[71] Donnelly, *Cork*, pp. 236-7.

[72] P.L.R. Horn, "The National Agricultural Labourers' Union in Ireland" in *Irish Historical Studies*, 17, no. 67 (March 1971).

1844-5 must have been only a fraction of the level during many earlier years, such as 1815, 1823, and 1831. Nevertheless, the annual number of outrages reported by the Constabulary for those two years was eighteen for every 100,000 persons in the population. It fell to thirteen during the Famine years of 1846-50, to nine during the years 1851-5, and to less than six during every subsequent five-year period until 1875.[73] Agrarian violence was still an important part of rural life in Ireland; and it was still the chief means by which laborers defended themselves.[74] Yet it was paltry in comparison with pre-famine violence.

Combinations formed by and claiming to represent the interests of tenant farmers became the predominant type of agrarian collective action in the post-famine period. Even before the Famine had passed, an organized political movement appeared, drawing its support from farmers, and seeking rent reductions and greater security of tenure. Although the Tenant League, as it was called, was a spent force by the mid-fifties, it laid the groundwork for continued political activity aimed at advancing the interests of tenant farmers. Beginning in the mid 1860s, there emerged local political associations composed mainly of farmers and demanding reforms in the system of land tenure. We can briefly describe these farmer movements, taking first the Tenant League.

THE TENANT LEAGUE   In 1847 several tenant organizations were formed in Ulster, the most important being the Ulster Tenant-Right Association, founded by James McKnight, a newspaper editor in Londonderry.[75] In County Cork a tenant-right league had been established in January of the same year and was trying to spread its influence to other parts of the country, meeting with some success in Wexford.[76] There was also tenant activity on a

[73] Excluding the years 1869-70 when a different method of reporting was used. See *Return of outrages 1844 to 1880*.

[74] Hoppen, "National politics and local realities." Hoppen notes that farmers continued to be the principal targets of agrarian violence; he cites agrarian outrages reported by the Constabulary in the four months beginning October 1858 to make the point. See also *Report from the select committee on Westmeath (unlawful combinations)*, H.C. 1871 (147), xiii; and, for a contemporary and highly opinionated analysis, J.L.W. Naper, *The Cause of Ribbonism and Its Continuance in the Province of Leinster* (Dublin, 1859).

[75] B. A. Kennedy, "The tenant-right agitation in Ulster, 1845-50" in *Bulletin of the Irish Committee of Historical Sciences*, no. 34 (17 May 1944).

[76] *Nation*, 20 March 1847, p. 376; 27 Nov. 1847, p. 949.

small scale in Meath, Waterford, Mayo, and Kilkenny,[77] while in Tipperary a "Central Tenant League" was founded in July 1847 and a large demonstration was held at Holy Cross in September.[78]

More successful efforts to organize a movement were made in 1849-50. In the autumn of 1849 a number of tenant defense associations were formed in Leinster and east Munster with the assistance of local Catholic clergymen. The first association was established in October at Callan, County Kilkenny, in response to evictions by the Earl of Desart. In the following month, a second one was established in Kilkenny, and two others in Tipperary and Wexford. By the middle of May 1850, at least twelve associations in Leinster and five in Munster had been formed.[79] At the same time, there was renewed activity in Ulster. Here as well the clergy were instrumental, in this case the Presbyterian clergy, from whom a petition for tenant right was presented to parliament in early 1850.[80] Finally, in August 1850 a land conference was held in Dublin. It was organized with the help of a handful of nationalists who had become discouraged with the failure of the Repeal movement and the fiasco of the 1848 rebellion. The result of the August conference was the inauguration of the Tenant League and the formulation of a program to be presented to parliament. Although it was a short-lived movement and did not realize any of its concrete goals, the Tenant League did succeed in mobilizing a large number of farmers into a single organization whose objectives were directly related to their interests. It even succeeded, for a brief period, in bringing together political activists from both the Protestant population in Ulster and the Catholic population in the South, certainly an unusual achievement in Irish politics.

Except for the role played by Protestants, the Tenant League agitation bore some resemblance to the Tithe War. Like the Tithe War, this movement depended heavily on clergymen to assist in local organization. And like the Tithe War, it drew dispropor-

[77] Ibid., 31 July 1847, p. 685; 15 Jan. 1848, p. 38. See also Whyte, The Independent Irish Party, p. 5, note 4.

[78] Nation, 31 July 1847, p. 685; 25 Sept. 1847, p. 807. The Holy Cross meeting has been assigned considerable importance by Irish historians because one of its organizers was James Finton Lalor, whose ideas on the relationship of the nationalist cause to the interests of the farming population became popular in later years and had some influence on those nationalists who supported the New Departure.

[79] Whyte, The Independent Irish Party, pp. 5-6.

[80] Ibid., p. 8. See also Kennedy, "The tenant-right agitation in Ulster."

tionate support from large farmers, from what one newspaper called the "class of respectable and sturdy farmers who were possessed of competent means."[81] These "respectable" farmers were reacting to a decline in agricultural prices and poor crop yields in the late 1840s, especially for wheat.[82] Most held long leases with fixed rents which were becoming increasingly difficult to pay. They were also faced with a decline in the value of land as a result of the Famine, which depreciated the value of their interests in their holdings. This was naturally a worry most of all to farmers in Ulster, where interests were worth far more than in the South, and the decline in the value of land goes a long way toward explaining their willingness to join the agitation.[83] All of these concerns were reflected in the demands laid out at the August conference: (1) a fair valuation of rent; (2) no disturbance so long as the rent was paid; (3) the right to sell their interests; and (4) a reduction of arrears and payments by installments.[84]

The regional distribution of the Tenant League was also similar to that of the Tithe War. Aside from support in Ulster, the strength of the League was centered mainly in Leinster and east Munster. During the winter of 1849-50, when local associations were being organized in all the other provinces, no such bodies were established in Connaught.[85] In March of 1850 the prospect of activity in Connaught was so bleak that a *Nation* editorialist was led to remark:

> We wish that the people of the West of Ireland could be induced to do something for themselves. Even sleep does not bear so close a resemblance to death as does the torpor that is upon Connaught. . . . All the other provinces are stirring. If their march is silent, and even slow, it is nonetheless steady. New 'tenant societies' are daily springing up in Ulster, in Munster, in Leinster. . . . The co-operation of Connaught is all that is wanted to make the movement strictly national.[86]

[81] *Kilkenny Journal*, 17 Nov. 1849. Quoted in Lee, *Modernisation of Irish Society*, p. 40.

[82] Lee, *Modernisation of Irish Society*, pp. 39-40.

[83] Adding to their concern was the failure in 1847 of Sharman Crawford's bill to legalize their right to sell their holdings. There was also talk that land-reform legislation might be passed in the House of Commons that would explicitly deny the legality of their "Ulster custom."

[84] Sullivan, *New Ireland*, pp. 314-5.

[85] Whyte, *The Independent Irish Party*, p. 6.

[86] *Nation*, 2 March 1850, p. 424.

Though tenant associations were formed at Castlebar and Tuam in time for the August conference, the Tenant League never did become "strictly national." Fewer than 5 percent of the delegates at the conference came from west of a line running from Cork to Derry.[87] Whereas in some counties in Leinster as many as ten societies were organized before the movement came to an end, in Connaught two or three clubs at the most were formed in any one county. By the spring of 1851 contributions to the central council of the League amounted to £810 from Leinster, £130 from Ulster, £170 from Munster, and nothing from Connaught.[88]

THE FARMERS' CLUBS   These clubs also drew their support primarily, though not exclusively, from large farmers. A meeting of the Queen's County Independent Club in 1871 was described by the *Nation* as "truly representative and influential," consisting of "priests and laymen, gentlemen of rank and station, men well known for sterling patriotism and great ability."[89] The Limerick and Clare Farmers' Club was founded in 1866 because, said the chairman at their first meeting, "we do not belong to the Chamber of Commerce, we would not be admitted into the club on George Street, and therefore we want a place for ourselves where we can all meet."[90] The first few meetings of the Limerick and Clare club were taken up with the problems of finding a suitable meeting house, arguing over whether dues should be set high enough to hire servants, and debating whether landowners should be admitted to membership.[91] The club continued to be dominated by substantial farmers. Even in 1878 it is possible to find members reacting angrily to a denunciation of "big graziers" by one of their own group, himself a large farmer and hotel proprietor. Another club member proudly stated that he considered himself a "big grazier," whereupon the presiding chairman asserted: "So am I, and so are we all, I fancy." "If we, by our own industry or by the industry of our forefathers have larger tracts of land . . . , we are not to blame for that. It is entirely owing to the energy and attention to business that such a state of things is in existence, and no slur should be cast upon us because we happen to be big graziers."[92] In a country

[87] Lee, *Modernisation of Irish Society*, p. 40.
[88] C. G. Duffy, *The League of North and South* (London, 1886), p. 181.
[89] *Nation*, 28 Jan. 1871, p. 84.
[90] *Limerick Reporter*, 30 Oct. 1866, p. 3.
[91] Ibid., 6 Nov. 1866, p. 4; 18 Dec. 1866, p. 4.
[92] Ibid., 18 June 1878, p. 3. The club member who had denounced big graziers

where the median size of land holdings was still less than twenty acres, it is likely that most farmers in these clubs had holdings of at least thirty acres.[93]

There were only a few farmers' clubs continuously active throughout the 1860s and 1870s. The more common pattern was for a club to meet regularly for a few years, then to languish, perhaps eventually to revive several years later. Overall there was a noticeable growth in the number of clubs from the 1860s to the 1870s. One very pronounced spurt in activity came in 1869-70 in connection with the forthcoming Land Act. On 16 September 1869 a conference was held in Cork city of delegates sent from several Munster farmers' clubs; on the 26th a large tenant meeting was held in Maryborough; and on the 29th, with Isaac Butt present, a Tenant League was formed at a meeting in the town of Tipperary.[94] In the remaining months of the year, public meetings were held to promote land reform in at least ten different counties.[95] At some, tenant associations were formed; and in December

---

was W. H. O'Sullivan, who was elected to parliament in 1874 as a Home Ruler with the support of the club and despite the opposition of the clergy. O'Sullivan had strong Fenian connections and in this regard was not typical of most of those who belonged to farmers' clubs.

[93] I selected a very small but random sample consisting of fourteen members belonging to three different clubs: the Queen's County Independent Club, the Limerick and Clare Farmers' Club, and the Wexford Independent Club. Among these fourteen, the median size of holdings was 99 acres and the median valuation was £74. Information on size of holdings was obtained from the Land valuation records in the Land Valuation Office, hereafter cited as V.O.

[94] *Limerick Reporter*, 17 Sept. 1869, p. 3; 1 Oct. 1869, p. 3. See also *Nation*, 2 Oct. 1869, pp. 103-4.

[95] Some of these meetings were also in support of amnesty for Fenian prisoners. The issues of the *Nation* in which reports of these meetings are given are as follows:

Kilkenny	9 Oct. 1869, p. 115
"	23 Oct. 1869, p. 148
Tipperary	9 Oct. 1869, p. 118
Limerick	16 Oct. 1869, p. 131
Cork	16 Oct. 1869, p. 131
"	13 Nov. 1869, p. 195
Wexford	30 Oct. 1869, p. 166
Mayo	6 Nov. 1869, p. 179
Cavan	6 Nov. 1869, p. 181
Galway	13 Nov. 1869, p. 195
King's	4 Dec. 1869, p. 243
Roscommon	4 Dec. 1869, p. 243

a meeting of the Tenant League was held in the Rotunda in Dublin.[96]

Contrary to Gladstone's hopes, the land bill he introduced did not dampen this activity. His bill proved to be as unpopular among tenant organizations as it was among landowners. Tenant spokesmen objected particularly to the fact that it contained no provisions to prevent increases in rents. They also objected to two provisions that excluded large farmers from the benefits of the act. First, the bill forced landlords to compensate tenants for eviction even in cases of non-payment of rent, but not if the valuation of the holding exceeded £15; second, tenants with leases of thirty-one years or longer were excluded entirely from protection under the act. Even before the bill was passed, it had been denounced by the Cork Farmers' Club, the Queen's County Independent Club, the Kilkenny Tenant League, and the Limerick and Clare Farmers' Club.[97] It was rejected at public meetings in eleven different counties, and tenant associations were formed to oppose it in at least two.[98] In the following three years, new associations were formed to protect tenants from so-called abuses of the act in the counties of Queen's, Tipperary, Roscommon, Wicklow, and Monaghan.[99]

The Land Act had another important effect on the farmers' clubs. It drew them closer to the Home Rule movement. This alliance was by no means inevitable. Deeply nationalistic as the members of these clubs were, land reform was their principal concern and they did not want to sacrifice it for any other. When the Limerick and Clare Farmers' Club had been founded in 1866, the members had resolved that "all political subjects should be avoided," excepting, of course, tenant right.[100] They were, not surprisingly, less than enthusiastic about Fenianism, since the Fenians were openly hostile to land reform. Although the farmers' clubs joined forces with the amnesty movement in 1869, they did so largely out of necessity and not because they were fully committed to the cause.[101] In reality, the farmers' clubs would have

[96] Nation, 18 Dec. 1869, p. 276.

[97] Nation, 5 March 1870, p. 452; Limerick Reporter, 22 March 1870, p. 3.

[98] Kilkenny Journal, 2 March 1870, p. 2; 5 March 1870, p. 2.

[99] Ibid., 13 Nov. 1872, p. 1; 7 Dec. 1872, p. 1; Roscommon Journal, 11 Jan. 1873, p. 2; Nation, 1 March 1873, p. 1; 30 May 1874, p. 3.

[100] Limerick Reporter, 6 Nov. 1866, p. 4.

[101] Even so, they were unable to avoid the hostility of many Fenian supporters who were determined that no special interest should receive a hearing alongside

much preferred that self-government and amnesty be forgotton until satisfactory land legislation had been obtained from the British parliament. Land reform was what really concerned them, and in late 1868 they promised the new Liberal government that if the land question were dealt with satisfactorily "the most un-doubted security would exist for the spread and maintenance of loyalty to the crown and institutions of the realm."[102]

When the land question was not dealt with to their satisfaction, the farmers' clubs were led to reconsider their priorities. Not en-tirely by coincidence, it was at this time that Butt was endeavor-ing to organize his Home Rule movement. In March 1870 the Tip-perary Tenant League combined its criticism of the land bill with approval of a proposal from Butt that the tenant societies reorgan-ize to agitate for Home Rule.[103] After the Land Act was passed, the Limerick and Clare Club denounced it and passed a Home Rule resolution. This occurred at a meeting of the club in October 1870, during which the chairman asserted that any doubts they might have had about the necessity of legislative independence had been dispelled by the Land Act. And another member stated that they should work for an independent parliament because "if we have home rule, a good land bill would inevitably be given."[104] In January 1871 the Queen's County Independent Club, which had never been enthusiastic about the Liberal alliance, affirmed its support for the Home Rule movement.[105]

The about-face in policy was hardly carried out without misgiv-ings.[106] It would have been strange indeed if the farmers' clubs had warmly embraced the Home Government Association. What no doubt bothered them was not just the elitism of the H.G.A., but also its obvious attempt to appeal to landed interests. Even after

---

the national question. Some extremists went so far as to break up tenant-right meetings at Limerick, Dundalk, and Dungarvan, and also forced the cancellation of a land meeting at Waterford. See *Nation*, 6 Nov. 1869, p. 179; 4 Dec. 1869, p. 243; *Kilkenny Journal*, 29 Jan. 1870, p. 3; *Nation*, 13 Nov. 1869, p. 197.

[102] *Limerick Reporter*, 21 Dec. 1868, p. 3. The argument I am making here is di-rectly opposite to that of E. D. Steele, who claims that in 1869 "it was plainer than ever that tenant-right and nationality were intertwined." See Steele, *Irish Land and British Politics*, p. 295.

[103] *Limerick Reporter*, 1 April 1870, p. 4.   [104] Ibid., 11 Oct. 1870, p. 4.

[105] *Nation*, 28 Jan. 1871, p. 80.

[106] *Limerick Reporter*, 5 Aug. 1873, p. 4; 9 Sept. 1873, p. 4. See also Thornley, *Isaac Butt*, p. 116 for an interesting letter written by Richard Lalor, president of the Queen's County Independent Club.

the association was reorganized in 1873 as the Home Rule League, the relationship between it and the farmers' clubs was far from harmonious. Throughout the 1870s the clubs complained bitterly that "tenant right had been left in the background in consequence of the great question of home rule."[107] They were especially dissatisfied with the performance of Home Rule members of parliament, many of whom could not be counted upon to support land bills. Yet the clubs remained part of the Home Rule movement and came to regard themselves as Home Rule clubs.[108] They stood loyal to Butt, whom they rightly considered to be a strong supporter of their interests. And they stayed firmly committed to the goal of self-government, invariably including it as part of their demands, and sometimes giving it priority over the land question.[109]

In addition to Home Rule, the major demands of the farmers' clubs were the same as those of the Tenant League, now known as the three Fs: fixity of tenure, fair rents, and free sale. Of these, they gave the greatest emphasis to fair rents. Even before the Land Act of 1870, rent arbitration was the principal point in their program. In a famous pamphlet written in the 1860s, Isaac Butt had proposed sixty-year leases based upon the independent revaluation of rents at periodic intervals.[110] At the conference in Cork city in 1869, the farmers' clubs had extended this proposal to a demand for rent arbitration on the basis of the average market value of agricultural produce for the previous twenty-one years.[111] The effect of the Land Act was to persuade them to give all the more emphasis to rent arbitration. It became clear that legal measures designed to provide greater security of tenure were ineffective unless accompanied by measures that would prevent landlords from raising rents. Throughout the 1870s, in almost any statement of their demands, the farmers' clubs included some reference to rent control. A tenant committee established in 1875 to draw up a land bill insisted on compulsory arbitration; and the most significant

[107] Limerick Reporter, 29 Sept. 1874, p. 4.

[108] For example, see Nation, 2 Feb. 1878, p. 13.

[109] Explicit statements to the effect that Home Rule should have priority over land reform may be found in reports of club meetings during this period. For the Kanturk Farmers' Club, see Cork Examiner, 29 Sept. 1873, p. 3; and for the Mallow Farmers' Club see Cork Examiner, 8 Oct. 1873, p. 3.

[110] Isaac Butt, Land Tenure in Ireland: A Plea for the Celtic Race (Dublin, 1866).

[111] Limerick Reporter, 17 Sept. 1869, p. 3.

part of Butt's land bill of 1876 was the inclusion of a provision for fixing rents. The essentials of land-reform thinking had been established with the Tenant League. Nevertheless, Butt and the farmers' clubs played an important role in keeping the demands alive and giving more priority than ever before to rent control.

Figure 3 provides a partial list of farmers' clubs or tenant defense associations mentioned in newspapers between 1875 and 1878. I have identified thirty clubs: ten in Ulster, seven in Leinster, six in Munster, and seven in Connaught. The list is not exhaustive, based, as it is, on references encountered in the course of investigating local agrarian politics in this period. Some of the clubs listed were noticed only once and were probably short-lived. Nevertheless, the mere mention of a club indicates that at least some efforts were being made in a district to form a political association to represent the interests of the farmer class. In addition to the clubs shown on this map, there were a number of Home Rule Associations, several of which were composed mostly of farmers. In the years 1875-8 the most active were the Edenderry, Cavan, and Wexford associations, but a few years earlier one of the most prominent groups had been the Roscommon Home Rule Association. Townsmen played leading roles in these clubs, but the bulk of their memberships came from the farming population. The organization of the Roscommon association in the early 1870s was a significant development that marked the beginning of a new political phase in the west. Subsequently, an increase in political activity by farmers in Connaught can be observed. It is true that only the Ballinasloe Tenants' Defence Association, formed in 1876, met regularly and was active in organizing land meetings during the late 1870s. But in December 1875 a tenant defense association had been formed in Louisburg.[112] In 1876 persons claiming to represent associations in Tuam, Leitrim, and Castlebar were present at land conferences in Dublin.[113] In early 1877 a tenant association was organized in Headford.[114] In late 1878 efforts were being made to form a club in Castlebar, and before long clubs had been established in Killannin and Clifden.[115] Collective action by and for tenant farmers was slowly but unmistakably expanding.

[112] *Nation*, 18 Dec. 1875, p. 3.

[113] Ibid., 18 March 1876, p. 5; 28 Oct. 1876, p. 5.

[114] *Galway Vindicator*, 3 Feb. 1877, p. 3.

[115] *Connaught Telegraph*, 9 Nov. 1878, p. 4; *Nation*, 30 Nov. 1878, p. 7; *Tuam News*, 7 Feb. 1879, p. 3.

FIGURE 3 · Farmers' Clubs, 1875-1878

NOTE: The most active clubs have been underlined. Some of the clubs listed were affiliates of others. For example, the Ballymena Tenants' Defence Association and the Ballyclare Tenants' Defence Association were both affiliates of the Antrim Central Tenants' Defence Association.

CONCLUSIONS

The interlude between the Great Famine and the Land War was one of the more tranquil periods in modern Irish history. Much of the bitter conflict that had plagued the land system before the Famine had subsided. Comparatively speaking, estates were now easier to manage, rents more often paid on time, and evictions fewer. A hard political contest was being waged between Catholic and Protestant interests, during which Catholics made substantial gains over Protestants. But there was not the routine violence, the waves of agrarian unrest, nor the mass political movements that were features of the pre-famine period. And there were no dramatic shifts in the distribution of power. In comparison with the period 1824-46 or 1879-1903, the immediate post-famine period was one of political stalemate.

Yet underlying this stalemate we can discern a fundamental contention. The Catholic church, though certainly the strongest, was not the only challenging collectivity in the 1860s and 1870s. Other combinations were actively pursuing goals that could only be realized if established power were undermined. The Fenian goal of total independence, the Home Rule goal of self-government within a federal system, and the three Fs of the farmers' clubs—all necessitated weakening the authority of the existing political elite. Some Home Rulers, it is true, were not prepared to attack vested interests. But the majority were in no doubt about the necessity of doing so if they wanted to achieve their goals. The same was true of most members of the farmers' clubs; and, needless to say, also of those who subscribed to the Fenian doctrine. For these political hopefuls the tranquillity of the post-famine period was indeed frustrating. Economic conditions, at least in the late 1860s and early 1870s, did not provide a good breeding ground for movements against the prevailing social order. Their efforts were not, however, in vain. When prosperity came to an end in the late 1870s, the groundwork had been laid by the challenging collectivities we have discussed in this chapter for the greatest challenge to established power in nineteenth-century Ireland.

Part C
The Land War

Seven · **Agricultural Crisis**

The year 1877 marked the peak of a period of economic advancement and the beginning of a period of economic decline. The 1876 harvest had been exceptionally good. Agricultural statistics showed an increase in the number of pigs, usually a reliable index of food surplus; and 1877 was the only year after the Famine during which the population of the country did not decrease. But it also rained heavily. In March and April it rained more than two out of every three days. Throughout the summer it was wet, and in August it rained almost the entire month. The weather was better in the summer of 1878, especially during the crucial month of July when the hay had to be saved, but the months of August and September were again unusually wet. The summer of 1879 was disastrous. The rainfall in June and July was far above the average for the preceding ten years, and the mean temperature of every month from January to September was below average.

The tillage sector of the economy suffered the greatest damage. Table 12 gives the yields per acre of the principal tillage crops in each year from 1871 to 1881. Most crops declined in yield between 1876 and 1877, recovered well in 1878, but then fell to record lows in 1879, not only in comparison with 1876, but even in comparison with the average yield for 1871-6. Furthermore, these losses were accompanied by depressed prices. Throughout western Europe grain prices had been falling in the 1870s as a result of increased imports from North America and the diminishing cost of shipping across the Atlantic. As a result, Irish farmers were not compensated by high prices for their crop failures in the late seventies.[1] At current prices, the value of the seven principal crops was depressed by an average of 20 percent in the years 1877-9 as compared with 1876, with the worst losses coming in 1879 when the value of the seven principal crops was 30 percent below the value in 1876.[2]

[1] Barrington, "A review of Irish agricultural prices," pp. 251-2; Solow, *The Land Question and the Irish Economy*, pp. 122-4.

[2] James S. Donnelly, Jr., "The agricultural depression of 1859-64" in *Irish Economic and Social History*, 3 (1976), pp. 52-3.

TABLE 12 · Crop yields per statute acre, 1871-81

	WHEAT (CWTS)	FLAX (CWTS)	OATS (CWTS)	BARLEY (CWTS)	HAY (TONS)	POTATOES (TONS)	TURNIPS (TONS)
1871	12.1	1.7	12.7	15.2	1.8	2.6	13.0
1872	11.4	2.8	11.4	14.3	1.9	1.8	11.4
1873	11.7	3.0	12.8	15.9	1.8	3.0	12.7
1874	15.4	3.4	13.5	19.2	1.8	4.0	13.2
1875	14.6	4.4	15.3	18.1	2.2	3.9	15.9
1876	17.0	4.1	14.3	17.6	1.9	4.9	13.2
Mean 1871-6	13.7	3.2	13.3	16.7	1.9	3.3	13.2
1877	13.6	3.6	12.1	15.5	2.3	2.0	10.7
1878	15.0	4.0	13.5	16.1	2.3	3.0	14.2
1879	11.4	3.0	11.7	12.8	1.9	1.3	6.5
1880	15.0	3.3	14.2	15.8	2.0	3.6	14.3
1881	14.9	3.9	14.1	15.8	2.0	4.0	12.9

SOURCES: *Preliminary report on the returns of agricultural produce in Ireland in 1879 with tables*, p. 7 [C 2495], H.C. 1880, lxxvi; and *The agricultural statistics of Ireland . . . 1881*, p. 43 [C 3332], H.C. 1882, lxxiv.

The agricultural depression of the late 1870s has been accepted by most historians as the principal cause of the Irish Land War. Yet it is possible to raise some serious questions about how and why it had this effect. As I shall argue in the concluding pages of this chapter, it is not clear that the hardships wrought by this depression were unprecedented. Moreover, in a country where livestock was the main agricultural product, it is, on the surface at least, rather puzzling that rural tenants should revolt against their landlords during a crisis which saw the greatest losses in the tillage sector. Altogether wheat, oats, and barley probably accounted for less than 10 percent of the gross value added in Irish agriculture.[3] In some parts of the country, especially in parts of the northeast, the midlands, and the southeast, losses in these crops may have been a major source of difficulty. But in most areas, and particularly in the west, livestock was a far more important source of income than commercial crops. Nonetheless, it was in the west that the land movement emerged and found its

[3] Solow, *The Land Question and the Irish Economy*, p. 171.

greatest support. How did the depression hurt farmers in this part of the country?

Rural Distress

By far the greatest damage resulted from the heavy dependence of western farmers on the potato. In December 1879 Constabulary reports from the west were unanimous in declaring a miserable crop. From the Ballymote district in Sligo it was stated that the wet season "prevented the crops ripening and caused great decay in the potatoes, which . . . in these parts of the country are a complete failure." In the Ballinasloe area in Galway, the potato was described as "a bad crop both in quantity and quality," except in a very few districts. In the countryside around Portumna, about 30 percent of the potato crop was "black," and in the Sixmilebridge district of Clare the potato was hit by a disease that "rendered the majority of the crop unfit for human use."[4] As shown in Table 12 the potato yield fell from a mean of 3.3 tons per acre in the period 1871-6 to 2.0 tons per acre in 1877. It recovered to 3.0 tons per acre in 1878 but then plummeted to 1.3 tons per acre in 1879.[5] In other words, the yield in 1879 was less than half of the mean for 1871-6, and less than a third of the yield in 1876. This was not only lower than the most recent poor potato crop (in 1872), but it also came after two years of below-average yields. The potato suffered more damage than did the main commercial crops. While the decline in yields per acre of wheat, oats, and barley (comparing 1871-6 with 1879) ranged from 12 percent for oats to 23 percent for barley, the decline in the yield per acre of potatoes was 61 percent.[6]

This potato failure was the main source of difficulty in the west in 1879, but it was compounded by several other factors. First, there was a declining demand for seasonal workers in England and Scotland. The demand had already been falling off during the 1870s, but it was abnormally low late in the decade as a result of the agricultural depression in Britain. One contemporary authority suggested that the loss from this source alone to the small

[4] *Preliminary report on agricultural produce in 1879*, pp. 42-8.

[5] These are national figures, but those for Connaught are almost identical. See *Agricultural statistics of Ireland . . . 1881*, p. 43.

[6] Ibid., p. 7.

farmers of Connaught was £250,000.[7] Certainly the estimate of
38,000 seasonal migrants in 1880 represents a drastic decline
from the annual rate of 100,000 that prevailed not much more
than ten years earlier.[8]

In addition, though the livestock sector of the economy was less
affected by the downturn than was the tillage sector, it also experienced substantial losses. Perhaps the greatest, especially in
the heavy dairying districts of Munster, came from the one-
quarter fall in butter prices between 1876 and 1879. The late
1870s marked the beginning of an almost steady decline in Irish
butter prices for several decades as a result of foreign competition.
In both 1877 and 1878 the lower prices were offset by relatively
high production, but in 1879 low output coincided with extremely depressed prices, the worst in ten years owing to sluggish
commercial and industrial activity in Britain.[9]

At the same time, the bad weather was having an adverse effect
on livestock production. The rains stimulated the growth of grass,
but also the spread of disease, especially liver-fluke disease which
ravaged the sheep population in the west in the spring of 1879.
The potato failures reduced the supply of feed available for pigs.
And, though the average yield per acre of hay in 1879 was not
below normal, most reports indicated that the quality was sub-
standard, and in some areas the hay was not saved without severe
damage. From the Ballinasloe district the Constabulary reported
that the hay crop was "light and badly saved; great quantities lost
by floods and constant wet." Around Ballymote, County Sligo, the
hay crop was "plentiful," but "to a great extent worthless, from
not being properly saved." Near Tulla, County Clare, it was described in similar language as "plentiful" but "of inferior quality." The damage to meadow and pasture appears to have been
especially serious in County Leitrim. From Carrick-on-Shannon,
the Constabulary reported that "hay is a fair crop, but much in-

[7] This estimate was made in January 1880 by the economist W. Neilson Hancock. See N. D. Palmer, The Irish Land League Crisis (New Haven, 1940), p. 66.

[8] Ó Gráda, "Seasonal migration," pp. 54-7.

[9] James S. Donnelly, Jr., "Cork Market: its role in the nineteenth-century Irish
butter trade" in Studia Hibernica, no. 11 (1971), pp. 154-5; Donnelly, Cork, pp.
253-4; Barrington, "A review of Irish agricultural prices," p. 252. The Barrington
butter price index for 1879 was 23 percent below the mean for 1871-6, and 27 percent below Barrington's figure for 1876. The May to November average price of
first-quality butter sold at the Cork market in 1879 was 29 percent lower than the
corresponding figure for 1876.

jured by continual wet during the time of saving." And about Ballinamore the hay was "considerably under an average as regards quantity and quality."[10]

Problems in keeping animals fed, together with the need to compensate for tillage losses, obviously put more than the usual pressure on farmers to dispose of their stock. Unfortunately, demand in the livestock market was down. According to the Barrington price index, prices for store cattle in 1879 fell 5 percent for 1-2 year olds and 8 percent for 2-3 year olds from the average for 1871-6. And prices for beef, mutton, and wool were down 17 percent, 8 percent, and 47 percent respectively.[11] The Barrington index actually underestimated the decline in prices for store cattle, since it was based on prices as reported from county fairs held in May and June only; in the second half of the year the market was worse, and farmers found it difficult to dispose of their stock.[12] At the Ballinasloe fair in October, prices for third and fourth-class cattle and sheep were good, but prices for first and second-class cattle and sheep were substantially lower than in previous years.[13] Further, the volume of livestock traded was considerably less than in earlier years. Table 13 shows that the number of sheep brought for sale at the Ballinasloe fair had been declining since 1873, and that in 1879 it fell to the lowest level recorded in the 1870s (primarily as a result of the sheeprot epidemic in the spring). The number sold, as a percentage of the number brought for sale, remained high in 1877 and 1878, but fell to 67 percent in 1879 as compared with a mean of 88 percent for the period 1871-6. In the case of horned cattle, the number brought for sale remained reasonably high in the late 1870s, and was slightly higher than average in 1879, but the percentage sold was only 65 percent as compared with a mean of 77 percent for the period 1871-6.

To understand the impact on small farmers of these losses in the livestock economy it may be helpful to magnify the economic differences between the typical pre-famine small landholder and the typical post-famine small landholder. The small landholder before the famine was poorer than his post-famine counterpart. But,

[10] Preliminary report on agricultural produce in 1879, pp. 42-8.
[11] Barrington, "A review of Irish agricultural prices," p. 252.
[12] Donnelly, Cork, pp. 253-4.
[13] Thom's, 1881, pp. 692-3.

TABLE 13 · Numbers of sheep and horned cattle brought for sale
and percentage sold at Ballinasloe fair in each of the years 1871 to
1881

	SHEEP		HORNED CATTLE	
	NUMBERS		NUMBERS	
	BROUGHT	PERCENT	BROUGHT	PERCENT
YEAR	FOR SALE	SOLD	FOR SALE	SOLD
1871	84,567	85	20,313	86
1872	74,621	85	18,142	78
1873	71,009	84	17,823	69
1874	65,130	91	18,018	81
1875	49,387	90	15,277	89
1876	59,809	95	19,525	59
Mean 1871-6	67,421	88	18,183	77
1877	55,588	94	17,352	74
1878	58,975	89	16,858	92
1879	45,901	67	18,213	55
1880	48,616	85	16,561	87
1881	42,118	85	15,687	76

SOURCE: Thom's, 1882, pp. 693-4.

partly as a result, he was also more self-sufficient. He obtained almost all his food from his own small holdings or from conacre
ground. Non-food consumption was modest and primarily based
on home production. Since wages were low, the majority of
people did not have sufficient income to engage in much purchasing. Most of the money that they did earn as laborers went to pay
their rents; in many cases, they did not even pay the rent in
money. This description is certainly an oversimplification, but it
helps to bring out the distinctive features of the pre-famine pattern. In the post-famine period many small landholders continued
to rely on home-grown food, particularly potatoes, but they also
engaged in considerable purchasing. They bought feed, clothing,
and even food; they also, of course, bought livestock. Thus, in
order to maintain his standard of living, the post-famine farmer
(even the small farmer) relied heavily on monetary income, which
in the west came largely from the sale of livestock and in some
cases from migratory labor. It has been said that there occurred a

revolution of "rising expectations" in post-famine Ireland.[14] People experienced an increase in standards of living and thereby acquired psychological aspirations for a better way of life. It is very possible that such a shift occurred, but I would suggest that a much more important change was that small landholders expected—indeed, came to depend on—more monetary income in order *just to preserve a constant standard of living*. Even if standards of living had not improved, there would have been expectations of increased purchasing power.

The situation was most serious for small farmers, particularly those in the west, many of whom had become dependent on a level of purchasing power beyond their means. Their increasing need for money had forced them to make heavy purchases on credit and to accumulate larger and larger debts. According to one estimate, by 1879 over £200,000 was owing to shopkeepers in the county of Mayo alone.[15] In December Henry Robinson of the Local Government Board suggested that the distress was "due not so much to the inclemency of the summer, as to the improvidence of bye gone years." "For it appears to be generally admitted," he continued in a tone of reprimand, "that such were the liabilities of many of the poorer tenant farmers that the year must have been an extraordinarily favourable one to have placed them in a position to extricate themselves from their very heavy incumbrances."[16]

The problem was in fact more complex than Robinson allowed. If the harvest had been favorable, most small farmers could have supported their debts. The tragedy was that their sources of credit were diminishing at the very time when they needed to borrow more. Formerly, credit had been relatively easy to obtain so long as farmers had met minimal payments. But faced with potentially bankrupt customers, shopkeepers were less willing in 1879 to extend credit, and in some cases would not grant advances unless a customer could settle his existing account. It is true that many shopkeepers did continue to extend credit as the only means by which their clientele could be maintained. In 1880 a parish priest in County Cork acknowledged that the "humane, merciful, and large-hearted shopkeepers of Castletown . . . kept all the people of

[14] Donnelly, Cork, pp. 249-52.

[15] P.A.E. Bew, "The politics of the Irish Land War, 1879-82," unpublished Ph.D. thesis, Cambridge University, 1974, p. 61.

[16] S.P.O., Chief Secretary's Office, Registered Papers: Report of H. A. Robinson of the Local Government Board, 16 Dec. 1879 (1879/22715).

this barony alive [on meal] for the last three years against great odds."[17] They could not, however, grant limitless amounts of credit without driving themselves into bankruptcy. "The shopkeepers who live by the custom of the farmers," remarked a member of the Ballinasloe Tenant Defence Association in 1878, "cannot meet their engagements if their accounts are not paid."[18] As purchasing declined and debts could not be collected, the resources available to shopkeepers to lend money greatly diminished. They must also have found it more difficult to secure bank loans, since the deposits of the joint stock banks fell by some 14 percent between 1876 and 1880, after rising almost steadily since the 1840s.[19] Many shopkeepers were forced to resist demands for credit and even to press for payment of debts.[20] A petition for rent reductions submitted in October 1879 by tenants on the Trinity College estate at Portmagee, County Kerry, complained of the cumulative effect of the potato failure, the decline in agricultural prices, and the restriction of credit:

> Owing to the failure of the potato crop during the past two years, we have been obliged to buy all the necessaries of life; and this together with the great fall in the value of all kinds of farm produce, coupled with the refusal of the traders and shopkeepers to give any credit as they used to do previously, has placed us all in a very embarrassed position.[21]

In 1880 the credit system was described by Thomas Baldwin, an authority on Irish agriculture, as "actually paralyzed in most parts of the country."[22]

[17] Donnelly, Cork, p. 245.

[18] Connaught Telegraph, 12 Jan. 1878.

[19] W. Neilson Hancock, Report on Deposits and Cash Balances in Joint Stock Banks in Ireland, 1840-1869 (Dublin, 1870), p. 5; W. Neilson Hancock, Report on Savings in Ireland (Dublin, 1877), p. 7; Thom's, 1886, p. 716.

[20] One index of this greater pressure for payment is afforded by the increase in processes for the recovery of small debts at the petty sessions. See Solow, The Land Question and the Irish Economy, p. 87.

[21] T.C.D., Trinity College papers: C. J. O'Connell to Board, 1 Oct. 1879 (MUN/P/23/1677[1]). Though the agent for this estate, Captain H. Needham, did not believe that rent reductions were, on the whole, justified, he agreed that "the shopkeepers have refused credit, in many cases." See Captain H. Needham to J. Carson, 12 Oct. 1879 (MUN/P/23/1677[2]).

[22] Minutes of evidence taken before her majesty's commissioners on agriculture, p. 89 [C 2778 I], H.C. 1881, xv.

The Opposing Interests of Landlords and Tenants

Landlords often claimed that the distress was exaggerated, insisting that rents would be paid if the government enforced the law and compelled tenants to meet their financial obligations. The Chief Secretary's office was swamped with letters asserting, as did one landlord in Sligo, that tenants "are well able to pay, but openly set me a defiance and will pay nothing."[23] Lord Lucan, the largest landowner in the Castlebar area, declared that "this general resistance to rents in Mayo cannot be attributed to poverty or distress; food is at a very moderate cost [and] there are no applications for relief from able bodied persons." "It is to communism alone," his lordship announced, "that the present state of things in the country is to be attributed."[24]

The allegation that Ireland was falling to the specter of communism could not have been more mistaken, but the assertion that most tenants were actually able to pay their rents is supported by reports from many government officials. G. E. Hillier, the inspector-general of the Royal Irish Constabulary, suggested in October 1879 that most tenants could pay their rents, but were not doing so because they were awaiting the result of the agitation to obtain better terms, or because they were afraid of punishment from the agitators. In January 1880 a resident magistrate in Galway related a case of tenants who refused to pay more than one-quarter of their normal rent, but among whom he saw "evidence of wealth in all the surroundings of their houses, and the amount of crops safely housed." Also in January 1880 a Clare magistrate, helping to serve processes on tenants in neighboring Galway, reported that "the people appeared to me to be well off—the son of one said his father would not sell a cob to which I took a fancy." And Henry Robinson declared in December 1879 that "in most instances the shortcomings of rent arise, not from an inability to pay, but from a species of mutual agreement to defer doing so as long as possible, in the hope of beneficial circumstances ultimately eventuating from the agitation movement."[25]

[23] S.P.O., Chief Secretary's Office, Registered Papers: Henry Brett to Under-Secretary, 2 Jan. 1880 (1880/180).

[24] Ibid.: Lord Lucan to Under-Secretary, 26 Sept. 1879 (1879/16272).

[25] Ibid.: Report of the inspector-general of the Royal Irish Constabulary, 30 Oct. 1879 (1880/13904); H. A. Blake, R.M., to Under-Secretary, 14 Jan. 1880 (1880/

Enough claims of this kind survive to call into question the school textbook history of the Land War as a desperate struggle of half-starving peasants against heartless landlords. But we should not too readily accept these statements at face value. Their authors were not unbiased. If the real situation was as I have come to perceive it, neither the image of the half-starving peasant nor the image of the rent-hoarding peasant accurately portrays the typical farmer who turned against his landlord in 1879. The problem was that most landlords, and even many government officials, had a different notion from tenants of what constituted hardship. Many people still thought in pre-famine terms. If Irish farmers were experiencing hardship, one should find them devoid of means. If they had livestock and crops that they could sell, then the seriousness of the situation was being misrepresented by agitators.

This view, however, fails to consider the changes that had taken place in the small-farm economy after the Famine. It is impossible to understand the consequences of the bad harvests of 1877-9 unless one recognizes that a post-famine small farmer had economic resources to protect, some of which were luxuries, but most of which were essential to his survival. Referring to distress in County Roscommon during the winter of 1879-80, an inspector of the Local Government Board indicated that:

> I do not mean so much the labourers and cottiers as the small farmers, those holding from four to sixteen acres of land and whose valuation runs up to about £15. These men are really the greatest sufferers having perhaps one or two cows, but who are now denied credit, even a stone of meal. Their position is much worse than that of the labourer, who if he has to go into the [work]house for a short period comes out in as good a position as he was before. But if these men are forced to part with their cow, involved as they are, they are utterly and hopelessly ruined.[26]

Whether or not we conclude that tenants were hoarding their rent depends, in the final analysis, on how we define *ability to pay*. If we mean, as some landlords meant, that a tenant must give his last pound or sell his only cow to fulfill his obligations to his landlord, then we are not using the term in the same way that tenants did.

1300); Hugh MacTernan, R.M., to Under-Secretary, 18 Jan. 1880 (1880/1495); Report of H. A. Robinson, 16 Dec. 1879 (1879/22715).

[26] Ibid.: Captain Straight to Local Government Board, 27 Feb. 1880 (1880/5368).

No doubt many tenants were earning income and holding livestock while at the same time claiming inability to pay rents. Their
use of monetary income had placed them in a position where, during hard times, they had to face a difficult choice between different types of expenditures. A fall in income and a withdrawal of
credit meant that purchases had to be curtailed and that they had
to reduce the number of their livestock. But (and this is the crux of
the matter) the extent to which they were forced to do so could be
mitigated by a reduction in their rent. In preceding years farmers
had become accustomed to a certain level of expenditure over and
above their rent; and, from their point of view, it was only right
that if their other expenditures should decline, so too should their
rent.

This was potentially a dangerous situation for landlords. On the
whole, they had managed to keep tenants relatively content for at
least several decades by granting privileges that went considerably beyond their legal obligations. Such privileges, however, were
generally regarded by tenants as customary rights to which they
had a traditional claim. In 1879 many tenants took the view that
they were entitled to rent reductions as a matter of right and that it
was the obligation of any "good" landlord to help them meet the
economic adversities they were facing. Indeed, on at least some
estates and perhaps on most, there was an expectation that the
landlord, if approached politely and provided with good reasons,
would grant abatements sufficient to help offset their economic
losses.

In 1878 tenants began to submit appeals for reductions. The
number increased further when the first gale became due in the
spring of 1879. When the second gale approached in the autumn
of that year, landlords were deluged with requests of this kind. A
memorial submitted by nine tenants on the Pratt estate in County
Kilkenny illustrates the general tone of these petitions:

> We the undersigned tenantry of the above townland hereby
> take the liberty of tendering you an unanimous petition for an
> abatement in the ensuing season's rent. In so doing we re-
> spectfully appeal without the aid or influence of orators, etc.,
> we do it from the calling of privation and the suffering of the
> many grievances of these trying occasions.
>
> As you are already aware that foreign importation has ren-
> dered prices so low that every department of agricultural

production is at its lowest ebb, consequently by taking full amount of the rent from us at this season could leave us unable to cope with the ensuing winter.

For in addition to rentals at this season there is the coal dealer and manure vendor's to be met with, together with almost an entire failure of potato produce.

With all these contentions the ensuing winter will be a hard one, should you now demand a full half rent on this trying occasion. But we hope and trust such won't be the case, but expect you will prove a good and generous landlord in the present as we have proved an honest and faithful tenantry in the past.[27]

Speeches and resolutions coming from land meetings were more militant, but they manifested the same expectation that landlords should reduce rents in view of the agricultural depression. As will be seen in the following chapter, the single most common demand of resolutions adopted at land meetings during 1879 was for a reduction in rents; it was only later that other demands and concerns assumed greater importance.[28] The Land War began primarily as an attempt to persuade landlords to accede to requests from their tenants for abatements. Resolutions tried "respectfully, but firmly, [to] press upon the landlords . . . the necessity of an immediate and general reduction of rents," or they "respectfully and earnestly" requested landlords "to make such a reduction . . . as will be adequate to meet the present crisis, so that their tenants may be able to retain their lands and pay in future an equitable rent."[29] Another resolution, addressed in August 1879 to "the several landlords and agents" of Ballingarry, County Tipperary, bears quoting in full:

We, the tenantry of the parish of Ballingarry, beg to express our gratitude to you, who with only one or two exceptions, have always treated us with benevolence and kindness. Many of us remember the famine years, and believe that in consequence of this kind and considerate treatment the parish contrasted favourably with many others in the safety with which landlord and tenant got through them.

[27] N.L.I., Pratt papers: Petition from the tenantry of the townland of Coolrainey, County Kilkenny, 14 Oct. 1879 (MS 13327).
[28] See Table 19 in Chapter Eight below.
[29] *Nation*, 27 Sept. 1879; 4 Oct. 1879; and 1 Nov. 1879.

A succession of previous bad years, and the very low prices of everything this year which we have for sale—wool, corn, pork, beef, store stock, and especially butter, on which we have mainly depended—have brought about a crisis similar to that of '47, and it is with great reluctance that we feel ourselves constrained to state to you our wants, and to beg of you humbly and earnestly that you will in your kindness give us a reduction in the rents of this year, and thus help to save us from utter ruin.

We all feel very much the great pressure of the times, and are, indeed, in many instances, very poor and embarrassed, and with our credit run out.[30]

It is difficult to make general statements about how landlords responded to these appeals, but it is clear that, on the whole, they reacted slowly and reluctantly. There was a widespread view among landlords that, for most tenants, the level of distress was insufficient to justify abatements. Many also felt that rents were already moderate, and that they were doing more than their share if they postponed increases that they had otherwise intended to introduce. Some landlords refused outright to grant abatements. Stephen Gibbons and Sir George O'Donel met with deputations of tenants on their estates in Mayo in June 1879, but both refused to grant any reductions.[31] Tenants in the neighborhood of Athleague, County Roscommon, sent memorials to their respective landlords in September 1879, but only one landlord agreed to an abatement.[32] A county inspector of the Royal Irish Constabulary reported in October 1879 from east Galway that "with one exception, the large landed proprietors have not declared any intention to abate their rents."[33]

Probably most landlords did grant at least some reduction. They were, as a rule, extremely reluctant to give equal abatements to all tenants, since this would drastically cut estate revenues, perhaps without relieving those in the most need. Many landlords, therefore, granted selective abatements. Sometimes reductions would go to particular tenants whom the landlord or his agent thought were suffering the greatest hardship. In other cases, abatements

[30] Ibid., 23 Aug. 1879.

[31] *Connaught Telegraph*, 21 June 1879, p. 5; 28 June 1879, p. 5.

[32] *Roscommon Journal*, 13 Sept. 1879, p. 2.

[33] S.P.O., Chief Secretary's Office, Registered Papers: Report of the inspector-general of the Royal Irish Constabulary, 30 Oct. 1879 (1880/13904).

varied systematically with the level of rent. In 1879 Sir Arthur
Guinness granted abatements on his Galway estate of 30 percent
for tenants whose annual rent was less than £20 and of 20 percent
for tenants whose annual rent was more than £20.[34] Still other
landlords gave preference to yearly tenants or to tenants whose
rent had been raised within the past ten or fifteen years. G. F.
Stewart proposed to Lord Leitrim in September 1879 that tenants
be divided into three "grades": (1) those with old leases, who
would be granted no abatement; (2) yearly tenants whose rent had
not been raised since 1868, who would also not receive any reduction; and (3) yearly tenants whose rent had been raised since 1868,
who would be granted an abatement.[35] Stewart was anxious to
avoid across-the-board reductions. Although he recognized that a
graduated reduction might not give as much "general satisfaction" as "a general equal abatement over the whole estate," he
preferred to deal with individual cases and indicated in one letter
to the bailiff on the Newtown Gore estate that he "need not tell
any tenant what his neighbour is paying and I am most anxious
that there not be any notice in the papers on the subject of the
abatement."[36]

Many landlords were in the end forced to concede general
abatements. Unavoidably, however, they were modest. The financial position of the typical Irish landlord had certainly improved
since the Famine, but he was still faced with family charges,
mortgages, head rents, taxes, management expenses, and general
debts that limited the revenue over which he had unfettered control.[37] Hence, only very moderate general reductions could be
granted without great difficulty. Most abatements reported in
newspapers in 1879 were less than 30 percent, and one can safely
assume that these were higher than the average.[38] In October 1879
the *Sligo Champion* asserted that seven-eighths of the landlords

[34] *Northern Whig*, 4 Dec. 1879, p. 5.

[35] N.L.I., Leitrim papers: Letter book of G. F. Stewart: Stewart to Lord Leitrim, 30
Sept. 1879.

[36] Ibid.: Stewart to Lord Leitrim, 30 Sept. 1879; Stewart to William Gibson, 10
Nov. 1879.

[37] For discussions of the financial difficulties faced by landlords in the late
nineteenth century, see Solow, *The Land Question and the Irish Economy*, pp.
181-4; and Vaughan, "Landlord and tenant relations."

[38] Donnelly found that about forty Cork landowners whose allowances were reported in local newspapers between August and December 1879 reduced their
rents an average of some 25 percent. See Donnelly, *Cork*, p. 255. A rough count

had refused to grant "significant" abatements; most of those who allowed any reduction had given 10 or 15 percent in order to avoid accusations that they were doing nothing.[39]

Reductions of this kind were simply insufficient to provide tenants with substantial relief. One can illustrate this hard fact by referring again to the family-budget estimates provided by inspectors of the Congested Districts Board in the early 1890s. In the electoral district of Moore, County Roscommon, the estimated total expenditure (including agricultural expenses) of a family in ordinary circumstances was almost £46, while the estimated rent (including taxes) was £6 to £7, or less than 15 percent of the total. In the Castlerea district the estimated total expenditure was £33, while the estimated rent (including taxes) was £4 to £5, or again just under 15 percent. And in the district of Partry, County Mayo, the total came to about £43, while rent and taxes were estimated at £5 to £6, once again less than 15 percent.[40] It is true that, even in cases such as these, rents could represent the critical margin between bankruptcy and solvency, and could be bitterly resented as a consequence. Still, for tenants in these circumstances, the reality was that an abatement on their rent of 30 percent would have reduced their total expenditures by less than 5 percent, while a reduction of 20 percent would have lowered their total expenditures by less than 3 percent. Although rents were higher in the 1870s than they were in the 1890s,[41] they could not have been so much higher as to alter the conclusions to which these estimates lead us: that abatements of from 10 to 30 percent were not much help to tenants in 1879 faced with crop failures, a depressed livestock market, a sharp fall in butter prices, a decline in the demand for migratory labor, and the loss of their major source of credit. The Sligo Champion noted that a farmer who paid a rent of £5 per annum saved only 10s. if granted an abatement of 10 percent. Expressing what was certainly the viewpoint of most tenants, the newspaper was morally outraged that a landlord should expect a family to live on 10s.[42] The irony was that, if competitive rents had been charged in earlier decades, these abatements would

that I made of abatements announced in local newspapers in 1879 (mostly in Connaught) showed that the majority were in the range of 15 to 30 percent.

[39] Sligo Champion, 25 Oct. 1879, p. 2.

[40] T.C.D., Congested Districts Board: Base line reports, pp. 388, 601, and 614.

[41] As a result of land legislation passed in the 1880s. See below, Chapter Nine.

[42] Sligo Champion, 25 Oct. 1879, p. 2.

have represented a more significant reduction in total tenant expenditures.

In any case, the rent reductions granted in 1879 manifestly failed to meet the needs of tenants. Most tenants now found their rents burdensome, and some began to fall into arrears. Figure 4 plots the level of arrears as a percentage of annual rents for the years 1876 to 1881 on nine estates. Perhaps the most striking feature of these graphs is that arrears reached their peak in 1881 when the worst hardships of the depression had passed. The explanation is that a refusal to pay full rents was part of the program promoted by tenant agitators during the Land War. The arrears in 1879, however, can only partly be explained in these terms, since the agrarian movement was just beginning in that year. On all nine estates, the level of arrears was higher in 1879 than in 1878. On some properties, for instance on the Earl of Erne's in County Donegal, the increase was small; but on others, such as Lord Crofton's Mote estate and the Stewart estate in Louth, the increase was considerable. On the average for these nine estates, arrears rose from 23 percent of the annual rental in 1878 to 34 percent in 1879, and to 41 percent in 1880 (using unweighted means). Landlords, when confronted with arrears of this magnitude, inevitably responded with notices to quit, ejectment processes, and evictions. Even in 1878 the number of evictions (without readmission) was over 800, higher than in any year since 1864. In 1879 there were more than 1,000, and in 1880 the figure was almost 1,900.[43]

In an earlier chapter I argued that the strength of the Irish land system lay in the power that landlords exercised over tenants, especially their power to grant non-contractual privileges. To the extent that such privileges were granted, the landlord's power was not a burden to tenants. On the contrary, it was a very real benefit. His control over land gave them moderate rents, security of tenure, and other related advantages, for which they were in most cases thankful. The depression of the late 1870s, however, reduced the value of these privileges. No longer did tenants enjoy what they regarded as moderate rents; no longer were they secure in the occupation of their holdings. Landlord power, which under different circumstances had been beneficial, became an obstacle to tenant interests.

[43] Return of evictions from 1849 to 1880, p. 3.

FIGURE 4 · Arrears as a percentage of annual rents on nine estates in each of the years, 1876-1881

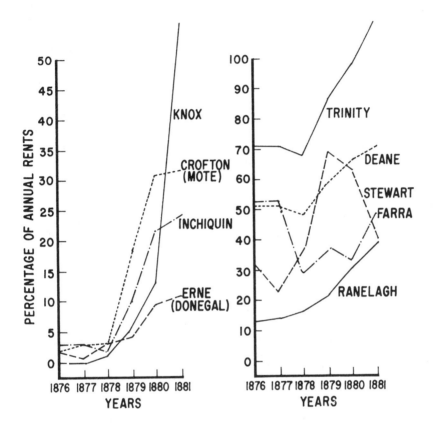

NOTE: Data for the Erne estate in Donegal, Inchiquin estate in Clare, and Knox estate in Roscommon have been taken from Vaughan, "Landlord and tenant rela-tions," p. 88. Other sources are as follows: N.L.I., Crofton papers: Rentals of the Mote estate, County Roscommon, May gale; Deane papers: Rentals of the Deane estate, County Kildare, 1876-81, Nov. gale (MS 14282); T.C.D., Incorporated Soci-ety papers: Rentals of the Ranelagh estate, County Roscommon, Nov. gale; Rentals of the Stewart estate, County Louth, 1876-81, Nov. gale (IS/5558); Rentals of the Farra estate, County Westmeath, 1876-81, Nov. gale (IS/5562); and Trinity College papers: Rentals of the Old Crown, Old Private, and Baldwin estates, 1876-81, Nov. gale (MUN/V/78/10).

THE DEPRESSION IN PERSPECTIVE

Too often social scientists have been satisfied with explaining rebellions by demonstrating the presence of hardship and discontent at the point in time that a rebellion breaks out. They suppose
that if they explain this high level of discontent, they have *ipso
facto* explained the rebellion.[44] Yet, in many societies, equally intense hardships had been experienced at earlier points in time
without revolutionary consequences. The agricultural depression
of the late 1870s was the immediate precipitating condition for
the Irish Land War, and the purpose of this chapter has been to
explain why this was the case. In doing so, I have run the risk of
conveying an impression that these hardships were somehow
unique, and so might possibly explain the unique characteristics
of the Irish Land War.

Yet one can easily avoid this mistake by viewing the depression
of the late 1870s within a larger historical perspective. Intense
rural hardship and discontent were often to be found in early
nineteenth-century Ireland. Pre-famine farmers were time and
again faced with falling agricultural prices and shrinking revenues that made their rents appear burdensome. Pre-famine cottiers did not have high aspirations and did not depend primarily
on money for their livelihood, but they did have certain expectations and needs that were just as important to them. They depended on a minimal level of employment, on their potato crop,
and on the continued occupation of their small holdings. The loss
(even the threat of losing) any of these could and did generate violent expressions of discontent, as we know from Chapter Three.
The economic depression that followed the Napoleonic Wars,
numerous potato failures in the pre-famine period, and above all
the Great Famine of the late 1840s cut rural sources of livelihood
more than did the depression of the late 1870s. Nor was there anything unique about post-famine expectations of non-contractual
privileges. Although I would argue that the refusal of landlords to
grant the rent reductions to which tenants believed they were entitled was the greatest source of discontent in 1879, I am not implying that this kind of discontent was unprecedented. If anything, pre-famine peasants had an even longer list of customary

[44] In an earlier publication I discussed this literature and endeavored to criticize
it by drawing on some of the themes also developed in this book. See my "The
political mobilization of Irish farmers" in *Canadian Review of Sociology and Anthropology*, 22, no. 4, pt. 2 (Nov. 1975).

privileges which they claimed as rights, which they were prepared to defend, and which they were repeatedly forced to defend
during the economic decline that followed the Napoleonic Wars.
No, neither the hardships of the late 1870s nor the moral passions
generated by these hardships surpassed the privations and passions of the first half of the nineteenth century.

Even in the post-famine period, the depression of the late 1870s
was not unique. Recent research has shown that the downturn of
1859-64 was quantitatively more damaging, though it had almost
no political repercussions.[45] Whereas during the crisis of 1877-9
the value of the seven major crops was depressed by an average of
20 percent for *three* years, in the earlier downturn their value was
reduced by an average of 21 percent for *five* years.[46] The potato
crop suffered, on the whole, more damage in the years 1860-62
than it did in the years 1877-9. And the critical livestock sector
suffered much greater damage in the early 1860s than it did in the
late 1870s: at average prices, the value of all cattle, sheep, and
pigs in Ireland decreased by less than 9 percent between 1876 and
1880, whereas between 1859 and 1864 their value fell by almost
16 percent.[47] It is true, and this qualification needs to be emphasized, that there was no one year during the depression of
1859-64 that was as bad as the year 1879. It is possible that the
crisis of the late 1870s generated more discontent than did the earlier depression because it concentrated the hardship in a shorter
space of time. But, given the fact that the downturn of the early
1860s was on the whole more severe, it is difficult to imagine that
hardships could have been so much greater in 1879 as to account
for the completely different political consequences of the two
depressions.

Still another way to gain some perspective on the crisis of the
late 1870s is to look at eviction statistics. Although the rate of
eviction rose in the late 1870s, the numbers reported in these
years were not record-breaking by earlier standards. Comparable
data are available only after 1848, but they nevertheless establish
the point. The annual average number of evictions (without
readmission) was roughly 7,000 in the years 1849-55, 1,000 in the
years 1859-64, and also 1,000 in the years 1877-80. Altogether,
there were nine years (1849-55 and 1863-4) in which the number

---

[45] Donnelly, "Agricultural depression of 1859-64."
[46] Ibid., pp. 52-3.   [47] Ibid., pp. 53-4.

of evictions exceeded 1,500, and there were five years (1849-53) in which they exceeded 3,000, as compared with 1,094 in 1879 and 1,893 in 1880.[48]

It should also be remembered that tenant farmers were not the only members of the society who suffered during the depression of the late 1870s. Laborers also experienced distress—non-farm workers as a result of the general economic deterioration, and farm workers as a result of a sharp fall in the demand for agricultural labor, especially in the hard-hit tillage sector. Many of the reports of sick and starving families in the west, which so shocked English and American readers, were actually descriptions of rural laborers, not farmers. The average daily number of persons receiving outdoor poor relief (to which laborers were more inclined to resort than were farmers) rose almost steadily from 1875 to 1881; by 1879 it was 31 percent higher than it had been in 1875, and by 1880 it was more than 100 percent higher than it had been in 1875.[49] While some observers believed that laborers fared better during the depression than farmers, most were emphatic in asserting the opposite. Many claimed that the greatest misfortune was to be found among the lower orders in the towns. In a report covering Galway and Roscommon in December 1879, a poor-law inspector offered the opinion that the "principal classes that will suffer are artisans, labourers and poor householders, residing in towns and villages, who are far more in need than the peasantry."[50] The town of Roscommon, wrote one champion of the laborers' cause, "has more idle hands which are in far greater distress than those in rural districts all put together."[51] Yet few political efforts were made during the crisis to protect the interests of laborers, particularly by laborers themselves.

The increase in hardship caused by the depression of 1878-9 cannot, taken alone, explain the Land War. It cannot explain why tenant farmers responded to this depression with collective action, whereas laborers did not. And it cannot explain why their

[48] Return of evictions from 1849 to 1880, p. 3.

[49] Annual report of the Local Government Board for Ireland . . . tenth report, p. 4 [C 3311], H.C. 1882, xxxi. The annual periods for which the data are given end in February. The number jumps dramatically in 1880 as a result of the Poor Relief Act of 1880, which made it easier for poor-law boards to grant out-door relief.

[50] S.P.O., Chief Secretary's Office, Registered Papers: Report of Dr. Roughan to the Local Government Board, 9 Dec. 1879 (1880/4653).

[51] Roscommon Journal, 2 July 1881, p. 2.

response, for the first time, assumed the form of a national movement against the land system. The depression was, to be sure, a critical factor. Its significance, however, lay not in the entire range or in the severity of hardship it created, but rather in its impact on a particular social group within the rural population. While tenant farmers may not have suffered the most in 1879, their suffering had the greatest political consequences owing to their strength in the rural society and to the gradually expanding efforts that were being made to form political associations to represent their interests. The underlying cause of the Irish Land War was not the depression of the late 1870s, but rather the long-term evolution of this social group. What the depression did was bring members of this group into direct confrontation with their landlords.

Eight · **The Challenging Collectivity**

It is difficult to identify a specific point in time when the Land War began. It evolved gradually through an increase in political activity by tenant farmers during the years 1878-80. In 1878 tenant-farmer spokesmen were only slightly more militant than in preceding years. Still, there was more activity than has often been recognized. Most of the existing farmers clubs met more regularly;[1] and several organized large demonstrations, especially in November when the Ballinasloe Tenants' Defence Association and the Kerry Tenants' Defence Association staged well-attended rallies.[2] At a political meeting in Castlebar in October it was suggested that a Mayo tenants' defense association should be formed; such a body was apparently "all but established" by the second week of November. And before the end of November a new tenants' defense association had been organized at Killannin, County Galway.[3]

Yet it was not until 1879 that political activity on behalf of tenant farmers grew by degrees and reached a scale that had not been seen since the Tithe War of the early 1830s. In January farmers' clubs were busy organizing public meetings in Tipperary and Meath. In the same month a tenant-right rally was held in the town of Donegal to demand rent reductions to meet the fall in agricultural prices. In February tenant farmers meeting in Clifden, County Galway, established the Connemara Tenants' Defence Association; and by April a new farmers' club had been formed in

[1] See, for example, meetings of the Central Tenants' Defence Association, the Ballinasloe Tenants' Defence Association, the Kerry Tenants' Defence Association, the Farney Tenants' Defence Association, and the Meath Tenants' Defence Association reported in the *Nation*, 4 May 1878, p. 2; 18 May 1878, p. 3; 21 May 1878, p. 3; 11 June 1878, p. 3; 3 Aug. 1878, p. 3; 14 Dec. 1878, p. 3; 21 Dec. 1878, p. 2; and 4 Jan. 1879, p. 6. See also meetings of the Kerry Tenants' Defence Association reported in the *Kerry Sentinel*, 6 Aug. 1878, p. 3; 17 Sept. 1878, p. 3; and 12 Nov. 1878, p. 3; as well as meetings of the Limerick and Clare Farmers' Club reported in the *Limerick Reporter*, 18 June 1878, p. 3 and 31 Dec. 1878, p. 3.

[2] *Nation*, 9 Nov. 1878, p. 3 and 23 Nov. 1878, p. 2.

[3] *Connaught Telegraph*, 26 Oct. 1878, p. 5; 9 Nov. 1878, p. 4; *Nation*, 30 Nov. 1878, p. 7.

Clare.[4] Also in April a large public meeting, reportedly attended by no less than 7,000 persons, was held in Irishtown, south of Claremorris in County Mayo.[5] In June demonstrations were organized in various places in Connaught (at Claremorris, Knock, Westport, and Milltown) to publicize tenant demands for abatements in rent. In July and August public land meetings took place almost every week, most frequently in Connaught, but also in Tipperary, Waterford, Monaghan, and Limerick.[6] At a meeting in Castlebar on 16 August a National Land League of Mayo was formed. In September and October still more land meetings were held and new tenant associations established. Then in Dublin, on 21 October 1879, the Irish National Land League was founded, claiming to represent most of the groups that had staged land demonstrations and most of the associations that existed or were being formed in the interests of agricultural tenants.[7]

The agitation continued to grow in 1880. Public demonstrations were held and hundreds of branches of the Land League formed. Candidates who endorsed the movement stood for public office in local-government elections and in the general election of that year. A small but determined band of M.P.s who were closely associated with the land agitation were elected to office and endeavored to promote the goals of the Land League at Westminster. Within Ireland itself the movement sought to disrupt the operation of the land system by assaulting landowners, bailiffs, process servers, and landgrabbers, by persuading tenants to withhold their normal rents, and by organizing tenants to resist evictions. The most effective sanctions used to enforce the authority of the League consisted of the threat of violence and various techniques of social ostracism. Ostracism was openly promoted by leaders of the agitation. In September 1880 Parnell himself proposed during a speech at Ennis, County Clare, that a landgrabber should be put

[4] *Nation*, 25 Jan. 1879, pp. 3 and 5; 18 Jan. 1879, p. 6; *Tuam News*, 7 Feb. 1879, p. 3; *Clare Independent*, 12 April 1879, p. 1.

[5] *Connaught Telegraph*, 26 April 1879, p. 3. See also Michael Davitt, *The Fall of Feudalism in Ireland or the Story of the Land League Revolution* (London, 1904), pp. 147-51.

[6] *Nation*, 14 June 1879, pp. 2-3; *Roscommon Journal*, 7 June 1879, p. 1; *Connaught Telegraph*, 14 June 1879, p. 2; 21 June 1879, p. 3; and 28 June 1879, p. 3; *Nation*, 19 July 1879, p. 2; 9 Aug. 1879, p. 2; and 16 Aug. 1879, p. 7; *Limerick Reporter*, 2 Sept. 1879, p. 4.

[7] *Nation*, 25 Oct. 1879, p. 5.

"into moral Coventry" and isolated "as if he was a leper of old."[8]
The best-known case in point was that of Captain Charles Boycott.
The "boycott" against him was organized by the Ballinrobe
branch of the Land League, which denied this unfortunate gentleman the use of laborers to harvest his crops as well as the privileges of receiving mail, making purchases at local shops, or getting his horses shod at the blacksmith.[9]

To combat the threat posed by the movement, the government
sought to enforce the land laws and protect individuals intimidated by the agitators. In late 1879 it prosecuted three of their
leaders, two of whom had been prominent organizers in the early
stages of the agitation. A year later it brought more than a dozen
key Land League figures to trial, including Parnell and four other
M.P.s. Both prosecutions failed to obtain convictions and served
mainly to increase sympathy for the movement. But in March
1881 parliament suspended *habeas corpus* under the Protection
of Person and Property Act, permitting the internment of hundreds of agitators during the years 1881-2.

At the same time the government tried to remove the grievances
on which the movement had been built. In the summer of 1880
Gladstone's ministry introduced, and the House of Commons
passed, a Compensation for Disturbance Bill, which temporarily
empowered the county-court judges to force a landlord to compensate a tenant who had been evicted for non-payment of rent if
the tenant could prove to the satisfaction of the court that he was
unable to pay as a result of the economic depression.[10] The House
of Lords overwhelmingly rejected this measure, with the result
that it was another year before significant land reform was enacted
to tranquilize the agitation. On 22 August 1881 a new law came
into effect that went further than any previous land legislation
toward meeting tenant demands, most directly by establishing a
Land Commission to adjudicate rents.[11] Together with an improved economic situation and the repression imposed on the
movement in 1881-2, the Land Act undercut support for the Land

---

[8] *Clare Independent*, 18 Sept. 1880, p. 2.

[9] Palmer, *Land League Crisis*, pp. 195-217.

[10] *A bill to make temporary provision with respect to compensation for disturbance in certain cases of ejectment for non-payment of rent in parts of Ireland*, H.C.
1880 (232), i. It was amended and reprinted as 1880 (271), i, and then further
amended and reprinted as 1880 (276), i, the title remaining the same.

[11] 44 Vict., c. 49.

League and brought about its decline. Diehards in the movement remained active, but by the spring of 1882 the larger mass support had so disintegrated that even the leadership felt it necessary, indeed advantageous, to come to terms with the government.

The process I have just described was fundamentally one in which an active collectivity slowly expanded, struggled with established power, and then contracted. The purpose of this chapter will be to identify the major characteristics of this challenging collectivity. From what social groups did it draw its members? How was it organized and what were its manifest goals? How did it differ from other active collectivities that we have discussed in this study?

Farmers

AN ANALYSIS OF ARRESTS

The best source of information on the social characteristics of those who participated in the Land War is a list of persons arrested under the Protection of Person and Property Act, 1881. This act gave the lord lieutenant the power to apprehend anyone reasonably suspected of intimidation, violence, or incitement to violence, and to hold a suspect in custody without trial.[12] Altogether 955 persons were interned. Occupational data are available for 845 of them.

Table 14 shows the percentage of suspects in various occupational categories. The same table also gives an occupational breakdown of the male labor force in 1881. The Land War, it is clear from this table, cannot be described simply as an "agrarian" or "rural" movement. It was specifically a farmers' movement. Admittedly, 62 percent of the suspects for whom we have data belonged to the agricultural labor force. But this is no more than would be expected by chance, since the agricultural sector constituted 65.9 percent of the total male work force. The only occupational groups in the agricultural sector that were significantly over-represented relative to their numbers in the work force were farmers and farmers' sons. Together they constituted over half of the suspects. It is true that herdsmen were slightly over-represented, but laborers and farm servants were under-represented. Laborers accounted for only 4.2 percent of the arrests. Yet they

[12] 44 Vict., c. 4.

TABLE 14 · Occupations of persons arrested under the Protection of
Person and Property Act, 1881, and the occupational distribution
of the male labor force: Detailed breakdown of agricultural sector

OCCUPATIONS	PERCENTAGE OF SUSPECTS	PERCENTAGE OF LABOR FORCE
Agricultural sector	62.0	65.9
Farmers	38.7	24.4
Farmers' sons	15.5	12.1
Herdsmen or shepherds	1.1	0.4
Laborers	4.2	12.6[a] / 8.5[b]
Farm Servants	0.5	6.0
Other agricultural	2.0	1.9
Commercial and industrial sector	32.6	23.2
Professional sector	4.6	4.4
Civil service and defense sector	0.2	4.3
Domestic sector	0.6	2.2
Total number	845	1,571,896

[a] "agricultural"

[b] "general"

NOTE: The sources are S.P.O., Irish crimes records, 1881; and *Census of Ireland, 1881: General report*. The basis for the occupational classification is given in Appendix B. Suspects whose occupation was given as "Land League organizer" or "clerk in Land League office" were not included, nor were members of parliament. Altogether 110 suspects were either excluded or could not be coded because no occupation was provided. This table has been adapted from Tables 2 and 3 in my "The social composition of the Land League" in *Irish Historical Studies*, 17, no. 68 (Sept. 1971). Differences in the percentages given are a result of a reclassification of several suspects and the transfer of general laborers from the commercial and industrial sector to the agricultural sector.

comprised 12.6 percent of the labor force if we include only "agricultural" laborers, or 21.1 percent of the labor force if we also
include "general" laborers.[13]

    Some readers may be bothered by the use of internment records
to sample participants in the movement. Aside from the fact that
this is the only large sample available, the justification for doing
so is that law-enforcement authorities no doubt arrested compara-

[13] The reader will recall that "general" laborers are those for whom it is unknown whether they were agricultural or non-agricultural workers.

tively active Land Leaguers. This kind of bias is not to be regretted, but rather is precisely what we want. At the same time it must
be admitted that there could be other biases in the data as well and
that we should temper our conclusions accordingly. It is probably
safe to assume, however, that the greatest distortion would be toward arresting those who had engaged in some form of violence.
And fortunately, we can control for this particular bias. If we do,
we find that our basic conclusions remain unaltered. When persons arrested on suspicion of having committed a violent crime
are excluded from the analysis, the number comprised by farmers
and farmers' sons declines from 54.2 to 52 percent, but the
number comprised by laborers declines even further, from 4.2 to 1
percent. Thus, we are still led to conclude that laborers were not
an important part of the challenging collectivity, and that rural
support for the land agitation came almost entirely from farmers.

This was the most important characteristic of the Land War. In
three earlier agrarian movements (the Tithe War of the early
1830s, the Tenant League of the early 1850s, and the farmers'
clubs of the 1870s) farmers were equally active. But this was not
true of pre-famine collective violence, in which farmers were outnumbered by laborers and in which an important class of farmers
(i.e., large farmers) hardly engaged at all. Many writers have failed
to see the significance of the preponderance of farmers in the Land
War because they have assumed that the same was true of all rural
unrest in nineteenth-century Ireland. Such a notion ignores critical differences between this violence and the Land War. It also
overlooks the transformation in rural class structure discussed in
Chapter Four. In the post-famine period farmers became the numerically dominant social group in rural Ireland. At the same
time they developed much stronger common interests because
of the decline in subletting and because the great majority of
them participated in the livestock economy. Some farmers and
many farmers' sons also engaged in periodic outside labor, but
this did not make them part of the class of laborers, which consisted of those engaged in labor for the better part of their working
day on a permanent basis. These permanent laborers were fewer
in number than farmers; they were often not tenants of agricultural land; and they did not directly engage in much livestock
trade. They had very few interests in common with farmers, and
some interests that were diametrically opposed to those of
farmers. It would have been surprising, under the circumstances,

to have found large numbers of them joining in collective action along with farmers.[14]

AN ANALYSIS OF REGIONAL VARIATIONS

As we might expect, there was considerable variation among farmers themselves in the extent to which they took part in the movement, and many did not support it at all. It would therefore be useful to identify what segments of the farming population were most active. Unfortunately, little systematic information is available concerning the attributes of those who participated, except for the occupational data we have just used. What we do have are data on the social characteristics of regions. This is quite a different thing from information about individuals, but it can nevertheless serve a useful purpose. The regional units I shall use are the counties of Ireland, excluding County Dublin. I measured the strength of the movement in the remaining thirty-one counties by a scale consisting of three variables: (1) number of land meetings per capita in 1879-80; (2) number of agrarian crimes per capita in 1879-80; and (3) number of arrests per capita under the Protection of Person and Property Act of 1881. Each of these variables was given equal weight in the scale, henceforth called the Agitation Scale.[15]

Table 15 presents the results of a correlation and regression analysis of the relationship between this Agitation Scale and a set of relevant variables. Let us begin by looking at the simple "zero-order" coefficients in Column A. There is a strong negative association between the Agitation Scale and a scale that I have formed to measure communication facilities (based on literacy, number of railway stations, and number of newspapers). The coefficient is −.56. In the decades after the Famine communications improved considerably in those parts of the country where the land agitation received its greatest support, but most of this region was still comparatively undeveloped in this regard. The next two variables, evictions and arrears, are both measures of conflict between landlords and tenants. Predictably, they have substantial positive associations with the Agitation Scale; the coefficients are .41 and

[14] Several of the former leaders of the National Agricultural Labourers' Union did participate in the Land War. See Horn, "National Agricultural Labourers' Union."

[15] The score for each country was the mean of its standardized scores on the three variables.

TABLE 15 · Correlation and regression analysis of Agitation Scale
(N = 31)

SOCIAL CHARACTERISTICS OF COUNTIES	A ZERO-ORDER COEFFICIENTS	B STANDARDIZED MULTIPLE REGRESSION COEFFICIENTS (LEVEL OF SIGNIFICANCE IN PARENTHESIS)	
Communications scale	−.56	−.15	(.387)
Number of evictions per holding in 1878-80	.41	.03	(>.500)
Percentage of holdings in arrears in 1882-3	.34	−.42	(.036)
Percentage of persons who were Roman Catholic in 1881	.66	.32	(.057)
Factor I (pasture and subsistence-tillage)	.80	.66	(.002)
Factor II (large-farm)	−.15	−.46	(.032)
Multiple correlation squared:		.76	
F ratio:		12.59	(<.001)

NOTE: For an explanation of Factors I and II see Chapter Four. The Communications scale was formed by standardizing and averaging three variables: (i) percentage of persons five years of age or older who were literate in 1881, (ii) number of railway stations per capita in 1869, and (iii) number of newspapers per capita in 1879. Sources for all variables are given in Appendix C.

.34 respectively. The reader should be warned, however, that the data on arrears are far from satisfactory for our purposes. They are based on applications made under the Arrears Act of 1882, which enabled tenants in debt to petition the Land Commission to pay a portion of their rents due. They obviously have two serious defects: first, they measure arrears *after* rather than before the agitation; second, they measure the number of tenants who applied to have a portion of their arrears paid by the Commission, which does not necessarily correspond to the number of tenants in arrears.

The next two variables obtain the highest coefficients in Column A: .66 for religion and .80 for Factor I. Factor I, as the reader may recall, identifies regional variations in types of land use and levels of poverty; high scores indicate that large proportions of land were devoted to livestock and subsistence tillage and that the county was comparatively poor. Factor II, on the other hand, measures the size of agricultural enterprises. As one would expect, Factor II has a negative correlation with the Agitation Scale, but the coefficient is very low: a mere −.15. This suggests a modest tendency for the movement to receive less support where farms were comparatively large.

The coefficients in Column A describe relationships that existed between the characteristics of counties and the intensity of the agitation. They help to identify the distinguishing features of those counties in which the movement caught on as compared with those in which it did not. One cannot, however, assume that these *descriptive* correlations necessarily represent *causal* relationships. Some correlations may be just coincidental. It is possible, for instance, that the movement was stronger in regions where communications were less developed simply because there were, say, more evictions or higher arrears in those counties. Or there was perhaps more unrest in counties that score high on Factor I simply because Catholics were more numerous in these counties. In this second case, the real causal variable would be religion; and the association between Factor I and the Agitation Scale would be merely "spurious." We can never completely eliminate the possibility that a relationship is spurious, but we can reduce the probability that it is being misinterpreted by controlling statistically for other variables in our list. We do this by computing a "multiple-regression equation," which tells us what the relationship would be between each of our variables and the Agitation Scale if the effects of the other variables in the list were held constant. Column B in Table 15 gives the standardized regression coefficients for this equation.

What do they indicate? First, they demonstrate that neither the Communications Scale nor the eviction rate has a strong independent relationship with the intensity of the agitation; the regression coefficients for these two variables are very low: −.15 and .03 respectively. Second, we no longer have a moderately high *positive* correlation with arrears as we did at the zero-order level; we now have a moderately high *negative* coefficient of −.42. It would obviously be a mistake to conclude from this that arrears tended to dampen the agitation, but we certainly cannot use these

correlations as evidence that they promoted it. In fact, to say anything about arrears with confidence we would need better data.

On the other hand, we can make some reasonably confident as-
sertions about the effects of the remaining variables. All three
have strong independent relationships with the Agitation Scale.
The regression coefficient for religion is not as high as the zero-
order coefficient, but it is still a convincing .32. The regression
coefficient for Factor II is −.46, which is much stronger than the
zero-order coefficient. And the regression coefficient for Factor I is
an impressive .66. Factor I is clearly the most important variable
in the list. This single item explains almost as much of the total
variance as all the other variables in the equation put together.
Moreover, since it holds up well when religion is controlled, we
can be certain that the relationship between Factor I and the Agitation Scale is not just a function of differences in the religious
composition of counties.

I have tried in Figure 5 to give the reader a visual impression of
regional variations in the strength of the movement by dividing
the counties of Ireland into five groups ranging from very low to
very high on the Agitation Scale. Although this map does not
provide the same insights as the statistical analysis, it demonstrates in a more striking way the patterns we have found. First,
the relationship between support for the movement and the
strength of Catholicism is clearly demonstrated by the concentration of all very low ratings in the northeastern part of the country.
This region had the highest proportions of Protestants; it is the
part of the island that today constitutes the state of Northern Ireland. Second, Figure 5 demonstrates the comparative popularity
of the movement in western districts. Here we see visually what
the statistical analysis has already told us—that the agitation was
greatest in those areas where the livestock economy coexisted
with poverty and subsistence tillage.

LARGE FARMERS

The strength of the movement in the west contrasts sharply with
earlier national movements representing the interests of tenant
farmers. The Tithe War, the Tenant League, and the farmers' clubs
of the 1870s were strongest in the province of Leinster, in eastern
parts of Munster, and with the exception of the Tithe War, in parts
of Ulster. These movements also drew their support disproportionately from the class of large farmers that was comparatively

FIGURE 5 · Strength of the Land Movement of 1879-1882 as measured by Agitation Scale

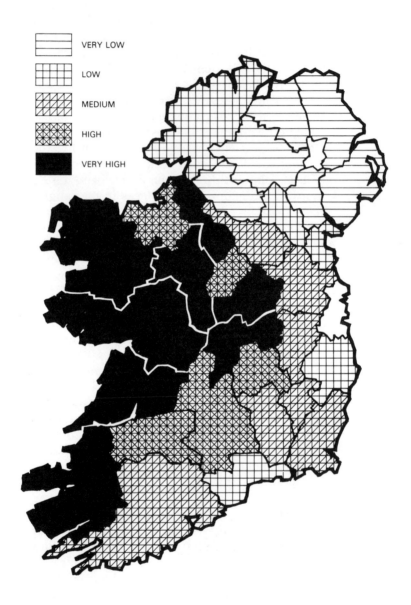

numerous in the east. As a result, they were particularly sensitive to the welfare of this class. They took up none of the grievances which small farmers and laborers had against large farmers, and which were evident in many of the demands made by violent combinations before the Famine (such as steady work, higher wages, lower conacre rents, and the breakup of large grazing holdings). The farmers' clubs of the 1870s were constantly on guard lest the interests of large farmers be neglected. In March 1877, for instance, a resolution was proposed at a meeting of the Limerick and Clare Farmers' club objecting to the exclusion of graziers from Isaac Butt's amended land bill.[16] In June 1878, during a quarrel to which I have already referred, club members defended their right to be big graziers when they were denounced by one of their own number.[17] In April 1878 Thomas Robertson of the Kildare Tenants' Defence Association argued against the suggestion that farmers with more than sixty acres should be excluded from land-reform legislation; he insisted, in the course of a heated newspaper exchange with Matthew Harris of the Ballinasloe Tenants' Defence Association, that large farmers deserved fixity of tenure as a matter of right.[18]

Yet it cannot be argued that these clubs fought for the interests only of the large-grazier class. Indeed, the few disputes I have cited suggest that there were at least some members who were prepared to give priority to the interests of small farmers at the expense of large ones. Those in the Ballinasloe club were, not surprisingly, the most likely to take this position, but it could occasionally be taken by members of clubs in big grazing counties such as Limerick. It is true that, on the whole, the clubs were not so inclined. Their members were determined to prevent the exclusion of large graziers from the benefits of land legislation. Yet they made no attempt to exclude small farmers or to propose legislation from which large farmers alone would benefit. They simply avoided issues on which large and small farmers might disagree; and they made the most of the interests they had in common. The basis of their program consisted of the three Fs: fair rents, fixity of tenure, and free sale. These were goals that could be supported by the entire tenant-farmer population, the social group that the clubs always claimed to represent.

[16] *Limerick Reporter*, 3 April 1877, p. 3.
[17] See above, p. 214.
[18] *Connaught Telegraph*, 16 March 1878, p. 5; 6 April 1878, p. 2.

When the welfare of tenant farmers became threatened by the economic downturn of the late 1870s, the first sign of a collective response came, as we have seen, from these clubs. They were already active in 1878 and they organized a land conference in February of 1879.[19] By midsummer their efforts had been eclipsed by the movement in Connaught, but they did not retire from the political scene. They continued to meet regularly; they organized public meetings;[20] and they took part in the establishment of the Irish National Land League in October.[21] They were naturally apprehensive about the character of the movement in the west, but they eventually joined, with some hesitation during the winter of 1879-80, and then with considerably less hesitation during the summer and fall of 1880, especially after the House of Lords rejected the Compensation for Disturbance Bill.[22] As the agitation spread from Connaught into Munster and Leinster, much of the leadership came from the existing farmers' clubs;[23] and many of the struggles involved disputes between landlords and large farmers.[24] Moreover, even in the west, large farmers played a prominent role. Perhaps the most important of the early meetings in Connaught was the Irishtown demonstration in April. More will be said about the organizers of this meeting in a moment, but we can note at this point that three Mayo farmers have been credited with helping to arrange it; two were comparatively large landholders with farms of over one hundred acres in the Irishtown district, and the third was the son of the largest grazier in the

[19] *Nation*, 15 Feb. 1879.

[20] See meetings organized by the following clubs:

Tipperary Independent Club	*Nation*, 25 Jan. 1879
Tipperary Farmers' Club	Ibid., 19 July 1879
Waterford Tenants' Association	Ibid., 9 Aug. 1879
Limerick and Clare Farmers' Club	*Limerick Reporter*, 2 Sept. 1879
Queen's County Independent Club	*Nation*, 11 Oct. 1879
Wexford Independent Club	Ibid., 1 Nov. 1879

[21] Members of these clubs can be found among the list of names comprising the founding committee of the Land League. See Davitt, *Fall of Feudalism*, pp. 172-3 for this list.

[22] Bew, "Politics of the Irish Land War," p. 172.

[23] Ibid., p. 185.

[24] One remarkable example was a meeting at Knockaroe in Queen's County to protest the eviction of a tenant who was in arrears for a large farm with an annual rent of over £100; he also had an adjoining holding which was larger still and which he retained. S.P.O., Chief Secretary's Office, Registered Papers: Report of Thomas Hamilton, R.M. (1880/5151).

Balla district.[25] During the following months there were land meetings in Connaught organized by "graziers"[26] or attended by "every class from the extensive grazier to the holder of one acre."[27] It is also possible to find petitions for rent reductions initiated by large farmers[28] and disputes between large farmers and their landlords.[29]

In order to obtain some idea of the size of farms held by members of western branches, I searched the *Nation* 1880-81 for reports of branch meetings that included the names and addresses of members. Reports containing such information were printed for seven branches in Connaught, yielding altogether a list of forty-four members for whom I was able to determine the approximate size of their agricultural holdings. Table 16 gives the results of this modest survey and compares the distribution of farm sizes for these branch members with the distribution of all agricultural holdings in the province of Connaught. First, we can note that tenants with less than sixteen acres accounted for about one-third (34 percent) of the branch members and that tenants with less than thirty-one acres made up well over half (61 percent). On the other hand, those over-represented relative to the distribution of all agricultural holdings in the province were tenants in the over 30-acre category. Those in the 16-30 acre category were almost proportionately represented, while those in the category of 1-15

[25] The two farmers from Irishtown were James Daly and Daniel O'Connor, with 108 acres and 200 acres respectively. See V.O., Kilvine, 1867. The other organizer was P. W. Nally; his father, William Nally, held several hundred acres near Balla. See V.O., Balla, 1869.

[26] The Claremorris demonstration at the beginning of June was first announced in the *Connaught Telegraph* as a meeting to be held by "the graziers of Mayo . . . for the purpose of calling upon their landlords for a reduction of rents." See *Connaught Telegraph*, 3 May 1879, p. 5. Given the dual forces operating within the movement, it is curious but not incredible that at this same meeting a resolution was adopted "calling upon the landlords to give the lands at present occupied by graziers to small farmers." See *Roscommon Journal*, 7 June 1879, p. 1.

[27] *Connaught Telegraph*, 12 July 1879, p. 4. The report of this meeting (which was held near Hollymount, County Mayo, on 7 July) went on to say that "the majority of those assembled appeared to belong to the better class of tenantry."

[28] Captain H. Needham, agent for the Trinity College property at Portmagee, County Kerry, believed that it was large farmers who originated the memorial from Portmagee that I have quoted in Chapter Seven. See T.C.D., Trinity College papers: Captain H. Needham to J. Carson, 12 Oct. 1879.

[29] Finlay Dun discusses one such case between a large farmer, who was Scottish, and Lord Lucan of Castlebar. See Dun, *Landlords and Tenants in Ireland*, pp. 239-40.

TABLE 16 · Members of seven Land League branches in Connaught distinguished according to size of holdings and compared with the distribution of all agricultural holdings in Connaught

SIZE OF HOLDINGS IN ACRES	PERCENTAGE OF BRANCH MEMBERS	PERCENTAGE OF AGRICULTURAL HOLDINGS IN CONNAUGHT OVER ONE ACRE
1-15	34	54
16-30	27	28
31-100	30	14
Over 100	9	4
Total number	44	112,504

NOTE: The branches were Ballinafad, Glentavine, Knockmore, Tulsk, Calry, Drumlease, and Brackloon / Tully. Size of holdings for members was obtained from V.O., Land valuation records. For ten branch members no acreage was given and it was necessary to estimate the size of their holdings from their land valuations. The distribution of agricultural holdings in Connaught was taken from *Census of Ireland, 1881: General report*, p. 199.

acres were actually under-represented. In other words, though tenants with more than thirty acres were in the minority, they were nevertheless the only over-represented group. Furthermore, not shown in Table 16 is the fact that eight of the fifteen members in this sample who belonged to the executives of their branches held more than thirty acres of land.

We can compare these results with those of an analysis carried out by William Feingold of voting patterns in a poor-law election in Tralee, County Kerry, in March of 1881.[30] This election was fought between clearly defined landlord candidates and clearly defined Land League candidates. It affords a rare opportunity to assess the class basis of the Land League's electoral following. Feingold finds that, among farmers, Land League support came primarily from those with between 4 and 19 acres of land, and from those with 50 or more acres; the fewest votes came from what he calls the "middling farmers," those with farms of 20 to 49

[30] Feingold, "Boards of guardians," pp. 160-74. This study is based on a sample of voters in Tralee. Feingold is currently engaged in a further analysis of this election based on the population of voters in Tralee rather than a sample.

acres.[31] We must be very cautious in whatever conclusions we draw from these two sets of data. First, both samples are small: mine with an n of forty-four, Feingold's with an n of sixty. Second, the two surveys are difficult to compare, since different categories were used in each. And third, they involve quite different types of political participation—in one case, branch membership, in the other, electoral support in a poor-law contest. Still, they are consistent on one point: both indicate substantial support from large farmers, as well as small ones. If this was true in the west, it was all the more true in Leinster and east Munster.

There is nothing mysterious about the foundations on which the Land War was built. Collective action in Ireland by and for tenant farmers had its precedents. Most recently, the Tenant League and the farmers' clubs had sought to advance the interests of this social group. In a sense, the farmers' clubs comprised the nucleus of the active collectivity that rose to challenge the land system during the Land War. These clubs were not mainly responsible for the organization of the agitation that eventually emerged, but they had been engaged in collective action on behalf of tenant farmers in the immediately preceding period, and the Land War began with an increase in political activity on their part. I have also argued that these clubs, and many persons in the large-grazier class from which they drew most of their members, played an active role in the Land League movement.

Yet the great significance of the Land War lies in the change that occurred in the social composition of the challenging collectivity during 1879. It came to differ in important respects from the farmers' clubs, the Tenant League, and even the Tithe War. In class terms, it embraced proportionately more small farmers than did these earlier collectivities. In regional terms, it included a greater number of farmers in the west. Far more than the earlier movements, the Land War succeeded in uniting farmers of different classes and different regions. The social origins of this union

[31] Actually Feingold classifies voters according to land valuation, not acreage. But since agricultural land in this particular union was, on the average, valued at £1 per acre, we can assume that his categories roughly correspond to equivalent acreage categories. His survey tells us nothing about the political inclinations of very small tenants, those with valuations of less than £4, since they were not entitled to vote in poor-law elections.

lay in the changes that occurred in the rural society during and
after the Great Famine and in the effect these changes had on
small farmers in the west. Like large farmers, these small farmers
held land directly from proprietors; like large farmers, they were
engaged in raising cattle and sheep for the commercial market.
Yet they were still poor and they still depended heavily on subsistence tillage for their livelihood. They were highly vulnerable
to economic depression, even an economic depression that was
more damaging to tillage than to the livestock economy. This is
what made the union of these small farmers with large farmers so
volatile.

Farmers' Allies

TOWNSMEN

The way in which urban groups can promote social change in
rural societies and the role they can play in agrarian political
movements have been complementary themes in much of the literature on peasant societies.[32] Great importance has been attached
to urban participation in peasant movements and to the conditions under which such participation occurs. Most writers regard
it as problematic, since the interests of the majority of people living in cities and towns do not usually coincide with the interests
of those living in the countryside. In most societies, there is an
underlying social cleavage between town and country. Well
rooted in history, this cleavage has intensified in the modern period as industrialization and the growth of the nation-state has
expanded the economic and political power of urban centers at
the expense of rural districts. The conflict has been between the

[32] For some early statements about the role of townsmen in promoting social
change, see Daniel Lerner, The Passing of Traditional Society (New York, 1958)
and Everett M. Rogers, Modernization among Peasants: Impact of Communication
(New York, 1969). For discussions of their political role, see Neale J. Pearson,
"Latin American pressure groups and the modernization process" in Journal of
International Affairs, 20, no. 2 (1966), p. 316; Henry A. Landsberger, "The role of
peasant movements and revolts in development" in Henry A. Landsberger (ed.),
Latin American Peasant Movements (Ithaca, 1969); Eric Wolf, Peasant Wars of the
Twentieth Century (New York, 1969); D. Frances Ferguson, "Rural/urban relations
and peasant radicalism: a preliminary statement" in Comparative Studies in Soci-
ety and History, 18, no. 1 (Jan. 1976); and David Sabean, "The communal basis of
pre-1800 peasant uprisings in western Europe" in Comparative Politics, 8, no. 3
(April 1976).

interests of established landed elites and rising urban elites. It has also pitted agricultural producers against agricultural processors and consumers. Frequently, this rural-urban cleavage has coincided with cultural cleavages, which have served to deepen and embitter the economic conflicts.[33]

It is possible to argue that this kind of rural-urban division underlay the antagonism between England and Ireland, and perhaps also, to a lesser extent, the division between England and other parts of its "Celtic fringe." England's increasing economic and political domination over Ireland was also the domination of an urban-industrial center over an essentially rural and agricultural periphery. Yet it is important to recognize that this rural-urban cleavage did not reproduce itself within Ireland. English domination was not represented in Ireland by urban elites, but primarily by a landed elite. The Irish challenge to English domination, as we have seen, did not emerge exclusively from the rural population; indeed, its leadership tended to come from the urban population. And the Land War was not a rural assault on urban power and interests, but rather a rural-urban coalition against a landed elite.

The basis for this coalition lay, first of all, in the social ties in Ireland between townspeople and country people. The urban trading class was largely recruited from the farming population. The two groups shared a common religion, close kinship bonds, and the familiarities that developed through stable economic exchanges. True, these integrative ties were in some ways weak in the pre-famine period. Even then, however, it would have been a mistake to talk about a rural-urban cleavage in Ireland. As shown in Chapter Four, after the Famine there was a marked increase in the integration of the rural and urban segments of the society and indeed of the nation as a whole. In addition to the incorporation of the majority of the rural population into the livestock economy, there was a tremendous increase in literacy, most likely considerable growth in newspaper readership, and a revolution (through the railways) in the national transportation system. And there was a noticeable strengthening of relationships between rural people and certain occupational groups in the agrarian towns. The relationships that became stronger at this time were based not only on

[33] For a discussion of this social cleavage, along with other types of cleavages that accompany industrialization, see "Introduction" to Lipset and Rokkan, *Party Systems and Voter Alignments*.

communal bonds resulting from constant interaction, but also on associational bonds resulting from economic interdependence. Though I cautioned against exaggerating the magnitude of change, I nevertheless insisted that the farmers who comprised the bulk of the rural population in the post-famine period were significantly more integrated into national and urban structures than were the small farmers and laborers who were numerically dominant before the Famine.

In contrast, a sharp social division existed between the urban population and the landed elite. Obviously this cleavage was largely a function of differences in social class and religion. Most townsmen, especially in the small agrarian centers, were far below landed proprietors in social rank and wealth. More important still, most townsmen were Catholic, whereas even in the late nineteenth century it would seem that at least half of the landed proprietors were Protestant, and in the case of large proprietors, probably a good deal more than half. Even Catholic landowners, however, had few friends among townsmen, and the friends they did have were drawn mostly from occupational groups with a vested interest in the land system, such as land agents and lawyers. Though landowners had once played an instrumental role in building and improving Irish towns, the Irish gentry class was nonetheless principally a rural gentry class; or to be more precise, it was absentee and rural. That is to say, the great majority of owners resided either outside the district in which they possessed land, or on estates in the countryside. Rarely did they live in towns, and by the mid-nineteenth century it had become less common for them to invest in towns. They typically occupied demesnes in the country or on the fringes of towns, protected by high walls from the unsightly abodes of their more humble neighbors.

What is more, townsmen were frequently tenants of landowners. This could be true in two ways. First, though Irish landowners no longer invested heavily in towns, the land on which the majority of Irish towns was situated was owned by large landed proprietors.[34] Second, it is well known that many townsmen were also tenants by virtue of holding agricultural land located outside towns. This is most certainly true if we include

[34] The importance of this fact should not be exaggerated. By the late 1870s town land was generally held on very long building leases which gave most businesses comparative security, usually at low rents.

among "townsmen" those who pursued urban-type occupations though they lived in the country or in small villages. The number of such people had declined since the pre-famine period, but there was still a significant number and they almost invariably practiced farming in addition to their non-agricultural businesses. Unfortunately, it is difficult to document this point. In the 1881 census only 10,382 farmers reported that they also pursued a non-agricultural occupation. It is worth noting that the largest group among these were shopkeepers (980), followed by publicans (912), carpenters (835), and grocers (655).[35] This return, however, obviously misses those shopkeepers and publicans who may have held farm land but failed to report a dual occupation to the census-takers. I suspect that many did in fact hold agricultural land, including even some of those who resided in towns. During an investigation of the landholdings of persons who participated in the land agitation in the town of Roscommon, I discovered a considerable number of town residents who were listed as occupiers of one or more agricultural holdings in the surrounding district.

For all these reasons, both the sympathies and the interests of townsmen tied them more closely to the farming population than to the landowning class. Consequently, they perceived the threat of the agricultural crisis of the late 1870s in much the same terms as did farmers. Townsmen who held agricultural land experienced directly the same difficulties as farmers, and almost all townsmen had to contend with these difficulties indirectly. As the buying power of the rural population declined, the trade enjoyed by the towns suffered greatly. Townsmen were quick to point this out and to complain that the misfortunes of farmers were also their misfortunes. "In Ireland," wrote the editor of the Connaught Telegraph in August 1879, "trade depends altogether on its agricultural class, and now that they are reduced to such extremities the consequence is that the business portion of the population are, if not in a worse, certainly in as bad a position, as those upon whom they must always depend."[36] Similarly, an editorial writer for the Limerick Reporter asserted that the hardships of the depression were not limited to the farming population, but also included "the numerous small commercialists, mechanics, labour-

---

[35] Census of Ireland, 1881: general report, p. 125.
[36] Connaught Telegraph, 9 Aug. 1879, p. 3.

ers and other industrialists whose material interests are bound up
with the wellbeing of tenant farmers."[37] An additional factor operated to translate this hardship into hostility toward the landowning class. Many people accepted the tenant farmer's argument
that his buying power was substantially reduced by his rent. This
argument was all the more disturbing to those traders who assumed, again to quote the *Connaught Telegraph*, that "the money
this country produces is spent out of it."[38] Though some traders
depended heavily on the patronage of local landowners, the
majority received very little business from the landed class and
believed that it was primarily in England, or at least in Dublin,
that large proprietors made their major purchases. In contrast,
local farmers were steady and loyal customers.

Admittedly, the agricultural crisis also had a negative impact
on relationships between shopkeepers and their customers, as
many shopkeepers began to refuse credit and to demand the settling of accounts. Some even took customers to court, and though
the number of such cases was small, they had a symbolic significance that seriously strained ties between the two social groups.
Even this conflict, however, did not deter shopkeepers from joining the land agitation. Indeed it may actually have promoted such
participation for at least two reasons. First, the land agitation offered the shopkeeper a possible means of balancing his accounts.
Since it was by refusing to pay their rents, or by winning large
abatements, that farmers hoped to maintain shop-purchasing during the depression, a trader was not altogether mistaken if he
thought that he was the one who would collect unpaid rents. The
point was made in uncomplimentary terms in June of 1879 by a
correspondent to a Connaught newspaper, who claimed that the
"gushing zeal and sympathy" of merchants, traders, and publicans for the anti-rent agitation could be explained simply by the
fact that "these gentlemen want their little bills paid."[39] Second,
in equally pragmatic terms, participation in the land agitation was
one way in which shopkeepers could offset the bad reputation

[37] *Limerick Reporter*, 6 June 1879, p. 3.

[38] *Connaught Telegraph*, 9 Aug. 1879, p. 3.

[39] *Tuam Herald*, 12 June 1879, p. 1. The point is also well illustrated by an inci-
dent cited by Donnelly in which tenants on two Cork estates, whose offer of a portion of the rents due was refused, took the money and "went directly for the shops,
where they paid for the provisions that sustained their families the past summer."
Cork Examiner, 18 Dec. 1880. See Donnelly, *Cork*, p. 279.

they were acquiring from the collapse of credit. A shopkeeper who joined the movement would thereby distinguish himself as a friend of the farmer. Particularly those merchants and publicans who had established themselves as local patrons could furnish political leadership to their clients as a way of compensating for the loss of the usual benefit they supplied. Or, if they were still able to give credit, they could join the land movement in order to supplement the benefits they provided in an effort to increase their clients' "indebtedness." Shopkeepers and publicans possessed considerable advantages over other members of the community in their capacity to organize political activity, and when the opportunity arose they could only be expected to use these advantages to advance their political importance, especially since the opposition was the traditionally dominant political group in the community.

Some overall measure of the participation of townsmen (and those with similar occupations who lived outside towns) can be obtained from the list of suspects interned under the Protection of Person and Property Act of 1881. We have already noted that the agricultural sector was slightly under-represented among these suspects;[40] in contrast, the commercial and industrial sector was substantially over-represented. No less than 32.6 percent of the suspects belonged to this sector, even though it comprised only 23.2 percent of the male labor force. For Connaught alone, the over-representation was even greater: 30.9 percent of the suspects came from the commercial and industrial sector, while only 9.5 percent of the male labor force belonged to this sector.[41]

Table 17 tries to provide a further breakdown of the commercial and industrial sector, as well as of professional groups. The purpose here is to indicate which non-agricultural occupations were most inclined to participate relative to their numbers in the society. Regrettably, the census classification of the commercial and industrial labor force was not especially useful for our purposes. It

[40] See Table 14 above.

[41] In my "Social composition of the Land League" and my "Political mobilization of Irish farmers" the numbers given differ from the above. The reason for these differences is that I have since transferred general laborers to the agricultural sector. As I indicated in the note for Table 14, I have also reclassified several suspects, which accounts for other differences between the percentages given here and those found in earlier publications.

TABLE 17 · Occupations of persons arrested under the Protection of
Person and Property Act, 1881, and the occupational distribution
of the male labor force: Detailed breakdown of two
non-agricultural sectors

OCCUPATIONS	PERCENTAGE OF SUSPECTS	PERCENTAGE OF LABOR FORCE
Agricultural sector	62.0	65.9
Commercial and industrial sector	32.6	23.2
Traders, business proprietors, and shopworkers	14.1	11.9
Innkeepers and publicans	8.1	0.4
Artisans and non-farm laborers	10.4	9.8
Other commercial and industrial	0.0	1.1
Professional sector	4.6	4.4
Clergy	0.1	0.5
Teachers	1.2	0.5
Newspaper editors and correspondents	1.6	0.02
General professional	1.2	0.6
Subordinate professional service	0.5	0.2
Students	0.0	2.6
Civil service and defense sector	0.2	4.3
Domestic sector	0.6	2.2
Total number	845	1,571,896

NOTE: See Table 14.

was divided according to type of commodity; that is, persons
working with a certain commodity were grouped together, often
with no indication as to how many were artisans, shopworkers,
clerks, shopkeepers, or managers. Fortunately, innkeepers and
publicans were grouped separately. And I have been able to provide a rough estimate of the portion of the male work force consisting of artisans and non-farm laborers. I have also estimated the
number of traders, business proprietors, and shopworkers. It is essential for the reader to know that the method by which these estimates were made involved assigning to the first of these two

categories only those occupations unambiguously connected with artisanal or manual (non-farm) work, while almost all remaining commercial and industrial occupations were placed in the second category. In other words, the method I have used underestimates the number of artisans and non-farm laborers in the male work force, while it overestimates the number of traders, business proprietors, and shopworkers.

A comparison of the two distributions in Table 17 shows that newspaper editors and correspondents constituted the most over-represented professional category among the suspects. Other professional categories were either under-represented or over-represented by degrees so small that it would be unsafe to draw any conclusions. In the commercial and industrial sector, innkeepers and publicans were vastly over-represented (8.1 percent versus 0.4 percent), while artisans and non-farm laborers were just slightly over-represented (10.4 percent versus 9.8 percent). Traders, business proprietors, and shopworkers were only moderately over-represented (14.1 percent versus 11.9), but since we have over-estimated their number in the male labor force it is remarkable that they were over-represented at all. Their actual number in the work force was certainly less than the estimate we have used, so in reality the difference between their percentage among the suspects and their percentage in the work force was greater than the difference shown in Table 17. The civil service and defense sector was under-represented, and so was the domestic sector.

To sum up, we have found that the commercial and industrial sector, taken as a whole, was over-represented among the arrests, and the occupational groups primarily responsible for this over-representation were: innkeepers and publicans; and traders, business proprietors, and shopworkers. We found that the professional sector was not, as a whole, over-represented, but that at least one category within this sector, namely, newspaper editors and correspondents, clearly contributed more than its share to the arrests. The reader should also be told that by grouping shop-workers with traders and business proprietors, I have obscured the particular contribution made by traders to the agitation. If the category could be broken down still further, one would discover that more than half of the traders, business proprietors, and shopworkers who were arrested were actually merchants or shop-keepers.

Again it should be acknowledged that these data may not be

truly representative of the challenging collectivity. In fact, we should be even more cautious now than we were when we used these arrests to assess the participation of farmers and laborers in the movement. The numbers then were rather overwhelming; the numbers here are not. Yet once more confidence in our conclusions is strengthened by controlling for what was undoubtedly the major bias affecting these data. If we exclude suspects arrested on suspicion of a violent crime, the percentages change, but our basic conclusions do not. Artisans and non-farm laborers drop from 10.4 percent to 6.9 percent. By contrast, innkeepers and pub-·licans increase from 8.1 percent to 10.3 percent; traders, business proprietors, and shopworkers increase from 14.1 to 17.8 percent; and newspaper editors and correspondents increase from 1.6 to 2.4 percent. The exclusion of persons arrested for violent activities raises the percentages contributed by the very town occupations I have suggested were the most important.

We can also use the list of suspects arrested under the Protection of Person and Property Act to obtain some idea of the role that townsmen played in the movement. Table 18 cross-tabulates type of arrest with occupation. The alleged crimes that were used to justify the arrest of innkeepers and publicans often fall into the category that I have called *threatening letters and notices* (which includes no-rent and boycott notices). Innkeepers and publicans contribute a larger percentage to this type of arrest than any other occupational groups in the table, primarily because their business establishments could be used for posting Land League placards. Their premises could also be used as gathering places, so it is not surprising that a relatively large percentage were arrested for *illegal meeting*. Traders and business proprietors were less energetic in these activities, but were ahead of all other townsmen in *non-violent intimidation*, no doubt partly because this category includes boycotting, which business proprietors were in an advantageous position to assist by refusing, as many did, to deal with boycott victims. Traders and business proprietors stand out even more in the category I have called *seditious speeches and writings*. Whereas seditious speeches and writings accounted for only 4.6 percent of the total arrests in this table, 9.6 percent of the traders and business proprietors were interned for activities of this kind. Newspaper editors and correspondents also had a relatively large percentage in this category. Their number is too small to allow for much generalization about their role, but this finding

TABLE 18 · Type of arrest under the Protection of Person and Property Act, 1881, by occupation

PERCENTAGE OF SUSPECTS BY OCCUPATION

Suspected crime	Farmers	Farmers' sons	General laborers	Other agricultural	Traders and business proprietors	Shopworkers and clerks	Innkeepers and publicans	Artisans and non-farm laborers	Newspaper editors and correspondents	Total
Violence	33.9	53.5	85.6	64.7	19.2	23.1	19.1	58.0	7.1	38.9
Non-violent intimidation	42.3	24.4	8.6	11.8	40.3	30.8	36.7	18.2	28.6	33.2
Illegal meeting	12.4	15.2	2.9	17.6	18.1	23.1	22.1	11.4	28.6	14.6
Threatening letters and notices	7.4	3.1	2.9	0.0	12.8	19.2	20.6	9.1	7.1	8.7
Seditious speeches and writings	4.0	3.8	0.0	5.9	9.6	3.8	1.5	3.4	28.6	4.6
Total number	324	131	35	17	94	26	68	88	14	797

NOTE: In order to keep this table to a manageable size, I have omitted occupational groups contributing less than 1.5 percent to the total. Whenever an individual's suspected activities extended to more than one of the above categories, he was coded according to whichever seemed to be the primary reason for his arrest. The source is S.P.O., Irish crimes records, 1881. Basically the same table appears in my "Social composition of the Land League." It differs slightly because a few occupations have been reclassified.

certainly makes sense, since the newspaper vocation could readily lend itself to seditious writings.

Perhaps the most striking finding in Table 18 is the relatively
low percentage of townsmen who were suspected of committing
violence. Whereas 38.9 percent of all arrests were for violent activities, only 19.2 percent of the traders and business proprietors
were interned for this reason. Similarly, only 23.1 percent of the
shopworkers and clerks, only 19.1 percent of the innkeepers and
publicans, and only 7.1 percent of the newspaper editors and correspondents were arrested on suspicion of committing violence.
This does mean that these groups had no connection with violence. On the contrary, dossiers on suspects reveal that the majority of internments for non-violent activities were justified on the
grounds that the suspect was responsible for instigating violence,
though he may not have committed any himself. One inference
that could be drawn from these data is that townsmen often
functioned as local leaders. I argued in Chapter Four that they
were socially integrated into rural society, but also that they were
different from farmers in important respects, enjoying a greater
range of social contacts both within and outside their own district. The implication was, of course, that they were consequently
in a better position to provide leadership in the community. Some
evidence will now be presented supporting this conclusion, but it
will also become apparent that there was considerable regional
variation in the leadership role townsmen played.

We have already noted that the Land War began with an increase in activity on the part of the political collectivity that had
been promoting the interests of tenant farmers in the late 1870s. In
Leinster and Munster, this collectivity consisted principally of the
farmers' clubs. In Connaught, where farmers' clubs were weaker,
the pre-Land War challenging collectivity consisted of a disproportionate number of townsmen. One farmers' club had met regularly in Connaught in the late 1870s (the Ballinasloe Tenants' Defence Association), but two of its most active members, Matthew
Harris and M. M. O'Sullivan, were not themselves farmers.[42] The
single most important local politician in Connaught in the late
1870s was James Daly of Castlebar, publisher of the *Connaught*

[42] Both men had farming backgrounds, but in the late 1870s Harris was a builder
and O'Sullivan a schoolteacher.

Telegraph. Daly spoke at a "meeting of electors" in Castlebar in August 1875, at a tenant-right demonstration in Louisburgh in the following December, and at another tenant-right meeting organized by the Ballinasloe club and held at Headford early in February 1877. During the Louisburgh meeting Daly proposed the formation of a tenants' defense association for Mayo; and he was behind a similar effort in the autumn of 1878.[43]

The collectivity primarily responsible for organizing the agitation in Connaught in the spring and early summer of 1879 consisted of a handful of townsmen, among whom Daly was the central figure. Some of these townsmen were Fenians, and they were assisted by Fenian politicians from outside Connaught, especially by Michael Davitt. In The Fall of Feudalism Davitt claims credit for initiating the Irishtown meeting, and he refers to four local individuals who helped to organize it: P. W. Nally, the farmer's son from Balla to whom I have referred once already,[44] J. W. Walshe, a commercial traveler, J. P. Quinn, a schoolteacher, and John O'Kane, a shopkeeper in Claremorris.[45] Actually, the chief person behind the meeting was probably not Davitt, but rather Daly, who later asserted in a letter to his own newspaper that he had proposed the idea of the Irishtown meeting to a group consisting of the two Irishtown farmers mentioned before (one of whom was also named James Daly), plus Thomas Sweeney, a shopkeeper in Claremorris, and the John O'Kane whom Davitt mentions.[46] If we put the lists together, the organizers of the Irishtown meeting consisted of two farmers, one farmers' son, a commercial traveler, a schoolteacher, and two shopkeepers—along with Daly and Davitt. Daly served as chairman of the meeting, and only one of the speakers was a farmer.[47]

[43] Nation, 21 Aug. 1875, p. 7; 18 Dec. 1875, p. 3; Galway Vindicator, 3 Feb. 1877, p. 3; Connaught Telegraph, 26 Oct. 1878, p. 5.

[44] See above, note 25.

[45] Davitt, Fall of Feudalism, p. 147.

[46] Connaught Telegraph, 15 Jan. 1881, p. 15. An announcement of a forthcoming meeting at Irishtown appears in the Connaught Telegraph in February 1879, which strongly suggests that Daly's version of who organized the meeting comes closer to the truth, since Davitt claims to have proposed the meeting in March. See Connaught Telegraph, 15 Feb. 1879, p. 2. See also Lee, Modernisation of Irish Society, pp. 72-4.

[47] Six Fenians took the floor, none of whom were farmers: J. W. Walshe, Thomas Brennan, M. M. O'Sullivan, John Ferguson, Matthew Harris, and John O'Connor Power, M.P. for County Mayo. The floor was also taken by Thomas Sweeney, the

Townsmen continued to be prominent at subsequent meetings in the west. The absence of farmers on the platform at the Milltown meeting in June was noted by the Chief Secretary in parliament.[48] Shortly afterwards, plans for a demonstration in Claremorris were made by "a large and very influential meeting of priests, merchants and tenant-farmers."[49] In September a meeting of "merchants and traders of Castlebar" was held to organize a county demonstration.[50] And in October a demonstration in the town of Roscommon was organized at a preliminary gathering where the floor was taken by three shopkeepers and a newspaper proprietor, but not one farmer.[51] At the founding meeting of the Mayo Land League (in Castlebar in August) a substantial number of farmers were present, but townsmen were also well represented. According to the minutes of this meeting, the speakers included Davitt, three shopkeepers, a barrister, and two farmers.[52] A five-man executive was appointed, consisting entirely of persons from Mayo, but the closest any of them came to being a farmer was P. W. Nally, who was a farmer's son.[53] The founding committee of the National Land League (established in October) included farmers from Leinster and Munster, while Connaught was represented by three clergymen and four townsmen, but no farmers.[54]

As support for the movement grew, farmers quickly came to

shopkeeper from Claremorris, John J. Louden, a barrister (and large landholder) from Westport, and Alex T. Leonard, Esq., who was, I assume, a tenant farmer, since he occupied a large agricultural holding in the Irishtown area. The son of James Daly of Irishtown has told me that Leonard was a physician, but I have not been able to find any supporting evidence. The meeting is reported in the *Connaught Telegraph*, 21 April 1879.

[48] *Hansard 3*, ccxlvii, cols. 434, 694-5.

[49] *Connaught Telegraph*, 21 June 1879, p. 5. This demonstration was eventually held on 13 July and should not be confused with an earlier demonstration at Claremorris on 1 June.

[50] Ibid., 20 Sept. 1879, p. 5. The demonstration itself took place on 28 September. See ibid., 4 Oct. 1879, p. 2.

[51] The meeting was reported in the *Roscommon Journal*, 25 Oct. 1879, p. 2. Two landowners also addressed the meeting, T.A.P. Mapother and Major J. T. D'Arcy, both Catholics and both active in Butt's Home Rule movement.

[52] *Connaught Telegraph*, 16 Aug. 1879, p. 5. The barrister was John J. Louden. The shopkeepers were William Judge of Claremorris, Thomas Reilly of Balla, and P. J. Monahan of Ballinrobe (who was also an innkeeper). The farmers were Patrick Ryan from Ballyhean and Stephen Hestkin from the Neale.

[53] The others were John J. Louden, James Daly, J. W. Walshe, and Hugh Feeney. The last-mentioned was a shopkeeper and publican from Castlebar.

[54] For a list of members of this committee, see Davitt, *Fall of Feudalism*, p. 173.

outnumber townsmen. But an intensive study I was able to make of the Land League in two localities in Connaught left me with the clear impression that townsmen continued to perform an important leadership role. By carefully reading issues of the *Roscommon Journal* and the *Connaught Telegraph* I became familiar with the major personalities in the movement in the districts surrounding the towns of Roscommon and Castlebar. In both, townsmen functioned as local leaders. The hard core of active Land Leaguers in the Roscommon district consisted of a half-dozen townsmen who were well known to the authorities and were regarded as responsible for activities often carried out by others.[55] Townsmen in Roscommon were especially active in boycotts (the most publicized of which was directed against James White, a large farmer and land agent, who was forced to buy supplies through Findlater's in Dublin);[56] and they were occasionally involved in helping farmers to organize branches of the League.[57] As already noted, townsmen of Castlebar were active in organizing many of the early Mayo meetings and responsible for the first large demonstration in their district; they also gave assistance to rural branches[58] and organized their own Castlebar branch, which was unquestionably the most active in the area.[59]

My intention, of course, has not been to argue that the Land War was in any sense a townsmen's movement. I have already demonstrated that it was clearly a farmers' movement. My point has been simply that many townsmen played an active role. To be sure, a large number of them (including many shopkeepers and publicans) did not support the Land League. The same can be said, however, of many farmers. The fact remains that townsmen constituted an important part of the challenging collectivity. They did so because they were socially integrated into the rural society and enjoyed strong social bonds and cooperative economic relationships with farmers. For reasons already indicated, rural-urban relations were less divisive in Ireland than in most other societies.

[55] *Roscommon Journal*, 5 Feb. 1881, p. 1.

[56] Ibid., 4 Dec. 1880, p. 2; and 19 March 1881, p. 2.

[57] *Roscommon Journal*, 4 Sept. 1880, p. 2; and *Nation*, 2 Oct. 1880, p. 13.

[58] A branch in nearby Crumlin was organized by J. B. Walsh of Castlebar. See N.L.I., Land League papers: Branch returns (MS 8291). In the absence of the president, a meeting of the Belcarra branch was chaired in February 1880 by James Daly. See *Connaught Telegraph*, 21 Feb. 1880, p. 5.

[59] See *Connaught Telegraph*, 17 Jan. 1880, p. 5; 20 March 1880, p. 4; 25 Sept. 1880, p. 3; 30 Oct. 1880, p. 2; and 6 Nov. 1880, p. 4.

This was true before the Famine, but it was even more so in the post-famine period when rural-urban ties became stronger as the country population became more integrated into national and urban structures. The result was an effective rural-urban coalition against the landowning class.

NATIONALIST POLITICIANS

Before the Land War, political movements seeking to obtain greater self-government for Ireland had been regionally imbalanced. They had failed, of course, to attract any substantial support from Ulster since the beginning of the century. But they had even failed to mobilize much support in Connaught and in west Munster; instead they had drawn their followers largely from Leinster and east Munster. Their strength had also come disproportionately from cities and towns. This statement does not deny that nationalism had considerable rural appeal. Indeed, in absolute numbers, the majority of its supporters must traditionally have lived in rural areas, if only because country people always constituted over three-quarters of the total population. Yet nationalist movements in Ireland had all begun in urban centers; the most active members had usually been city or townspeople; the bulk of the leadership had invariably come from urban districts; and the countryside was generally not as well organized as were cities and towns.

In view of the greater national and urban integration of the rural population in the post-famine period, one might expect to find these regional and rural-urban differences diminishing. More communication and contact among different parts of the country, as well as between town and country, would surely have increased the attention given by western and rural people to the politics that eastern and urban people had tended to dominate. These same developments should also have made it easier for politicians to organize those areas that had been comparatively less mobilized in the past. The level of nationalist political activity by people in the west, and by rural people in general, should therefore have increased.

This did not happen immediately. Neither the Fenians nor the Home Rulers could claim to have rallied western support or rural support more successfully than did O'Connell in the 1840s. In fact, until the late 1870s both Fenianism and Home Rule were characterized by discernable anti-agrarian elements, and some of their leaders were even prepared to solicit the patronage of the landed gentry at the expense of support from tenant farmers. Most notably, the Home Government Association made undisguised attempts to woo supporters from among the Protestant Ascendancy.

Given the prevailing social structure, this conservative gambit inevitably failed. The reasons should be clearly understood since they reveal the underlying structural conditions that have shaped the political evolution of modern Ireland. Irish nationalism had been supported mainly by Catholics, and movements for self-government had been led primarily by members of the mostly Catholic urban middle class. An alliance between these urban Catholics and any significant number of Protestant landowners would have had to overcome the social cleavage in the society that divided the two major religious groups. Protestants were separated from Catholics by religious bigotry and by differences in social status. They were also separated by well-recognized differences in interests: because they constituted a numerical minority, Protestants believed that their social position depended on the preservation of the British connection. The situation might have been entirely different—the whole course of Irish history during the past hundred years might have been entirely different—if the landed class in Ireland had been composed or had come to be composed mostly of Catholics. Under these circumstances, a nationalist alliance between the landed gentry and the urban middle class would have been at least conceivable. And if such an alliance had been formed, Irish nationalism would not have taken an agrarian direction. The point is, of course, that an alliance of this kind was impossible. The dominant lines of integration and cleavage in the society separated the urban middle class from the rural elite, while they drew together the urban middle class and the rural masses. This was true in O'Connell's time; and as a result of the social changes that had occurred during and after the Famine, it was even more true on the eve of the Land War.

The unavoidable failure of conservative nationalism in the 1870s was followed by the re-emergence, in a stronger form than ever before, of the basic political affinity between rural and urban Irish Catholics on the question of self-government. At the same time, and perhaps even more significantly, there also occurred the beginnings of an adjustment in the regional distribution of nationalist strength. It is now possible, with the advantage of hindsight, to detect events taking place in the 1870s that we can recognize as the antecedents of these two developments. The appeal of nationalism was gaining ground among the rural electorate; the farmers' clubs became more closely identified with the Home Rule movement; a small Fenian network was established in Connaught; several farmers' clubs and even a few Home Rule Associations appeared in the west; and some nationalist politicians were giving serious consideration to a program that would seek directly to attract tenant farmers.

Then, in 1879, a considerable number of nationalist politicians joined the emerging land movement. The way in which they became involved was not the same in all parts of the country. It differed greatly between Connaught and other regions. In Connaught it was primarily through the intermediary role of townsmen that nationalist politicians from outside the province were brought in. These townsmen served to link the rising land agitation with the nationalist movement. They were able to do so because a number of them had recently become involved in nationalist politics and had acquired connections with nationalist leaders. Some of these townsmen, in fact, were part of the Fenian network. The core of Fenians that had begun operating in Connaught during the 1870s included, among others, Matthew Harris and M. M. O'Sullivan, the two townsmen already cited as active members of the Ballinasloe Tenants' Defence Association. It also included Thomas Brennan, who worked for several years in the office of a milling company in Castlebar, and P. W. Nally, the farmer's son from Balla, mentioned several times already in connection with the Irishtown meeting. These men were the organizers behind the 1874 campaign to elect John O'Connor Power to parliament.[60] Power was himself a Fenian, and his election is, as suggested before, the best evidence we have that Fenians were making genuine progress in the west at that time.

The presence of this active Fenian network in Connaught had a profound impact on the land agitation that emerged in 1879. In March of that year Michael Davitt made a trip to Connaught to visit friends. Davitt was well known as a Fenian, though he did not enjoy a position of great influence in the Fenian organization. He had been in Paris in January, unsuccessfully trying to obtain the endorsement of the Supreme Council of the Irish Republican Brotherhood for the "New Departure" (the proposed alliance between Fenians and constitutionalists). Land agitation was only

[60] Ryan, *Fenian Memories*, pp. 37-9, 44-6.

part of the New Departure program, but Davitt's visit to the west persuaded him that an unusual opportunity was emerging for nationalists to join forces with an agrarian movement. As a result, the land question became for him the central plank of the new program. He returned to Dublin to face a second meeting of the Supreme Council, but this time hoping to persuade them to help organize a land movement. "What he now demanded," wrote John Devoy many years later, "was not the support of the scheme discussed in Paris, but a new one that was wholly agrarian."[61]

The Supreme Council was no more receptive on this occasion than it had been earlier in Paris. On the other hand, Davitt was able to find at least some Fenians who shared his views. Most of them were members of the Fenian network in Connaught. Aware of the discontent in the west, they too were of the opinion that Fenians should take an enterprising part in the rising land agitation. A few, such as Harris and O'Sullivan, had already been doing so. All four persons whom Davitt mentions as helping to organize the Irishtown meeting were Fenians, and so were six of those who spoke at the meeting. While it does not appear true, as Davitt implies, that he was primarily responsible for this meeting, it is true that he and other Fenians were very much involved in it. The Irishtown demonstration is generally regarded as the beginning of the Land War. Yet several land meetings had been held and new tenants' defense associations formed during the months prior to it. The Irishtown meeting did, however, mark a crucial turning point in the early evolution of the agitation. It was at this gathering that Fenians from outside Connaught began to play an influential role. From then on, they were active at most (though not all) of the meetings in the west. They helped to arrange an important one at Westport in June and another at Claremorris in July.[62] And it was principally Davitt who organized the gathering in Castlebar on 16 August at which the Mayo Land League was founded.

Elsewhere in the country the involvement of nationalist politicians in the movement followed a different pattern. First, in the eastern and southern counties, the farmers' clubs, more than townsmen, provided the critical link between the land agitation and the nationalist movement. Second, since these farmers' clubs

[61] *Gaelic American*, 8 Sept. 1906.

[62] They used the occasion of the Claremorris meeting to hold a secret conference of the Mayo council of the Fenian brotherhood. See John Devoy's recollections, ibid.

were more closely associated with the constitutionalist Home
Rule party than with the Fenians, it was primarily the constitutionalist faction that joined forces with the land movement in
Leinster and Munster, whereas in Connaught it was the Fenian
faction. Although Davitt is usually given more credit than Parnell
for helping to initiate the land movement, in fact Parnell had
taken an interest in the agitation before Davitt had any notion of
what was happening. Parnell spoke at two demonstrations
mounted by farmers' clubs in November 1878 (in Galway and in
Kerry), and participated in discussions held by the Central Tenants' Defence Association in Dublin in January and February
1879. He was subsequently persuaded by Davitt to address the
Westport meeting in June, which inaugurated the coming together of the two separate factions of the nationalist movement in
the Land War. Historians have only been able to speculate as to
Parnell's motives for accepting Davitt's invitation. The most likely
explanation is that he was aware of the role Fenians had played at
the Irishtown meeting, and he feared that unless he attended at
Westport, he would risk losing to them the opportunity of becoming leader (and hence political beneficiary) of the rising agrarian
unrest.

If Davitt's major contribution in 1879 was to help organize early
meetings in Connaught, Parnell's was to take a leading part in
uniting this movement in the west with the activities of the
farmers' clubs in Leinster and Munster. One of the political advantages that Parnell had over Davitt was a closer affiliation with
groups interested in the land question in Leinster and Munster,
primarily as a result of the close tie between the farmers' clubs
and the Home Rule movement. Thus Parnell could help to provide the movement with a national organization in a way that
Davitt could never have done. It was Parnell who organized the
founding meeting of the Irish National Land League in October. It
was he who was elected its president. Along with his public
popularity and his position in the Irish party, this presidency gave
him more influence over the agitation than any one other person.
Yet the Fenian faction was by no means pushed out of the movement by Parnell. It remained powerful not only in western districts, but also in the central executive, which was staffed mainly
by Fenians throughout its two-year history.[63] The central direc-

[63] In addition to Parnell, who was a Home Ruler, the executive included W. H.
O'Sullivan and Joseph Biggar, who were Home Rule members of parliament, but

tion of the agitation provided by this body was perhaps the most important contribution made by nationalists to the movement. Nationalist politicians also spoke regularly at rallies in various parts of the country. Indeed, one of the functions performed by the central executive was to arrange for nationalist politicians to address local meetings in response to requests from branches.[64] And, as will be discussed in the following chapter, these politicians provided tenant farmers with a slate of parliamentary candidates who stood on a tenant-right platform in the election of 1880 and endeavored to present the tenant's case in parliament.

For years afterwards, there was an inclination to exaggerate the significance of nationalist politicians in the Land War. The worst offenders were Fenians, some of whom liked to pretend that they deserved most of the credit for rescuing Ireland from landlords. Their habitual claim was that the New Departure was the seed from which the land agitation grew. Such a view confuses two distinguishable historical developments and greatly overstates the value of their role.[65] Nevertheless, the leadership provided by nationalist politicians was one of the most important characteristics of the Land War, and the consequences of it are still felt today. While not responsible for the movement, nationalist politicians made noteworthy contributions to it. By so doing, they acquired an unprecedented amount of power over the rural population.

THE CATHOLIC CLERGY

We saw how salient religious cleavages and integrative bonds were in pre-famine society and what effect they had on collective action. Nothing happened in the post-famine period to lessen the weight of religious structure. Religion continued to divide and unite people, with tremendous consequences for the nature of ac-

---

also had Fenian connections. The other Fenians were Patrick Egan, Michael Davitt, and Thomas Brennan. Also on the executive was A. J. Kettle, president of the Central Tenants' Defence Association. Along with O'Sullivan, who was a member of the Limerick and Clare Farmers' Club, Kettle represented the older farmers' clubs. See Davitt, Fall of Feudalism, p. 172.

[64] N.L.I., Land League papers: Branch returns. Many of these returns contain requests for prominent nationalist politicians to attend meetings planned by local branches.

[65] Moody, "The new departure in Irish politics, 1878-9." See also Moody, "Irish-American nationalism" in Irish Historical Studies, 15, no. 60 (Sept. 1967), pp. 444-5.

tive collectivities. Sectarian rioting in working-class Belfast was almost endemic until the 1870s; altogether there were at least four major eruptions in which lives were lost during the second half of the century.[66] A Protestant religious revival in Ulster in 1859 mobilized more persons in sustained common activity than any other movement in rural Ulster in the nineteenth century.[67] A small, but significant, temperance movement appeared in Connaught in the late 1870s, which was organized chiefly by members of the Catholic clergy.[68] Religious fervor swept the country during the years 1879-80 in response to reports of an apparition of the Virgin Mary on the wall of the Catholic chapel in the village of Knock, County Mayo.[69] And finally, it is obvious that the Land War itself was not free of religious bias. Regional variations in the intensity of the agitation correlated strongly with the percentage of the population that was Catholic. There tended to be more unrest in Catholic counties and the least unrest of all in the six Ulster counties in the northeast. Like so many earlier movements in Ireland, the Land War was a Catholic movement.

In most of the earlier movements the Catholic clergy had performed a critical role. What part did they play in the Land War? The answer, in brief, is that they played an active role, but one that contained a basic contradiction. On the one hand, the capacity of the clergy to organize collective action, as they had done so frequently in the past, made it difficult for them to avoid becoming part of any extremely large political movement involving their parishioners. On the other hand, it was inevitable that the clergy would seek to control such a movement and to direct the activities of its members and sympathizers in the way they had done before. More than any other constituent group, the Catholic clergy formed a relatively autonomous segment within the challenging collectivity, possessing their own organization and resources. They not only belonged to communities formed by themselves and their parishioners; they also belonged to a large and bureaucratically organized religious institution. As representatives of this institu-

---

[66] Gibbon, *Origins of Ulster Unionism*, pp. 67-8.   [67] Ibid., pp. 44-66.

[68] See *Galway Vindicator*, 16 May 1877, p. 3; 13 June 1877, p. 4; 18 July 1877, p. 4; 8 Sept. 1877, p. 4; 13 March 1878, p. 3; 22 June 1878, p. 3; 6 July 1878, p. 3.

[69] The apparition was first sighted in August 1879, five days after the Mayo Land League was founded in nearby Castlebar. It was reportedly seen again early in 1880, and for much of the remainder of 1880 it competed with the land agitation for the attention of the people.

tion, priests were able to exert influence over people, but their position in the church also curtailed their freedom of action.

It would be a mistake to assume that these institutional constraints operated entirely through pressures exerted by the church hierarchy. Part of the political convictions of all but a few members of the Catholic clergy was a fundamental belief in the values of the religion to which they belonged—not only its teachings, but also its combined strength and the authority on which that combined strength rested. Nevertheless, there certainly did exist considerable pressure to conform to the policies laid down by the church leaders. The consequence of this was a tendency for clerical participation to vary from region to region, depending on the attitude of the local bishop. In the dioceses of Cashel, Clonfert, Achonry, and several others, the attitude of the bishop was positive and the clergy were comparatively active. But in the majority of dioceses, the bishops opposed the land agitation and the involvement of the clergy was more limited. Edward McCabe, the archbishop of Dublin, was sympathetic to the need for reductions in rent, but was almost unqualified in his opposition to the agitation, arguing that tenants should "pray for clement weather," and in the meantime pay their just debts.[70] McCabe restricted clerical participation in the Dublin diocese and even sought to curtail the encouragement given to the movement by pro-Land League bishops.[71] Several bishops in Connaught were out of sympathy with the leadership of the Land War, including John MacHale, the aged archbishop of Tuam. For over forty years MacHale had been the radical cleric, the tenant-righter and the protector of his clergy's freedom to participate in politics. Yet he now opposed the land agitation and tried to dissuade his clergy from participating in it. He denounced the Westport meeting, and issued a stinging attack on the movement in reply to an invitation to attend a land meeting in Ballyhaunis in July 1879. In words that reverberated through the country, John of Tuam warned the people not to be deceived by "a few unknown strolling men."[72]

MacHale's philippics were not just the spiteful grumblings of

[70] C. J. Woods, "The politics of Cardinal McCabe, archbishop of Dublin, 1879-85" in Dublin Historical Record, 26, no. 3 (June 1973), p. 102. See also Emmet Larkin, The Catholic Church and the Creation of the Modern Irish State, 1878-1886 (Philadelphia, 1975).

[71] Woods, "Politics of Cardinal McCabe."

[72] Nation, 12 July 1879, p. 12.

an old man. To begin with, there was no real inconsistency between his position now and his earlier radicalism. His radicalism
had always been founded on the belief that the Catholic clergy
had a right and a duty to direct the political activities of
parishioners and to protect parishioners from political control by
other groups. In 1879 he was genuinely concerned that people
were falling prey to those who were, from his point of view, unknown men. He was worried most of all about the role that Fenians were playing in the agitation, but more generally he was
alarmed by the rise of an energetic lay leadership that sought to
assume a relationship with the people which the clergy had always claimed as their own. MacHale's views on this subject were
certainly shared by other bishops in Connaught who opposed
the agitation, such as John MacEvilly, bishop of Galway, and
Laurence Gillooly, bishop of Elphin. But even a prelate sympathetic to the movement, such as Francis MacCormack, bishop of
Achonry, could find reason to fear the threat posed by this emerging lay leadership. In one notable instance, MacCormack responded to Parnell's decision in April 1880 to contest one of the
Mayo parliamentary seats by accusing him and his associates of
infringing on the political domain of the Catholic clergy.

> The bishops and priests of Ireland are, let me assure him, very
> united, and the heart of Catholic Ireland is still loyal to its
> Church; and the bubble of Mr. Parnell's popularity might at
> any moment burst before the indignant spirit of Irish faith
> and fatherland. The evident tendency of his recent political
> action is to sever Irish priests and people. But he miscalcu-
> lates his power when he steps, as an apostle of discord, be-
> tween us and our flocks.[73]

Nor should we assume that this clerical apprehension was felt
only by the bishops. There is good reason to believe that many
members of the lower clergy were equally afraid of the influences
that were directing the new movement. Even those who could endorse its aims were unhappy with the fact that it was not sufficiently under their control. MacHale's opposition alone does not
explain the hostility that the movement encountered among the
clergy of Connaught in the early months. According to Davitt, before MacHale publicly condemned the agitation "many of the al-

[73] *Sligo Champion*, 17 April 1880, p. 4.

tars rang with warnings and denunciations" against it.[74] There were no priests present at the Irishtown, Westport, or Milltown meetings. Some clergymen attended meetings in July and August, but they were the exception rather than the rule. No priest was present at the founding of the Mayo Land League in August.[75]

The fact was that the clergy had something real to fear. The agitation was initially organized by laymen, many of whom were in favor of building a movement independent of clerical assistance. The early meetings in Connaught were organized without the solicitation of clerical endorsement that was customary for political gatherings of this kind. It was no accident that the Irishtown demonstration was held specifically to embarrass a local priest, who was acting as land agent for his nephew. And it was not entirely with regret that the agitators greeted MacHale's denunciation of the Westport meeting. MacHale thereby handed them the chance to carry on the agitation without the clergy. They were aided in this endeavor by Parnell's decision to address the Westport meeting despite MacHale's opposition. They regarded his decision as a major step forward because it signaled to the clergy that the movement would not accept political subservience to a Catholic prelate.[76] Although Parnell eventually won the confidence of most Catholic churchmen, this did not come about until the summer of 1880 (even later in some places), and not before Parnell and the priests had fought openly in several constituencies during the general election of 1880.[77]

The clergy had been presented with a serious dilemma. When they took part in the agitation, they faced opposition to their authority from lay organizers.[78] When they did not, they only

[74] Davitt, Fall of Feudalism, p. 151.

[75] One priest, William Joyce of Louisburgh, County Mayo, sent a letter of support.

[76] Davitt, Fall of Feudalism, pp. 152-4.

[77] Lyons, Charles Steward Parnell, pp. 118-21.

[78] John Devoy describes the preparatory meeting in June 1879 for the Claremorris demonstration in July and recalls that the clergy were told by lay organizers that religious questions were not to be introduced. See C. J. Woods, "Catholic church and Irish politics, 1879-92," unpublished Ph.D. thesis, University of Nottingham, 1968. His account is based on Devoy's recollections of this meeting. Between the June meeting and the July demonstration, the chief cleric who helped to organize the demonstration, Canon Ulick Bourke, came under attack from Daly in the pages of the Connaught Telegraph. See Connaught Telegraph, 28 June 1879, p. 4.

strengthened lay control over the movement. The absence of the clergy during the early months of the agitation seriously aggravated their relations with those among their parishioners who supported it. A Constabulary report from Galway in October 1879 observed that "the disposition of the people is bad towards . . . the Roman Catholic clergy who have not taken part in the anti-rent agitation."[79] In November the *Northern Whig* observed that some of the agitators have assumed "a very antagonistic attitude to the priests, who have generally spoken with moderation." "This war against the landlords," the *Whig* lamented, "has shown some indications of also becoming a war against the Roman Catholic clergy."[80]

It did not turn into a war against the Roman Catholic clergy. At different times, in different parts of the country, clergymen were gradually drawn into the movement in significant numbers. Given their social position in local communities, it would have been difficult for them to do otherwise. If townsmen were socially integrated into rural society, Catholic clergymen were doubly so. Initially, most priests hoped that good weather would return and the agitation would subside. When it became clear that this was not going to happen, they had to make the difficult choice between joining the movement or losing influence over many of their parishioners. In varying degrees, probably the majority chose the first option, recognizing that only in this way would they have any chance of controlling the agitation and undercutting the dangerous power that they felt was influencing their flocks. "Whether the priest will it or no," Bishop MacEvilly wrote Tobias Kirby, rector of the Irish College in Rome, "the meetings will be held. Their people will assemble under the pressure of threatened famine to expound their wrongs to landlords and government; if the priests keep aloof, these meetings will be scenes of disorder; if the priests attend they will keep the people attached to them."[81] No doubt, those who chose to participate also felt a genuine sympathy for the plight of their parishioners. Yet it is essential to recognize that they were primarily motivated by a fear that the struggle between landlords and tenants would create an irreparable gulf between themselves and their people.[82]

[79] S.P.O., Chief Secretary's Office, Registered Papers: Report of the inspector general of the Royal Irish Constabulary, 30 Oct. 1879 (1880/13904).

[80] *Northern Whig*, 22 Nov. 1879, p. 4.

[81] Quoted in Larkin, *Catholic Church and Creation of Modern Irish State*, p. 29.

[82] I have borrowed this argument from two writers. Larkin uses it to explain the

In fact, clerical efforts to control the agitation began early, before priests came to participate in the movement itself. While laymen were organizing land meetings in the spring and summer of 1879, many Catholic clergymen were busy helping to organize tenants who were petitioning their landlords for reductions in rent. The bailiff on the Manor Hamilton estate of Lord Leitrim believed that a petition submitted by tenants in April 1879 was the work of the local Catholic curate.[83] In June a group of tenants on a property near Ballinasloe met with their curate to organize a petition.[84] And in September tenants in the neighborhood of Athleague, "acting on the advice of the parish priest," sent memorials to their respective landlords asking for abatements in rent.[85] Through activities of this kind, clergymen hoped not only to assist their parishioners in a time of need, but also to head off more radical types of action. On several occasions during 1879, assemblies of Catholic clergymen passed resolutions calling upon landlords to reduce their rents.[86]

Yet it was only a matter of time before Catholic priests would yield to pressure from their parishioners to provide some direct assistance to the agitation. It was advantageous for any group planning to hold a demonstration to obtain the endorsement of local clergymen. Many land meetings took place near Catholic chapels; and most were held on Sundays. In such cases the clergy could be tremendously helpful as organizers, especially if they were willing to announce during mass that a demonstration would be held, or to make special arrangements to accommodate it.[87] Pressures were also exerted on clergymen to attend land

---

fact that some bishops, one of whom was MacEvilly, came to support the agitation, though they were originally opposed. See Larkin, *Roman Catholic Church and Creation and Modern Irish State*, especially pp. 25, 29-30, and 49-50. Woods employs the same argument to explain the participation of the clergy in general. See Woods, "Catholic church and Irish politics."

[83] N.L.I., Leitrim Papers: Letter book of G. F. Stewart: Stewart to H. T. Clements, 15 April 1879.

[84] *Tuam Herald*, 21 June 1879, p. 2.

[85] *Roscommon Journal*, 13 Sept. 1879, p. 2.

[86] *Connaught Telegraph*, 24 May 1879, p. 5; *Tuam Herald*, 7 June 1879, p. 1; 21 June 1879, p. 2; *Sligo Champion*, 15 Nov. 1879, p. 4.

[87] In September 1880, for instance, a priest granted a request from the local Land League branch to say mass at eight o'clock in order to enable his parishioners to attend a demonstration in Newmarket-on-Fergus. See *Clare Independent*, 18 Sept. 1880, p. 3. By the same token, of course, clerical opposition to a land meeting represented a serious obstacle, especially if a priest was moved to condemn a demonstration from the altar, as some did. For examples of clergymen who denounced

demonstrations, thereby lending respectability to the proceedings. The extent to which they obliged is revealed by a sample I selected of 153 land meetings reported in the *Nation* from June 1879 through August 1881. For no less than 62 percent of these meetings some reference was made in the newspaper report to at least one priest being present. Given their initial hesitation, and given also the continued opposition to the movement of most bishops, this figure is remarkably high. (And there may well have been some priests present at other meetings in the sample but not mentioned in the newspaper report.) Frequently only one or two clergymen attended, but those who did usually took the chair. Occasionally, more than a dozen clergymen were listed as present. As a rule, priests were willing to take part in land meetings only if they were approached at an early stage and given some say about who would speak and what resolutions would be proposed. When they refused, it was often because they had not been sufficiently consulted in advance.[88]

Although there were exceptions, priests normally insisted that the temper of meetings be kept moderate. The role they most often played is well illustrated by two demonstrations cited by Emmet Larkin, both of which occurred in County Kilkenny in November 1880. At one, the crowd demanded the expulsion of two uniformed policemen, but they were allowed to remain at the insistence of the clergy. At the other, when one of the speakers remarked that there "were bad landlords amongst them" and several persons cried out "Down with them," the priest who was chairing the meeting ordered the crowd raisers off the platform, and declared: "There will be no cries of down with them where I am chairman. I am responsible for the maintenance of order. I will not have the Tory press of England putting me down as sanctioning assassination by sanctioning such cries."[89]

These two functions—organizing petitions and attending land demonstrations—were supplemented by a third function performed by priests in the Land War: they sometimes helped to organize and manage Land League branches. Again they were in a unique position to provide assistance. As with land meetings,

---

meetings from the altar, see *Nation*, 20 Oct. 1880, and *Clare Independent*, 4 Dec. 1880.

[88] See reports of meetings at Killeenadeema, County Galway, and Shrule, County Mayo, in *Nation*, 2 Oct. 1880 and 6 Nov. 1880.

[89] Larkin, *Catholic Church and Creation of Modern Irish State*, p. 50.

they could, if they chose to do so, promote local branches during sermons. A landowner in County Sligo complained in May 1880 that in church he had recently heard "the usual Sunday announcement made from the altar" that a meeting of the Land League would be held after mass.[90] Clergymen could be even more effective if they were willing to serve on the executives of local branches. In doing so, they would provide the branch with both respectability and badly needed administrative skills. In the summer of 1880 the Land League branch on the Arran Islands reported that it had "been thrown into some confusion" as a result of the removal of the local Catholic curate, who had been its vice-president and treasurer.[91] The growth of the Ennistymon branch in County Clare during 1880 was ascribed to "the timely action of the clergy of the county who have stepped in at the critical moment to give the dignity of their presence and the wisdom of their council in the struggle of the nation."[92]

It is possible that most clergymen were less than enthusiastic about the formation of these branches, reasoning, as did one, that "the matter could be managed more efficiently by the priests and the people of each parish working together with a general farmers' club for the whole county."[93] The formation of a branch posed the danger to the local clergyman that lay leaders would acquire a strategic political position in the community. By the same token, however, should a branch be formed, it was clear to many priests that they must have some influence over it. One indication of their level of involvement is provided by the branch returns sent to the central executive in Dublin. Of a sample of 115 branches, 32 percent submitted reports that were signed by at least one clergyman acting as president, vice-president, or secretary of the branch.[94] Only by accepting such positions could clergymen hope to prevent the movement from falling completely under the control of what they often perceived to be dangerous parties. As Davitt claimed in his account of it, the Land League produced a "new spirit among the sons of farmers and country traders which

---

[90] *Sligo Champion*, 29 May 1880, p. 3.

[91] N.L.I., Land League papers: Branch returns (MS 8291).

[92] *Clare Independent*, 4 Dec. 1880, p. 3.

[93] Statement by Thomas Nolan, P.P., Abbeyleix, objecting to a resolution by the Queen's County Independent Club advocating the formation of local tenant committees. See *Nation*, 8 Nov. 1879, p. 5.

[94] N.L.I., Land League papers: Branch returns.

involved local lay leaders who became in many districts rivals to the parish priest or curate for the headship of a league branch."[95] Usually this rivalry was camouflaged by pretenses of homage and professions of reverence, but occasionally it produced open clashes between the two groups.[96]

That large numbers of Catholic priests took part in the Land War is beyond question. Yet one of the characteristics of the Land War that sets it apart from earlier national movements in Ireland was that the clergy formed a less vital part of the local leadership. Only two priests were present when the National Land League was formed in October 1879. It is true that thirteen of the fifty-three members of the founding committee were Catholic clergymen,[97] but this statistic can be compared with the number of Catholic clergymen among delegates to the Tenant League convention in 1850, nearly 50 percent of whom were priests.[98] Their role had been no less important in the Emancipation campaign, the Tithe War, and the Repeal movement. There was probably not a great deal of difference between the functions the clergy performed in these earlier movements and their participation in the Land War. The new development was that during the Land War priests were faced with "rivals," to use Davitt's term, and their whole approach to the unrest was governed by this fact. As one church historian has observed, during the agitation of 1879-82 the "priest figured not as coachman, but as fellow-traveller."[99]

Thus far in this chapter we have examined the social composition of the collectivity that challenged landlordism during the Land War. Plainly it did not draw its members from a single social group, but from several groups. These groups could overlap, as did farmers and Catholics, or townsmen and nationalist politicians; or they could be largely distinct, as were farmers and townsmen. Also important to recognize is that the active collectivity did not embrace any social group entirely, not even farmers. It is impossible, of course, to draw a sharp line between those we

[95] Davitt, *Fall of Feudalism*, p. 466.

[96] In the Ennis district, several clergymen waged a prolonged battle for control of local associations, primarily against T. R. Cleary, editor of the *Clare Independent*. See *Clare Independent*, 6 Sept. 1879, p. 3; 5 June 1880, p. 3; 24 July 1880, p. 3; 23 Oct. 1880, p. 2.

[97] Davitt, *Fall of Feudalism*, p. 173.

[98] Lee, *Modernisation of Irish Society*, p. 90.

[99] Woods, "Catholic church and Irish politics," p. 435.

include in an active collectivity and those we do not. Yet were we to define the active collectivity even in broad terms as consisting of persons enrolled in Land League branches, probably not more than one-fifth of all farmers and farmers' sons in the country would be included.[100] This actually constitutes a rather impressive figure, but it reminds us that the Land League (like almost all social movements) mobilized only a small portion of the social group that it sought to represent.

The composition of the challenging collectivity was a function of the prevailing cleavages and integrative bonds in the society. The most significant social division in nineteenth-century Ireland was the sectarian cleavage. It divided the society into two identifiable religious groups and made it unlikely that persons of different religions would join together in collective action. The challenging collectivity we have been discussing was to be found mainly in Catholic Ireland; it extended only barely into the Protestant counties of the northeast. Second, the composition of our challenging collectivity was a function of class cleavages in the rural society, primarily the division between landowners and farmers, but also that between farmers and laborers. The movement was supported mostly by farmers, less than a representative number of laborers, and very few landed proprietors. At the same time, the integrative bonds linking farmers with certain urban groups made it likely that these groups would be over-represented in the challenging collectivity; I have focused especially on the roles of shopkeepers and publicans, and nationalist politicians. Finally, the integrative bonds that existed between farmers and the Catholic clergy made it difficult for priests to avoid involvement in the movement.

Organization and Goals

ORGANIZATION

At both the national and the local level, members of the active collectivity that fought the Land War were brought together by an as-

[100] This conclusion is based on Davitt's estimate that in February 1881 the Land League had some 200,000 members in Ireland. Let us further assume that 54 percent or 108,000 of them were farmers or farmers' sons, since farmers and farmers' sons comprised 54 percent of the suspects arrested under the Protection of Person and Property Act. This 108,000 would represent 19 percent of the total number of farmers and farmers' sons in the male labor force. Obviously this is an extremely rough estimate. See Davitt, *Fall of Feudalism*, p. 301.

sociation known as the Land League, which was established for
the specific purpose of coordinating their activities and pursuing
their common goals. Essentially it consisted of a central committee and a large number of local branches. While Davitt's claim that
about 1,000 branches were eventually formed may have been an
exaggeration,[101] he could legitimately have boasted that a larger
number of local organizations were affiliated with the Land
League than with any previous tenant association in Ireland. The
number of Land League branches certainly exceeded five hundred. The central committee was established when the Land
League was founded in October 1879. It went through a number of
changes in the course of the agitation, but initially consisted of
seven executive members and fifty-one committee members (virtually all of whom were nationalist politicians, members of
farmers' clubs, or Catholic clergymen). The central committee
held weekly meetings, which were usually attended by less than a
dozen members. With the exception of Parnell, who appeared ir-
regularly, executive officers were the most constant in attendance
at these meetings, particularly Thomas Brennan, Michael Davitt,
and Patrick Egan—all former Fenians. These three performed the
bulk of the administrative work that fell upon the central committee, and next to Parnell, were the most powerful persons in the
association.

The Land League was not a tightly organized body. The formation of branches depended on local initiatives; and the headquarters was not in a strong position to enforce its regulations or
supervise branch activities. Yet it did endeavor to exercise a
measure of control over branches and to work closely with them.
Occasionally it became involved in the strategies and maneuvers
of branches engaged in especially difficult or important battles
with landlords in their districts. In such cases the central committee could even assume direct command by issuing orders from
Dublin by telegraph.[102] The rules of the League required the
branches forward monthly financial statements to the central
executive and report cases of "rack renting" and contemplated
evictions in their district. It is instructive for any student of
the Land League to go to the National Library and examine the
thousands of branch returns that have survived. What one finds

[101] Ibid., p. 301.
[102] For example, see S.P.O., Chief Secretary's Office, Registered Papers: Arthur
Wise to Chief Secretary, 12 Dec. 1879 (1880/264).

are numerous reports of finances, rents, and evictions, usually filled out on printed forms with "Irish National Land League" inscribed in bold letters at the top of the page. There are also a great number of appeals to the central executive for assistance. These appeals fall into four categories: (1) pleas for financial assistance, which are the most numerous; (2) requests for advice, usually about the interpretation of Land League regulations or the prevailing land laws; (3) submissions for the arbitration of disputes over which the branch itself was divided; and (4) requests for speakers to address local meetings.

According to regulations established by the central committee, every branch was to have an executive committee composed of a president, vice-president, treasurer, and secretary, plus at least seven other members. This committee was supposed to be elected annually by all members who had paid their subscriptions.[103] It is difficult to say how well branches conformed to these rules, but most took them seriously enough that when they issued reports to the central committee or to newspapers the impression was invariably given that the official regulations were being followed closely. As a result, one does not find much evidence of deviations, though many must have occurred.[104] Most branches convened monthly, but committees were usually active in the interim and some met weekly.[105]

The natural territorial unit on which to base local branches was the Catholic parish. People living in the same parish routinely came together for Sunday mass at a time when they were comparatively free from their daily labors. Thus the church provided agitators with a ready-made assembly that could be utilized for political meetings. Both branch meetings and large demonstrations were typically held on Sundays, after mass, and often in the vicinity of the Catholic chapel. The central committee fully appreciated the strength of the parish as a unit of social organization. Thus in January 1880, it recommended that branches should be formed on a parish basis and that they should meet "in the

[103] N.L.I., Land League papers: Rules for the guidance of branches (MS 9219). See also Nation, 27 Nov. 1880, p. 13.

[104] In early 1881 the attention of the central committee was called to a case in which the president of a branch, a Catholic clergyman, had undertaken to appoint the executive himself rather than to permit elections. See Nation, 8 Jan. 1881, p. 4.

[105] Nation, 29 May 1880, p. 4; Clare Independent, 4 Dec. 1880, p. 1; N.L.I., Land League papers: Minutes of Rathvilly branch, 21 Nov. 1880 and 1 Jan. 1881 (MS 842).

chapel yard on a Sunday if no other place of meeting be available."[106] The central committee also urged that "sub-branches or tenants' clubs" should be formed upon every large estate and that separate "land clubs" should be established by all those who were sympathetic toward the movement in towns and cities throughout Ireland as well as in the centers of Irish population in England, Scotland, and America.

As it turned out, the majority of branches were indeed formed on a parish basis. In my sample of 115 branches, no fewer than 73 bore the same name as a Catholic parish.[107] Yet in several other respects, the territorial units on which branches were based differed from what had been envisaged by the central committee.

Let us first consider rural branches. Some rural branches encompassed farmers living in a group of adjacent townlands, often corresponding to a poor-law electoral division, such as, for example, the Drumcolumb branch in the Sligo Union.[108] More often branches were co-extensive with parishes or half-parishes (a half-parish being the district embraced by a chapel and often called the "chapel area"). These parish or half-parish branches frequently appointed delegates from each townland within the parish boundary.[109] Not once in my research did I discover a Land League branch or sub-branch that claimed to represent tenants living on a specific estate. In some ways this is surprising, since the central committee had recommended the formation of such branches and since tenants on the same estate did often join together to request abatements or to resist evictions. But Land League branches, it seems, conformed more closely to the prevailing social structure; and the landed estate in Ireland was a less important communal structure than the parish or the townland.

Similarly, the organization of town branches departed noticeably from what had been proposed by the central committee. The original idea had been that "land clubs" in towns would assume a supportive yet clearly separate role, much like that played by sympathetic groups outside Ireland. The central committee even

[106] *Nation*, 3 Jan. 1880.

[107] This is the same sample cited above on p. 289 and taken from the returns of branches to the central executive.

[108] *Sligo Champion*, 5 June 1880, p. 4.

[109] In May 1880, for instance, a Land League branch was formed in Ballisodare, County Sligo, and a committee was appointed consisting of delegates to represent the various townlands within the parish. See ibid., 1 May 1880, p. 4.

left these town clubs the option of establishing their own rules and not being bound to those of the Land League.[110] As it happened, town branches came to perform a much more critical function than had been anticipated. Numerically, they may have comprised between a third and a half of all branches; in my sample of 115 branches, fifty bore the same name as a town.

Townsmen were naturally active in town branches, which normally held their meetings within towns. Yet rarely were these branches composed exclusively of townsmen. Indeed it was precisely because they were not separate clubs reserved exclusively for townsmen that they came to play a critical role in the movement. Most town branches defined their territory as both the urban and rural portions of the parish in which they were located. The Rathvilly branch in County Carlow, for instance, regarded itself as the branch of the parish of which the town of Rathvilly was the center.[111] So did the Ballymote branch in County Sligo, which was established in May 1880 in an effort to unite several small branches that had already been formed in other parts of the parish.[112] Most town branches resulted from collaboration between townsmen and farmers, though some were initially organized by townsmen alone. In any case, they typically appointed delegates to represent different districts (usually townlands) in the surrounding parish.[113]

Some town branches went further and sought to operate as a central branch for areas encompassing more than one parish and sometimes even more than one town. In Westport, County Mayo, when a Land League branch was being formed in November 1879, circulars were issued calling on farmers in the surrounding parishes to appoint delegates to attend the founding meeting.[114] The branch centered in the town of Castlebar tried to embrace the united parishes of Castlebar, Ballyhean, and Breaffy as well as "the surrounding parishes"; and it encouraged delegates from branches in still other parishes to attend its meetings.[115] The

[110] Nation, 3 Jan. 1880.

[111] N.L.I., Land League papers: Minutes of the Rathvilly branch, 21 Nov. 1880.

[112] The organizers of the Ballymote branch believed that "the union of these branches into one having Ballymote for its centre would be able to effect much more good than could be worked out of the division of the parish into small branches." See Sligo Champion, 29 May 1880, p. 3.

[113] Nation, 29 May 1880, p. 4; Roscommon Journal, 18 Dec. 1880, p. 2.

[114] Connaught Telegraph, 15 Nov. 1879, p. 5.

[115] Ibid., 17 Jan. 1880, p. 5; 28 Feb. 1880.

Ennis club in County Clare adopted a similar practice and appointed delegates from smaller branches to be present when it met.[116] When a branch was established in the town of Roscommon in the autumn of 1880 some people wanted it called the "Roscommon and Athleague Branch of the Land League" since efforts to form a branch in the nearby town of Athleague had been unsuccessful. The Roscommon agitators decided, however, to call theirs simply the "Roscommon branch," while they encouraged persons from other districts to join and promised them the protection of the League.[117] Eventually a body was established in Boyle that claimed to be a central organization for the entire county of Roscommon and sought to oversee the activities of a large number of smaller branches.[118] To take one last example, the Kanturk branch in County Cork appealed in August 1880 to the central executive for help because the area which it represented was so large. Noting that many small towns and villages in the district had no associations, the chairman of the Kanturk branch complained that "the inhabitants of these places look to Kanturk to undertake the work of organization, and are constantly coming before us asking our assistance and advice. A good deal has already been done, but it would be absolutely impossible for a branch like ours to carry out, unaided, the organization of a district twenty miles in circumference."[119]

Given what we know about the social integration of town and country, as well as the role that townsmen played in the agitation, it comes as no surprise that the organization of Land League branches followed this pattern. To have separated town branches from rural ones and to have relegated the former to a merely supportive role would have deprived the movement of perhaps its strongest organizational base. It was both advantageous for the movement and inevitable for social reasons that the associational structure would reflect the structure of the local agrarian society. This society was defined primarily by towns and parishes, and thus most Land League branches were formed on the basis of one or the other of these two structures, or more often both.

[116] Clare Independent, 31 July 1880, p. 2; 7 Aug. 1880, p. 3.

[117] Roscommon Journal, 16 Oct. 1880, p. 2.

[118] Nation, 8 Jan. 1881, p. 13.

[119] N.L.I., Land League papers: Kanturk branch to executive, 31 Aug. 1880 (MS 17, 706-8).

GOALS

The goals of a social movement do not necessarily correspond to the objectives of every individual or faction within the active collectivity. People do not all participate in a social movement for the same reason. They usually hold a great variety of notions about what the aims of the movement should be and an even wider range of personal interests that they seek to advance through participation. The goals of a social movement—at least those explicitly proclaimed as such and manifestly pursued by the active collectivity—are generally a function of those beliefs and interests which are shared by the people who participate in it.

Although there was disagreement among the agitators on some aspects of their program, on the whole, one could not accuse the Land League of failing to make clear what it wanted. Carefully worded statements were passed both at the founding of the Mayo Land League in August 1879 and at the founding of the National Land League in October.[120] The central committee in Dublin frequently reaffirmed its demands and provided declarations of policy on numerous issues related to the land question. The Dublin land conference of April 1879 outlined a program of legislative reform which became the official platform of the League.[121]

In addition, resolutions were passed at hundreds of land meetings held during the period of the agitation. Table 19 provides the results of a content analysis of resolutions adopted at 153 land meetings sampled from the *Nation* for the period from June 1879 through August 1881. I have classified these resolutions into two groups: those expressing basic goals, which I have called declarations of *demands*, and those encouraging support or stating tactical goals, which I have called declarations of *policy*.

The demands clearly reflect the interests of tenant farmers, the largest social group in the movement. Farmers would be the main beneficiaries if the objectives of the first four types of resolutions were realized: the three Fs, a halt to ejectments, reductions in rent, and peasant proprietorship, which together accounted for about one-quarter of the resolutions. And the enforcement of these demands was the unmistakable purpose of at least two types of policy resolutions, namely, a refusal to pay normal rents and opposition to landgrabbing, which accounted for an additional 19.3

[120] Davitt, *Fall of Feudalism*, pp. 162-3; 172.   [121] Ibid., pp. 240-44.

TABLE 19 · Content analysis of resolutions passed at 153 land
meetings reported in *Nation*, June 1879 through August 1881.

CONTENT OF RESOLUTION	PERCENTAGE OF RESOLUTIONS			
	1879 JUNE-DEC.	1880 JAN.-DEC.	1881 JAN.-AUG.	TOTAL
Declarations of demands	57.1	38.7	22.2	38.2
Three Fs	3.6	3.5	0.0	2.7
Halt to evictions	3.6	8.7	4.2	6.6
Reductions in rent	28.6	4.1	2.8	8.3
Peasant proprietorship	5.4	8.1	1.4	6.0
Laborers' interests	10.7	5.2	2.8	5.7
Self-government	5.4	9.3	11.1	9.0
Declarations of policy	28.6	50.3	66.7	50.2
Support for movement	7.1	17.3	16.7	15.3
Refusal to pay normal rents	1.8	1.2	4.2	2.0
Opposition to landgrabbing	14.3	19.7	13.9	17.3
Pressure on politicians	3.6	9.3	12.5	9.0
Opposition to government measures	1.8	2.9	19.4	6.6
Other	14.3	11.0	11.1	11.6
Total number	56	173	72	301

NOTE: See Appendix A for an explanation of the categories used in this table.

percent of the resolutions. In the first year of the agitation, reductions in rent stood out as the single greatest concern of the movement, but then declined (at least relative to other concerns) in the following two years.

There were far fewer resolutions that sought to advance the interests of laborers, but there were enough to deserve some explanation. The explanation cannot be that laborers were active in formulating Land League goals. Few if any resolutions passed at land meetings were drafted by laborers or with their assistance. The main reason for resolutions of this kind is that the farmers who dominated the movement were afraid of the laboring population—on the one hand, fearful of the costs that they might have to pay for any improvements won by laborers, but at the same time anxious about what laborers would do if the League made no attempt to promote their interests. Fear of offending laborers was especially likely to find expression in resolutions adopted at land meetings, since these meetings were usually well attended by these agricultural workers, who were typically the most vocal members of audiences. Along with fear, there was also the recognition that added strength would be gained for the movement by enlisting their support. Eventually, in September 1881, the Land League changed its name to the "Land League and the Labour and Industrial Movement."[122] But this concession came belatedly and was sheer pretense. The movement was overwhelmingly a tenant farmers' movement, and its goals were primarily those of its largest group of members.

A significant number of resolutions expressed viewpoints on the national question. Here, of course, the explanation lies in the strong and growing support for Irish nationalism among farmers, as well as the involvement of nationalist politicians in the land movement. It is also worth noting that the proportion of resolutions demanding self-government rose from one year to the next in the course of the agitation; though we should be careful in what we conclude from this, it is consistent with the argument that the Land War increased the strength of nationalism among the rural population. Yet at no time during the Land League agitation did self-government gain priority over the land question. The reason was simply that tenant farmers dominated the challenging collectivity, and their most pressing concern was land. The great majority of these farmers were ardent nationalists, but they were also determined not to be diverted from their principal goal. This order of priorities cost them the support of some active nationalists, but there were as many others who were willing to agitate for land reform in the short run as the first step toward self-government. "When they had rooted the cultivator in the soil," one nationalist politician told a large gathering of farmers, "they would have laid the foundation for what must be the ultimate goal of Irish politics—National Independence."[123] "Their social en-

---

[122] Palmer, Land League Crisis, p. 286.

[123] Roscommon Journal, 16 Oct. 1880, p. 1. The speaker was Andrew Commins, one of the M.P.s for County Roscommon, addressing a rally in Roscommon town in October 1880.

franchisement," said another, "would lead to their political enfranchisement."[124]

If all one knew about the challenging collectivity was that it
consisted mostly of farmers, one would be astonished to find no
anti-urban resolutions in the sample. Anti-urban demands, characteristic of agrarian movements in so many other countries,[125]
were conspicuous by their absence in the Land War. Not one of
the 301 resolutions in my sample was anti-urban—no demands
for better terms of credit, no condemnations of profiteering by
middlemen, no complaints about prices charged by retailers.[126]
Ultimately the explanation for this lies in the social bonds and
cooperative relationship that existed between farmers and
townsmen. Yet we should keep in mind that this social tie did not
erase all sources of conflict between the two groups. There was
considerable strain in the shopkeeper-farmer relationship—certainly enough, one would have thought, to have generated at least
a few resolutions denouncing high interest rates or high retail
prices. What the social relationship between townsmen and
farmers did, however, was to draw a sizable number of townsmen
into the movement. Not only were they numerically over-represented in the challenging collectivity, but they often assumed
leadership roles and were active, especially in the first year of the
agitation, in organizing land demonstrations. Under these circumstances, it is less surprising that very few resolutions censur-
ing townsmen were endorsed at these demonstrations.

Similarly noteworthy is the absence of resolutions expressing
hostility toward large farmers. The sample contained no resolutions denouncing graziers, nor any demanding the breakup of

[124] Ibid., 8 May 1880, p. 1. The speaker in this case was J. J. O'Kelly, the other
M.P. for County Roscommon, addressing a rally at Balla, County Mayo, in May
1880.

[125] See, for example, Hugh Borton, *Peasant Uprisings in Japan of the Tokugawa
Period* (New York, 1937), especially pp. 29-30; Jean Burnet, "Town-country relations and the problem of rural leadership" in *Canadian Journal of Economics and
Political Science*, 13, no. 3 (Aug. 1947); S. M. Lipset, *Agrarian Socialism: The
Cooperative Commonwealth Federation in Saskatchewan: A Study in Political
Sociology* (Berkeley, 1950); George D. Jackson, "Peasant political movements in
eastern Europe" in Henry A. Landsberger (ed.), *Rural Protest: Peasant Movements
and Social Change* (London, 1974); and Nicos Mouzelis, "Greek and Bulgarian
peasants: aspects of their sociopolitical situation during the interwar period" in
Comparative Studies in Society and History, 18, no. 1 (Jan. 1976).

[126] The only resolutions making any explicit reference to townsmen were several calling on shopkeepers to support boycotts.

large farms into smaller holdings. I was able to find several such
resolutions adopted at meetings that did not happen to fall into
my sample. For instance, at a demonstration at Mayo Abbey in
January 1880 it was resolved that "we firmly believe that the grazing system which prevails in this country is antagonistic to the
welfare of the Irish people."[127] Several of the League's leaders
were openly hostile to graziers and suggested schemes for the redistribution of land. The most vocal were militant men in the
movement, such as Matthew Harris and John Dillon, but even Parnell proposed a scheme for settling some of the surplus western
population on eastern grasslands.[128] More than occasionally opposition to graziers prompted outrages or at least found expression in threatening notices. This was especially true in the west.
One newspaper correspondent reported that in parts of Galway
and Mayo "a sort of dead set is being made against grazing
farmers." Citing several attacks on the property of graziers during
the winter of 1879-80, he concluded that "the object in all cases
seems to have been to 'hunt' the injured persons out of the country
in order that the neighbours might turn their cattle on to his grazing land."[129]

Yet the truly remarkable thing is that there was not more activity of this kind. The majority of farmers who participated in the
Land War would personally have benefited from a redistribution
of land and probably favored such a step. But here we see how
necessary it is to distinguish between the individual aspirations
of those who participate in a social movement and its manifest
goals. Although the mass of small farmers may have had an interest in land redistribution, it did not become a principal goal of the
Land League movement. The most obvious reason is that large
farmers, like townsmen, were active in the agitation, especially in
leadership roles, and so were in a position to prevent it from turning in directions contrary to their interests. Usually they could
ensure that resolutions demanding the breakup of large farms did

[127] *Connaught Telegraph*, 3 Jan. 1880, p. 3. Similar sentiments were expressed
either in resolutions or speeches at meetings reported in the *Clare Independent*, 28
Aug. 1880, p. 3 and *Connaught Telegraph*, 25 Dec. 1880, p. 5. For still more examples, see note 26 above and Bew, "Politics of the Irish Land War," pp. 114-16.

[128] See Bew's extensive discussion of this subject, especially pp. 13-19, 107-16
and 194-204.

[129] B. H. Becker, *Disturbed Ireland: Being the Letters Written during the Winter
of 1880-81* (London, 1881), pp. 78-9; quoted in Donnelly, *Landlord and Tenant*,
pp. 42-3.

not often come before land meetings. And they had enough influence in most branches to prevent the organization from pressing
such a demand or supporting those who did. This appears to have
been the case from the beginning, but it became all the more true
as the agitation spread outside Connaught.

Furthermore, and this may have been the most critical factor,
the goals that large and small farmers shared in common had the
longest and most continuous place in the collective consciousness of the rural population. Historically, one can trace collective
action in pursuit of them to agrarian combinations in the late
eighteenth and early nineteenth centuries. More directly, one
can trace the pursuit of these goals to the Tenant League of the
1850s and the farmers' clubs of the 1870s. Both these post-famine
movements were comprised disproportionately of large farmers,
with the result that they tended to emphasize the objectives upon
which large and small farmers could agree. The post-famine tenant organizations were responsible for articulating these aims as
the three Fs: fair rents, fixity of tenure, and free sale. Whether referred to in this language or in other terms, these were longstanding agrarian claims. They also corresponded, it may be recalled, to
the three foremost non-contractual privileges that tenants enjoyed
and that they had come to regard as customary rights.

The same goals became the core of the Land League program—with one noteworthy difference: the demand for free sale
was no longer as prominent as before, while peasant proprietorship now emerged as a major objective. "When I first became
president of the [Limerick and Clare] Farmers' Club," William
Bolster told the Bessborough commission in 1880, ". . . our idea
was a thirty-one years' lease. That is sixteen years ago. We crept
from that to sixty-one years' lease. Then Mr. Butt came in, and it
was the three Fs, and we forgot these two things which we
thought at one time would be satisfactory, and now we believe we
must sweep the landlords away altogether."[130] Peasant proprietorship was stressed especially by nationalist politicians directing
the agitation, who believed that the pursuit of this goal would assist the nationalist cause.[131] As a result, the abolition of the existing land system received special attention in declarations of goals
over which the central leadership had the most influence, such as

[130] Bessborough commission, vol. i, p. 16.
[131] Bew, "Politics of the Irish Land War," pp. 48-9, 65-71.

policy statements adopted at major land conferences, including the official platform formulated in April 1880.[132] We must, it is true, be careful not to exaggerate the emphasis given to peasant proprietorship during the Land War. In my sample of resolutions there were, taking all three years combined, fewer resolutions calling for this than for reductions in rent or a halt to evictions, even if we fail to include policy resolutions expressing opposition to landgrabbing and advocating a refusal to pay normal rents. Also, the percentage of resolutions demanding peasant proprietorship did not rise steadily from one year to the next during the unrest; it increased from 5.4 percent in 1879 to 8.1 percent in 1880, but then fell in the last year of the agitation to 1.4 percent, a finding that casts doubt on the argument made by at least one historian that the Land League created the aspiration for peasant proprietorship in the course of the Land War.[133] As we shall discover in the following chapter, the response of tenants was less than overwhelming to the opportunities that became available for them to purchase their holdings under the land acts of the 1880s and 1890s, and they certainly showed little sign that they came out of the Land War totally convinced of the need to "sweep the landlords away altogether." Nevertheless, the emphasis historians have given to the Land League's call for peasant proprietorship is justified. Demands for ownership were certainly heard more often in the years 1879-82 than during any previous agrarian movement in Ireland, and from that time on they were to be heard more frequently still.

Considerable variation can be observed among social movements in the manner by which they acquire an ideology. Some movements emerge along with—perhaps partly as a result of—the conversion of people to a new set of beliefs and goals. Far more often, people are mobilized in the name of principles which they already hold and in the pursuit of objectives to which they have long before committed themselves.[134] The Land War was, for the

---

[132] Davitt, *Fall of Feudalism*, pp. 240-44.

[133] Lee, *Modernisation of Irish Society*, p. 96.

[134] Collective-behavior theory sees most social movements as belonging to the first type. The best example from this literature is Smelser, *Theory of Collective Behavior*. In contrast are those writers, particularly in the mobilization perspective, who believe that most social movements fall into the second type. See Oberschall, *Social Conflict and Social Movements*; and Tilly, Tilly, and Tilly, *Rebellious Century*.

most part, a movement of the second type. With the significant exception of peasant proprietorship, nothing was novel about the major demands of the Land Leaguers. It would be patently absurd to try to explain the Land War as a consequence of the conversion of great numbers of tenant farmers to the notion of fair rents and fixity of tenure. They had always claimed these rights, as had their ancestors before them.

Nine · **The Struggle for Power**

There are several possible frameworks that one could use to give meaning to the variety of activities undertaken by participants in the Land War. The framework used here is derived from my general argument that the Land War resulted from the emergence of a new challenging collectivity. The goals this collectivity sought to achieve were contrary to the interests of certain established holders of power, and the behavior of its members during the years 1879-82 can be understood as an attempt to undermine this established power and advance the power of the emerging collectivity. The power that came under greatest attack was plainly that of landowners. Precisely to whom power was being transferred was not so clear, since the challenging collectivity was expanding, fluid, and not unanimously defined. For most people, however, the challenging collectivity was represented by the Land League.

Power over the Land

To undermine landlord control over the use of land, the Land League had to persuade people to defy laws supporting the land system and to obey its own laws instead. In place of the legal right of landlords to repossess a holding, the League tried to substitute its own law that no evictions should occur, or that when they did occur the farm should be left vacant. And in place of the legal right of landlords to set and collect rents, the League tried to substitute its own law that all landlords should reduce their rents to the official valuation,[1] and that no occupier should pay more than the official valuation or the level collectively agreed upon by his fellow tenants. In practice this meant that tenants were expected to pay the rent demanded by their landlord only when the sheriff

[1] The official valuation of land for tax purposes was carried out between 1853 and 1865 under the direction of Richard Griffith and was thus often known as "Griffith's valuation." It was based on the average prices for 1849-51 and was not readjusted in subsequent years to conform to the increased value of agricultural land. Even by the year in which it was completed (1865), it was probably 15 percent below the real letting value of land. See Solow, *The Land Question and the Irish Economy*, pp. 61-8.

arrived with a force sufficient to remove them from the property. Known as "paying rent at the point of the bayonet," this was the official policy of the League until very late in the agitation when the central leadership began to insist that tenants let their farms go altogether without paying.[2]

It was no easy matter to convince people to obey these laws. Many tenants were quite willing to honor their rents in order to remain on good terms with their landlord. Frequently, they considered it an acceptable price to pay for the non-contractual privileges they enjoyed. For numerous tenants, the landlord was not an obnoxious oppressor, but the very basis of their economic security. Landlords, as we saw in Chapter Five, had considerable resources that they could employ to coax or coerce tenants into "good" behavior. Needless to say, they had no hesitation in using these resources to defend their interests when they came under attack by the Land League. A landlord could offer a tenant all sorts of inducements to defy the League and pay his rent (a larger farm, a long-term lease at a modest rent, grazing or turf rights, secure title to a disputed holding, and so on). Almost all landlords tried to use abatements to wring rents from tenants; they did this by making reductions conditional on prompt payment of the abated rent and perhaps also on the liquidation of arrears.[3] Naturally, many landlords also threatened to evict tenants who failed to pay up or in other ways defied their authority. In five west-coast counties (Clare, Cork, Kerry, Galway, and Mayo) the number of ejectment decrees and writs obtained by landlords was 2,889 in 1879; the figure rose to 3,395 in 1880 and 7,882 in 1881.[4] Alternatively, a landlord could attempt to distrain the property of a defaulting tenant, a maneuver to which landlords resorted more frequently when the Land League began to make evictions difficult.[5]

It is important to keep in mind that in this struggle for power, the Land League was the underdog. Unlike the League, landlords did not have to take the offensive, but could, initially at least, rely

[2] Bew, "Politics of the Irish Land War," pp. 176-8, 260-66.

[3] For examples, see T.C.D., Trinity College papers: Board register, 25 June 1881 (V MUN/5/14), p. 190; and N.L.I., Leitrim papers: Letter book of G. F. Stewart: Stewart to James McCullagh, 27 Oct. 1879.

[4] Returns showing, for the counties of Clare, Cork, Kerry, Galway, and Mayo respectively, the number of civil bills in ejectment . . . for each of the years from 1879 to 1888 inclusive . . . , pp. 3-7, H.C. 1889 (211), lxi.

[5] Bew, "Politics of the Irish Land War," pp. 235-6.

on their existing powers, since these powers were supported by
the prevailing order and land laws. For this reason landlords were
slow to form combinations for their defense. They were certainly
capable of doing so, but the legal position they already had made
such combinations appear unnecessary. In hundreds of letters to
newspapers and to Dublin Castle they insisted, often indignantly,
that there would be no problem if the government enforced the
existing laws. The only noteworthy landlord combination to appear in the first year-and-a-half of the agitation was a propaganda
organization known as the Irish Land Committee. It was originally
established in November 1879 to collect and present evidence to a
government commission on agriculture, but subsequently it
played a more general role in a verbal battle with the Land
League. It is most noted for a series of eleven pamphlets present-
ing the landlord's side of the story.[6]

Eventually, the effectiveness of the Land League's campaign
prompted some landlords to launch a better organized counter-
attack. In October 1880, as boycotting was spreading rapidly
throughout Connaught and parts of Munster, over one hundred
landlords and agents met in Dublin. They adopted a series of resolutions and appointed a deputation to present their case to the
Lord Lieutenant and the Chief Secretary.[7] In the following December two associations were formed to represent landed interests. The first, known as the Orange Emergency Committee, was
established in Ulster and played upon Protestant opposition to
any movement that was nationalistic and supported mainly by
Catholics. The second organization, the Property Defence Association, was founded in Dublin and was the more effective and better financed of the two. These associations tried to combat the
Land League in a number of ways: by helping landlords serve
processes despite intimidation; by sending representatives to
sales of distrained property in order to frustrate boycotts of such
sales; by providing laborers to boycotted persons or offering protection to those laborers who remained with their employers; by
obtaining supplies and services for boycotted persons; and by
furnishing caretakers to occupy holdings for which no tenant
could be found.[8] As of October 1881 the Emergency Committee
had reportedly attended nearly six hundred sales of distrained

[6] Palmer, Land League Crisis, pp. 219-20.
[7] Ibid., p. 223.   [8] Ibid., pp. 227-9.

property and supplied laborers to boycotted persons in nineteen different counties.[9]

Ultimately, as landowners knew only too well, their survival depended on the government. It was the government that possessed both the resources and the duty to safeguard property rights. The government supplied the police to defend their bailiffs and process servers; it carried out their evictions; and it arrested their opponents. Not infrequently, hundreds of police were deployed, at great cost, to protect a process server delivering a half-dozen processes or to assist the sheriff removing two or three tenants. It was also the responsibility of the government to defend landlords and their supporters from violent attack. On 31 December 1880 there were 153 persons in Ireland receiving personal police protection and no fewer than 1,149 being specially watched by the police to guard them against outrage.[10] Although most of the political leaders and civil administrators who authorized these measures were from the higher ranks of society, we should not assume that they wholeheartedly supported those whose interests they were expected to defend. On the contrary, at all levels of government it was possible to find at least some individuals who were hard pressed to justify what landlords were doing. Yet they were bound to enforce the existing land laws, and thus, willingly or not, they found themselves in opposition to the challenging collectivity.[11]

Essentially, then, there were two sets of protagonists who fought against one another in the Land War: those who endeavored to advance the interests of tenants and those who undertook to defend the interests of landowners. Ironically, sometimes tragically, tenants were the main targets of both contenders, since both sought to control their behavior. Collective action commanded by landlords had existed before any landlord associations as such were organized, in fact long before the Land War broke out. It existed in the routine control that landlords had for centuries exercised over the majority of tenants and to a considerable extent still maintained during the Land War. In this sense, not only gov-

[9] Ibid., p. 228.

[10] Return of the number of persons receiving special police protection in each county in Ireland on 31st December 1880, H.C. 1881 (1), lxxvi.

[11] Richard Hawkins, "Liberals, land and coercion in the summer of 1880: the influence of the Carraroe ejectments" in Journal of the Galway Archaeological and Historical Society, 34 (1974-5).

ernment officials, but even tenants themselves were part (the subordinate part) of the landlord collectivity. The objective of the challenging collectivity was to persuade or coerce them into switching sides.

Four types of activity stand out as the principal methods employed for this purpose: (1) the open-air meeting or public demonstration; (2) the boycott; (3) assistance to tenants; and (4) violence.

PUBLIC DEMONSTRATIONS   Today we have become so accustomed to public demonstrations that we may find it hard to imagine political processes being carried out without them. Yet in fact, as a widespread form of activity by political combinations, demonstrations are a comparatively recent historical development. They evolved along with associational (as opposed to communal) collective action: a demonstration is usually organized in advance and publicized by a special-purpose association, which calls upon all those sharing specific goals to come together at a certain time and place to promote them. In western Europe public demonstrations were common in some places during the eighteenth century; they became more effective and spread during the nineteenth century; and finally they became routinely accepted during the twentieth century. In Ireland, they first acquired significance in the late eighteenth century and in the early decades of the nineteenth, most often as part of organized electoral politics. The greatest development did not occur, however, until the O'Connell movements and particularly until the Repeal campaign of the 1840s. Subsequently, the demonstration became an accepted, indeed apparently necessary, feature not only of election campaigns, but of almost any large-scale political activity. Demonstrations held during the Land War were smaller than those of the O'Connell period; at least they were certainly smaller than the monster meetings of the Repeal movement. Estimated attendance at land meetings during the Land War ranged from 100 to 100,000, but probably most were of the order of several thousand. On the other hand, there may have been more public meetings held during the Land War than during any earlier political movement in Ireland. From October 1879 (when the National Land League was founded) until the end of 1880, the Constabulary reported an average of forty-six land meetings a month.[12]

[12] Return showing for each month of the years 1879 and 1880 the number of

The most obvious purpose of a public demonstration was to outline and express the demands of the movement. In the preceding chapter we have already examined the demands set forth in resolutions adopted at 153 land meetings during the Land War. This sample also indicates another function of these meetings. Look again at Table 19 and notice that the percentage of resolutions concerned with basic demands declined steadily from one year to the next, while the percentage of resolutions concerned with "policy" increased, reaching 66.7 percent in 1881 and constituting for the period as a whole 50.2 percent of the resolutions. Public demonstrations, it is clear, were used to promote means as well as ends, and especially to encourage support for the movement and to reaffirm the rule that the holdings of evicted tenants should be left vacant. These two types of resolutions were the most common in the sample.

Another less well recognized function of land meetings was intimidation. Demonstrations were often held to intimidate opponents of the League or anyone who had violated or intended to violate its laws. Many of these "indignation meetings," as they were called, were convened to protest against evictions that had already occurred or to denounce a tenant who had taken a farm from which the previous occupier had been evicted. The intention of such after-the-fact meetings was to frighten the wrongdoer and to dissuade anyone contemplating similar action. The message was usually conveyed by staging the meeting near the evicted farm and by placing on record resolutions condemning both the eviction and the new tenant who had taken possession of the holding.[13] On other occasions land demonstrations were held before an eviction was to occur in an effort to prevent it from being carried out. At such meetings resolutions would be passed expressing "our deep sense of indignation at the issue of ejectment processes" or pledging "to assist by every means in our power our brothers who have been served with ejectments."[14] One of the ear-

---

Land League meetings held and agrarian crimes reported to the Inspector General of the Royal Irish Constabulary in each county throughout Ireland, p. 11, H.C. 1881 (5), lxxvii.

[13] See report of a meeting held near Ballymote, County Sligo, in early June 1880. A few weeks later a similar meeting was held at Dromore West to denounce a landgrabber. Sligo Champion, 12 June 1880, p. 4; 26 June 1880, p. 4; 17 July 1880, p. 3.

[14] Nation, 6 July 1879; Connaught Telegraph, 27 Dec. 1879, p. 2.

liest and most impressive of these eviction-obstructing assemblies was the Dempsey demonstration in County Mayo in November 1879, which was made famous by Parnell's presence. In this instance the members of the assembly were described by a resident magistrate as "much more determined and earnest than on any former occasion, and much more under the control of the persons directing their movements."[15] Landowning interests were quick to recognize the effect that intimidation meetings could have on tenants and consequently the threat they posed to the established order. As early as December 1879 the magistrates of Mayo sent to the government a petition which included the following resolution:

> That we beg to call the attention of the government to the new phase into which the land meetings have entered. That now they are held for the purpose of terrorism wherever ejectments are to be executed and to denounce individuals where farms are taken after being given up even where voluntary by their former occupiers. That these cannot be considered legal or constitutional meetings and we now call upon the government to stop them.[16]

THE BOYCOTT   Without a doubt the best-known tactic employed by the Land League was boycotting. The practice was obviously not invented by Irish farmers in 1880. For centuries, in all parts of the world, it had been employed by active combinations for a variety of purposes. In rural Ireland itself the practice of refusing to bid for involuntarily vacated farms or for distrained livestock had a long history, as did the ostracism of landgrabbers.[17] Even during the Land War, the tactic was used well before the Boycott affair; and it had been advocated on numerous occasions before Parnell recommended it in September 1880.[18]

What was novel in the autumn of 1880 was not the idea or even the use of boycotting, but the spread and development of this type

[15] S.P.O., Chief Secretary's Office, Registered Papers: Arthur Wise to Chief Secretary (copy), 23 Nov. 1879 (1880/12061).

[16] Ibid.: Petition from magistrates meeting in Castlebar, 30 Dec. 1879 (1880/580).

[17] Some examples from the late eighteenth century can be found in Donnelly, "Rightboy movement." For examples in 1852, see O'Neill, "Famine to near famine," p. 166.

[18] See Connaught Telegraph, 3 Jan. 1880, p. 3; Sligo Champion, 17 July 1880, p. 4; Palmer, Land League Crisis, p. 196; and Lyons, Charles Stewart Parnell, p. 135.

of collective action on a scale so enormous that the coining of a
new term for it was necessary. Boycotting was becoming the most
awesome feature of the agitation. Not only was it the chief method
by which the Land League now tried to enforce its authority, but it
also came to represent the clearest evidence of the degree to
which the League was actually able to do so. The effectiveness of a
boycott depends on whether the behavior of a large number of
people can be controlled. The success with which the Land
League employed boycotting is a measure of how many people,
voluntarily or involuntarily, accepted its orders. Boycotting also
indicates the extent to which the League was firmly grounded in
the stable structure of social relationships in agrarian communities. The interdependence necessary to make a tactic of this
kind effective can exist only among people who are bound together by strong communal and/or associational ties. It was especially, to take one such relationship as an example, because
farmers depended on shopkeepers for credit and because shopkeepers depended on farmers for business that members of both
groups could be persuaded to support the movement through fear
of boycotting. In an anomic society, consisting of many isolated,
alienated, or "uprooted" people (the social environment that has
often been depicted as most prone to social movements) boycotting campaigns such as those conducted by the Land League
would be much less effective because there would not be the same
fear of social ostracism.

It was the policy of the Land League to divide communities into
pro- and anti-League factions and to create as much ill-feeling as
possible between the two. To facilitate this polarization the central executive in Dublin issued membership cards to those who
had paid their dues; these cards became immensely popular and
served as an aid in recruiting members.[19] Some branches went so
far as to publish the names of those in their area who declined to
join.[20] The understanding, of course, was that supporters of the
League should avoid associating with non-members and should
certainly not assist them in any way. Usually, this very general

[19] N.L.I., Land League papers: Rules for the guidance of branches; and Branch
returns: Returns from Bohola branch, County Mayo, and Baslicke branch, County
Roscommon (MSS 8291, 17706).
[20] N.L.I., Land League papers: Minutes of Rathvilly branch, 23 Jan. 1881. See
also report of the Knockcroghery branch, County Roscommon, in Nation, 24 Sept.
1881, p. 7.

kind of boycotting was not well organized, but sometimes it was. A branch in County Cork, for instance, decided that only members of the Land League would be permitted to use the one threshing mill in the parish, which happened to belong to an active branch member. "When the threshing season came every farmer in the parish had joined," recalled an elderly resident. "The owner of the machine would not agree to thresh for any man until he had first produced his membership card of the League."[21]

As distinct from those who merely failed to join the Land League, those who actively opposed it or violated its rules might face more explicit and earnest boycotting. Obviously landlords, land agents, and bailiffs were frequently ostracized as opponents of the League, but many tenants were treated in the same way, usually for paying their rents or for landgrabbing. And almost anyone—from the biggest shopkeeper down to a struggling laborer—could be boycotted for failing to observe a boycott. Boycotts aimed at enforcing compliance with an original boycott were far more common than one might imagine and provide an indication of the importance attached by the agitators to controlling the population. Another significant type of boycotting was the League's prohibition against bidding for distrained property. As an increasing number of landlords began to seize stock for unpaid rents, the boycotting of sheriffs' sales became a prominent part of the Land League's campaign.

How were boycotts initiated? In most cases, local branches took it upon themselves to consider accusations that a League law had been broken and to determine whether or not sanctions should be imposed. In a difficult case, a branch might hold a "court," which would hear evidence from witnesses and even from the accused himself should he choose to obey his summons to attend. The climax of the agitation in and around the town of Roscommon was reached in March 1881 with the trial of James White, who was summoned to a court at which Matthew Harris presided in the offices of the *Roscommon Messenger*. White was convicted of landgrabbing, and the sentence of the court was that a land meeting should be held on his property and that he should be boycotted.[22] The secretiveness with which most of these courts operated makes it difficult to judge their extent, but they were

[21] Irish Folklore Commission: MS 1174, pp. 441-3.

[22] *Roscommon Journal*, 19 March 1881, p. 2; see also Chapter Eight above for a reference to White in the discussion of the role of townsmen.

undoubtedly widespread in Connaught and west Munster. They were especially active in southeast Clare. People in this region were subject to the rulings of a county court operated by the Ennis branch as well as to the decrees of courts sponsored by smaller branches at Thradaree, Sixmilebridge, and Quin.[23] Early in December 1880 three tenants had to stand meekly before the president of the Thradaree branch while he thundered:

> Mr. Kelly, I charge you with paying your rent, which is over the Government valuation. You ought not to have paid it until you came with your fellow-tenants and offered the Government valuation. It was wrong of you to break the rules, and you are called on now to explain why you did it. . . .
>
> James Garvey, you are charged by your fellow-tenants that you went to Limerick and paid your rent, which is over the Government valuation, after you agreeing with them that you would not do so. Are you guilty? . . .
>
> Mr. Lynch, you are charged with paying your rent, which is over the Government valuation, when you should have gone with your fellow-tenants and offered the valuation. . . .[24]

If a decision was taken to declare a boycott, the next step was to ensure that this became public knowledge and that the boycott was rigorously pursued. If a branch was daring enough, it might publish an announcement in a local newspaper.[25] Typically, a notice was posted in an appropriate place, usually in the vicinity of the convicted individual's property. A notice posted in Boyle in December 1880 demanded the boycott of certain shopkeepers in the town and called on the people to "leave the grass growing at the doors of these traitors and flunkies."[26] William Bence Jones, the most famous victim of boycotting in the province of Munster, complained that notices were sent to his laborers by post and that his tenants were threatened at the fair.[27] Fairs were favorite places for declaring and enforcing boycotts; often the bellman would be instructed to call attention to the targeted individual and to dis-

[23] *Clare Independent*, 13 Nov. 1880, p. 3; 4 Dec. 1880, p. 3.

[24] *Nation*, 4 Dec. 1880, p. 4.

[25] *Clare Independent*, 16 Oct. 1880, p. 3.

[26] *Roscommon Journal*, 4 Dec. 1880, p. 2.

[27] W. B. Jones, *The Life's Work in Ireland of a Landlord Who Tried to Do His Duty* (London, 1880).

Recollections of boycotting by a Kerry farmer

The Land League "court" . . . was a committee of Land League
men who held meetings, and they tried cases of people being
evicted and grabbers. If a person was put in an evicted farm,
he would get a notice to attend the meeting. If he didn't turn
up for three meetings, he would be declared boycotted. His
name would be written down in papers and put on walls and
trees telling the people not to work for him or buy any of his
cattle, etc. This notice would be signed "by the order of Captain Moonlight". Then if the boycotted person went to a fair
selling his cattle, pigs or horses, one of the moonlighters
would be around the fair and if any buyer would come to the
man and be buying his animals, the moonlighter would say
"there is a smell from that animal". The buyer would then
walk away. . . . The boycotted people were called 'roasters'.

SOURCE: Irish Folklore Commission: MS 782, p. 333.

courage anyone who might want to do business with him.[28] And
in important cases, a land meeting might be called, as was done in
Roscommon to publicize the boycott against James White and in
Mayo to denounce Captain Boycott himself.[29]

Not all boycotts were decreed by Land League courts. Many
emerged more informally and sometimes without the approval of
the League. The League tried to exercise as much control as possible, but there was little to stop small groups from trying to organize a boycott on their own initiative. Even a single individual
might take it upon himself to post boycott notices against a person
who he thought had violated the land code or against whom he
had some personal grudge. The central committee began an investigation in January 1881 into a case in which a tenant was being
boycotted, though he claimed that he had supported the League

[28] For an example of a bellman performing such a role, see Roscommon Journal,
4 Dec. 1880, p. 12. See also Roscommon Journal, 18 Dec. 1880, p. 2 and 5 Feb.
1881, p. 1 for reports of state prosecutions of bellmen for intimidation.
[29] Connaught Telegraph, 25 Sept. 1880, p. 5. For still another example, see a
newspaper report of a demonstration in Ballymacurly, County Roscommon, in
November 1880. Roscommon Journal, 20 Nov. 1880, p. 2.

and that the president of the local branch knew nothing of the matter.[30] In October of the same year, a member of the Roscommon branch admitted that the League had received a large number of letters from people fearful of being boycotted, though the League had no such intention.[31] The Monasterevan branch in Queen's County provided a tenant with a statement in September 1881 declaring that he was not boycotted. "He has done nothing," the document read, "to deserve such punishment. We take this opportunity of warning members against the practice of private 'boycotting'. Members should await a formal sentence of the executive."[32]

ASSISTANCE TO TENANTS   The Land League did not rely entirely on negative sanctions. It also endeavored to give people some positive inducement to support the movement. For every landlord or landgrabber who was denounced, there was a tenant, perhaps many, whose cause was thereby championed. The central committee also furnished money for legal defense against landlords and often made its own solicitor available to tenants for counsel.[33] League branches were instructed by the central committee to use their funds to defend any of their members who might have to resist rack renting, arbitrary disturbance, or any other "unjust action" in connection with a landholding.[34] As noted in an earlier chapter, the Land Act of 1870 afforded tenants some means by which to bargain with their landlord in court. Land Leaguers sought to renew these legal hostilities; in particular, they tried to utilize a provision in the act that could force a landlord to compensate a tenant for disturbance even though the tenant had not paid his rent, if the annual rent did not exceed £15 and if the court deemed the rent to be exorbitant.[35] Although it was contrary to the policy of the central committee to finance legal defense for tenants who were not members of the League, it did so on occasion and branches did so quite frequently.[36] There was, however, a strong

[30] *Nation*, 8 Jan. 1881, p. 4.   [31] *Roscommon Journal*, 15 Oct. 1881.

[32] Quoted in M. E. Collins, *The Land Question, 1879-82* (Dublin, 1974), p. 40.

[33] *Nation*, 21 Feb. 1880, p. 2; 15 May 1880, p. 4; 22 May 1880, p. 12; 20 Nov. 1880, p. 4.

[34] *Nation*, 3 Jan. 1880.

[35] Bew, "Politics of the Irish Land War," pp. 126-7; see also 33 and 34 Vict., c. 46, section 9.

[36] *Nation*, 21 Feb. 1880, p. 2; 20 Nov. 1880, p. 4; *Connaught Telegraph*, 20 Dec. 1879, p. 4; 25 Sept. 1880, p. 3.

feeling in the central committee that legal defense was not a wise use of their resources. (Some members were convinced that it only put money into the hands of lawyers, since most cases were lost and tenants eventually had to settle with their landlord.) An effort was made to curtail this type of expenditure in the summer of 1880, but requests from tenants for legal aid were so numerous that it was impossible for the League to eliminate it altogether.[37]

Perhaps the most effective type of financial assistance offered by the Land League was relief to destitute tenants, usually in the form of food, clothing, and seed. In order to appreciate the significance of this kind of aid, it should be understood that other associations were also active in supplying relief, including the government. State assistance came not only by way of the poor law, but also through an extension of loans to landowners for making improvements on their estates, through the distribution (at cost price or less) of "champion" seed potatoes, and through grants for local public works.[38] This extensive government relief was supplemented by private charity, which totaled an estimated £830,000 by early October 1880.[39] Contributions came largely from America, Australia, and England, and were channeled primarily through four relief agencies: the Duchess of Marlborough's Committee, the Mansion House Relief Committee, the New York *Herald* Fund, and the Land League Relief Fund.[40] By August 1880 the Land League had distributed more than £47,000.[41]

It is interesting to observe how jealously those in the Land League regarded the relief efforts of others. They were greatly annoyed that only landowners were entitled to government loans.[42] They tended to see other relief organizations as rivals and did little to assist or to cooperate with them. Parnell's American tour in the early months of 1880 was originally undertaken to collect funds for political purposes, but he broadened the scope of the

[37] *Nation*, 12 June 1880, p. 3; 19 June 1880, p. 3. For a more extensive discussion of this whole subject, see Bew, "Politics of the Irish Land War," pp. 124-8, 155-6, 160-61, and 181. And for the attitude of the Ladies' Land League on legal defense, see T. W. Moody, "Anna Parnell and the Land League" in *Hermathena*, no. 117 (1974), pp. 13-14; and R. F. Foster, *Charles Stewart Parnell: The Man and His Family* (Hassocks, Sussex, 1976), pp. 264-84.

[38] Donnelly, *Cork*, pp. 260-61.

[39] Palmer, *Land League Crisis*, p. 104; see also Donnelly, *Cork*, pp. 261-2.

[40] Palmer, *Land League Crisis*, pp. 83-105.

[41] *Nation*, 7 Feb. 1880, p. 2; 14 Aug. 1880, p. 4.

[42] *Clare Independent*, 3 Jan. 1880, p. 3; *Nation*, 21 Feb. 1880, p. 2.

mission to include collection for relief in order not to be outdone
by the private agencies that were being organized at that time.[43] In
the course of this tour Parnell went so far as to denounce the Mansion House Relief Committee, suggesting that only tenants who
had paid their rent would receive assistance from this body. He
called for the removal of landlords from the Mansion House
Committee and declared that "it is not to be expected that any
man will continue to work for land reform when the daily bread of
his wife and children depends on a committee of landlords."[44]
Similar charges were made in north Mayo and in Sligo, where it
was suggested that relief money was distributed more liberally to
tenants who had paid their rent or who had voted for the landlord's candidate in parliamentary or poor-law elections.[45]

For their part, opponents of the land movement repeatedly alleged that the Land League employed relief money for political
purposes.[46] In April 1880 a Sligo priest refused to cooperate with
the League's relief efforts in his district, claiming that it had been
known not to assist tenants unless they had paid up their membership fees.[47] The Castlebar branch came under fire in June 1880
for giving assistance itself rather than channeling funds through a
local non-political relief committee.[48] In another case, a Catholic
curate in Longford charged that £10 sent to Cloontuskert for al-
leviating distress had been used by the Land League branch to pay
the expenses of a demonstration.[49] And the Balla branch was accused of refusing aid to persons in want if they had paid their
rent.[50] The League stoutly disputed such accusations. It insisted
that relief money was distributed fairly and impartially through
local committees, clergymen of all denominations, the St. Vincent
de Paul Society, and the Association for the Relief of Distressed
Protestants.[51] In conjunction with almost all reports of meetings
of the central committee, the League printed lists of local committees that had received grants, and of the amounts allocated to
them.

[43] Bew, "Politics of the Irish Land War," pp. 92-7.
[44] Ibid., pp. 98-9.
[45] Nation, 21 Feb. 1880, p. 2; Sligo Champion, 24 April 1880, p. 2; 22 May 1880, p. 2.
[46] Nation, 7 Feb. 1880, p. 2; 24 April 1880, p. 2.
[47] Bew, "Politics of the Irish Land War," pp. 130-31.
[48] Connaught Telegraph, 26 June 1880, p. 5.
[49] Roscommon Journal, 3 July 1880, p. 2.
[50] Nation, 21 Feb. 1880, p. 2.   [51] Ibid., 7 Feb. 1880, p. 2.

What the charges and countercharges evince is not that any of the agencies grossly misused money, but rather a recognition on both sides that the distribution of relief could not be totally impartial. Inevitably some variation occurred in the kinds of cases that came to the attention of different relief bodies and in the degree of sympathy that each organization felt for them. Supporters of the Land League could naturally expect more consideration from it than could non-supporters. Although the central committee vigorously denied that it was biased in its distribution of aid, one of its members did become concerned in February 1880 that people were joining the movement just to obtain relief.[52] In addition, as might be expected, the League directed its funds to the support of evicted families more often than did other agencies. Initially the central committee tried to support dispossessed families out of its general operating account and to avoid using money from the Relief Fund for this purpose. By June 1880, however, it had become clear that there were more applications for assistance to help evicted tenants than could be met from this source, and so £10,000 was transferred from the Relief Fund to a special fund to be used solely for the support of evicted families.[53] Subsequently, the central committee regularly voted sums of money for this purpose.[54]

As Davitt himself remarked in his own account of the Land War, the Land League's relief operations raised its prestige among tenants and especially among the clergy. In some districts, he noted, local clergymen organized branches of the League in order to distribute relief money that it provided, and consequently "the work of combination kept pace with the relief operations."[55] A resolution passed by the Ballisodare branch of the League in County Sligo boasted that "in discharging the double functions of a political organization and a medium of distributing relief, our committee has at once succeeded in evoking a popular spirit antagonistic to landlordism."[56] Although Irish landlords had never been noted for their charity, they had sufficient resources to assist tenants, as well as sufficient influence over other sources of relief, to worry

[52] Ibid., 6 March 1880, p. 2.

[53] Ibid., 12 June 1880, p. 13. See also Bew, "Politics of the Irish Land War," p. 157.

[54] Nation, 19 June 1880, p. 13; 14 Aug. 1880, p. 4; 20 Nov. 1880, p. 4; 28 May 1881, p. 4; 11 June 1881, p. 5; 25 June 1881, pp. 4-5; 17 Sept. 1881, p. 13.

[55] Davitt, Fall of Feudalism, p. 211.

[56] Sligo Champion, 29 May 1880, p. 3.

the Land League. There is no doubt that the League became involved in the business of relief not only in a genuine effort to assist the poor, but also in an effort to offset the goodwill which its opponents were fostering through relief efforts. This dual purpose explains the apparent contradiction that can be found in one remarkable statement by its treasurer, who most righteously asserted that relief money was not used by the Land League for political ends, but rather "for the purpose for which it was subscribed—that was for the rooting out of the system of landlordism."[57]

VIOLENCE Although most people who took part in the Land War engaged primarily in non-violent activities, a significant segment within the challenging collectivity committed violent acts, and the overall level of agrarian violence during the Land War was high, indeed higher than in any years since the Constabulary began to publish statistics in 1844. A comparison of figures for a few specific years is startling. The number of agrarian outrages reported in 1880 was more than double the number reported in 1849, though there were four times as many evictions in 1849 as in 1880. In the years 1861-4, as a result of a serious downturn in Irish agriculture, evictions were almost as frequent as they were during the Land League agitation; yet in the peak year of violence during the early 1860s, the number of agrarian outrages was less than a tenth of the total reported in 1881.[58] Quite simply, this means that the amount of violence associated with the Land War was vastly greater than can be explained by the degree of hardship. It would seem (at least in the period for which Constabulary data are available) that upsurges in agrarian violence tended to coincide more closely with increases in the intensity of non-violent political activity than with increases in distress. This alone suggests that violence was very much a part of this political movement. The point is worth making both because it reveals an important characteristic of the Land War, and also because a similar pattern has been found by researchers studying other societies, particularly France.[59]

Violence helped to enforce the laws of the Land League. Most often the objective was to prevent or punish landgrabbing, the

[57] Nation, 24 April 1880, p. 2.
[58] Return of outrages 1844 to 1880.
[59] Tilly, Tilly, and Tilly, Rebellious Century, especially pp. 287-90.

payment of normal rents, or the eviction of tenants; in addition, violence or the threat of it was often employed during boycotts. According to Constabulary figures, these were the four most common motives for agrarian crimes committed in County Galway during 1880. Altogether they constituted about three-quarters of the approximately 400 offenses reported in the county in that year.[60]

Who were the major targets of this violence? Whose behavior were the terrorists seeking to control? The single most common motive for outrage was the prevention or punishment of land-grabbing, and the victims in such cases were almost always tenants. Typically, the occupant of a holding from which the previous tenant had been ejected was assaulted, or some property belonging to him was damaged, or he was threatened with personal injury or death unless he surrendered the farm. Tenants were also the usual victims of violence or threats of violence aimed at preventing the payment of normal rents. In some instances, a general threat would be issued to all tenants on an estate warning them not to pay their rents or to pay no more than a certain portion, usually the official valuation.[61] In other cases, specific tenants would be singled out for threats or rough treatment because they had paid their rents. A tenant was actually murdered near Athlone in December 1881 for having settled with his landlord.[62] In Galway during 1880 tenants were the victims of nearly two-thirds of the violent crimes seeking to prevent the payment of rents.[63]

Next to tenants, the most common victims of outrage were landlords, their agents, or their bailiffs. A notorious assault on a landlord occurred in September 1880 when Viscount Mountmorres, a small proprietor in Galway, was murdered near his home, his

---

[60] Return of all agrarian outrages which have been reported by the Royal Irish Constabulary between the 1st day of January 1879 and the 31st day of January 1880 . . . , pp. 66-8, H.C. 1880 (131), lx; Return . . . of all agrarian outrages reported by the Royal Irish Constabulary between the 1st day of February 1880 and the 31st day of October 1880 . . . , pp. 88-106, H.C. 1881 (6), lxxvii; similar return for the month of November 1880, pp. 55-61, H.C., 1881 (6-I), lxxvii; similar return for the month of December 1880, pp. 79-89, H.C. 1881 (6-II), lxxvii. (These returns will hereafter be cited as Outrages, 1880.)

[61] For example, see the report of a notice posted in the Castleisland district in County Kerry in October 1880. S.P.O., Chief Secretary's Office, Registered Papers: 1880/29854.

[62] Roscommon Journal, 10 Dec. 1881, p. 1.   [63] Outrages, 1880.

body riddled with bullets.[64] But other attacks, equally daring if
not so brutal, were also directed at landlords. In the same month
as Lord Mountmorres was slain, a resolute band of rebels issued a
notice warning all tenants on C. W. Stoughton's estate in Kerry
not to pay their rents; they sent a warning to the landlord himself
that his life would be taken if he did not grant an abatement of 25
percent; and they eventually fired a shot through the window of
Stoughton's sitting room.[65] The most frequent reason for attacking
landlords was to prevent the payment of rents or the eviction of
tenants, particularly the latter. Attempts to check evictions or to
punish landlords for having carried them out apparently figured
in nearly half of the offenses directed at landlords in Galway in
1880.[66] Similarly, land agents, bailiffs, and process servers often
faced attack, or the threat of it, as a result of evictions. In March
1880 a bailiff was dragged from his house by four men, and a portion of his ear cut off in retaliation for the part he had played in
raising rents and issuing ejectments on an estate in County
Sligo.[67]

The most romanticized violence of the Land War was that
committed by crowds. These combinations tended to evolve naturally (some might say "spontaneously") out of kinship and neighborhood groups. Typically, they endeavored to defend their holdings by assaulting process servers, resisting the execution of
ejectments, or forcibly retaking possession of their homes. Resistance of this kind can be contrasted with the intimidation demonstrations discussed above, which had a similar purpose, but were
more formally organized (public announcements beforehand, a
fixed time, a chairman who presided over the gathering, and
speakers who addressed an audience and proposed resolutions).
The more traditional crowd was not as widespread as some popular accounts of the Land War would lead us to believe, but there
were numerous instances: in the country as a whole as many as
360 violent encounters reported by the Constabulary in 1880-81
could have involved activities of this kind.[68] From the very first

[64] Palmer, Land League Crisis, p. 188.

[65] S.P.O., Chief Secretary's Office, Registered Papers: 1880/22493.

[66] Outrages, 1880.   [67] Sligo Champion, 6 March 1880, p. 4.

[68] To arrive at this figure I have included the following types of agrarian offenses: assaults on police (36), assaults on bailiffs and process servers (82), taking
and holding forcible possession (147), riots and affrays (64), and resistance to legal
process (31). The sources are Return of the number of agrarian offences in each

days of 1880, reports of excited crowds contesting evictions appeared in newspapers and were received at Dublin Castle, particularly from Galway and Mayo. A resident magistrate reported from Galway early in January 1880 that he had been forced to delay the serving of processes on one estate until he received reinforcements because the process server and several members of the Constabulary had been "attacked by a large and infuriated mob armed with stones."[69] Later in the same month a famous encounter took place at Carraroe, County Galway: police protecting a bailiff were routed by a mob said to have numbered some 3,000 persons "armed with sticks, stones, reaping hooks, spades, scythes and in fact every weapon they could lay their hands on."[70] In March an under-sheriff for County Roscommon, after reporting how he had faced "an excited mob of men, women and children" in Cloontuskert, remarked that in his thirty-four years of service he had "never met this sort of opposition before."[71]

Finally, we can note that violence aimed at enforcing boycotts could fall on almost anyone. In this category of crime, no particular social groups stood out as the most common victims. Threatening notices warning people not to deal with a certain individual were usually phrased in very general terms and were meant to apply to everyone in the community and to cover a wide range of transactions. Yet there was some tendency for shopkeepers, publicans, and car-drivers to be threatened or punished more often than others, obviously because they provided important services that needed to be cut off if a boycott were to be effective. More frequent still were threats or attacks on laborers, servants, and herdsmen, who were invariably expected to withdraw from the employment of any person who had been declared boycotted by the League.[72] Almost all the threats or attacks on such workers reported in County Galway in 1880 were aimed at persuading them

---

county in Ireland reported to the Constabulary office in each month of the year 1880 . . . , pp. 2-3, H.C. 1881 (12), lxxvii; Return of the number of agrarian offences in Ireland reported to the Constabulary office in each month of the year 1881 . . . , pp. 2-3, H.C. 1882 (8), lv.

[69] S.P.O., Chief Secretary's Office, Registered Papers: 1880/403.

[70] Nation, 10 Jan. 1880, p. 12. This was but one of several violent affrays at Carraroe which have been immortalized in a number of accounts. See Davitt, The Fall of Feudalism, pp. 213-19; and Hawkins, "Liberals, land and coercion in the summer of 1880."

[71] S.P.O., Chief Secretary's Office, Registered Papers: 1880/13150.

[72] Ibid.: 1880/29854; Roscommon Journal, 4 Dec. 1880, p. 2.

to quit work because their employer was deemed to be an enemy
of the movement.[73]

The leadership of the Land League took pains to dissociate itself
from this violence, and even to condemn it, in an effort to protect
its status as a lawful organization. Yet in fact violence was frequently committed by persons who belonged to the League. Furthermore, the non-violent activities of the movement did much to
incite the violent activities. Often the incitement was direct, as
when a person denounced at a land meeting or declared boycotted
by the League would become the victim of violence. Even if the
speakers did not condone such actions or recommend specific
penalties, their act of singling out an offender could lead others to
draw their own conclusions as to what should be done. It was not
unusual for speeches at land meetings to be punctuated with
shouts from the crowd of "Shoot them!" or "Down with them!"

More generally, the movement established a mood which encouraged lawlessness and gave those inclined to commit outrages
ample excuses for doing so. Not only was agrarian violence more
frequent than it had been for at least forty years, but the level increased steadily from one year to the next during the Land War,
though economic conditions improved over the same period.
Moreover, it is undeniable that violence helped the League in its
campaign against landlords. The most common motives for outrage were, as we have seen, in harmony with its goals. Violence,
and the threat of it, served to increase the power of the League
both by intimidating its enemies and by coercing tenants into
obeying its laws. In Galway during the year 1880, there were even
fifteen cases of agrarian offenses designed to force people to join
the Land League or to attend demonstrations.[74]

All this does not mean, however, that the Land League exercised tight control over this unrest. In this regard it is useful to
compare violence with other activities associated with the land
movement, since there was considerable variation in the extent to
which various activities were subject to control and regulation
either by the central executive or by local branches. The central
executive maintained the most (though far from complete) control
over the channeling of relief funds to local committees and over
the official activities of local branches, especially with respect to

[73] Outrages, 1880.   [74] Ibid.

finances. Considerable control was also exercised by the central executive or by branches over demonstrations, though it is possible to find Land League branches disapproving of land meetings not held under their auspices and it is also possible to find a small number of land meetings at which the League itself was denounced.[75] Boycotting often escaped control. Theoretically it was regulated by Land League courts, but we have already noted that private or unofficial boycotts were common.

Least of all was the control exercised over violence. Some persons who broke the rules of the League were attacked; others were not. In most instances, whether an offender would incur such treatment depended on whether there was an aggrieved party willing to commit violence. Those responsible for agrarian crimes usually had some personal stake in the case, or were friends of individuals who were personally involved. It is partly for this reason that opposition to landgrabbing was the most frequent motive for violence. Landgrabbing entailed a gain on the part of one tenant at the expense of another. Paying one's rent or ignoring a boycott may have offended the collective will of the community, but it did not antagonize a particular individual in the way that landgrabbing did. The aggrieved party was most often the previous tenant, but not always. Many assaults on so-called landgrabbers were calculated not to restore a former occupant, but to promote the interest of one or more parties seeking to obtain a vacated piece of land.[76] Not a few outrages involved disputes among relatives over the inheritance of land, or attacks on parents (typically widows) for not turning land over to their children.[77] I counted almost one hundred agrarian crimes motivated by landgrabbing in Galway in 1880, but also a further thirty cases arising from disputes among individuals over who was entitled to a holding.[78]

We should not assume that the Land League failed to control violence because violence is somehow, by its very nature, impossible to institutionalize. Secret societies in pre-famine Ireland

[75] *Clare Independent*, 4 Sept. 1880, p. 2; 18 Sept. 1880, p. 3; *Roscommon Journal*, 3 June 1880, p. 1.

[76] See Appendix A for several illustrations.

[77] For examples, see *Return . . . of all agrarian outrages . . . between the 1st day of February 1880 and the 31st day of October 1800*, pp. 95-6, and *Northern Whig*, 24 Nov. 1879 and 29 Jan. 1880.

[78] *Outrages*, 1880.

often institutionalized it at a local level. All governments, by definition, institutionalize violence and use it to support the prevailing social order. But the Land League was not the government, nor did it seek to defend the prevailing order. On the contrary, to reach its objectives it had to challenge the established power structure. In its efforts to do so it often failed to control the conduct of its own supporters. An inevitable lack of authority exists within any challenging collectivity. On the one hand, members of the collectivity encourage one another to reject established practices and even laws. At the same time they try to convince one another to accept a new authority and a new set of rules. That so many people accepted the Land League as the association entitled to represent tenant farmers demonstrates the extent to which a consensus had emerged about where the new authority should lie. And that so much of the activity associated with the Land War— even most of the violence—conformed to a common set of goals indicates the extent to which a consensus had been reached about what the new rules should be. But any organization that invites people to defy the established order will inevitably have difficulty controlling many of its members.

Power in Politics

POOR-LAW POLITICS

If the Land War was indeed a struggle for power between a challenging collectivity and an established holder of power, then we would expect to find members of the challenging collectivity taking advantage of every opportunity available to weaken their opponents. One of the most revealing aspects of the Land War, which until recently has gone largely unnoticed by historians, was the Land League's campaign to overthrow landlords on the poor-law boards. There was at best only an indirect connection between the operation and function of these boards and the land system, and so it is difficult to explain the takeover by tenants as a necessary part of the struggle over land. Clearly, the purpose of this campaign was simply to attack landlord power wherever it was vulnerable.

Chapter Six included a brief discussion of the control exercised by the landed class over the boards as late as the 1870s. That control was due, first, to the requirement that half the membership should be ex *officio* chosen from among justices of the peace, and second, to the influence that landowners exercised over the election of the remaining guardians. As a consequence, the vast majority of the 163 poor-law boards in Ireland were dominated by landowners and those who supported landed interests.[79] This dominance, however, was neither complete nor unassailable. Although they were usually outnumbered, at least a few individuals opposed to landed interests were regularly elected to most boards. They frequently tried to use the boards as forums for advancing favorite political causes. Along with town councils and city corporations, the poor-law boards were the only popularly elected institutions in which farmers and shopkeepers had a chance to play statesmen. (Often, they were contemptuously referred to as "local parliaments.") And indeed the routine affairs of most boards were in the hands of the elected members, since the absenteeism rate was much higher among ex *officio* than among elected guardians.[80] This was true for a number of reasons: landowners had numerous other kinds of business (including other official functions) for which their attendance was required; they often lived far away from the union; and in many cases, they were simply bored by the undistinguished role of poor-law guardian. This absenteeism meant that landed power over the boards usually depended on the return of a critical number of elected guardians who supported landed interests. Ultimately, then, power on the boards lay with whoever could command the support of the tenant electorate.[81]

Landed control over poor-law boards survived for more than forty years. Yet as time passed it became more and more precarious. On some boards, guardians became increasingly political, and landowners found it steadily more difficult to resist activist guardians who wanted to use the boards to promote causes with which most landowners were not in sympathy. The earliest-known political activity by boards occurred in 1843 when the Abbeyleix, Thurles, and Enniscorthy boards submitted petitions endorsing the Repeal movement.[82] In 1854 the Bailieborough and North Dublin unions passed resolutions applauding G. H. Moore's

---

[79] See above, pp. 191-2.   [80] Feingold, "Boards of guardians," pp. 45-9.

[81] Ibid., pp. 56-63.

[82] Ibid., p. 102. The Enniscorthy petition was signed by twenty-five members of the board.

land bill.[83] In 1869 several boards passed resolutions on the land question; in 1871 three boards in Mayo signed a petition supporting amnesty for Fenian prisoners; in 1872 at least twenty-six boards passed resolutions backing Home Rule; and in 1876 a total of twenty-nine boards petitioned the House of Commons in favor of Butt's land bill.[84] Significant attempts to remove landowners from officer positions were to come later, but even in the 1870s a few instances could be found. In 1870 the president of the Limerick and Clare Farmers' Club won the chairmanship of the Kilmallock board; and in 1872 all three of the officers chosen by this board were tenants. Also in 1872 an unsuccessful bid was made by guardians connected with the Home Rule movement to unseat the ex *officio* officers of the Roscommon board.[85] By 1877 fifty-nine tenants (including urban tenants) were serving as officers of poor-law boards. The largest occupational groups among them were shopkeepers and merchants (20 percent), and farmers (36 percent); the majority of the farmers were large graziers and many belonged to one or another of the farmers' clubs.[86]

The real assault on the poor-law boards began during the Land War. The first round of elections came in March 1880 in the heat of a parliamentary election campaign when the energies of the Land League and its supporters were focused on more important political victories. Nevertheless, the number of poor-law seats that were contested rose substantially, perhaps doubled, in comparison with 1877; more anti-landlord guardians were elected; and subsequently, tenants were chosen to fill 21 percent of the officer positions as compared with only 12 percent in 1877.[87] The assault in 1881 was more determined and certainly better organized. For the first time the central executive of the Land League took an interest. The forthcoming poor-law elections were discussed at meetings of the central committee in December, February, and early March. A notice was circulated to League branches requesting that they convene special meetings to make arrangements for

[83] Ibid., p. 103.

[84] *Nation*, 13 Nov. 1869, pp. 200 and 204; Feingold, "Boards of guardians," pp. 103-4; and *Nominal return of the municipal corporations and boards of guardians in Ireland that have sent petitions to this House in favour of the Land Tenure (Ireland) Bill*, H.C. 1876 (320), lx.

[85] Feingold, "Boards of guardians," pp. 104-13; see also Feingold, "Tenants' movement to capture the Irish poor law boards."

[86] Feingold, "Boards of guardians," pp. 40, 82-3, 104-11.

[87] Ibid., pp. 127-35.

promoting the election of Leaguers as poor-law guardians.[88] And a letter written by Parnell appeared in the *Freeman's Journal* advocating that branches should "see that all exertions are made to secure the return of Land League candidates as poor law guardians, and to drive from office the agents, bailiffs, and landlord nominees who have hitherto been allowed to fill these important positions."[89] Many branches followed this directive, selected candidates, and canvassed energetically for their election. And they were successful enough that in the aftermath of this contest 28 percent of the officer positions went to tenants.[90]

These two poor-law elections, but especially that of 1881, initiated a gradual process in which anti-landlord forces expanded their power on the boards of guardians. In 1882 tenants further increased their representation in officer positions to 35 percent; by 1884 they had reached 39 percent; and by 1886 they constituted 50 percent.[91] Victory on the poor-law boards was largely prestigious. True enough, greater tenant strength made it easier to get political resolutions adopted. It also reduced landlord control over a very useful kind of government spending and source of local patronage. The assault on the boards of guardians was undertaken, however, not just for these pragmatic sorts of reasons, but also because it accorded unprecedented status in the local community to the shopkeepers and large farmers who came to manage these government bodies so recently under the patronizing rule of the landed elite.

PARLIAMENTARY POLITICS

Yet the real basis of landlord power lay elsewhere and could be undermined only through a direct attack on the political center of the state. It was at this political center that the laws were made which kept the landowning class in control, and it was only here that those laws could be changed to bring the landowning class down. The land movement was, however, comparatively weak in this vital political arena when the agitation began in 1879. The farmers' clubs did enjoy the sympathy of some members of parliament, but their supporters comprised a minority even within the Irish party. Furthermore, the Irish party was so loosely structured by 1879 that it is really a misnomer to call it a party; it was

[88] Ibid., pp. 142-3.
[90] Ibid., pp. 146, 158, and 219.
[89] Ibid., p. 143.
[91] Ibid., p. 219.

not united on any issues except Irish self-government and
Catholic interests. Isaac Butt's death in May 1879 served to make
it, as a whole, even less attuned to tenant demands. His successor,
William Shaw, was distinguished primarily by his lack of sympathy for popular causes. Along with most members of the Irish
party, he refused to have anything to do with the emerging land
movement.

On the other hand, the allies that farmers did have were strong
allies; those Irish M.P.s who supported the land agitation in 1879
were not submissive in nature. They included the most aggressive
Irish representatives, the very M.P.s who had been creating chaos
in the House of Commons and arousing public opinion by their
obstructionist tactics. Moreover, some were not just sympathetic,
but had directly participated in the movement and helped to organize it. W. H. O'Sullivan was an active member of the Limerick
and Clare Farmers' Club. John O'Connor Power had been involved
in the organization of the early demonstrations in Connaught.
And Parnell, as we have seen, had addressed several meetings organized by farmers' clubs in 1878; he had also participated in discussions held by the Central Tenants' Defence Association in
early 1879. The Westport meeting in June did not represent Parnell's first contact with the emerging agitation, but did constitute
an important step forward in his attachment to it. When the National Land League was founded in October 1879, the central
committee included no fewer than eight Irish M.P.s.[92]

During the winter of 1879-80, the critical question in Irish parliamentary politics was whether Parnell and his parliamentary
followers would remain an aggressive clique within the Irish
party, or whether they would win over enough M.P.s to dominate
it. Until the spring of 1880 the answer seemed to be that majority
control would stay in the hands of Shaw and the moderate Home
Rule members. The general election of 1880, however, shifted the
balance of power by substantially altering the make-up of Irish
parliamentary representation.

In terms of social composition, there was a decline in the
number of landowners elected for Ireland from forty-two in 1874
to twenty-one in 1880; within the Irish party the decline was from

[92] Davitt, Fall of Feudalism, pp. 172-3. There were three M.P.s on the executive
(Biggar, O'Sullivan, and Parnell) and another five on the central committee
(O'Gorman, Power, Finigan, Mahon, and Ennis).

eighteen in 1874 to eight after the election of 1880.[93] Eminent landowners such as Captain H. S. Vandeleur in Clare, George Browne in Mayo, K. T. Digby in Queen's County, Colonel E. R. King-Harman in Sligo, and the O'Conor Don in Roscommon went down to defeat. By contrast, there was an increase in the number of Home Rule representatives drawn from middle-status social groups, particularly the lower professions, which rose from zero in 1874 to eight in 1880.[94] In terms of political allegiance, there were now more Irish representatives who were willing to follow Parnell. This became clear shortly after the general election when the choice of Parnell (in place of Shaw) as sessional chairman of the Irish party indicated that Parnell could count for support on at least twenty-four of its members.[95] And there was an increase in the number of M.P.s who were sympathetic toward the land movement. Indeed, along with Parnell, some dozen Irish representatives were now connected with the agrarian agitation.[96]

The significance of this shift in power within the Irish party should not be exaggerated. It was enough to make Parnell chairman, but it was not enough to bind all party members to him in the House. Twenty-four supporters was a bigger handful than he had had before the election, but it was still only a handful. The general election of 1880 in Ireland was by no means a Parnellite landslide. One reason may well be that neither Parnell nor the Land League were yet as popular as we tend to assume. But it is also clear that Parnell went into this election with a handicap: the Land League had not yet reached its full organizational strength;

[93] Thornley, *Isaac Butt*, p. 207; Conor Cruise O'Brien, *Parnell and His Party* (Oxford, 1957), pp. 14-18. Data are for owners of over 1,000 acres. I have relied on Thornley for 1874 and C. C. O'Brien for 1880. O'Brien also gives figures for 1874, but they differ slightly from those provided by Thornley. As O'Brien notes, the decline in the number of landowners elected to parliament really underestimates the decline in the landed interest, since it does not include the disappearance of several members without land but with important landed affiliations.

[94] C. C. O'Brien, *Parnell and His Party*, pp. 14-18.

[95] Parnell was actually elected chairman by twenty-three votes to eighteen for Shaw, but at least one Parnell supporter was absent and he should be included in the Parnell group. See ibid., pp. 25-6. For a list of those who voted for Parnell, see R. B. O'Brien, *The Life of Charles Stewart Parnell, 1846-1891* (London, 1898), I, pp. 223-4.

[96] The Irish representatives who had some connection with the land movement were Parnell, T. P. O'Connor, Thomas Sexton, John Dillon, Richard Lalor, Arthur O'Connor, J. J. O'Kelly, Andrew Commins, Joseph Biggar, Lysaght Finigan, T. D. Sullivan, W. H. O'Sullivan, and John O'Connor Power.

what is more, its policy at the time was to avoid participation in parliamentary politics. This policy existed primarily in order to satisfy the Fenian element in the League, whose members were particularly strong in the central executive. Though a secret financial donation was made to Parnell, and many members of the Land League were personally active in the election campaign, the League officially took no part, except for issuing a manifesto urging members to vote against landlord candidates.[97] As in 1874, the greatest influence over the nomination of Home Rule candidates was enjoyed by the Catholic clergy; and the clergy generally supported non-Parnellite Home Rulers. Inevitably, many non-Parnellite Home Rule candidates were nominated and only six were opposed by Parnellites.[98]

Whatever the exact explanation, the election did not give Parnell enormous strength in parliament. He could not stop other members of the Irish party from sitting with the government or from taking its side in House debates, as some did. When the government introduced a bill in June 1880 to provide tenants with financial compensation for eviction, Parnell was unable to have several objectionable clauses deleted, and he could not prevent many non-Parnellite Home Rulers from supporting the motion to go into committee.[99] And he was, of course, totally powerless to prevent the House of Lords from rejecting the bill, which they did in August.

Until the defeat of this bill there had been some measure of cooperation between the Parnellites and the new Gladstone ministry. Thereafter, the two sides were locked in a determined and steadily more embittered struggle. In late August nineteen members of the Irish party obstructed the Royal Irish Constabulary estimates; in November the government prosecuted five Irish M.P.s (along with nine other Land Leaguers); and in December the Irish party voted that all Home Rule members should sit in opposition.[100] When the 1881 session began, Parnell and his allies put forward one amendment after another to the speech from the throne; and shortly afterwards they vigorously obstructed the Pro-

[97] Davitt, *Fall of Feudalism*, p. 234; C. C. O'Brien, *Parnell and His Party*, pp. 120-21.

[98] C. C. O'Brien, *Parnell and His Party*, pp. 24, 42-3.

[99] Ibid., pp. 48-9; see also R. B. O'Brien, *Life of Parnell*, I, pp. 231-3.

[100] C. C. O'Brien, *Parnell and His Party*, pp. 52-7; R. B. O'Brien, *Life of Parnell*, I, p. 254.

tection of Person and Property Bill. It was in the course of the debate on this measure that the speaker's intervention brought the discussion to an end, and the government gave notice that it would introduce a "closure" resolution which would destroy the tactic of obstruction.[101] Even before closure came into effect, however, thirty-six Irish members were ejected from the House during an uproar over the arrest of Michael Davitt. The view taken by some of Parnell's supporters was that the occasion should be used for Irish members to secede from the House, but Parnell chose to return, possibly for a number of reasons, but almost certainly because he realized that at best only twenty Irish members would have obeyed a decision to secede.[102] Without obstruction, however, the Parnellites could do little to prevent the passage of the Protection of Person and Property Bill as well as a supplementary measure to restrict the use of arms.

The major victory in parliament for the land movement was the land bill, which was finally passed in July and received the royal assent in August. Although Parnell and his closest allies in the House denounced many of its features and refused to vote for it on second reading, this piece of legislation was nevertheless a great accomplishment for them. There was never any serious intention by the Parnellites to destroy it;[103] and a number of them earnestly endeavored to make it as beneficial to tenants as possible. They persuaded the government to accept several amendments, and they successfully defended the government text against amendments from landowning interests.[104] The Parnellites could be outvoted and even prevented from obstructing the business of the House, but it was decidedly more difficult to ignore the widespread unrest in Ireland that they could, with considerable justification, claim to represent. This unrest raised the strength of Parnellites in the House far above what their numbers alone would have allowed. Indeed Parnell's political power in 1880-81 derived less from his position as leader of the Irish party and more from his leadership of the land movement. By 1881 the government realized that some substantial land reform was necessary to ap-

[101] R. B. O'Brien, *Life of Parnell*, I, pp. 267-83.

[102] C. C. O'Brien, *Parnell and His Party*, pp. 57-61; see also Lyons, *Charles Stewart Parnell*, pp. 146-9.

[103] Lyons, *Charles Stewart Parnell*, p. 161.

[104] C. C. O'Brien, *Parnell and His Party*, p. 68; see also Davitt, *Fall of Feudalism*, pp. 321-9.

pease Irish tenants. Whereas Ireland had been almost totally ignored in the speech from the throne in May 1880, the Queen's
speech in January 1881 was concerned primarily with Ireland.
The sovereign threatened her Irish subjects with coercion, but she
also promised them land reform. Ironically, these very measures,
for which the land movement was most responsible, helped to destroy the movement and eventually to reverse the basis of Parnell's power.

The Outcome

DECLINE

The challenging collectivity that emerged in the years 1879-80
contracted during the winter of 1881-2. There were three reasons.
First, economic conditions gradually improved. Many tenants
were still in arrears and the number of evictions continued to rise
from one year to the next, but the economic recovery was nevertheless sufficient to reduce the level of discontent. The potato
yield climbed from 1.3 tons per acre in 1879 to 3.6 tons in 1880
and 4.0 tons in 1881, when its was as high as in any year during
the 1870s with the exception of 1876.[105] In addition, by 1880
prices for cattle and sheep had almost recovered and sales at the
Ballinasloe fair were much better than in the previous year.[106] Yet
economic conditions alone do not explain the decline of the
movement. If economic discontent were the only factor, the unrest
should have begun to taper off in 1880 when conditions were
distinctly better than they had been in 1879. The improvement between 1879 and 1880 had, however, no noticeable effect on the
agitation.[107]

A second reason was "coercion." As we have just seen, two
laws were enacted in the spring of 1881 making it easier for law-
enforcement agencies to combat the agitation. The most damaging
was the Protection of Person and Property Act, which gave the

[105] See Table 12 in Chapter Seven above.

[106] Barrington, "A review of Irish agricultural prices," p. 252; Thom's, 1881, pp.
692-3.

[107] In many western counties potato yields were still low in 1880, especially in
Roscommon where only 1.9 tons were harvested per acre. But in no county was the
crop as bad in 1880 as it had been in 1879. See Agricultural statistics of Ireland . . .
1881, pp. 39-42. Furthermore, livestock and butter prices were much better in 1880
than in 1879, indeed better in 1880 than in 1881.

lord lieutenant wide-ranging powers to arrest and detain persons without trial.[108] This act dealt the agitation a serious blow by putting many of the most important activists behind bars; by the end of 1881, a total of 568 persons had been arrested, 420 of whom were still in jail.[109] Less important, but still worth noting, was the second measure, officially titled the Peace Preservation Act, but better known as the Arms Act, which empowered the lord lieutenant to prohibit the possession of arms within any specified part of Ireland except in special cases.[110]

The third reason for the collapse of the movement was the Land Act of 1881. Basically it sought to legalize the so-called three Fs: fair rents, fixity of tenure, and free sale. The most revolutionary provisions were those which provided for the arbitration of rents. Applications to have rents adjudicated could be made either to the ordinary county courts or to a newly established Land Commission. Once settled, rents were to remain fixed for a period of fifteen years. The act also provided that a yearly tenant should have fixity of tenure so long as he paid his rent, did not commit persistent waste, and did not sublet, subdivide, or erect buildings without the consent of the landlord. Yearly tenants were to have the right to sell the interest in their holdings at the best price they could obtain, subject to the right of the landlord to reject the sale on reasonable grounds. Finally, the act empowered the Land Commission to lend up to three-quarters of the purchase price to a tenant who wanted to buy his holding, repayable over thirty-five years at an annual interest rate of 5 percent. It was without question the most far-reaching piece of land reform enacted for Ireland during the nineteenth century.[111]

These three factors—economic improvement, coercion, and land reform—did not have a uniform effect on the movement. They served to weaken it, but they also helped to stimulate more radical activity designed to prevent this result. In response to an increasing tendency for tenants to come to terms with their landlords, agrarian violence rose during the winter of 1881-2; some 3,500 outrages were reported between October 1881 and April 1882 compared with about 2,600 during the equivalent period in the winter of 1880-81.[112] Led by Parnell, the Land League initially

---

[108] 44 Vict., c. 4.   [109] S.P.O., Irish crimes records, 1881.
[110] 44 Vict., c. 5.   [111] 44 Vict., c. 49.
[112] Lee, *Modernisation of Irish Society*, p. 86.

chose to "test" the Land Act, that is, to discourage tenants from
rushing into court and instead to put forward in each district several selected cases that would enable them to assess how well they
would fare under the new legislation.[113] In other ways, however,
the Land League behaved as though it were trying to undermine
the act. During the summer the central executive had decided that
the existing policy of "paying rent at the point of the bayonet"
had become ineffective and too costly in the face of determined
action by landowners; since then the policy had been that tenants
should submit to eviction rather than settle with their landlords—which also meant, of course, that they would be unable to
take advantage of the new act.[114] In September it was decided that
two tenants in each district should be chosen to determine what
was a fair rent for all the holdings, a blatant attempt to usurp the
powers of the forthcoming Land Commission.[115] And no sooner
had Parnell persuaded the Land League to adopt the program of
testing the act than he sent a cable to the president of the Land
League of America stressing that tenants had been advised to
"rely on the old methods to reach justice" and alleging that the
test cases were intended to expose "the hollowness of the Act."[116]
Parnell used similar language in public speeches in September
and October, resulting in his arrest on 13 October. Within a few
days the government also arrested his principal lieutenants after
they had vehemently denounced its action against their leader.
The vicious circle of radicalism and repression continued when
the new internees issued the "No Rent Manifesto" calling for a
universal strike against rents and taking the Land League closer to
open rebellion than it had been at any point during the preceding
two years of agitation. On 20 October the Land League was proclaimed an illegal organization.

The No Rent Manifesto was a failure. It was condemned by the
Catholic clergy, even by the archbishop of Cashel, until then a
strong supporter of the movement. And it was deplored in varying
degrees by almost the entire Irish press. The truth was that opposition to the new land law by leaders of the Land League did not
coincide with the sentiments of many of the League's own members and supporters. Even in Land League strongholds, such as

[113] Palmer, Land League Crisis, pp. 283-6.
[114] Bew, "Politics of the Irish Land War," pp. 261-70, 297; see also Donnelly,
Cork, p. 289.
[115] Donnelly, Cork, p. 289.   [116] R. B. O'Brien, Life of Parnell, I, p. 306.

the counties of Roscommon and Mayo, the Land Act was regarded by most supporters as the fruit of their victory rather than as an occasion for renewed agitation. In Roscommon the movement split over the act, with each side finding a voice in one of the major county newspapers. The diehard faction was led by the *Roscommon Herald*, which rejected the act and welcomed the No Rent Manifesto. But an opposing faction had already met in September and decided to use the act rather than obstruct it. They reacted angrily to the No Rent Manifesto, which was denounced violently in the pages of the *Roscommon Journal*.[117] In Castlebar the Land Act was strongly endorsed by James Daly, the father of the movement in Connaught. During the last four months of 1881, Daly's editorials in the *Connaught Telegraph* indicated an increasing alienation from the Land League, which he believed had fallen into the hands of unscrupulous opportunists who "know as much about land as a crow does about Sunday."[118] In November a Tenants' Defence Association was established at Castlebar to instruct farmers on the benefits to be obtained from the Land Act.[119]

By November 1881 the movement was in disarray. Much of the central leadership was in jail. The parliamentary party "had no corporate existence during this period"; those aggressive Parnellites who were not in prison carefully remained in England in order to avoid arrest.[120] According to the Land League's own sources of information, many of its branches had already disintegrated by early October;[121] after 20 October they were illegal. An organizational structure was maintained by a "Ladies' Land League," which had been established in January 1881. Although the significance of this Ladies' League should not be underestimated, it was powerless to prevent the defections from the movement that were occurring. The Land Commission began hearings in October and was immediately swamped with applications from tenants to have their rents arbitrated.[122] It would be a number of years before judicial rents would be fixed for more than a small

[117] *Roscommon Journal*, 15 Oct. 1881, p. 2; 22 Oct. 1881, p. 2.

[118] *Connaught Telegraph*, 13 Aug. 1881; 20 Aug. 1881; 3 Sept. 1881; 1 Oct. 1881; 8 Oct. 1881; 15 Oct. 1881; 22 Oct. 1881; 26 Nov. 1881; and 5 Dec. 1881. A good discussion of Daly's withdrawal from the movement can be found in Feingold, "Boards of guardians," pp. 184-5.

[119] *Connaught Telegraph*, 22 Nov. 1881, p. 5.

[120] C. C. O'Brien, *Parnell and His Party*, p. 74.

[121] Lyons, *Charles Stewart Parnell*, p. 174.

[122] Palmer, *Land League Crisis*, p. 301.

portion of Irish tenants, but the successful operation of the courts had a dramatic impact on the political mood of the country. The committed agitators soldiered on, but the majority of farmers turned their attention from political meetings to land courts, whose deliberations they carefully watched and discussed. The No Rent Manifesto proved to be merely the death spasm of the movement, as its leader knew it would be. "Politically it is a fortunate thing for me that I have been arrested," Parnell wrote his mistress five days *before* he signed the Manifesto, "as the movement is breaking fast, and all will be quiet in a few months, when I shall be released."[123]

The violence did not break as fast as he expected and it was actually more than six months before he was released. In what has come to be known as the "Kilmainham Treaty" between Gladstone and Parnell, the Irish leader undertook to use his influence against further outrages and not to resume the agitation, in return for an understanding that the government would make an effort to overcome several deficiencies in the Land Act, the most serious of which was that tenants in arrears did not enjoy the right to have their rents arbitrated.[124] In order to effect the treaty, the government set free Parnell and two close associates on 2 May 1882. Several days later, the Chief Secretary and the Under Secretary were assassinated in Phoenix Park. This deed at first threatened to destroy the political understanding between Parnell and the Liberals. (And it did force the government to renew coercion with a far more repressive measure than they had originally intended.)[125] Yet ultimately the murders served to strengthen Parnell's hand over those in the movement who favored a resumption of the struggle. Moreover, Gladstone did honor the most important part of his commitment to Parnell. In August the Arrears Act became law, giving the Land Commission authority to pay a portion of the arrears due on holdings where the tenant was deemed unable to discharge the debt.[126]

ROUTINIZATION

The contraction of the challenging collectivity did not mean its total disappearance. It is true that mass demonstrations, boycotting, and agrarian violence all declined. (After the savage winter of

[123] Quoted in Lyons, *Charles Stewart Parnell*, p. 175.
[124] R. B. O'Brien, *Life of Parnell*, I, pp. 262-3.
[125] 45 and 46 Vict., c. 25.   [126] 45 and 46 Vict., c. 47.

1881-2, the number of agrarian offenses reported by the Constabulary fell steadily—from 3,433 in 1882 to 870 in 1883 and 762 in 1884.)[127] On the other hand, many other activities continued, primarily those which were relatively institutionalized. Rather than continue fighting landlords by refusing to pay their rents or resisting the serving of writs, many tenants now tried to outmaneuver them in the land courts. The struggle to weaken the landed interest on the poor-law boards also continued.[128] So did the strengthening of Parnellite control over the Irish party. Even the Land League was resurrected, and became a more unified and tightly controlled organization.

The Land League was declared illegal in October 1881, but a replication of its institutional form was maintained during the winter of 1881-2 by the Ladies' Land League. An American Ladies' Land League had been set up in October 1880, but it was not until January 1881 that an Irish organization was established, which began to organize branches in the following months.[129] Superficially, it appeared to be simply an arm of the men's league. Its leader was one of Parnell's sisters and its president was the cousin of one of his lieutenants. It shared its head office with the men's League and had a similar organizational structure. Recent research[130] has shown, however, that the leaders of the Ladies' League were not always on amicable terms with the leaders of the men's association. The Ladies' League was in large measure an independent organization with a different set of priorities and a different program, and composed of a noticeably different social class and persuasion of persons. The Ladies' League drew more of its support from middle-class and urban groups, and its members were inclined to be more radical.[131] In any case, its most impor-

---

[127] *Return by provinces of agrarian offences throughout Ireland . . . 1882*, H.C. 1883 (12), lvi; similar return for 1883 [C 3950], H.C. 1884, lxiv; and similar return for 1884 [C 4500], H.C. 1884-5, lxv.

[128] See above p. 000.

[129] In Connaught, branches were formed in the towns of Castlerea and Claremorris in February, as well as in the towns of Roscommon and Keadue, County Leitrim, in March. See *Roscommon Journal*, 12 Feb. 1881, p. 2; 19 Feb. 1881, p. 2; 5 March 1881, p. 2; and 12 March 1881, p. 1.

[130] Moody, "Anna Parnell and the Land League"; Finola A. Collins, "The Ladies' Land League," unpublished M.A. thesis, University College Cork, 1974; and Foster, *Parnell: The Man and His Family*, pp. 264-84. All three make effective use of Anna Parnell's unpublished account of the Land War.

[131] Collins, "Ladies Land League," pp. 233-4.

tant contribution was simply that it stayed alive. When it became clear in October and November of 1881 that the men's movement was losing support, the Ladies' League began to give less emphasis to promoting the agitation as such and elevated to first priority its function of maintaining a national organization.[132] It was able to perform this function because it was founded nine months before the suppression of the men's League and because it was more than a mere auxiliary of the older association. As the men's League gradually fell apart, the Ladies' League remained remarkably well organized and centralized. It was more solidly opposed to the Land Act than was the men's League and more committed to the No Rent Manifesto. The entire credit for the survival of the organizational structure of the Land League cannot be given to the ladies' association; on the other hand, it would be difficult, without taking the Ladies' League into account, to explain how the Land League could be outlawed, how the mass support for the movement could contract during the winter of 1881-2, and how, nevertheless, the Land League could reappear under a different name in late 1882. After Parnell came out of prison in May he crushed the Ladies' League. Yet it was partly the organizational continuity maintained by the Ladies' association that enabled him to revive the Land League the following October.

The new association was called the Irish National League. It was formed on the basis of reconstituted Land League branches, and many people continued to refer to them as "Land League" rather than "National League" branches. It was, however, a vastly different kind of organization. It was far more integrated into the political party system and much more centrally directed than the Land League had been. It was, in fact, an electoral organization for the Irish parliamentary party.

The original constitution of the National League provided for a governing council of forty-eight members, sixteen of whom were to be nominated by the parliamentary party, while the remaining thirty-two were to be elected at county conventions by delegates from local branches.[133] This council was, as it happened, never elected; and the National League instead remained governed by an organizing committee consisting of thirty members, the majority of whom were either members of parliament at the time or later elected to parliament.[134] The National League became the instru-

[132] Ibid., pp. 236-7.   [133] Davitt, *Fall of Feudalism*, p. 377.
[134] C. C. O'Brien, *Parnell and His Party*, pp. 127-8.

ment by which the Irish party took over the selection of parliamentary candidates, which formerly had been controlled by
independent associations or by the clergy operating in each constituency. These independent associations and the clergy were
not so much replaced as they were incorporated into the structure
of the National League. The county conventions, at which parliamentary candidates were nominally chosen, consisted of four delegates from each branch of the National League in the county, any
members of the Catholic clergy in the county who wished to attend, and two or three representatives of the parliamentary party.
When a general election was held in 1885, what occurred in practice was that candidates were selected by a caucus of the parliamentary party meeting in Dublin, and then, by means of a variety
of autocratic tactics, were imposed on the conventions.[135] By this
time the Irish party bore little resemblance to the loose band of
political aspirants that had faced the electorate in 1880. It was instead a well organized political party composed of pledge-bound
parliamentary candidates, an organizing committee, county conventions, and local branches. Altogether Parnell's machine won
85 of the 103 Irish seats.

The routinization of the land movement into a political party
changed the character of the active collectivity. The membership
of the National League looked slightly more like that of the old
farmers' clubs of the 1870s. The large-farm element was stronger
and the small-farm element weaker in comparison with Land
League branches; and there were more branches in Leinster and
Munster relative to the number in Connaught than under the Land
League. These, however, were small changes in degree. More
dramatic was the shift in goals of the active collectivity. First, the
National League was obviously more "constitutionalist"; radical
elements were weaker and the movement was dominated by those
who believed that their political objectives could be achieved
through institutionalized politics. At the center of the organization, the old Fenian "triumvirate" of Davitt, Brennan, and Egan,
which had largely managed the Land League, was now replaced
by a coterie of men closer to Parnell and to his view of politics.[136]
Second, there was now greater attention given to Irish independence and less attention to land reform. The political party that
took over from the land movement was a nationalist party, and

[135] Ibid., pp. 128-32.
[136] Davitt, *Fall of Feudalism*, p. 378; R. B. O'Brien, *Life of Parnell*, I, pp. 365-78.

it sought to return the emphasis to the goal of self-government with which the members of this party had originally been most concerned.

Yet nothing could be more mistaken than to assume that the routinization of the Land War resulted in a return to the political situation as it existed in the 1870s. The Land War had generated a new political force in Irish politics that did not disappear even after the movement as such had collapsed. The presence of this new political power is clearly evident in the social characteristics of politicians elected in the mid-1880s, both in local government and to the British parliament. We have already seen that 50 percent of the officers of local poor-law boards were tenants by this time; in terms of occupation, the largest increase occurred among farmers, who had risen from 7 percent in 1877 to 26 percent in 1886, and among shopkeepers, publicans, and innkeepers, who had risen from less than 2 percent in 1877 to 10 percent in 1886.[137] In the Irish parliamentary party, the new members elected in 1885 came almost entirely from two groups: (1) farmers, shopkeepers, and wage earners, which went from two in 1880 to twenty-two in 1885; and (2) the lower professions, which increased from eight in 1880 to nineteen in 1885.[138] Recall that (with the exception of wage earners) these were the very social groups that were most actively involved in the Land War. In saying this, I am obviously referring primarily to farmers and shopkeepers, but some of the lower professions were also well represented in the agitation of 1879-82, especially newspaper editors and correspondents. It was not until the mid-1880s that significant numbers of persons drawn from these groups began to win their place in institutionalized politics, but the emergent stage in the evolution of this political force was the Land League agitation.

Moreover, though nationalism rather than land reform was now the principal goal of the Irish party, and even of the National League, the fact remained that the National League was largely an agrarian organization. A comparison with the situation in the 1870s makes the point. Butt's Home Rule Party drew its support disproportionately from the cities and towns. It had no official associations in the counties and only a handful of unofficial organizations. There were thirty or more farmers' clubs, but most were not active for more than a few continuous years, and they had to

[137] Feingold, "Boards of guardians," p. 267.
[138] C. C. O'Brien, *Parnell and His Party*, p. 152.

struggle to get their voices heard in the Home Rule party. The Irish parliamentary party of the 1880s was altogether different. Still popular in the large urban centers, its strength rested primarily on an association consisting of hundreds of branches in small towns whose members were drawn mainly from the farming population. The mere existence of an organization of this kind tells us that a new political force had come into existence.

It is helpful to think of the 1880s as a period when a new political collectivity, which had emerged during the Land War, was now in a position to contend with other political collectivities in defense of its interests. Its adversaries had by no means disappeared. The rise of a new political force does not necessarily mean the elimination of opposing forces. In the case we are examining, it meant nothing of the kind. The strength of the landed interest had been severely reduced among Irish members of parliament; and it was steadily declining in local government. But landed proprietors still possessed considerable power. They could yet look to many English M.P.s in the House of Commons and to the overwhelming majority of peers in the House of Lords to stand behind them. Although they had been displaced on half of the poor-law boards, they were still running the other half and they retained complete control over the grand juries, which remained the most powerful institutions in local government until 1898 when the structure of local administration was reformed by the Local Government Act. And they still owned the land, which had always been the immediate and direct source of their control over the rural population.

There has been an unfortunate tendency in some historical accounts to exaggerate the effects of the Land Act of 1881. The act did have a tranquilizing effect on the agitation of 1879-82, but its impact on the actual operation of the land system was more limited. Admittedly it placed severe constraints on landlords; it made the management of estates much more troublesome; and in a few cases, it drove landowners into bankruptcy. But it would be reading Irish history backwards to assume that it destroyed the basis of landlords' control over their estates and made the ultimate abolition of the nineteenth-century land system inevitable. Landlords still had the power to grant or withhold customary privileges, to claim arrears, to evict or distrain for nonpayment of rent, and even to set rents. A few statistics indicate the extent to which they were still able to determine what rents their tenants would pay. From the time the Land Act came into operation in 1881 until August 1885, the rents of only some 85,000 holdings (representing 17 percent of all holdings over one acre) were fixed by the courts, and the average reduction was 20 percent.[139] It is true, of course, that the act also had an influence on rents settled outside the land courts. But if we can judge this effect by those private agreements that were registered with the Land Commission, it is clear that proprietors fared slightly better out of court. There were roughly 84,000 rent agreements lodged with the commission by August 1885, and the average reduction was 17 percent.[140]

Neither one side nor the other had emerged clearly victorious from the struggle of 1879-82. The Land War had not resolved a conflict, but rather had intensified it. During the Land War a new challenging collectivity had been formed while the opposing established collectivity remained, besieged as it had never been before, but still not defeated. Thus the Land War set the stage for a further struggle between two formidable antagonists, both ready to engage in battle. The occasion for the renewal of hostilities came in the mid-1880s when economic conditions again deteriorated, as a result of a combination of bad weather and a decline in agricultural prices. Unlike the downturn of the late 1870s, the weather was now too dry rather than too wet, particularly in the summers of 1884 and 1887. And unlike the preceding depression, cattle producers as well as dairy farmers and grain growers were now faced with shrunken demand and falling prices.[141]

[139] K. Buckley, "The fixing of rents by agreement in County Galway, 1881-5" in *Irish Historical Studies*, 7, no. 27 (March 1951), pp. 150-51.

[140] Ibid. That less than one-quarter of the tenants of Ireland took their landlords to court in the years 1881-5 can be explained by a number of factors. First, the courts could hardly have handled more cases than they did; as it was, they were fixing the rents of an average of more than 1,500 holdings per month. Second, virtually all leaseholders were excluded in practice from the rent-fixing provisions of the act; and they may have constituted more than a third of all holdings over one acre. Third, the reductions commonly granted by the commissioners were not all that enticing, especially for tenants with small holdings, who would have to bear legal costs of £3 to £4 in order to obtain a reduction that might save them less than £1 a year. And fourth, taking a landlord to court could result in the loss of non-contractual privileges. Many landlords allegedly threatened tenants who were planning to have their rents fixed (or punished those who did so) with immediate demands for arrears, refusal to allow the normal six months to pay, loss of turbary rights, or denial of permission to sell the interest in the holding at more than the value assessed by the court.

[141] This was true especially in 1886, but perhaps also in 1887. See Donnelly, *Cork*, pp. 308-13; Barrington, "A review of Irish agricultural prices," p. 252.

But the greatest difference between the two depressions was in the speed with which they sparked a land movement. Tenants were poorly organized when economic conditions deteriorated in the late 1870s; it took over a year for the agitation to build and for them to mobilize a collective defense. By contrast, a collective response to the downturn that began in 1884 developed quickly, indeed as early as the spring of 1885. This time farmers were both politically experienced and extensively organized. Specifically, the National League provided a base on which the active anti-landlord collectivity could again expand, especially since the League was simultaneously organizing in anticipation of a general election. In July 1885 the police noted "a perceptible increase in the power of the league" and reported the existence of 818 branches; by January 1886 there were reportedly no less than 1,261 branches.[142] Throughout 1885 and 1886 many local bodies began boycotting campaigns in their districts and held land courts. Many also helped to organize rent strikes. On some estates tenants agreed to withhold their rents until their landlords granted satisfactory abatements. They typically raised "defense funds" to meet legal costs and to support evicted tenants. On a smaller number of estates, they went so far as to contribute their rents (less the abatement they demanded) to such funds, which were lodged in the hands of trustees.[143]

Initially, neither the Irish parliamentary party nor the central executive of the National League provided leadership for this new agitation. The Irish party's energies were directed almost entirely toward winning seats in the general election of 1885, and subsequently, during the spring of 1886, toward obtaining Irish self-government, which seemed a very real possibility as a result of Gladstone's Home Rule bill introduced in April. Only after this bill was defeated in the Commons in June, and after the Liberals were ousted from power at the general election in July, did the Irish parliamentary party give more attention to the land question. In October 1886 the central executive of the National League initiated "A Plan of Campaign," which called on tenants to place rents in the hands of trustees in the manner that had been tried on some estates during the winter of 1885-6. Under the leadership of several members of the parliamentary party, the most active of whom

[142] C. C. O'Brien, *Parnell and His Party*, pp. 132-3.
[143] Donnelly, *Cork*, pp. 317-22; see also Donnelly, *Landlord and Tenant*, pp. 85-6.

were John Dillon and William O'Brien, the agitation spread rapidly, drawing its strength from much the same parts of the country as had the Land League seven years earlier. (Of the estates affected by the Plan, almost half were located in Connaught, while most of the remainder were in Munster.)[144] The movement was stoutly resisted by landowners, who organized a syndicate to support estates besieged by rent strikes. It also faced determined opposition from the government, which enacted a far-reaching crimes act in the summer of 1887. By 1890 thirty-two members of Parnell's party had faced prosecution and a total of 116 estates had been affected by the Plan.[145]

As a result of the Plan of Campaign, Irish tenant farmers made some very real gains in their struggle for control over the land. Yet they were still far from winning that struggle. In conjunction with the crimes act, a new land act was offered to them in 1887. It granted leaseholders the right to have their rents adjudicated by the Land Commission, and also permitted the commission to revise judicial rents fixed before 1886, in consideration of the fall in agricultural prices.[146] Nonetheless, the essential powers of landlords persisted. As long as this was the case, tenants could be expected to participate in collective efforts to undermine these powers. Consequently, the government (particularly when the Conservative party was in office) was becoming convinced that agrarian unrest in Ireland would only be broken by transferring ownership of land to the occupiers. Unfortunately, legislation enacted in the 1880s and 1890s and aimed at promoting this transfer had limited impact, primarily because tenants insisted that their annuities be substantially less than their current rents. An act of 1885 enabled the Land Commission to lend tenants the full purchase price of their holdings, repayable over a period of forty-nine years by an annuity of 4 percent per annum; and four amending acts had been passed by 1896. But there was nothing to force landowners to sell. And the price demanded by most of those willing to do so was rarely low enough to give tenants the reduction in annual payments which they sought. Altogether,

[144] *Report of the Evicted Tenants' Commission*, appendix, pp. 95-6 [C 6935], H.C. 1893-4, xxx.

[145] F.S.L. Lyons, *John Dillon: A Biography* (London, 1968), pp. 82-112. See also L. P. Curtis, Jr., *Coercion and Conciliation in Ireland, 1880-1892: A Study in Conservative Unionism* (Princeton, 1963), p. 236.

[146] Donnelly, *Cork*, pp. 340-41.

only about 74,000 holdings were purchased under these and earlier acts, with the result that landlordism still prevailed over the vast majority of agricultural holdings in Ireland.[147]

There was, then, no clear sign that landlords were either withdrawing or being driven from the struggle as the nineteenth century came to a close. To be sure, they were quite visibly tired of receiving abuse where they thought they were entitled to deference; they were finding the administration of their estates exceedingly worrisome and costly; and they were faced with increasing difficulties in obtaining credit as the value of their properties declined and as lenders lost confidence in the security of Irish land.[148] These difficulties are important to recognize because they help to explain the willingness of landowners to surrender their estates when, as did happen eventually, they were offered an acceptable price. During the 1890s, however, landed power was still unmistakably the stronger of the two contending forces. Indeed, for most of the 1890s it was not subject to any effective attack by tenants, despite several years of bad weather and slack demand for agricultural produce.

In January 1898, however, after two consecutive years of potato failures, a new tenant association was formed in Mayo called the United Irish League (U.I.L.). With the appearance of this association, the very real differences in interests that existed between large and small farmers finally came into the open. Initially at least, the U.I.L. drew its support almost entirely from small farmers in Connaught, most of whom had more to gain from an assault on graziers than from any further reductions in their rents. For the first two years of its campaign, the U.I.L. was unequivocally an anti-grazier movement, and its principal demand was the breakup of large farms. Its supporters challenged large farmers in Mayo by interfering with auctions of grazing land, turning up pasture, and boycotting graziers.[149] Here and in other parts of the west, agitators made effective use of the hostility that small farmers had always felt toward large ones.

This kind of program could be maintained only as long as the

[147] J. E. Pomfret, *The Struggle for Land in Ireland, 1800-1923* (Princeton, 1930), p. 307. See also Solow, *The Land Question and the Irish Economy*, pp. 184-94; and Donnelly, *Cork*, pp. 367-72, 384.

[148] Donnelly, *Cork*, pp. 304-7.

[149] *Connaught Telegraph*, 13 May 1899, p. 1; 8 July 1899, p. 2; 19 Aug. 1899, p. 5; and 10 March 1900, p. 2.

agitation remained largely confined to Connaught and independent of the Irish parliamentary party. During 1899, however, the movement began to find strength in other provinces, and in June of 1900 the Irish parliamentary party adopted the U.I.L. as its national electoral organization. By this time the association had grown to 653 branches with 63,000 members. Within a year it had reached 989 branches with nearly 100,000 members.[150] Although the movement in Connaught continued to emphasize the breakup of large holdings, the program of the expanded organization consisted of the typical anti-landlord demands of the tenant population. Land redistribution would re-emerge as a political issue later, but on this occasion, as in both 1879-82 and 1884-90, shared interests prevailed and served to unite large and small farmers against a common enemy and toward a common goal. When several large landowners indicated a willingness to come to terms with the agitators on land purchase, the leaders of the land movement accepted the offer and a conference was held in December 1902 between a small group of landowners representing their class and four politicians representing the tenants. The recommendations of this conference formed the basis for the "Wyndham Act" of 1903, which finally established terms for land purchase that proved to be agreeable to both landlords and tenants.

The Wyndham Act made it possible to bridge the gap between the price that most landowners were willing to accept and the price that most tenants were ready to pay. It did so by providing the landlord with a bonus of 12 percent on the selling price, payable out of Irish revenues.[151] Some tenant spokesmen, including Michael Davitt, argued that the arrangement was far too generous to landlords. It is certainly true that individually they were as much the beneficiaries of the legislation as were tenants. In a more important sense, however, they were destined to be the losers, for in their zeal to take advantage of the lucrative terms now offered for relinquishing their estates, they were fated to dissolve themselves as a social class. Under the Act of 1903, and amending

[150] Lyons, *John Dillon*, pp. 201 and 223.

[151] The act also reduced the interest rate to 3¼ percent, extended the period of repayment to sixty-eight and one-half years, and stipulated that the annuities had to give tenants paying judicial rents a reduction of 20 to 40 percent on first-term rents or 10 to 30 percent on second-term rents. See Pomfret, *Struggle for Land in Ireland*, pp. 291-6.

legislation enacted in 1909, tenants became the owners of more than 326,000 holdings by the early 1920s, when nearly two-thirds of Ireland's total area had ceased to be the property of land-lords.[152] The struggle was coming to a close. The power of land-lords was being destroyed in Ireland.

[152] Donnelly, Cork, p. 384.

Ten · Conclusion

How Did Collective Action Change?

It is now time to offer some general observations on social structure and rural unrest in nineteenth-century Ireland. Our first task is to arrive at whatever conclusions we can about how collective action changed in the course of the century in order that we can identify the features of the Land War that distinguished it from earlier varieties of unrest. One thing clearly not distinctive about the Land War was the *amount* of collective action. This is true even if we compare it only with other cases in which rural people organized themselves free of control by established elites. Active collectivities drawn from rural classes and representing their interests can be found both before and after the Famine. Indeed, there was actually much more collective action of this kind before 1845. The Land War was certainly a massive collective effort. But the vast number of small combinations that terrorized people in the pre-famine period (not to mention several enormous waves of rural protest) make it impossible to argue that the Land War represented an unprecedented level of collective activity in the countryside. Nor can it be said that there was more violence in the second half of the century. Unfortunately, we do not have satisfactory data with which to make direct and accurate comparisons. Yet what evidence we have strongly suggests that collective violence in an average pre-famine year was much greater than in an average post-famine year, and that the violence which accompanied major outbreaks of unrest before the Famine, such as those of 1821-4 or 1830-34, undoubtedly far exceeded the violence of the Land War. In this sense, pre-famine laborers and small farmers were more militant, more rebellious than the farmers who participated in the Land War.

The point is not that the Land War was a minor or insignificant revolt. But it would clearly be a mistake to assume that the most important feature of the Land War was that it was bigger than anything coming before it, and that this is what needs to be explained. Any such assumption nourishes a serious historical misconception. It also diverts attention from much more interesting differences between pre-famine collective action and the Land

War, differences that were more qualitative than quantitative, having more to do with how the character of social unrest changed than with a rise or fall in the amount of unrest. Unfortunately, almost regardless of which society is under investigation, most sociologists today tend to be interested primarily in explaining variations in the amount of unrest. Why does rebellion break out in a society that was formerly peaceful? Why is there more political protest in some periods than in others? They may attribute an increase in rebellious activity to the breakdown of social institutions; they may argue that it results from relative deprivation; or they may emphasize differences in the capacities of discontented populations to become mobilized. But whatever theoretical explanation is provided, there is, in most of this literature, a far greater concern with understanding changes in the magnitude of unrest than changes in its nature.

Lately, however, more attention has been paid to variations in character. Such an orientation can be found, in particular, among those historians and sociologists who, in the tradition eminently represented by Hobsbawm, Thompson, and Rudé,[1] have been studying qualitative changes in collective action in western Europe over the last three or four hundred years. The best recent work has come from Charles Tilly and his collaborators. They have been analyzing the effect on collective violence of major structural transformations, especially urbanization and industrialization. Tilly argues that, as a result of these structural transformations, the social organization of groups contending for power in western European countries has changed over the past several centuries, and the nature and targets of their goals have changed. There has been a decline in collective violence by small communal groups, either struggling for power with one another or trying to resist the centralization of power in national states, in favor of a transition to collective violence that erupts as broadly based interest groups, organized associationally, seek to influence the national state and make claims to rights not previously enjoyed. The contrasting prototypes are food riots in the eighteenth century, strikes and demonstrations by newly formed worker associations in the late nineteenth, and student demonstrations in the twentieth.[2]

[1] E. J. Hobsbawm, *Primitive Rebels* (Manchester, 1959); E. P. Thompson, *The Making of the English Working Class* (Harmondsworth, Middlesex, 1963/68); Rudé, *Crowd in History*; and Hobsbawm and Rudé, *Captain Swing* (London, 1969).

[2] See especially, Tilly, Tilly, and Tilly, *Rebellious Century*, pp. 17-23.

In more than one way, the present work constitutes an attempt to describe and analyze this fundamental transition in another western European country, and in the process, to make a small contribution to the much larger academic enterprise of explaining how collective action has changed in western Europe as a whole. Progress in answering this larger question will come only through the combined efforts of a great number of scholars researching different countries and periods. In this study of rural unrest in nineteenth-century Ireland, we have been able to consider only one geographical area, and even within it, only a portion of the longer transformation in which we are interested. Collective action had begun to change significantly in Ireland (as it did elsewhere in western Europe) several centuries before the point at which this study began. Nevertheless, a crucial part of the total transformation occurred in the nineteenth century. Essentially, three changes in the character of collective action can be discerned. Active collectivities became (1) less often local and more often national in their scope, (2) less often reactive and more often proactive in their aims, and (3) less often communal and more often associational in their organizational basis and structure. One can see these changes most clearly by comparing pre-famine violence with the other forms of collective action we have discussed.

LOCAL TO NATIONAL   Most of the oath-bound agrarian combinations and feuding factions of the 1820s and 1830s were comparatively localized, confined to one county or even part of one county. Even the broader regional combinations of the day, such as the Rockites and Terry Alts, did not embrace as much of the country as did, say, the Emancipation campaign or later the Land War. Furthermore, most of the local combinations and even many of the regional ones did not focus their efforts directly on the government that ruled over the entire country in the way that the Emancipation campaign or the Land War did. The United Irishmen, the Emancipation campaign, the Tithe War, the Repeal agitation, the Tenant League, to a lesser extent the farmers' clubs, but certainly the Home Rule movement and the Land War—these were what I have called *national* movements because they contended for power on the national stage rather than at local or regional levels. Collective action of this kind was to be found in Ireland both in the first and in the second half of the nineteenth century. Nevertheless, there was a difference between the two periods in the relative number and importance of local, as opposed to national, active collectivities. Oath-bound agrarian combinations and feuding factions had all but disappeared by the 1860s.

REACTIVE TO PROACTIVE   The transition from local to national collective action had a noticeable effect on the goals of active collectivities. In his celebrated work on popular disturbances, George Rudé made a distinction between "backward-looking" and "forward-looking" crowds; and Charles Tilly has reformulated this distinction into one between "proactive" and "reactive" collective action.[3] In Tilly's terms, proactive collective action involves an attempt by a group to lay claim to rights, privileges, or resources not previously enjoyed, while reactive collective action involves an attempt by a group to defend rights, privileges, or resources previously accorded to them. Tilly also identifies a third category called "competitive" collective action, which involves two or more groups engaged in routine struggles over conflicting goals without attempting to claim or usurp the recognized rights or privileges of others. According to Tilly, the competitive form predominated in western Europe during the fifteenth and sixteenth centuries, while the competitive and reactive forms were the most common during the seventeenth and eighteenth centuries. During the nineteenth and twentieth centuries, reactive collective action declined, while the proactive variety became predominant and new forms of competitive collective action began to emerge.[4]

At first glance, it would seem that rural unrest in Ireland did not undergo this transition, at least not during the nineteenth century. Faction fights and sectarian clashes in the early part of the century do indeed look much like competitive collective action, but the transition from reaction to proaction is not immediately evident. The Land League's major goals (fair rents and security of tenure) had been pursued by agrarian combinations before the Famine; these goals were also, both before and after the Famine, regarded by most tenants as customary rights to which they had a traditional claim. The obvious conclusion is that agrarian unrest in Ireland remained, for the most part, backward-looking throughout the nineteenth century. This would be consistent with what many historians and sociologists see as the general pattern: that rural

[3] Rudé, *Crowd in History*; and ibid., pp. 48-55.
[4] Tilly, *From Mobilization to Revolution*, p. 148.

populations have been most responsible for collective reaction, while urban populations have usually been responsible for collective proaction. Such a conclusion also accords with the common view that small commodity producers have been a dying class in the nineteenth and twentieth centuries and that they participate in social movements in a desperate attempt to resist the march of time.

It is certainly true that the small commodity producers who joined the Land League were trying to resist the destruction of the social group to which they belonged. Yet there is an important sense in which their struggle to do so was proactive. Pre-famine agrarian combinations almost invariably assumed that their goals were accepted as legitimate by most people in the society, at least most people of their own social rank. Indeed these combinations habitually claimed that they were defending the natural laws of the rural community. They took on functions that would normally be performed by the state; they promulgated laws in notices posted in public places ("by the order of Tommy Downshire"), and they sought to enforce these laws by threatening or punishing those who disobeyed them. Precisely the same kind of activity was also widespread during the Land War, but there was then something more. In a way that pre-famine secret societies only occasionally did, the Land League also focused attention on the state. Specifically, it tried to force the central government to enact laws recognizing the right of tenant farmers to fair rents and security of tenure. The Land League, in other words, insisted that the demands of tenant farmers be legalized and protected by the government itself. This is clearly proaction. And it contrasts sharply with the activities of pre-famine agrarian combinations, which could not hope to realize and did not generally make demands of this kind. Only the broad national and some of the regional movements before the Famine could seek to influence the state in such a manner; and, if we consider just agrarian movements, they did so almost exclusively with respect to tithes. The evolution of collective action laying claims on the central government in the name of tenant farmers began with pre-famine anti-tithe agitation. It developed slowly and sporadically in the aftermath of the Famine, and then moved to the center of the political stage with the Land War.

These observations may help to resolve a disagreement among historians over the origin of the aspiration in Ireland for peasant proprietorship. There is a difference of opinion as to whether this aspiration was created by the Land League.[5] Unfortunately, the argument can very easily become semantic, hinging on what one means by "aspiration." If one means a wish not only that rents be lowered, but that no rents be collected at all, then it is clear that such hopes (articulated or not) pre-dated the Land War by generations. If, however, one means that tenants demanded that the government make new laws transferring ownership from landlords to occupiers, then this aspiration did not pre-date the Land League. Indeed, I would argue that it did not become a high priority in tenant aspirations until *after* the Land League. The legal abolition of Irish landlordism could only be realistically demanded by tenants when they were represented by a national movement, and would only become a major aspiration for them as they came to realize that they had the national strength to put it within their reach. That conviction developed slowly in the latter part of the nineteenth century. The land movement of 1879-82 was a critical step in this development, but it did not create the conviction overnight.

COMMUNAL TO ASSOCIATIONAL   Most pre-famine violent combinations rested primarily on communal bonds, especially those of neighborhood and kinship. This was obviously true of factions and very small agrarian gangs, but even large secret societies relied heavily on communal relations for their solidarity. At the same time, many violent combinations, particularly the large clandestine societies, also had associational features. Leagues such as the Rightboys, the Caravats, the Rockites, and the Terry Alts united substantial numbers of persons spread over broad regions, but sharing common interests and goals.

In addition, of course, associational organization was to be found in pre-famine national movements, which were all organized on the basis of very specific objectives—the "emancipation" of Catholics, the abolition of tithes, or the repeal of the Act of Union. The principal bond that brought people together in each case was the pursuit of a common goal. In another sense, however, even these movements relied on a foundation that was communal. Let us again note that a common characteristic of pre-famine na-

[5] The respective positions in this debate can be found in Lee, *Modernisation of Irish Society*, p. 96 and in a review of Lee's book by James S. Donnelly, Jr. in *Irish Historical Studies*, 20, no. 78 (Sept. 1976).

tional movements was their religious connection. The parish priest was the foremost instrument of local organization for all three; and the goals of these movements were, in each instance, distinctly Catholic goals. This feature points to the fact that local religious communities provided these campaigns with their most effective organizational base. The church was both a communal and an associational structure: a large national association was built on top of a great number of communal parishes. The link between the two levels was provided by the Catholic clergy, who were thus in a unique position to utilize communal ties to mobilize support for national associational movements.

In the post-famine period there was still a mixture of communal and associational organization. We have already observed the effect of parish structure on the organization of local Land League branches. Nevertheless, associational organization was clearly predominant during the Land War, and indeed during the entire second half of the nineteenth century. In contrast to the pre-famine period, when local communal combinations were very real contenders for power, in the post-famine period nearly all important power struggles were waged by active collectivities tied together primarily by common interests and objectives rather than by communal bonds. In fact, the first national body organized in the name of tenant farmers did not appear in Ireland until the early 1850s with the Tenant League. The farmers' clubs maintained some continuity of associational organization on the part of tenant farmers during the 1860s and 1870s. And then the Land League emerged as the largest associational structure ever formed by Irish farmers. We can also perceive a contrast between the role of religion in the Land War and its role in the earlier national movements. Though the Land League drew its support primarily from Catholics, religion was incidental to its major goals. Moreover, the critical social relationship on which the movement depended was not provided by the religious structure: whereas the center of local political organization during the O'Connell movements had been the parish priest, the closest equivalent during the Land War was what C. M. Arensberg called the "shopkeeper-publican-politician."[6] This personage occupied a central position in the network of common interests which the land agitation rep-

[6] C. M. Arensberg, *The Irish Countryman: An Anthropological Study* (London, 1937), p. 179.

resented and provided an invaluable link that enabled these interests to be united in a national associational structure.

The critical functions performed by priests and townsmen in
national movements in nineteenth-century Ireland does not,
however, mean we should endorse the position, often taken by
students of peasant movements, that peasants lack the capacity to
organize themselves effectively. Although this notion is now usually accompanied by sympathy and even considerable respect for
rural people, it actually descends from a European tradition of
urban disdain and hostility toward peasants. Marx had little more
than contempt for them, and his prejudices have survived among
many present-day scholars, some of whom never seem to tire of
repeating after him that peasant societies are "formed by the simple addition of homologous magnitudes, much as potatoes in a
sack form a sack of potatoes," and that consequently "they cannot
represent themselves, they must be represented."[7] Only with the
assistance of more educated and politically experienced town and
city dwellers, so the argument goes, can the political potential of
peasants be realized. Peasants are incapable of effective political
action unless they are mobilized by means of an "exogenous organizing force."[8] Otherwise, their discontent is usually spent in
sporadic violence, or occasionally explodes in a spontaneous jac-
querie, which is unorganized, lacks clearly defined goals, and is
inevitably repressed.

By far the most serious mistake in this line of argument is the
conception of "primitive" rebellion as unorganized. In fact, traditional rural unrest is usually well organized. It can, however,
seem unorganized because the basis for its organization is normally communal rather than associational. Since the most powerful active collectivities in modern society are associational, we
have a tendency to assume that people in such collectivities are
"better" organized than people in communally based collectivities. Yet if by organization we mean the efficient coordination
of human efforts, then most pre-famine Irish crowds, factions, and
secret societies were as well if not better organized than associational combinations such as the Land League. The same claim

[7] Karl Marx, *The Eighteenth Brumaire of Louis Bonaparte* (New York, 1963), pp.
123-4. Let me confess that this is not the only time I have quoted this passage myself.
[8] Ferguson, "Rural/urban relations."

could be made for peasant revolts in the middle ages,[9] English crowds in the eighteenth century,[10] or Mexican village rebels in the twentieth.[11] What does appear true is that communal organization is invariably stronger when it remains local than when it extends over wide areas. But it is simply ethnocentric for us to dismiss communally based rural unrest as unorganized "turmoil."

On the other hand, the argument that peasants need the help of townsmen to mount effective political action cannot be discounted so easily. It is not so much wrong as in need of reformulation. As a rule, the case is made very carefully by defining "effective" political action in such a way as to exclude all those types of collective action in which peasants can and have engaged on their own. Once this is done, we are left with a proposition that is technically correct, but which misses the more general point and leaves the important questions unanswered. It is not the necessity of urban participation in peasant movements that should be emphasized, but rather the effect of such participation. The character of peasant movements in the nineteenth and twentieth centuries has varied significantly according to whether or not the peasants involved have formed alliances with urban groups, and if so, with which urban groups they were allied. Indeed, one of the lessons sociologists learned from Barrington Moore is that the nature of alliances formed by peasants can have an effect on the entire political and economic course that societies follow.[12] In any study of a peasant movement involving townsmen it is necessary to ask: What structural conditions brought these townsmen to ally themselves with peasants, and what consequences did their participation have? It may be true that peasants (and maybe townsmen for that matter) cannot support broad revolutionary movements on their own. This observation is, however, simply one corollary of the more general proposition that the coalitions into which people enter have a decisive impact on the character of their col-

[9] Rodney H. Hilton, "Peasant society, peasant movements and feudalism in medieval Europe" in Henry A. Landsberger (ed.), Rural Protest: Peasant Movements and Social Change (London, 1974) pp. 89-94; see also his Bond Men Made Free: Medieval Peasant Movements and the English Rising of 1381 (London, 1973).

[10] Thompson, "Moral economy of the English crowd."

[11] John Womack, Jr., Zapata and the Mexican Revolution (New York, 1968); and Paul Friedrich, Agrarian Revolt in a Mexican Village (Englewood Cliffs, N.J., 1970).

[12] Moore, Social Origins of Dictatorship and Democracy.

lective action. Urban involvement in a peasant movement may
make it radical, reformist, utopian, parochial, reactionary, or nationalistic, as well as impart a whole host of other characteristics.
The effect townsmen have depends on a variety of factors, among
which the most critical is usually their class position and ideology. In the case of the Irish Land War, the alliance between
farmers and townsmen had a noticeable impact on the organization and goals of the agitation; here I am referring particularly to
the prominent role played by town branches and to the absence of
anti-urban demands. Townsmen were also instrumental in forg-
ing the union of the agrarian with the nationalist movement.
Without the help of townsmen, there would still have been an
Irish Land War, but it would have been significantly different
from the movement that in fact emerged.

Challenging Collectivities

Collective action changes over time because the active collectivities contending for power change. Active collectivities, as the
term has been used in this book, are not the same as social groups.
Nevertheless, their composition is determined by the social
groups from which they are drawn; and these social groups are a
product of the integrative bonds and social cleavages in the prevailing social structure. A transformation in the social structure
will give rise to a shift in the boundaries of social groups, which
in turn will cause a change in the composition of collectivities
that are active in the society. Admittedly, it is possible for the social structure to remain stable for generations, but this is rare. In
most societies, there is enough structural change that the active
collectivities in one period of time are not identical to those in
earlier or later periods.

    If it is true that they evolve and succeed one another in this
manner, then in most periods one should find two types of active
collectivities: new and old. An active collectivity would be new in
the sense that its characteristics (goals, social composition, etc.)
differed significantly from active collectivities to be found in previous periods, though a new collectivity may well have evolved
from an earlier one. An active collectivity would be old in the
sense that it formed part of a continuous tradition of collective action by people having much the same social characteristics and
interests, and pursuing much the same goals. Usually, though not

always, old collectivities enjoy a considerable measure of power that they seek to maintain, while new collectivities have relatively less power and are struggling to acquire more. When such is the case, the old collectivity may be termed "established" and the new collectivity "challenging."[13]

In this study we have directed our attention mostly at challenging collectivities. Some pre-famine violent combinations could, however, constitute exceptions, or at least marginal cases. To be certain about it, we would have to select particular combinations and trace their individual histories. In one sense we would probably decide to classify nearly all of them as challenging, since they almost all represented challenges to the established order. But in another sense some could be considered as established, since on closer examination it would be discovered that they had long histories, were well entrenched in their localities, and possessed considerable power that they were actively trying to keep. Others would be found who were newer and constituted challenges both to more established combinations and to established elites.

There is no need to hesitate in classifying movements such as the Emancipation campaign, the anti-tithe agitation, and the Repeal movement as challenging collectivities. At the most general level, one could argue that there was essentially one challenging collectivity that emerged in nineteenth-century Ireland. The defining feature of this collectivity was that it drew its members primarily from the Catholic population and sought to advance the interests of this social group. Whatever aspect of nineteenth-century Irish history one is studying, the most outstanding political development in that century was the growing collective organization of Catholics in opposition to the Protestant establishment, and the increasing collective resistance by Protestants to this Catholic challenge.

Nevertheless, the characteristics of the collectivities that took part in each of the Catholic movements we have discussed, despite this common element, were by no means identical. The strength of the Emancipation campaign and the Repeal movement came primarily from the Catholic urban middle class. In both, members of this social group were over-represented in the challenging collectivity relative to their numbers in the society; and in both, they provided the bulk of the leadership. Although they

[13] See Tilly, "Revolutions and collective violence," p. 502; and Gamson, *Strategy of Social Protest*.

succeeded (with the help of the Catholic clergy) in mobilizing mass rural support, control over these movements remained largely in their hands, a fact reflected in the goals that these movements pursued. In the Tithe War, on the other hand, we see the beginnings of the evolution of the challenging collectivity that has been our main concern. The anti-tithe movement shared some important characteristics with the Emancipation campaign and the Repeal movement, but in this case tenant farmers, not the Catholic urban middle class, constituted the core of the active collectivity and their interests were paramount. The Tithe War drew support from virtually all classes of tenant farmers. Relative to their numbers in the society, however, large farmers may have been the most over-represented. The agitation was strongest in Leinster and east Munster, which were parts of Catholic Ireland where the rural population was comparatively well integrated into urban society and where large farmers were comparatively numerous. The Tenant League of the early 1850s and the farmers' clubs of the 1870s were strongest in roughly the same regions and were also supported disproportionately by large farmers.

Challenging collectivities do not mobilize spontaneously, and one of the tasks I set myself in this study was to describe the development of the challenging collectivity that fought in the Land War. There was considerable continuity between the Land League and earlier tenant-right agitation, particularly as represented by the farmers' clubs. Their goals were similar, and the first signs of protest in the face of the depression of the late 1870s came from these farmers' clubs. Nevertheless, what made the Land War a turning point in Irish history were the differences between the challenging collectivity that emerged in 1879-80 and any previous national movements in Ireland. The most outstanding difference was the extent to which poor landholders in the west became mobilized. The unprecedented feature of the Land War was the formation of a national-associational active collectivity composed of tenant farmers, and drawing more support from those in the west than from those in Leinster and east Munster.

The formation of this new active collectivity was the result of structural changes that occurred in Irish society during and after the Great Famine. In somewhat simplified terms, we can say that these changes entailed an increase in the level of integration within the tenant population, including a decline in class and

communal cleavages that had formerly divided agricultural tenants. This came about largely as a consequence of a fall in the
number of laborers. But it also resulted from greater national integration of poor tenants, and especially the greater integration of
poor tenants into the commercial livestock economy.

Much has been written about the spread of the market economy
into peasant societies. A common theme in recent studies is that
rural communities experience severe dislocation with the advance of agricultural commercialization, which exposes peasants
to the vagaries of market prices and undermines the security provided by traditional institutions, including traditional bonds between peasants and their masters. Agricultural commercialization
also forces a shift in resources from the service of local to urban
needs. More of the land, for instance, that was formerly used to
ensure that all members of local communal groups were provided
with a means of livelihood becomes devoted to generating a
surplus for an urban market. And within the rural society itself,
two distinguishable groups evolve: those whose interests lie in
maintaining resources for local needs; and those whose interests
lie in extracting as large a surplus as possible and exchanging it
with an outside market.[14]

Neither the first nor the second half of the nineteenth century
marked the beginning of agricultural commercialization in Ireland. Irish agriculture was already highly commercialized by the
end of the eighteenth century. What did happen in the early nineteenth century was that the segment of the society that was less
actively engaged in trade with the urban market expanded in size
and became much larger than the segment that was directly involved in commercialized agriculture. The source of this important change was population growth, which increased the number
of small farmers and laborers, and reduced proportionately the
number of large farmers. It was in the interest of the former to
maintain resources for local needs (by obtaining higher wages and
by preserving land for subsistence agriculture), while it was in the

[14] For instance, see Wolf, *Peasant Wars of the Twentieth Century*; Charles Tilly,
"Do communities act?" in *Sociological Inquiry*, 43, nos. 3-4 (1973); Daniel Chirot
and Charles Ragin, "The market, tradition and peasant rebellion: the case of
Romania in 1907" in *American Sociological Review*, 40, no. 4 (Aug. 1975);
Mouzelis, "Greek and Bulgarian peasants: aspects of their sociopolitical situation
during the interwar period"; Ferguson, "Rural/urban relations," and Scott, *Moral
Economy of the Peasant*.

interest of the latter to direct resources toward serving the demands of the outside market (by keeping wages low and by utilizing as much land as possible for commercial production). Hence, the separation that existed between large and small landholders in pre-famine Ireland coincided with differences among the rural population in the extent of national and urban economic integration. It is thus not surprising that collective efforts by small farmers and laborers to defend their interests against large farmers were frequently hard to distinguish from collective action based on local communal groups and serving the interests of such groups. It is also not surprising that collective action at the national level drew its support disproportionately from large farmers. In the second half of the nineteenth century, however, the division of the agrarian population into these two groups diminished as the segment of the society that was directly involved in commercialized agriculture became numerically the largest. The majority of landholders were now farmers, who—both large and small—profited from the export of agricultural produce to the urban society and abroad. To be sure, class differences among tenant farmers still remained. But this very fact is what made the integration of farmers into a common group so consequential. One of the most significant features of the post-famine farmer social group was that it included both large farmers who were economically secure and small farmers who were not.

In an effort to explain the participation of small farmers in the Land War, it is tempting to cite economic changes in their living standards resulting from greater involvement in commercialized agriculture. One of two arguments could be made. We could take a conventional relative deprivation position and claim that post-famine commercialization raised standards of living and thus expectations, which were then disappointed by the depression that began in the late 1870s—a pattern that conforms precisely to Davies' J-curve. Alternatively, we could argue that the Land War was a consequence of greater economic insecurity resulting from commercialized agriculture; though standards of living may have improved, these standards were not as secure as those of less commercialized pre-famine peasants.

As I suggested in Chapter Seven, the problem with the relative deprivation argument is that it overlooks the bitter and repeated disappointments experienced by farmers and laborers in the decades preceding the Famine. These disappointments were no less infuriating because deprivation was often absolute and not just relative. The economic crisis that came after the Napoleonic Wars resembled a J-curve in many ways, except that the decline which followed the wartime prosperity was far worse than the kind of situation the J-curve is normally meant to describe. We would expect it to generate more discontent and to arouse greater moral indignation than the depression of the late 1870s. And the magnitude of pre-famine violence affords ample evidence that it did.

Much the same response can be given to the suggestion that post-famine agricultural commercialization increased the economic insecurity of small farmers. This sort of argument is probably the most widely respected among students of peasant movements.[15] Yet it seems to me that the whole idea underestimates the insecurities of peasant life in less commercialized systems. I do not deny that agricultural commercialization has increased hardship or made life more precarious in some societies, but I do not believe that it has done so often enough and consistently enough to explain the nature of rural unrest among commercializing peasantries. In any event, commercial insecurities contribute very little toward explaining the Irish Land War. That the post-famine livestock economy did create new kinds of insecurities for Irish small farmers was certainly true and was one of the contentions of Chapter Seven in this book. But it would be absurd to carry the argument to the point of insisting that post-famine small farmers were more vulnerable to economic disaster than pre-famine peasants. The risks that the pre-famine cottier faced when he went searching for a piece of conacre ground and when he planted his potato crop were far greater than the risks a post-famine small farmer took when he bought and sold cattle. Whether or not standards of living rose after the Famine—and I think they clearly did—it is absolutely certain that post-famine small farmers were no worse off, and their insecurities no greater, than the pre-famine rural poor.

What agricultural commercialization did to living standards after the Famine had far less long-run impact on Irish society than what it did to the shape of social groups. The most important development of the post-famine period was not that anyone became more or less economically secure, nor that anyone's ex-

[15] The most influential statement of this view is in Wolf, *Peasant Wars of the Twentieth Century*. See also Chirot and Ragin, "Market, tradition and peasant rebellion" and Scott, *Moral Economy of the Peasant*.

pectations were raised or lowered, but that a segment of the rural population that had been and remained comparatively insecure became integrated, at the national level, into the same social group as a more secure segment. In this way the social basis was laid for an active collectivity that drew its support from both. The insecure segment was vulnerable less because it was involved in commercialized agriculture than because it remained dangerously dependent on subsistence tillage. In the late 1870s it was not the commercial livestock market that failed small farmers so much as the potato.

The Mobilization of Challenging Collectivities

During the years 1879 and 1880 the active collectivity in which we are interested expanded and assumed a new form. In 1878 collective action seeking to advance the interests of tenant farmers consisted of little more than two or three dozen farmers' clubs, which had no formal connection and were only loosely affiliated with the languishing Home Rule movement. Within two years collective action on behalf of tenant farmers was being undertaken by a large and extensive organization with hundreds of branches and several hundred thousand supporters.

Rapid mobilization of this kind constitutes a dramatic process which, in varying degrees, is characteristic of all social movements. In the space that remains, I want to suggest that what makes this process so special is the effect that it has on established social institutions and on the distribution of power.

SOCIAL INSTITUTIONS AND CHALLENGING COLLECTIVITIES Over the past twenty years sociologists have done a volte-face in their thinking about the relationship between social institutions and social unrest. In the 1950s and early 1960s, when collective-behavior theory was king, the predominant view was that the two were antithetical phenomena. Social unrest consisted of a rejection and departure from social institutions; it also occurred as a result of the breakdown of prevailing institutions and their consequent failure to restrain anti-institutional behavior. This conception was, as I suggested in the opening chapter, stated most explicitly in mass-society theory, but it underlay most writings in those years. More recently, it has come under steady criticism, especially from those who adopt a "mobilization" approach and argue that alienation or disaffection is not sufficient to generate protest movements. Disaffected people must also be collectively organized into action and this process, a mobilization theorist would argue, cannot take place in a vacuum. It requires an organizational base, which is typically provided by existing social institutions.[16]

The theory of mass society and similar approaches did indeed overlook the fact that social institutions can have mobilizing as well as restraining effects. Writers in the 1950s and early 1960s commonly forgot that institutions themselves often come into conflict with one another. They consequently failed to recognize the implications of the almost obvious fact that social integration restrains opposition not to all institutions, but only to the particular institutions into which a person is integrated. The integration of Irish people into the Catholic church, for example, restrained opposition to this particular institution, but did not restrain opposition to British rule. On the contrary, the attachment of the Irish to their church helped to mobilize resistance to British rule. Social integration may impede collective action with one set of goals, while mobilizing collective action toward another set. On this point the critics of mass-society theory are absolutely right.

Yet the underlying argument of mass-society theory is not altogether mistaken. If people are well integrated into institutions that support the established order, then there is less probability of challenges to that order; and the danger that people will rebel against established institutions does increase if their integration into these institutions weakens. Not unique to mass-society theory, this principle is a cherished belief in a tradition of sociology that goes back to Emile Durkheim and is best known in modern sociology in the work of Talcott Parsons and Neil Smelser. If reduced to its fundamentals and freed of its usual social psychological misconceptions, it is valid. Rebellion against established institutions results from social disintegration; in fact, it can only occur through social disintegration. Here, of course, social disintegration does not refer to psychological maladjustment or personal disorganization, but to a decline in bonds that tie people to social institutions. The expansion of a challenging collectivity is possible only if the hold of established institutions over people has been weakened so that they can be disengaged *from* collective

---

[16] See Chapter One above.

action in which they have participated as members of established institutions and mobilized *into* opposing collective action.

Mobilization theorists all too often talk as though people who are not engaged in protest are involved in no collective action at all. This is plainly untrue. People are always participating in collective action of some kind. Thus mobilization is a process not of organizing collective action where none existed before, but rather of pulling people away from one kind of collective action and convincing them to engage in another. The expansion of the land-reforming collectivity in Ireland in the years 1879-80 necessitated drawing people from active collectivities that were under the control of established elites and inducing them to behave in ways that promoted diametrically opposed interests. This process was facilitated by serious structural weaknesses which had long existed in the Irish landlord-tenant relationship and which had already put limits on the level of integration of tenants into the land system. Nonetheless, tenants were sufficiently bound to this system (through both contractual and non-contractual privileges) that they did not fall easily and smoothly into the challenging collectivity, and a great many of them did not fall into line at all. Tenants who year after year had paid their rents, and perhaps voted for candidates of their landlord's choice, needed to be persuaded to withhold their normal rents and to vote for anti-landlord candidates. Tenants who thought nothing wrong with taking the land of an evicted occupier had to be convinced not to do so. Great numbers of tenants who had enjoyed reasonably harmonious relationships with their landlords had to be persuaded to attend anti-landlord demonstrations, to join the Land League, and to support boycotts of landlords, land agents, and landgrabbers. In place of the laws and regulations of the land system, they had to be convinced to obey the laws of the Land League. And in place of the authority of their landlords and even of the state, they had to be persuaded to obey a rival authority.

All this comes very close to what is meant by "collective behavior." People were being persuaded to reject some aspect of the prevailing institutional structure. To be sure, their behavior was also built around existing beliefs and institutions; the basic ideology of the Land League had been solidly fixed in the peasant culture for generations. But these traditional beliefs were in opposition to those of the established order. And the process by which people began to act on such beliefs and to defy established institutions necessarily involved a sharp alteration in their behavior. There was inevitably a lack of consensus on what the new rules should be, on whose authority should be accepted, and on what the goals of the active collectivity were. This does not deny that some agreement prevailed within the anti-landlord collectivity concerning its rules and goals, as well as fairly general acknowledgment that the new authority lay in the Land League—but there was no unanimity on any of these points. Here we have the very characteristics of social movements emphasized by collective-behavior theory. Despite its errors and omissions, this theoretical perspective does identify an important kind of collective action, for which we do need theoretical concepts. The expansion of a challenging collectivity of necessity forces people to reject social institutions to which they have until recently conformed.

POWER AND CHALLENGING COLLECTIVITIES   There is a circular relationship between power and collective action. Power begets collective action and collective action begets power. To take a simple illustration, the powers possessed by governments make possible such organized collectivities as standing armies and police forces, which in turn are a source of power to governments. Similarly, the legal and political powers that an Irish landlord held over his tenants enabled him to organize them into collective action, which was in turn a source of economic and political power to him. The most blatant example was the way in which landlords controlled the collective votes of their tenants in order to acquire power for themselves in both national and local government. But in similar, if less obvious, ways other collective activities by tenants (paying rents, improving the value of the estate) also served to enhance a landlord's wealth and social position.

It follows that whenever we see people shifting from conventional behavior to some alternative collective action, we are witnessing a transfer of power. Conceptually we can recognize two processes at work, though empirically they may be indistinguishable. In the first, the established power controlling the conventional collective action is attacked, indeed must be attacked, in order to undermine the integrative bonds that have coerced or persuaded people to engage in the conventional behavior. Thus, much of what the Land League and its supporters did in the years 1879-82 consisted of attempts to weaken established power by rewarding tenants who disobeyed their landlord and punishing those who remained loyal. In the second process, the challenging collective action becomes more and more a source of power itself. As people switch sides and join the challenging collectivity, its power increases, and this greater power can be used to induce still more people to change allegiance, as well as to convince those who have already switched to remain on the challenging side. The power acquired by the Land League movement through its own expansion enabled it to persuade even greater numbers of people that they should join the League, or to coerce them into doing so through boycotts, violent assaults, and intimidation.

In concrete terms one can identify without great difficulty *from whom* power is being transferred in a struggle of this kind, be- cause established power is usually well institutionalized in norms and regulations, often in the laws of the state. *To whom* power is being transferred is rarely so clear because the challenging collec- tivity is not well institutionalized. It is usually difficult to be pre- cise about who within the challenging collectivity receives and exercises the power. During the expansion of a challenging col- lectivity there is invariably, as I have argued, a lack of consensus about whose authority should be obeyed; and it is common to find struggles taking place within the challenging collectivity for con- trol over the new collective action.

Power struggles were waged at all levels among members of the challenging collectivity during the Land War. Locally, these bat- tles were most often between the Land League branch and those who did not accept its authority, or between different factions within the League for control of the local branch. On the whole, however, there was clearly a transfer of power to those individ- uals who assumed a leading role in the League, especially those who held executive positions within branches or were elected to the local poor-law boards. Many of these people were shopkeep- ers, publicans, or large farmers; and it was no accident that these social groups came to dominate Irish county politics in later years. At the center of the organization, the most visible struggle within the challenging collectivity was between the con- stitutionalists, led by Parnell, and the more radical (or Fenian) fac- tion led by Davitt. Before 1882 the two sides were reasonably well matched. The Parnell faction was politically more powerful, but the Davitt faction had more direct control over the Land League's organization. After the agitation had subsided, however, the situation changed dramatically. At the national level the new power generated during the Land War became institutionalized in the National League and in the Irish parliamentary party, both of which were controlled by Parnell and his associates.

In any case, whoever controlled it, after 1882 the challenging collectivity became a recognized part of the existing political system; within this system it exercised a substantial claim to influence. The established landed interest remained a powerful force in Irish politics, but it was now compelled to defend its position against a new political collectivity. Theoretically, the landed interest could have continued for years to wage a constant battle against inroads by its new rival. As we know, it did not. Both contenders had sufficient strength in the polity that a legislative measure was enacted to satisfy their mutual interests. But this solution entailed the destruction of landlords as a social group.

The ultimate consequences of the Land War, however, went even further than the destruction of Irish landlordism. Two outstanding features of the challenging collectivity that emerged in the years 1879-80 had monumental long-run significance. First, it was a national collectivity, but the nation it comprised was not coterminous with the state that ruled over this nation. Whenever I have referred in this book to national collective action, I have obviously meant collective action that embraced not the entire United Kingdom, but Ireland, and more precisely, Catholic Ireland. What emerged during the Land War was, therefore, an active collectivity that was national and sought to influence the central government, but which did not represent all parts of the population ruled by that government. The nation from which it drew its support and which it could claim to represent was only a segment within that larger population.

Second, one of the goals of this challenging collectivity was to transform the existing political system. Not only did most of those who belonged to the challenging collectivity accept this goal, but the politicians who directed the Land League were committed above all to this objective and only undertook to lead the land agitation in order to revitalize the nationalist movement. For some, like Davitt, the means occasionally became an end in itself; at times land reform could be given the same status as national independence. Yet for many others self-government always remained the foremost objective. Parnell frankly admitted in October 1880 that he "would never have taken off [his] coat" over the land question if he had not thought that it would lay the foundations for the legislative independence of Ireland.[17] Subsequently, during the routinization of the Land League movement, the goals of the challenging collectivity shifted and independence was given priority over land reform. In the post-Land League period, therefore, two giant struggles were actually being fought simultaneously in Ireland: an agrarian-reform collectivity waged a battle against the landed interest for power *within* the existing political system; and almost the same collectivity sought to destroy the existing political system and establish a new system in its place.

Beyond its significance for Irish landlordism, the larger importance of the Land War lay in the rise of an active collectivity that would fight for and in itself embody the modern Irish nation-state. Though eventually dethroned, Parnell ruled during the 1880s as "uncrowned king" over this political collectivity. Indeed, one historian argues that in the brief period from 1878 to 1886 Parnell fashioned a *de facto* state in Ireland, more real than the official British state.[18] This places the demise of the old order too early, but it is certainly true that after the 1880s the great political question remaining was not only whether Ireland would attain self-government, but also what form independence would take if and when it came, and who would hold power in the new state. The active collectivity that had emerged under Parnell constituted an enormous source of power over which Irish nationalist politicians fought for more than thirty years.

[17] Lyons, *Charles Stewart Parnell*, p. 138.
[18] Larkin, *Catholic Church and Creation of Modern Irish State*.

Appendix A

Supplementary Notes

PAGE 108, TABLE 2

The medians in Table 2 have been computed from grouped data. For 1841 they have been adjusted on the basis of P. M. Austin Bourke, "The agricultural statistics of the 1841 census of Ireland: a critical review" in *Economic History Review*, second series, 18 (Aug. 1965). This correction entails doubling the medians that one obtains from the figures in the 1841 census. These figures were given for holdings of over one acre, but since we have doubled the medians we should assume that we are talking about holdings of over two acres for that year. We can compare the median size of holdings computed in this manner with the median computed from the poor-law return for 1844, which was 12.1 acres for holdings of over two acres and 10.8 for those of over one acre. For 1844 the data are available for each poor-law union and for the entire country, but not for each province.

PAGE 111, NOTE 6

For all of the computations on number of livestock I have used 1847 as the base year. This was, of course, during the Famine, and the reader could object that the size of herds would be unusually low at that time. We should not too readily assume, however, that the Famine had this effect. Taking 1847 as the starting point, the number of sheep declined from one year to the next during the Famine, but the number of cattle actually increased. Moreover, one encounters even more serious problems if one tries to use some other year as the base. The only statistics available for before the Famine are for 1841; and they are known to underestimate the number of livestock (or at least the number of cattle), and so would also inflate the rate of increase. See Bourke, "Agricultural statistics of the 1841 census." If we nevertheless compute the increase using 1841 as the base year, we obtain the following: the national rate of growth was 121 percent for cattle and 90 percent for sheep; the rate in Connaught was 120 percent for cattle and 125 percent for sheep. These data, then, suggest that the increase for cattle in Connaught was the same as the national rate and that for sheep it exceeded the national rate. On the other hand, if one were to take some year in the early 1850s as the base, one would obtain somewhat different results. This procedure would give higher rates for the country as a whole than for Connaught. To use a year after the Famine as the base, however, ignores the impact of the Famine itself in promoting the shift to pasture, particularly in the west. Furthermore, whatever year is used as the base, one still finds that the rate of increase of the herds was nearly as great, if not greater, in the west as in the east. This is sufficient to confirm my argument that small farmers in the west were not left out of the post-famine adjustment in Irish agriculture.

PAGE 114, TABLE 4

The figures in this table were obtained by combining occupational returns with data on size of holdings. In order to do this, I had to make several problematic assumptions. First, it was necessary to assume that the largest landholdings were occupied by farmers. And, in order to avoid including the wives, daughters, and young sons of landholders among landless laborers, I was forced to restrict the analysis to the adult male labor force, which meant that I assumed that all landholders were adult males. Though the exceptions would be few, we can be certain that there were at least some cases that did not conform to these assumptions. Furthermore, serious methodological problems were encountered in trying to determine the number of laborers and adult farmers' sons. The number of farmers' sons in 1881 is given in the census, but, as the reader already knows, for 1841 it was necessary to estimate the number of adult farmers' sons since many were included with laborers in the census. See above Chapter Two, note 44 for an explanation of how I estimated the number of farmers' sons and laborers in 1841. For 1881 I had difficulty calculating the number of laborers for a different reason: many agricultural workers found their way into a separate census category called "general laborers." I assumed that two-thirds of these were farm workers and included them in Table 4 among laborers (and among the total number of adult males in the agricultural labor force). Yet it has to be admitted that, as a result, I may be slightly overestimating the number of laborers in 1881. For both years, to estimate the number of laborer-landholders, I simply subtracted the number of adult-male farmers from the total number of landholders (including those with less than one acre); and to get the number of landless laborers I subtracted these laborer-landholders from the total estimated number of laborers. Hence, what the overestimation of laborers in 1881 distorts is the estimate of landless laborers. I would like to thank Joseph Lee for advice in the computation of these estimates.

PAGE 133, TABLE 8

This table is for brides only. A comparable table for grooms was constructed, but is not presented because it is more difficult to interpret. In Ireland, as elsewhere, marriages normally take place near the residence of the bride. We must therefore assume that almost all grooms who married someone living outside the area covered by the Roscommon registrar were lost from the sample; by the same token, included in the sample were grooms who were not from Roscommon. The table for grooms obtains results similar to those in Table 8, and so it would seem that these problems do not seriously affect occupational differences. Nevertheless, it is safer to draw conclusions from the marriage patterns of brides, for whom no similar problems exist, since they normally wed near home regardless of where their partner lived.

Another difficulty with these data has to do with arranged matches. It could be argued that the reason traders' daughters were more out-marrying than farmers' daughters is that farmers arranged the marriages of their daughters more often than did traders. Two responses can be made to this kind of reasoning. First, we do not know and have no basis for assuming that farmers arranged marriages more often than traders. Second, there is no good reason to believe that arranged marriages were more likely to be within the poor-law union than free marriages; in fact, if such were the case, it would then be very difficult to explain why farmers' daughters out-married more frequently than daughters of laborers and artisans, since we can be fairly certain that matches were more often arranged for the former than for the latter.

Furthermore, there is one feature of the data used here that undoubtedly exaggerates the out-marrying rate of farmers' daughters as compared with traders' daughters. The major towns in each of our unions (Roscommon, Glenamaddy, and Mount Bellew) were located approximately in the centers of their respective unions. Thus in order to qualify as out-marrying, most traders' daughters had to wed someone who lived further away than was the case for most farmers' daughters. Indeed, it is quite possible that at least

some farmers' daughters who were counted as out-marrying took
a husband who lived only a short distance away on the other side
of the union line.

PAGE 164, NOTE 29

G. F. Stewart had been land agent to the third Earl of Leitrim
and continued to manage the properties in County Leitrim after
the third Earl had been murdered. Stewart experienced considerable difficulty collecting rents and protecting property rights on
the estate in the latter part of 1878. Lord Leitrim had bequeathed
his land to his second cousin, Colonel H. T. Clements, rather than
to his nephew who inherited the peerage. There thus ensued a period of ambiguity about the ownership of the land, and some tenants on the estate, claiming that the new owner did not have clear
title, began to cut turf and trees. Stewart was helpless to prevent
this cutting for most of 1878, but his right to represent the ultimate owner was sufficiently established by the spring of 1879 that
he was able to reassert his control. During most of 1878-9 he was
acting as agent for the fourth Earl of Leitrim as well as Colonel
Clements, so letters from Stewart to both men can be found in his
letter book.

PAGE 298, TABLE 19

"Three Fs" refers to resolutions that simultaneously demanded
fair rents, fixity of tenure, and free sale. "Laborers' interests" includes all resolutions making any reference to improving the welfare of laborers, as well as resolutions containing demands that
would be in the interest of laborers (such as public works), even if
laborers were not explicitly mentioned. "Support for the movement" refers to resolutions endorsing the agitation or calling on
people to join it or to form branches of the League. "Pressure on
politicians" consists of resolutions expressing support for politicians sympathetic to the movement, or alternatively, denouncing politicians who opposed it. "Opposition to government
measures" consists primarily of resolutions denouncing land bills
or repressive measures adopted by the government to combat the
agitation.

Occasionally, a resolution covered more than one of the above
categories, and in such cases it was coded according to whichever
sentiment was expressed first. Any resolution expressing the
same sentiment as a preceding resolution adopted at the same
meeting was placed in the "other" category. The total of 301 reso-

lutions does not represent all resolutions passed at the 153 meetings, since some resolutions were not transcribed in the *Nation's* reports. The sample of meetings from which these resolutions were taken is the same sample referred to earlier in Chapter Eight in connection with the clergy.

PAGE 325, NOTE 76

Two examples will illustrate the kind of outrages to which I am referring. In April 1879 a tenant who had recently come into possession of a holding on the Mohill estate of Lord Leitrim received a threatening letter, and the house on this holding was set on fire; the outrage was apparently committed not by the former occupant, but by the adjoining tenant, who had been trying to obtain the farm. N.L.I., Leitrim papers: Letter book of G. F. Stewart: Stewart to James Stewart, 13 April 1879. In August 1880 property belonging to a tenant who had taken a farm in County Galway was damaged not because anyone wanted the farm returned to its previous occupant, but because the new tenant lived in a different townland and people in the neighborhood believed that they were entitled to it. *Return . . . of all agrarian outrages . . . between the 1st day of February 1880 and the 31st day of October 1880*, p. 102.

Appendix B

Occupational Classification Scheme

1. farmers
2. farmers' sons (includes farmers' grandsons, brothers, nephews)
3. herdsmen
4. farm servants
5. unspecified or general laborers (includes cottiers)
6. other agricultural: agriculturalist, bailiff, cattle dealer, cattle jobber, dairyman, dealer in pigs, fisherman, gamekeeper, gardener, horsedealer, nurseryman, plowman, sheepjobber, steward
7. traders and business proprietors: auctioneer, baker, bookseller, builder, butcher, car owner, commercial traveler, contractor, distillery manager, draper, eggdealer, general dealer, grocer, hardware dealer, hatter, hawker, manufacturer, merchant, miller, pawnbroker, peddler, printer, provision dealer, shopkeeper, stationer, trader, vintner
8. shopworkers and clerks: builder's clerk, clerk, draper's assistant, journeyman baker, printing compositor, railway clerk, shop assistant, shopboy, store clerk, store porter, telegraph clerk
9. innkeepers and publicans (includes hotel keepers)
10. artisans and non-farm laborers: asphalter, barber, blacksmith, boilermaker, bookmaker, bootmaker, cabinet maker, car driver, carpenter, carrier, coachbuilder, coachman, cooper, cork cutter, cotton spinner, dyer, electroplater, engine fitter, farrier, file maker, flax scutcher, foreman, gunsmith, hackler, harness maker, iron molder, ivory turner, mason, nailer, night watchman, organ builder, painter, plasterer, plumber, pump borer, rope maker, saddler, sawyer, shipwright, shoemaker, slater, smith, stone cutter, tailor, tinsmith, turner, watchmaker, weaver
11. other commercial and industrial

12. clergy
13. teachers
14. newspaper editors and correspondents (includes newspaper reporters, publishers, proprietors, and managers)
15. general professional: solicitor, barrister, medical doctor, lawyer, engineer
16. subordinate professional service: law clerk, sexton
17. civil service and defense: postmaster, postmessenger, constabulary, process server, surveyor
18. domestics: servant, waiter, porter, caretaker
19. gentry

Appendix C

Sources for Variables Used in Table 9 and Table 15

VARIABLES USED IN THE FACTOR ANALYSIS

1. Ratio of pasture to land under crops in 1881: *Census of Ireland, 1881*: pt. ii, *General Report* [C 3365], H.C. 1882, lxxvi.

2. Median size of landed properties in 1876: *Summary of the returns of owners of land in Ireland, showing, with respect to each county, the number of owners below an acre, and in classes up to 100,000 acres and upwards, with the aggregate acreage and valuation of each class*, H.C., 1876 (422), lxxx.

3. Agricultural valuation per acre in 1881: same as Variable 1.

4. Percentage of tillage land under potatoes: ibid.

5. Average class of houses in 1881:
Census of Ireland, 1881: pt. i . . . vol. i, *Province of Leinster* [C 3042], H.C. 1881, xcvii.
Census of Ireland, 1881: pt. i . . . vol. ii, *Province of Munster* [C 3148], H.C. 1882, lxxvii.
Census of Ireland, 1881: pt. i . . . vol. iii, *Province of Ulster* [C 3204], H.C. 1882, lxxviii.
Census of Ireland, 1881: pt. i . . . vol. iv, *Province of Connaught* [C 3268], H.C. 1882, lxxix.

6. Ratio of number of sheep to number of cattle in 1881: same as Variable 1.

7. Percentage of tenants who had leases in 1870: *Return showing the total number of agricultural holdings and the tenure by which they are held by the occupiers*, pp. 16-17 [C 32], H.C. 1870, lvi.

8. Percentage of land owned by absentee proprietors in 1870: *Return for 1870 of number of landed proprietors in each county*, H.C. 1872 (167), xlvii.

9. Median size of holdings over one acre in 1881: same as Variable 1.

10. Number of migratory laborers per capita in 1881: *Report and tables relating to migratory agricultural Irish labourers for 1881* [C 3150], H.C. 1882, lxxiv.

11. Percentage of occupiers who held in fee in 1870: same as Variable 7.

12. Ratio of number of farmers and farmers' sons to number of laborers in 1881: same as Variable 5.

13. Agricultural valuation per holding: same as Variable 1.

THE AGITATION SCALE

14. Number of land meetings per capita in 1879-80: *Return showing for each month of the years 1879 and 1880 the number of Land League meetings held and agrarian crimes reported to the Inspector General of the Royal Irish Constabulary in each county throughout Ireland*, H.C. 1881 (5), lxxvii.

15. Number of agrarian crimes per capita in 1879-80: ibid.

16. Number of arrests under the Protection of Person and Property Act of 1881: S.P.O., Irish crimes records, 1881.

OTHER VARIABLES

17. Percentage of holdings in arrears in 1882-3: *Number of holdings comprised in applications under the Arrears of Rent (Ireland) Act, 1882* [C 3904], H.C. 1884, lxiv.

18. Number of evictions per holding in 1878-80: *Return by provinces and counties (compiled from returns made to the Inspector General, Royal Irish Constabulary), of cases of evictions which have come to the knowledge of the Constabulary in each of the years from 1849 to 1880 (inclusive)*, H.C. 1881 (185), lxxvii.

19. Percentage of persons who were Roman Catholic in 1881: same as Variable 1.

20. Percentage of persons five years of age or older who were literate in 1881: same as Variable 5.

21. Number of railway stations in 1869: W. W. Browning (ed.), *Handbook of Railway Distances Compiled by the Direction of the Secretary of State for War* (London, 1869).

22. Number of newspapers per capita in 1879: Thom's, 1879, p. 1022.

Bibliography

A. Contemporary Sources

I. MANUSCRIPT MATERIAL

Cashel Diocesan Archives
   Diary of Rev. James O'Carroll, C.C., Clonoulty, County Tipperary, Jan. 1862-July 1864.
   Slattery papers: Michael Slattery to Daniel O'Connell, 8 April 1842.
Custom House
   Registry of births, deaths, and marriages.
Irish Folklore Commission
   MSS 782 and 1174.
Land Valuation Office
   Land valuation records.
McGill University Library
   Hardinge papers: The correspondence of Sir Henry Hardinge, 1st Viscount Hardinge of Lahore, 1785-1856.
National Library of Ireland
   Crofton papers: Rentals of the Mote estate, County Roscommon, 1852-81 (MSS 5632-3, 4074-94).
   Deane papers: Rentals of the Deane estate, County Kildare, 1876-81 (MS 14282).
   Land League papers:
   Branch returns
   Rules for the guidance of branches (MS 9219).
   Minute book of Rathvilly branch of the Irish National League (MS 842).
   Leitrim papers:
   Rentals of the Mohill estate, 1809-29 (MSS 12792-804).
   Second Earl of Leitrim's directions, 1839 (MS 3829).
   Rentals of the Mohill, Manor Hamilton, and Newtown Gore estates, 1845-80 (Packing Crate 156).
   Letter book of G. F. Stewart, agent for the estates of Colonel H. T. Clements in County Leitrim, Nov. 1878-Feb. 1880 (Packing Crate 156).

Pratt papers: Petition from the tenantry of the townland of Cool-rainey, County Kilkenny, 14 Oct. 1879 (MS 13327).

Rutland papers: Rentals of the Cork, Tipperary, Wicklow, and Queen's County properties (MSS 12769-78).

Public Record Office of Ireland

Midleton papers: Descriptive report and survey, with maps, by Charles Bailey, Cheltenham, England, of the Irish estates of Viscount Midleton, 1839-40 (978/2/4/1).

O'Brien rentals: Estates of the Duke of Leinster, Kildare (vol. 76, ID/24/20).

State Paper Office of Ireland

Chief Secretary's Office, Registered Papers: MSS 1879/16272, 22715; 1880/180, 403, 580, 1300, 1495, 1510, 5368, 12061, 12174, 13150, 13904, 22493, 23957, 29854.

Fenianism, Index to Names, 1866-71.

Irish crimes records, 1881.

State of the country papers: MSS 1815/1682/3 and 41; 1815/1711/14; 1820/2176/37; 1820/2188/10; 1825/2731/4.

Trinity College, Dublin

Congested Districts Board: Base line reports of inspectors for the Congested Districts Board, 1892-8.

Incorporated society papers:

Rentals of the Farra estate, County Westmeath, 1876-81 (IS/5562).

Rentals of the Ranelagh estate, County Roscommon, 1832-81 (IS/5520-31).

Rentals of the Stewart estate, County Louth, 1876-81 (IS/5520-31).

Trinity College papers:

Descriptive survey and valuation of the Trinity College estate, 1845 (MUN/V/78/46-61).

Rentals of the Old Crown, Old Private, and Baldwin estates, 1876-81 (MUN/V/78/10).

Letters from land agents, 1879 and 1888 (MSS MUN/P/3/124; MUN/P/23/1677[1-2]).

II. CONTEMPORARY PUBLICATIONS

1. Parliamentary papers (in chronological order)

First report from the select committee on districts of Ireland under the Insurrection Act, H.C. 1824 (372), viii, 1.

Poor Inquiry (Ireland): appendix (D) containing baronial examinations relative to earnings of labourers, cottier tenants, employment of women and children, expenditure; and supplement containing answers to questions 1 to 12 circulated by the commissioners [36], H.C. 1836, xxxi, 1.

A return of all crimes and outrages reported by the stipendiary magistrates and officers of police in Ireland . . . as having been perpetrated in their respective districts from the 1st January 1836 to the 12th December 1837 . . . , H.C. 1837-8 (157), xlvi, 427.

Outrages reported to the constabulary office, Dublin, as having occurred during January and February, 1837, H.C. 1837-8 (214), xlvi, 457.

Return of the total amount of county cess levied in each county, &c., in Ireland, in each year since 1824, H.C. 1839 (353), xlvii, 533.

Report of the commissioners appointed to take the census of Ireland for the year 1841 [504], H.C. 1843, xxiv, 1.

Appendix to minutes of evidence taken before Her Majesty's commissioners of inquiry into the state of law and practice in respect to the occupation of land in Ireland [672], H.C. 1845, xxii, 1.

Account of the total amount levied for all purposes by grand juries in Ireland, and amount of repayments to government, for the years 1843 to 1849, inclusive, H.C. 1850 (630), li, 466.

A bill to encourage and facilitate the granting of leases on encumbered estates in Ireland, H.C. 1851 (109), iii, 563.

The census of Ireland for the year 1851, pt. ii: Returns of agricultural produce in 1851 [1589], H.C. 1852-3, xciii, 1.

Report from the select committee appointed to inquire into the destitution alleged to exist in the Gweedore and Cloughaneely district in the county of Donegal . . . , H.C. 1857-58 (412), xiii, 89.

General rules and orders of the Landed Estates Court, H.C. 1859 (83-sess. 1), xxii, 139.

Return of the average weekly earnings of agricultural labourers in Ireland for the last six months previous to the 1st day of January 1861, H.C. 1862 (2), lx, 105.

Reports from the poor law inspectors on the wages of agricultural labourers in Ireland [C 35], H.C. 1870, xiv, 1.

Royal commission of inquiry into primary education (Ireland), vol. i, pt. i, *Report of commissioners* [C 6], H.C. 1870, xxviii, pt. i, 1.

Reports from poor law inspectors as to the existing relations between landlord and tenant in respect of improvements on farms, drainage, reclamation of land, fencing, planting, etc. . . . [C 31], H.C. 1870, xiv, 37.

Return showing the number of agricultural holdings in Ireland and the tenure by which they are held by the occupiers [C 32], H.C. 1870, lvi, 737.

Report from the select committee on Westmeath (unlawful combinations), H.C. 1871 (147), xiii, 547.

Report from the select committee of the House of Lords on the Landlord and Tenant (Ireland) Act, 1870; together with the proceedings of the committee, minutes of evidence, appendix, and index, H.L. 1872 (403), xi, 1.

Return for 1870 of number of landed proprietors in each county, H.C. 1872 (167), xlvii, 776.

Nominal return of the municipal corporations and boards of guardians in Ireland that have sent petitions to this House in favour of the Land Tenure (Ireland) Bill, H.C. 1876 (320), lx, 709.

The agricultural statistics of Ireland for the year 1871 [C 762], H.C. 1873, lxix, 375.

Abstract return of the number of civil bill ejectment processes entered, heard and decided in each of the years 1866-73, H.C. 1875 (260), lxii, 5.

Judicial statistics of Ireland for the year 1875: pt. ii, common law; equity; civil and canon law [C 1563], H.C. 1876, lxxix, 273.

Summary of the returns of owners of land in Ireland, showing, with respect to each county, the number of owners below an acre, and in classes up to 100,000 acres and upwards, with the aggregate acreage and valuation of each class, H.C. 1876 (422), lxxx, 35.

Census of Ireland, 1871: pt. iii, General report [C 1377], H.C. 1876, lxxxi, 1.

Report from the select committee on Irish Land Act, 1870; together with the proceedings of the committee, minutes of evidence, and appendix, H.C. 1877 (328), xii, 1.

The agricultural statistics of Ireland for the year 1876 [C 1749], H.C. 1877, lxxxv, 413.

Report from the select committee on Irish Land Act, 1870; to-

gether with the proceedings of the committee, minutes of evidence and appendix, H.C. 1878 (249), xv, 1.

A bill to make temporary provision with respect to compensation for disturbance in certain cases of ejectment for non-payment of rent in parts of Ireland, H.C. 1880 (232), i, 427.

—— (amended), H.C. 1880 (271), i, 431.

—— (amended), H.C. 1880 (276), i, 435.

Return showing the number of officers, and constables, in the Royal Irish Constabulary on 1st January 1880, distinguishing Protestants and Roman Catholics, H.C. 1880 (256), lix, 505.

Return of all agrarian outrages which have been reported by the Royal Irish Constabulary between the 1st day of January 1879 and the 31st day of January 1880 . . . , H.C. 1880 (131), lx, 199.

Preliminary report on the returns of agricultural produce in Ireland in 1879 with tables [C 2495], H.C. 1880, lxxvi, 893.

Minutes of evidence taken before her majesty's commissioners on agriculture [C 2778 I], H.C. 1881, xv, 1.

Report of her majesty's commissioners of inquiry into the working of the Landlord and Tenant (Ireland) Act, 1870, and the acts amending the same [C 2779], H.C. 1881, xviii, 1 (Bessborough commission).

——, vol. ii: Digest of evidence; minutes of evidence, pt. i [C 2779-I], H.C. 1881, xviii, 73.

——, vol. iii: Minutes of evidence, pt. ii; appendices [C 2779-II], H.C. 1881, xix, 1.

Return of the number of persons receiving special police protection in each county in Ireland on 31st December 1880, H.C. 1881 (1), lxxvi, 641.

Return . . . of all agrarian outrages reported by the Royal Irish Constabulary between the 1st day of February 1880 and the 31st day of October 1880 . . . , H.C. 1881 (6), lxxvii, 273.

Return of all agrarian outrages . . . between the 1st day of November 1880 and the 30th day of November 1880 . . . , H.C. 1881 (6-I), lxxvii, 409.

Return of all agrarian outrages . . . between the 1st day of December 1880 and the 31st day of December 1880 . . . , H.C. 1881 (6-II), lxxvii, 487.

Return of the number of agrarian offences in each county in Ireland reported to the Constabulary office in each month of the year 1880 . . . , H.C. 1881 (12), lxxvii, 619.

Return by province and counties (compiled from returns made to the Inspector General, Royal Irish Constabulary), of cases of evictions which have come to the knowledge of the Constabulary in each of the years from 1849 to 1880 (inclusive), H.C. 1881 (185), lxxvii, 725.

Return showing for each month of the years 1879 and 1880 the number of Land League meetings held and agrarian crimes reported to the Inspector General of the Royal Irish Constabulary in each county throughout Ireland, H.C. 1881 (5), lxxvii, 793.

Return of the outrages reported to the Royal Irish Constabulary office from 1st January 1844 to 31st December 1880 [C 2756], H.C. 1881, lxxvii, 887.

The agricultural statistics of Ireland for the year 1880 [C 2932], H.C. 1881, xciii, 683.

Census of Ireland, 1881: pt. i . . . vol. i, Province of Leinster [C 3042], H.C. 1881, xcvii, 1.

Report and tables relating to Irish migratory labourers for 1880, H.C., 1881 [C 2809], xciii, 807.

Return of the number of agrarian offences in each county in Ireland reported to the Constabulary office in each month of the year 1881 . . . , H.C. 1882 (8), lv, 1.

The agricultural statistics of Ireland . . . 1881 [C 3332], H.C. 1882, lxxiv, 93.

Report and tables relating to migratory agricultural Irish labourers for 1881, H.C. 1882 [C 3150], lxxiv, 189.

Census of Ireland, 1881: pt. ii, General report [C 3365], H.C. 1882, lxxvi, 385.

Census of Ireland, 1881: pt. i . . . vol. ii, Province of Munster [C 3148], H.C. 1882, lxxvii, 1.

Census of Ireland, 1881: pt. i . . . vol. iii, Province of Ulster [C 3204], H.C. 1882, lxxviii, 1.

Census of Ireland, 1881: pt. i . . . vol. iv, Province of Connaught [C 3268], H.C. 1882, lxxix, 1.

Return by provinces of agrarian offences throughout Ireland . . . 1882, H.C. 1883 (12), lvi, 1.

Return by provinces of agrarian offences throughout Ireland . . . 1883 [C 3950], H.C. 1884, lxiv, 1.

Number of holdings comprised in applications under the Arrears of Rent (Ireland) Act, 1882 [C 3904], H.C. 1884, lxiv, 91.

Return by provinces of agrarian offences throughout Ireland . . . 1884 [C 4500], H.C. 1884-5, lxv, 1.

Return for each county, city and borough in Ireland, giving names *of the persons holding the commission of the peace* . . . , H.C. 1886 (20-sess. 2), liii, 417.

Returns showing, for the counties of Clare, Cork, Kerry, Galway, and Mayo respectively, the number of civil bills in ejectment . . . for each of the years from 1879 to 1888 inclusive . . . , H.C. 1889 (211), lxi, 417.

Report of the Evicted Tenants' Commission, appendix [C 6935], H.C. 1893-4, xxx, 107.

Report of the departmental committee on agricultural credit in Ireland [Cd 7375], H.C. 1914, xiii, 1.

2. Newspapers and periodicals

Annual Register
Clare Independent
Connaught Journal
Connaught Telegraph
Cork Examiner
Drogheda Journal
Dublin Evening Post
Ennis Chronicle
Gaelic American
Galway Vindicator
Irish Farmer's and Gardener's Magazine and Register of Rural Affairs
Kilkenny Journal
Limerick Reporter
Northern Whig
Roscommon Journal
Sligo Champion
Tuam Herald
Tuam News
Waterford Mirror

3. Directories and maps

Thom's Irish Almanac and Official Directory (Dublin, 1844-).
Ordnance survey maps.

4. Other contemporary publications

Abram, W. A. *Irish People at Home* (London, 1890).
Barker, F., and Cheyne, J. *An Account of the Rise, Progress and*

Decline of Fever Lately Epidemical in Ireland. 2 vols. (Dublin, 1821).

Beaumont, Gustave de. *Ireland: Social, Political and Economic*, ed. W. C. Taylor, 2 vols. (London, 1839).

Becker, B. H. *Disturbed Ireland: Being the Letters Written during the Winter of 1880-81* (London, 1881).

Browning, W. W. (ed.). *Handbook of Railway Distances Compiled by the Direction of the Secretary of State for War* (London, 1869).

Butt, Isaac. *Land Tenure in Ireland: A Plea for the Celtic Race* (Dublin, 1866).

Carleton, William. *Traits and Stories of the Irish Peasantry* (London, 1867).

Coote, Charles. *Statistical Survey of the County of Monaghan* (Dublin, 1801).

"Correspondence" in *New Ireland Review*, 1, no. 6 (Aug. 1894).

Coulter, Henry. *The West of Ireland: Its Existing Condition and Prospects* (Dublin, 1862).

Davitt, Michael. *The Fall of Feudalism in Ireland or the Story of the Land League Revolution* (London, 1904).

Devoy, John. *Recollections of an Irish Rebel* (New York, 1929).

Duffy, C. G. *The League of North and South* (London, 1886).

Dun, Finlay. *Landlords and Tenants in Ireland* (London, 1881).

Dutton, Hely. *A Statistical and Agricultural Survey of the County of Galway* (Dublin, 1824).

Finlay, T. A. "The usurer in Ireland" in *New Ireland Review*, 1, no. 5 (July 1894).

Gorman, Peter. *A report of the proceedings under a special commission of Oyer and Terminer in the counties of Limerick and Clare in . . . 1831* (Limerick, 1831).

Hancock, W. Neilson. *The Usury Laws and the Trade of Lending Money to the Poor in Ireland* (Dublin, 1850).

————. *Report on Deposits and Cash Balances in Joint Stock Banks in Ireland, 1840-1869* (Dublin, 1870).

————. *Report on Savings in Ireland* (Dublin, 1877).

Hansard

Hill, Lord George. *Facts from Gweedore* (Dublin, 1845).

Irish Landlords, Rents and Tenures . . . by an Irish Roman Catholic Landowner (London, 1843).

Irish Magistrate. *The Irish Magistracy* (Dublin, 1885).

Jones, W. B. *The Life's Work in Ireland of a Landlord Who Tried to Do His Duty* (London, 1880).

Kimmis, Henry. "An inquiry into those causes which have tended to produce the existing relation between proprietors and occupiers of land, and have affected the social condition of the people in the rural districts of Ireland" in *Proceedings of the Evening Meetings of the Royal Dublin Society* (May 1855).

Lewis, George C. *On Local Disturbances in Ireland, and on the Irish Church Question* (London, 1836).

McKenna, P. J. "On the criminal jurisdiction of courts of quarter sessions in Ireland" in *Journal of the Dublin Statistical Society* (April 1856).

Naper, J.L.W. *The Cause of Ribbonism and Its Continuance in the Province of Leinster* (Dublin, 1859).

Nicholson, Samuel. *Report upon the general state of agriculture in the district of the country adjoining the middle Shannon; compromising parts of the counties of Tipperary, Galway, Roscommon, Westmeath and King's County* (Dublin, 1841).

O'Leary, John. *Recollections of Fenians and Fenianism.* 2 vols. (London, 1896).

Rice, Thomas. *An inquiry into the effects of the Irish grand jury laws, as affecting the industry, the improvement and the moral character of the people of England* [should read Ireland] (London, 1815).

Ridgeway, William. *A report of the proceedings under a special commission of Oyer and Terminer, and Gaol Delivery for the counties of Sligo, Mayo, Leitrim, Longford and Cavan in the month of December 1806* (Dublin, 1807).

Rogers, Jasper W. *The Potato Truck System of Ireland* (London, 1847).

Ryan, Mark. *Fenian Memories* (Dublin, 1945).

A Statement of the Management of the Farnham Estates (Dublin, 1830).

Staunton, Michael. *Reasons for a Repeal of the Legislative Union between Great Britain and Ireland* (Dublin, 1845).

Sullivan, A. M. *New Ireland, Political Sketches and Personal Reminiscences of Thirty Years of Irish Public Life* (London, 1882).

Tavern committee. *Report of the committee for the relief of distressed districts in Ireland, appointed at a general meeting held at The City of London Tavern on 7th May, 1822* (London, 1822).

Tocqueville, Alexis de. *Journeys to England and Ireland* (London, 1958).

Wakefield, Edward. *An Account of Ireland, Statistical and Political*. 2 vols. (London, 1812).

Weld, Isaac. *Statistical Survey of the County of Roscommon* (Dublin, 1832).

B. Later Works

I. WRITINGS IN IRISH STUDIES

Akenson, Donald H. *The Irish Education Experiment: The National System of Education in the Nineteenth Century* (London, 1970).

Arensberg, C. M. *The Irish Countryman: An Anthropological Study* (London, 1937).

Arensberg, C. M., and Kimball, S. T. *Family and Community in Ireland* (Cambridge, Massachusetts, 1940).

Barrington, Thomas. "A review of Irish agricultural prices" in *Journal of the Statistical and Social Inquiry Society of Ireland*, 15 (1927).

Beames, M. R. "Cottiers and conacre in pre-famine Ireland" in *Journal of Peasant Studies*, 2, no. 3 (1975).

———. "Peasant movements: Ireland 1785-95" in *Journal of Peasant Studies*, 2, no. 4 (1975).

Bew, P.A.E. "The politics of the Irish Land War, 1879-82," unpublished Ph.D thesis, Cambridge University, 1974.

Bourke, P. M. Austin. "The agricultural statistics of the 1841 census of Ireland: a critical review" in *Economic History Review*, second series, 18 (Aug. 1965).

Boyle, J. W. "The rural labourer" in *Threshold*, 3, no. 1 (Spring 1959).

Broderick, J. F. *The Holy See and the Irish Movement for the Repeal of the Union with England, 1829-47* (Rome, 1951).

Broehl, W. G. *The Molly Maguires* (Cambridge, Massachusetts, 1965).

Brown, Thomas N. *Irish-American Nationalism* (New York, 1966).

Buckley, K. "The fixing of rents by agreement in County Galway, 1881-5" in *Irish Historical Studies*, 7, no. 27 (March 1951).

Burns, R. E. "Parsons, priests and the people: the rise of Irish anti-clericalism, 1785-1789" in *Church History*, 31, no. 2 (June 1962).

Butler, W. F. "Irish land tenures: Celtic and foreign" in *Studies*, 13, no. 52 (Dec. 1924).

Carney, F. J. "Pre-famine Irish population: the evidence from the Trinity College estates" in *Irish Economic and Social History*, 2 (1975).

Christianson, Gale E. "Secret societies and agrarian violence in Ireland, 1790-1840" in *Agricultural History*, 46, no. 4 (Oct. 1972).

Clark, Samuel. "The social composition of the Land League" in *Irish Historical Studies*, 17, no. 68 (Sept. 1971).

———. "The political mobilization of Irish farmers" in *Canadian Review of Sociology and Anthropology*, 22, no. 4, pt. 2 (Nov. 1975).

———. "The importance of agrarian classes: agrarian class structure and collective action in nineteenth-century Ireland" in *British Journal of Sociology*, 29, no. 1 (March 1978).

Collins, Finola A. "The Ladies' Land League," unpublished M.A. thesis, University College Cork, 1974.

Collins, M. E. *The Land Question, 1879-1882* (Dublin, 1974).

Connell, K. H. *The Population of Ireland, 1750-1845* (Oxford, 1950).

Cousens, S. H. "The regional variations in population changes in Ireland, 1861-1881" in *Economic History Review*, second series, 17, no. 2 (Dec. 1964).

Crawford, W. H. "Landlord-tenant relations in Ulster, 1609-1820" in *Irish Economic and Social History*, 2 (1975).

Crotty, Raymond D. *Irish Agricultural Production: Its Volume and Structure* (Cork, 1966).

Cullen, L. M. "Problems in the interpretation and revision of eighteenth century Irish economic history" in *Transactions of the Royal Historical Society*, 5th series, 17 (1967).

———. "Irish history without the potato" in *Past and Present*, no. 40 (1968).

———. *An Economic History of Ireland Since 1660* (London, 1972).

Curtis, L. P., Jr. *Coercion and Conciliation in Ireland, 1880-1892: A Study in Conservative Unionism* (Princeton, 1963).

———. "The Anglo-Irish predicament" in *Twentieth Century Studies* (Nov. 1970).

Dardis, Patrick G. *The Occupation of Land in Ireland in the First Half of the Nineteenth Century* (Dublin, 1920).

Donnelly, James S., Jr. "Cork Market: its role in the nineteenth century Irish butter trade" in Studia Hibernica, no. 11 (1971).

————. Review of The Land Question and the Irish Economy, 1870-1903 by Barbara L. Solow in Studia Hibernica, no. 13 (1973).

————. Landlord and Tenant in Nineteenth-Century Ireland (Dublin, 1973).

————. "The journals of Sir John Benn-Walsh relating to the management of his Irish estates, 1823-64" in Cork Historical and Archaeological Society Journal, 79, no. 230 (1974) and 80, no. 231 (1975).

————. The Land and the People of Nineteenth-Century Cork: The Rural Economy and the Land Question (London, 1975).

————. "The agricultural depression of 1859-64" in Irish Economic and Social History, 3 (1976).

————. Review of The Modernisation of Irish Society by Joseph Lee in Irish Historical Studies, 20, no. 78 (Sept. 1976).

————. "The Rightboy movement, 1785-8" in Studia Hibernica, nos. 17-18 (1977-8).

————. "The Whiteboy movement, 1761-5" in Irish Historical Studies, 21, no. 81 (March 1978).

Drake, Michael. "Marriage and population growth in Ireland, 1750-1845" in Economic History Review, second series, 16, no. 2 (1963).

————. "Population growth and the Irish economy" in L. M. Cullen (ed.), The Formation of the Irish Economy (Cork, 1969).

Duignan, Michael. "Irish agriculture in early historic times" in Journal of the Royal Society of Antiquaries of Ireland, series seven, 14, pt. 3 (30 Sept. 1944).

Edwards, Ruth Dudley. An Atlas of Irish History (London, 1973).

Evans, E. Estyn. "Some survivals of the Irish openfield system" in Geography, 24 (1939).

————. Irish Folkways (London, 1957).

Feingold, William L. "The Irish boards of poor law guardians, 1872-86: a revolution in local government," unpublished Ph.D. thesis, University of Chicago, 1974.

————. "The tenants' movement to capture the Irish poor law boards, 1877-1886" in Albion, 7, no. 3 (Fall 1975).

Foster, R. F. Charles Stewart Parnell: The Man and his Family (Hassocks, Sussex, 1976).

Fox, J. R. "Kinship and land tenure on Tory Island" in Ulster Folklife, 12 (1966).

Freeman, T. W. *Ireland, A General and Regional Geography* (London, 1950).

———. *Pre-Famine Ireland: A Study in Historical Geography* (Manchester, 1957).

Gibbon, Peter. *The Origins of Ulster Unionism: The Formation of Popular Protestant Politics and Ideology in Nineteenth-Century Ireland* (Manchester, 1975).

Gibbon, Peter, and Higgins, M. D. "Patronage, tradition and modernisation: the case of the Irish 'Gombeenman' " in *Economic and Social Review*, 6, no. 1 (Oct. 1974).

———. "The Irish Gombeenman: re-incarnation or rehabilitation?" in *Economic and Social Review*, 8, no. 4 (July 1977).

Green, E.R.R. "Agriculture" in R. Dudley Edwards and T. Desmond Williams (eds.), *The Great Famine* (Dublin, 1956).

———. "Industrial decline in the nineteenth century" in L. M. Cullen (ed.), *The Formation of the Irish Economy* (Cork, 1969).

Handley, J. E. *The Irish in Modern Scotland* (Cork, 1947).

Haughton, J. P. "The livestock fair in relation to Irish country towns" in *Irish Geography*, 3, no. 2 (1955).

Hawkins, Richard. "Liberals, land and coercion in the summer of 1880: the influence of the Carraroe ejectments" in *Journal of the Galway Archaeological and Historical Society*, 34 (1974-5).

Hoppen, K. T. "Tories, Catholics and the general election of 1859" in *Historical Journal*, 13, no. 1 (1970).

———. "Landlords, society and electoral politics in mid-nineteenth-century Ireland" in *Past and Present*, no. 75 (May 1977).

———. "Politics, the law and the nature of the Irish electorate 1832-1850" in *English Historical Review*, 92, no. 365 (Oct. 1977).

———. "National politics and local realities in mid-nineteenth-century Ireland" in A. Cosgrave and D. Macartney (eds.), *Studies in Irish History Presented to R. Dudley Edwards* (Naas, 1979).

Horn, P.L.R. "The National Agricultural Labourers' Union in Ireland" in *Irish Historical Studies*, 17, no. 67 (March 1971).

Hughes, T. Jones. "The origin and growth of towns in Ireland" in *University Review*, 2, no. 7 (1960).

Inglis, Brian. *The Freedom of the Press in Ireland, 1784-1841* (London, 1954).

Johnston, E. M. *Ireland in the Eighteenth Century* (Dublin, 1974).

Jupp, P. J. "Irish parliamentary elections and the influence of the Catholic vote, 1801-20" in *Historical Journal*, 10, no. 2 (1967).

Kennedy, B. A. "The tenant-right agitation in Ulster, 1845-50" in *Bulletin of the Irish Committee of Historical Sciences*, no. 34 (17 May 1944).

Kennedy, Liam. "A sceptical view on the reincarnation of the Irish 'Gombeenman' " in *Economic and Social Review*, 8, no. 3 (April 1977).

Lampson, G. Locker. *A Consideration of the State of Ireland in the Nineteenth Century* (London, 1907).

Lane, P. G. "The Encumbered Estates Court, Ireland, 1848-1849" in *Economic and Social Review*, 3, no. 3 (April 1972).

———. "The general impact of the Encumbered Estates Act of 1849 on Counties Galway and Mayo" in *Journal of the Galway Archaeological and Historical Society*, 33 (1972-3).

Large, David. "The wealth of the greater Irish landowners, 1750-1815" in *Irish Historical Studies*, 15, no. 57 (March 1966).

Larkin, Emmet. "The devotional revolution in Ireland, 1850-75" in *American Historical Review*, 77, no. 3 (June 1972).

———. *The Catholic Church and the Creation of the Modern Irish State, 1878-1886* (Philadelphia, 1975).

———. "Church, state and nation in modern Ireland" in *American Historical Review*, 80, no. 5 (Dec. 1975).

Lee, Joseph. "Marriage and population in pre-famine Ireland" in *Economic History Review*, second series, 21, no. 2 (1968).

———. "The dual economy in Ireland, 1800-50" in *Historical Studies*, 8 (1971).

———. *The Modernisation of Irish Society, 1848-1918* (Dublin, 1973).

———. "The Ribbonmen" in T. Desmond Williams (ed.), *Secret Societies of Ireland* (Dublin, 1973).

Lowe, W. J. "Landlord and tenant on the estate of Trinity College Dublin, 1851-1903" in *Hermathena*, no. 120 (Summer 1976).

Lúing, Séan Ó. "Aspects of the Fenian rising in Kerry: I. The rising and its background" in *Journal of the Kerry Archaeological and Historical Society*, 1, no. 3 (1970).

Lynch, P., and Vaizey, J. *Guinness's Brewery in the Irish Economy, 1759-1876* (Cambridge, 1960).

Lyons, F.S.L., "Vicissitudes of a middleman in County Leitrim, 1810-27" in *Irish Historical Studies*, 9, no. 35 (March 1955).

———. *John Dillon: A Biography* (London, 1968).

———. *Charles Stewart Parnell* (Oxford, 1977).

McCaffrey, L. J. "Irish Federalism in the 1870's: a study in conservative nationalism" in *Transactions of the American Philiosophical Society*, new series, 52, pt. 6 (1962).

McCourt, D. "The rundale system in Donegal: its distribution and decline" in *Donegal Annual*, 3 (1955).

MacDonagh, Oliver. "The Irish Catholic clergy and emigration during the Great Famine" in *Irish Historical Studies*, 5, no. 20 (Sept. 1947).

————. "The politicization of the Irish Catholic bishops, 1800-1850" in *Historical Journal*, 18, no. 1 (1975).

McDowell, R. B. *The Irish Administration, 1801-1914* (London, 1964).

MacGeehin, Maureen. "The Catholics of the towns and the quarterage dispute in eighteenth-century Ireland" in *Irish Historical Studies*, 8, no. 30 (Sept. 1952).

Mac Giolla Choille, Breandán. "Fenians, Rice and Ribbonmen in County Monaghan, 1864-67" in *Clogher Record*, 6, no. 2 (1967).

Macintyre, Angus. *The Liberator: Daniel O'Connell and the Irish Party, 1830-1847* (New York, 1965).

MacLysaght, Edward. *Irish Life in the Seventeenth Century* (New York, 1939/1969).

MacNeill, Eoin. "Communal ownership in ancient Ireland" in *Irish Monthly*, 47 (Aug.-Sept. 1918).

Mac Niocaill, Gearóid. *Ireland Before the Vikings* (Dublin, 1972).

Maguire, W. A. *The Downshire Estates in Ireland, 1801-1845* (Oxford, 1972).

————. "The 1822 settlement of the Donegall estates" in *Irish Economic and Social History*, 3 (1976).

Masterson, Harold T. "Land-use patterns and farming practice in County Fermanagh, 1609-1845" in *Clogher Record*, 7, no. 1 (1969).

Miller, David W. "Irish Catholicism and the Great Famine" in *Journal of Social History*, 9, no. 1 (Fall 1975).

Montgomery, W. E. *The History of Land Tenure in Ireland* (Cambridge, 1889).

Moody, T. W. "The new departure in Irish politics, 1878-9" in H. A. Cronne, T. W. Moody, and D. B. Quinn (eds.), *Essays in British and Irish History in Honour of James Eadie Todd* (London, 1949).

————. "Irish-American nationalism" in *Irish Historical Studies*, 15, no. 60 (Sept. 1967).

————. (ed.), *The Fenian Movement* (Cork, 1968).

Moody, T. W. "The Fenian movement in Irish history" in T. W. Moody (ed.), *The Fenian Movement* (Cork, 1968).

———. "Anna Parnell and the Land League" in *Hermathena*, no. 117 (1974).

Moody, T. W. and Ó Broin, Leon. "The I.R.B. supreme council, 1868-78" in *Irish Historical Studies*, 19, no. 75 (March 1975).

Murphy, J. A. "The support of the Catholic clergy in Ireland, 1750-1850" in *Historical Studies*, 5 (1965).

Nowlan, K. B. "Travel" in R. B. McDowell (ed.), *Social Life in Ireland, 1800-45* (Cork, 1957).

———. *The Politics of Repeal: A Study in the Relations between Great Britain and Ireland, 1841-50* (London, 1965).

O'Brien, Conor Cruise. *Parnell and His Party* (Oxford, 1957).

O'Brien, R. B. *The Life of Charles Stewart Parnell, 1846-1891*. 2 vols. (London, 1898-1900).

O'Brien, William, and Ryan, Desmond (eds.). *Devoy's Post Bag, 1871-1928*. 2 vols. (Dublin, 1948).

Ó Corráin, Donncha. *Ireland Before the Normans* (Dublin, 1972).

O'Donnell, Patrick. *The Irish Faction Fighters of the 19th Century* (Dublin, 1975).

O'Donoghue, Patrick. "Causes of opposition to tithes, 1830-38" in *Studia Hibernica*, no. 5 (1965).

———. "Opposition to tithe payments in 1830-31" in *Studia Hibernica*, no. 6 (1966).

Ó Fiaich, Thomás. "The clergy and Fenianism, 1860-70" in *Irish Ecclesiastical Record*, 109 (Feb. 1968).

Ó Gráda, Cormac. "Seasonal migration and post-famine adjustment in the west of Ireland" in *Studia Hibernica*, no. 13 (1973).

———. "Agricultural head rents, pre-famine and post-famine" in *Economic and Social Review*, 5, no. 3 (April 1974).

———. "The investment behaviour of Irish landlords, 1850-1875: some preliminary findings" in *Agricultural History Review*, 23, pt. ii (1975).

———. "Some aspects of nineteenth-century Irish emigration" in L. M. Cullen and T. C. Smout (eds.), *Comparative Aspects of Scottish and Irish Economic and Social History 1600-1900* (Edinburgh, 1977).

———. "On some aspects of productivity change in Irish agriculture, 1845-1926." Paper presented at the Seventh International Economic History Congress, Edinburgh, Aug. 1978.

O'Neill, Thomas P. "Food problems during the great Irish famine" in *Journal of the Royal Society of Antiquaries of Ireland*, 82 (1952).

———. "Rural life" in R. B. McDowell (ed.), *Social Life in Ireland, 1800-45* (Cork, 1957).

———. "From famine to near famine, 1845-1879" in *Studia Hibernica*, no. 1 (1961).

O'Neill, Timothy P. "The state, poverty and distress in Ireland, 1815-45," unpublished Ph.D. thesis, University College Dublin, 1971.

Ó Tuathaigh, Gearóid. *Ireland Before the Famine, 1798-1848* (Dublin, 1972).

Palmer, N. D. *The Irish Land League Crisis* (New Haven, 1940).

Pomfret, J. E. *The Struggle for Land in Ireland, 1800-1923* (Princeton, 1930).

Reynolds, James. *The Catholic Emancipation Crisis in Ireland, 1823-1829* (New Haven, 1954).

Robinson, O. "The London companies as progressive landlords in nineteenth-century Ireland" in *Economic History Review*, 15 (1962-3).

Senior, Hereward. *Orangeism in Ireland and Britain, 1795-1836* (London, 1966).

Solow, Barbara L. *The Land Question and the Irish Economy, 1870-1903* (Cambridge, Massachusetts, 1971).

Steele, E. D. *Irish Land and British Politics: Tenant-Right and Nationality, 1860-75* (London, 1974).

———. "Cardinal Cullen and Irish nationality" in *Irish Historical Studies*, 19, no. 75 (March 1975).

Thornley, David. *Isaac Butt and Home Rule* (London, 1964).

Tierney, Mark. *Murroe and Boher: The History of an Irish Country Parish* (Dublin, 1966).

Tucker, G.S.L. "Irish fertility ratios before the Famine" in *Economic History Review*, second series, 23, no. 2 (1970).

Vaughan, W. E. "A study of landlord and tenant relations in Ireland between the famine and the Land War, 1850-78," unpublished Ph.D thesis, Trinity College Dublin, 1974.

Wall, Maureen. "The rise of a Catholic middle class in eighteenth-century Ireland" in *Irish Historical Studies*, 11, no. 42 (Sept. 1958).

———. *The Penal Laws, 1691-1760* (Dublin, 1961/1967).

———. "The Whiteboys" in T. Desmond Williams (ed.), *Secret Societies in Ireland* (Dublin, 1973).

Whyte, J. H. *The Independent Irish Party, 1850-9* (Oxford, 1958).

———. "The influence of the Catholic clergy on elections in nineteenth-century Ireland" in *English Historical Review*, 75, no. 295 (April 1960).

———. "Landlord influence at elections in Ireland, 1760-1885" in *English Historical Review*, 80, no. 317 (Oct. 1965).

Woods, C. J. "The Catholic Church and Irish politics, 1879-92," unpublished Ph.D. thesis, University of Nottingham, 1968.

———. "The politics of Cardinal McCabe, archbishop of Dublin, 1879-85" in *Dublin Historical Record*, 26, no. 3 (June 1973).

II. OTHER WRITINGS IN SOCIAL SCIENCE

Aveni, Adrian F. "The not-so-lonely crowd: friendship groups in collective behavior" in *Sociometry*, 40, no. 1 (1977).

Black-Michaud, Jacob. *Cohesive Force: Feud in the Mediterranean and the Middle East* (Oxford, 1975).

Blumer, Herbert. "Collective behavior" in A. M. Lee (ed.), *Principles of Sociology* (New York, 1951).

Borton, Hugh. *Peasant Uprisings in Japan of the Tokugawa Period* (New York, 1937).

Burnet, Jean. "Town-country relations and the problem of rural leadership" in *Canadian Journal of Economics and Political Science*, 13, no. 3 (Aug. 1947).

Chirot, Daniel and Ragin, Charles. "The market, tradition and peasant rebellion; the case of Romania in 1907" in *American Sociological Review*, 40, no. 4 (Aug. 1975).

Clark, Samuel, Grayson, J. P., and Grayson, L. M. (eds.), *Prophecy and Protest: Social Movements in Twentieth-Century Canada* (Toronto, 1975).

Coser, L. A. *The Functions of Social Conflict* (Glencoe, Illinois, 1956).

Dahrendorf, Ralph. *Class and Class Conflict in Industrial Society* (Stanford, 1959).

Davies, James C. "Toward a theory of revolution" in *American Sociological Review*, 27, no. 1 (Feb. 1962).

———. "The J-curve of rising and declining satisfactions as a cause of some great revolutions and a contained rebellion" in H. D. Graham and T. R. Gurr (eds.), *The History of Violence in America* (New York, 1969).

———. *When Men Revolt and Why* (New York, 1970).

Deutsch, Karl W. *Nationalism and Social Communication* (Cambridge, Massachusetts, 1953).

————. "Social mobilization and political development" in *American Political Science Review*, 55 (Sept. 1971).

Feierabend, Ivo K., Feierabend, Rosalind L., and Nesvold, Betty A. "Social change and political violence: cross-national patterns" in H. D. Graham and T. R. Gurr (eds.), *The History of Violence in America* (New York, 1969).

Ferguson, D. Frances. "Rural/urban relations and peasant radicalism: a preliminary statement" in *Comparative Studies in Society and History*, 18, no. 1 (Jan. 1976).

Foltz, W. J. "Ethnicity, status and conflict" in W. Bell and W. F. Freeman (eds.), *Ethnicity and Nation-Building: Comparative, International, and Historical Perspectives* (Beverly Hills, 1974).

Foster, George M. "The dyadic contract in Tzintzuntzan, II: patron-client relationship" in *American Anthropologist*, 65, no. 6 (Dec. 1963).

Frank, André G. "The development of underdevelopment" in *Monthly Review*, 18, no. 4 (Sept. 1966).

Friedmann, Harriet. "World market, state, and family farm: the social bases of household production in the era of wage labor" in *Comparative Studies in Society and History*, 20, no. 4 (Oct. 1978).

Friedrich, Paul. *Agrarian Revolt in a Mexican Village* (Englewood Cliffs, N.J., 1970).

Gamson, William. *The Strategy of Social Protest* (Homewood, Illinois, 1975).

Gerlach, Luther P. and Hine, Virginia H. *People, Power, Change: Movements of Social Transformation* (Indianapolis, 1970).

Grove, D. J. "A cross-national examination of cross-cutting and reinforcing cultural cleavages" in *International Journal of Comparative Sociology*, 18, nos. 3-4 (Sept.-Dec. 1977).

Gurr, T. R. *Why Men Rebel* (Princeton, 1970).

Hanham, H. J. *Elections and Party Management: Politics in the Time of Disraeli and Gladstone* (London, 1959).

Hardy, M.J.L. *Blood Feuds and the Payment of Blood Money in the Middle East* (Leiden, 1963).

Hilton, Rodney H. *Bond Men Made Free: Medieval Peasant Movements and the English Rising of 1381* (London, 1973).

————. "Peasant society, peasant movements and feudalism in

medieval Europe" in Henry A. Landsberger (ed.) *Rural Protest: Peasant Movements and Social Change* (London, 1974).

Hobsbawm, E. J. *Primitive Rebels* (Manchester, 1959).

Hobsbawm, E. J., and Rudé, George. *Captain Swing* (London, 1969).

Holland, Stuart. *Capital versus the Regions* (London, 1976).

Homans, George. *English Villagers of the Thirteenth Century* (New York, 1941/1960).

Jackson, George D. "Peasant political movements in eastern Europe" in Henry A. Landsberger (ed.), *Rural Protest: Peasant Movements and Social Change* (London, 1974).

Johnson, Chalmers. *Revolutionary Change* (Boston, 1966).

Kautsky, Karl. *Die Agrarfrage* (Stuttgart, 1899).

Kornhauser, William. *The Politics of Mass Society* (New York, 1959).

Landsberger, Henry A. "The role of peasant movements and revolts in development" in Henry A. Landsberger (ed.) *Latin American Peasant Movements* (Ithaca, 1969).

Lerner, Daniel. *The Passing of Traditional Society* (New York, 1958).

Lipset, S. M. *Agrarian Socialism: The Cooperative Commonwealth Federation in Saskatchewan: A Study in Political Sociology* (Berkeley, 1950).

―――. *Political Man: The Social Basis of Politics* (New York, 1963).

Lipset, S. M. and Rokkan, S. (eds.), *Party Systems and Voter Alignments* (New York, 1967).

McCarthy, J. D. and Zald, M. N. "Resource mobilization and social movements" in *American Journal of Sociology*, 82, no. 6 (May 1977).

McPhail, Clark, and Miller, David. "The assembling process: a theoretical statement and empirical examination" in *American Sociological Review*, 38, no. 6 (Dec. 1973).

Marx, Karl. *The Eighteenth Brumaire of Louis Bonaparte* (New York, 1963).

Moore, Barrington, Jr. *Social Origins of Dictatorship and Democracy: Lord and Peasant in the Making of the Modern World* (Boston, 1966).

Mouzelis, Nicos. "Greek and Bulgarian peasants: aspects of their sociopolitical situation during the interwar period" in *Comparative Studies in Society and History*, 18, no. 1 (Jan. 1976).

Oberschall, Anthony. *Social Conflict and Social Movements* (Englewood Cliffs, N.J., 1973).

Olson, Mancur. *The Logic of Collective Action* (Cambridge, Massachusetts, 1965).

Paige, Jeffery M. *Agrarian Revolution: Social Movements and Export Agriculture in the Underdeveloped World* (New York, 1975).

Paine, Robert. *Patrons and Brokers in the East Arctic* (St. John's, Newfoundland, 1971).

Pearson, Neale J. "Latin American pressure groups and the modernization process" in *Journal of International Affairs*, 20, no. 2 (1966).

Peters, E. M. "Some structural aspects of the feud among the camel-herding Bedouin of Cyrenaica" in *Africa*, 37, no. 3 (July 1967).

Pinard, Maurice. "Mass society and political movements: a new formulation" in *American Journal of Sociology*, 73, no. 6 (May 1968).

———. *The Rise of a Third Party: A Study in Crisis Politics* (Englewood Cliffs, N.J., 1971).

Rogers, Everett M. *Modernization among Peasants: Impact of Communication* (New York, 1969).

Rudé, George. *The Crowd in History: A Study of Popular Disturbances in France and England, 1730-1848* (New York, 1964).

Sabean, David. "The communal basis of pre-1800 peasant uprisings in western Europe" in *Comparative Politics*, 8, no. 3 (April 1976).

Scott, James C. "Patron-client politics and political change in Southeast Asia" in *American Political Science Review*, 66, no. 1 (March 1972).

———. *The Moral Economy of the Peasant: Rebellion and Subsistence in Southeast Asia* (New Haven, 1976).

Shorter, Edward, and Tilly, Charles. *Strikes in France, 1830 to 1968* (New York, 1974).

Smelser, N. J. *Theory of Collective Behavior* (New York, 1963).

Snyder, David, and Tilly, Charles. "Hardship and collective violence" in *American Sociological Review*, 37, no. 5 (Oct. 1972).

Stavenhagen, Rodolfo. *Social Classes in Agrarian Societies* (New York, 1975).

Stinchcombe, Arthur. "Agricultural enterprise and rural class relations" in *American Journal of Sociology*, 67, no. 2 (Sept. 1961).

Stirling, Paul. "A death and a youth club: feuding in a Turkish village" in *Anthropological Quarterly*, 33 (1960).

Thompson, E. P. "The moral economy of the English crowd in the eighteenth century" in *Past and Present*, no. 50 (Feb. 1971).

Tilly, Charles. "Collective violence in European perspective" in H. D. Graham and T. R. Gurr (eds.), *The History of Violence in America* (New York, 1969).

———. "The changing place of collective violence" in Melvin Richter (ed.), *Essays in Theory and History: An Approach to the Social Sciences* (Cambridge, Massachusetts, 1970).

———. "Do communities act?" in *Sociological Inquiry*, 43, nos. 3-4 (1973).

———. "Revolutions and collective violence" in Fred I. Greenstein and Nelson Polsby (eds.), *Handbook of Political Science* (Reading, Massachusetts, 1975).

———. *From Mobilization to Revolution* (Reading, Massachusetts, 1978).

Tilly, Charles, Tilly, Louise, and Tilly, Richard. *The Rebellious Century, 1830-1930* (Cambridge, Massachusetts, 1975).

Turner, Ralph, and Killian, L. M. *Collective Behavior* (Englewood Cliffs, N.J., 1957/1972).

Weingrod, Alex. "Patrons, patronage, and political parties" in *Comparative Studies in Society and History*, 10, no. 4 (July 1968).

Wilson, John. *Introduction to Social Movements* (New York, 1973).

Wolf, Eric R. "Kinship, friendship, and patron-client relations in complex societies" in Michael Banton (ed.), *The Social Anthropology of Complex Societies* (London, 1966).

———. *Peasant Wars of the Twentieth Century* (New York, 1969).

Womack, John, Jr. *Zapata and the Mexican Revolution* (New York, 1968).

Worsley, Peter. *The Trumpet Shall Sound: A Study of "Cargo" Cults in Melanesia* (New York, 1968).

Index

abatements in rent: as a non-contractual privilege, 69, 165, 180, 235, 242; demanded by tenants, 69, 211, 235-7, 246, 266, 294, 297-8, 303, 306, 345-7; landlords' reluctance to grant (1879), 237-40; requested by Catholic clergy (1879), 287. See also rents

Abbeyleix, Queen's County, 289n

Abbeyleix poor-law board, 327

Abercorn, 1st Duke of: estates of, 159

absenteeism, see landlords, absenteeism

Achonry, diocese of, 283, 284

active collectivities, 15-16, 359. See also challenging collectivities; collective action

Agitation Scale, 252-6

agricultural cooperation, 42-3

Agricultural Labourers' Union, see National Agricultural Labourers' Union

agriculture: depressions, 28, 225-45, 262, 265-6, 344-5, 363-4; extent of commercialization, 51-6, 362-5; post-famine adjustment, 107-12, 140-49; output, 111-12, 226, 243; recovery (1880-82), 334. See also livestock; pasture; potato; tillage

amnesty movement, 205, 216-17, 328

Antrim, county of, 50

Antrim Central Tenants' Defence Association, 220

Armagh, county of, 80, 93, 154n, 169

Armagh Tenants' Defence Association, 220

arms, raids for, 74, 84

Arms Act of 1881, see Peace Preservation Act

Arran, 4th Earl of: estate of, 42

Arran Islands, 289

arrears, see rents, arrears

Arrears Act of 1882, 253, 338

artisans, 244, 375; marriage patterns, 118-19, 133-4; number (1841-81), 127-8; in Fenian movement, 203-4; in Land War, 268-71. See also townsmen

Ascendancy, Protestant, 57, 182-93, 198, 277. See also Protestants; religious structure

assistant barristers, see county court judges

associational organization, 8-9, 264, 309, 312, 351-2, 355-7. See also names of specific associations

Athleague, County Roscommon, 237, 287, 296

Athlone, County Westmeath, 52, 178, 321

Aughrim, County Galway, 71, 72

Bailieborough poor-law board, 327

Baldwin, Thomas, 232

Balla, County Mayo, 259, 273, 274n, 278, 300n, 334; Land League relief efforts in, 318

Ballina, County Mayo, 45, 123

Ballinamore, County Leitrim, 229

Ballinasloe, County Galway, 227, 228, 287

Ballinasloe fair, 111, 229, 230

Ballinasloe Tenants' Defence Association, 219-20, 232, 246, 257, 272-3, 278

Ballingarry, County Tipperary, 236

Ballinrobe, County Mayo, 137, 248, 274n

Ballisodare, County Sligo, 294n, 319

Ballot Act of 1872, 200

Ballyclare Tenants' Defence Association, 220

Local Government Act, 343
Londonderry, county of, 50, 81, 159, 211, 214
Londonderry Tenants' Defence Association, 220
Longford, county of: 84, 113n, 318
Lorton, 1st Viscount: estate of, 31
Louden, John J., 274n
Louisburgh, County Mayo, 136, 273
Louisburg Tenants' Defence Association, 219-20
Louth, county of, 80, 89, 90n, 146, 204, 240, 241
Louth Tenants' Defence Association, 220
Luby, T. C., 201n, 202
Lucan, 3rd Earl of, 233, 259n

McCabe, Edward, archbishop of Dublin, 283
MacCormack, Francis, bishop of Achonry, 284
MacEvilly, John, bishop of Galway, 284, 286, 287n
McGeough Bond, J. P., 168-9
MacHale, John, archbishop of Tuam, 96, 196, 283-5
McKnight, James, 211
MacManus, T. B., 204
magistrates, see justices of the peace; resident magistrates
Magpies, 75
Mahon, the O'Gorman, 330n
Mallow Farmers' Club, 220
Manchester, 7th Duke of: estate of, 154n
Manchester Martyrs, 205
Manor Hamilton, County Leitrim, 154n, 287
Mansion House Relief Committee, 317-18
markets, see fairs
Martin, John, 199
Marx, Karl, 357
Maryborough, 215
mass society, theory of, 10, 365-6
Mayo, county of, 53n, 154n, 159; hamlets in, 45; collective action in, 90n,

205, 210, 212, 282, 328, 347; trade in, 125; seasonal migration from, 142; economic conditions in, 147n, 231, 233; new owners in, 173n; rent reductions in, 237; family budgets of tenants in, 239; Land War in, 247, 258, 259n, 273-5, 284, 295, 301, 311, 315, 323; distribution of relief in, 318; ejectment decrees issued in, 306; decline of Land League in, 337
Mayo Abbey, 301
Mayo Land League, see Land League of Mayo
Mayo (Castlebar) Tenants' Defence Association, 219-20, 246
Meath, county of, 50, 80, 90n, 95, 199, 207, 212, 246
Meath Tenants' Defence Association, 220
merchants, see townsmen
middlemen: transformation in late 1700s and early 1800s, 26-7; opposition of landowners to, 30; economic difficulties of, 28-9. See also subletting
Midleton, 5th Viscount: estate of, 35, 36n
migration: seasonal, 50-51, 116, 119, 142, 144-6, 227, 230, 239; internal, 50-51, 124-5. See also emigration
Milltown, County Galway, 247, 274, 285
Mitchel, John, 207n
mobilization, social, 151-2
mobilization, theory of, 12-16, 303n, 351, 365-7
Mohill, County Leitrim, 31, 65, 154n, 377
Molly Maguires, 65, 66
Monaghan, county of, 80, 89, 96, 204, 216, 247
Monaghan Tenants' Defence Association, 220
Monahan, P. J., 274n
Monasterevan, Queen's County, 316
Moore, Barrington, Jr., 358
Moore, County Roscommon, 239
Moore, G. H., 205, 327-8

Moriarty, David, bishop of Kerry, 199
Mote, County Roscommon, 154, 240, 241
Mount Bellew, union of 118n, 375
Mountmorres, 5th Viscount, 321-2
Munster, province of: subdivision in, 47; trade in, 53; towns, 56; economic and social conditions, 53, 107-10, 139-43, 228; collective action in, 74, 75, 79, 85, 90, 95, 97, 99, 204, 210, 212-15, 219, 255, 276, 361; townsmen in, 127-8; Land War in, 258, 261, 272, 274, 280, 307, 314; National League in, 341; Plan of Campaign in, 346
Murray Stewart, H. G.: estate of, 154n

Nally, P. W., 259n, 273, 274, 278
Nation, 97-8, 213-14, 259, 288, 297, 298, 377
National Agricultural Laborers' Union, 210, 252n
National Association, 196
National Council of 1853, 196
National League, Irish, 340-42, 345, 370
Neale, County Mayo, 274n
neighborhood ties, 40-43, 63, 85-6, 322, 355
New Departure, 209, 212n, 278-9, 281
Newmarket-on-Fergus, County Clare, 287n
Newport, County Mayo, 136
newspaper editors (proprietors), 88n, 203, 268-9, 270-72, 274, 342
newspapers, 49, 123, 252, 253n, 314
Newtown-Gore, County Leitrim, 154, 192, 238
New York Herald Fund, 317
Nolan, John, 201n
non-contractual privileges, 164-71, 184, 242, 306, 344n, 367; not respected by new owners, 172-4; and land acts, 175-6; claimed by tenants as customary rights, 179-81; undermined during depression of late 1870s, 235, 240; basis of three Fs, 302
No Rent Manifesto, 336-7, 338, 340
North Dublin poor-law board, 327
Northern Whig, 286

notices to quit, 168-70, 240. See also ejectment decrees; ejectment processes; evictions

O'Brien, William, 346
O'Connell, Daniel, 59, 88-90, 94, 95-7, 100, 101, 185, 199, 276, 277, 309, 356
O'Connor, Arthur, 331n
O'Connor, Daniel, 259n
O'Connor, T. P., 331n
O'Conor Don, the, 331
O'Donel, Sir George, 237
O'Kane, John, 273
O'Kelly, J. J., 300n, 331n
O'Leary, John, 201n, 206
O'Mahony, John, 201n
opposition, social, 9
Orange Emergency Committee, 307
Orange Order, 80-82, 202
O'Sullivan, M. M., 272, 273n, 278, 279
O'Sullivan, W. H., 199, 215n, 280, 281n, 330, 331n

Palmerston, 3rd Viscount, 31
parliamentary party, Irish, 337, 340-43, 345, 348, 370. See also Home Rule movement
Parnell, C. S., 247-8, 292, 311, 336-41, 369-71; early years in parliament, 207-8; New Departure, 209; organizes Land League, 280, 330n; clashes with Catholic clergy, 284, 285; attacks private relief organizations, 317-18; advocates return of Land League poor-law guardians, 329; and election of 1880, 330-32, 331n; and Land Act of 1881, 333-6; arrest of, 336; organizes National League, 340
Parsons, Talcott, 366
Partry, County Mayo, 239
pasture: post-famine shift to, 108, 109, 110; regional variations, 144-5, 148. See also grazing; livestock
patron-client ties, 21-2, 129, 267
Peace Preservation (Arms) Act of 1881, 333, 335
peasant proprietorship, 202, 297-8, 302-4, 355
Peel, Sir Robert, 69

418

Library of Congress Cataloging in Publication Data

Clark, Samuel, 1945-
   Social origins of the Irish land war.

   Bibliography: p.
   Includes index.
   1. Ireland—Rural conditions.   2. Land reform—
Ireland—History.   I. Title.
HN400.3.A8C57   301.35′2′09415   79-83980
ISBN 0-691-05272-7
ISBN 0-691-10068-3 pbk.